Tl

Me

wr

Ka

ROUGH GUIDES

www.roughguides.com

Contents

Foodies' Melbourne
colour section
following p.112

Colour map section
following p.256

3

Introduction to
Melbourne

Capital of the state of Victoria and Australia's second-largest city, Melbourne prides itself on being a place that knows how to live well and offers a quality of life that other Australian cities find difficult to match. It regularly gets voted one of the world's top five "most liveable cities" and with a population of around 3.8 million, it's the fastest growing city in Australia. Magnificent landscaped gardens and parklands have made Melbourne one of the greenest cities in the world, while beneath the skyscrapers of the arresting Central Business District (CBD) elegant Victorian-era facades present Melbourne on an agreeably human scale.

And it's an enjoyable place to visit too. Widely considered the most European and successfully multi-ethnic of all of Australia's cities, Melburnians and tourists alike can frequent some of Australia's coolest cafés and bars, dine out in fabulous restaurants and enjoy the fruits of its leading role in Australian cultural and sporting life. Melbourne is a passionate consumer, whether of art, footy or food.

For close on a century Melbourne was a rather staid, Anglo-Celtic city, but postwar immigration shook up its old ways for good. Reminders of former conservatism linger on in the city's uniform layout and relentless suburbanization, but in the inner-city neighbourhoods you'll experience urban life at its most diverse. Thanks to the influx of people from Vietnam, China, Greece, Italy, Turkey, Lebanon and the rest of Europe, the city's formerly inward-looking and parochial character has been enriched and energized.

In the last decade, Melbourne has also undergone a remarkable renaissance in everything from architecture and design to fashion, food and literature, thanks to forward-thinking state governments and massive private investment. The city is growing too, with an extra million people expected to live in Melbourne within the next twenty years. The government's **Melbourne 2030** plan hopes to prepare for this by developing compact residential, working and retail hubs such as Docklands, and increasing shopping and service hours.

Popularity and progress do not come without their pitfalls, however – older buildings have been demolished to

> **Melbourne is the most European and successfully multi-ethnic of all Australia's cities**

make way for Manhattan-style high rises and apartment blocks, and the public transport system is often pushed to the limit at peak times. But, despite these problems, regenerated Melbourne is today, more than at any other time in its history, looking forward to a confident and prosperous future.

What to see

Melbourne straddles the Yarra River, just before it flows into Port Phillip Bay. On the northern banks of the river and about five kilometres from the bay, the **Central Business District (CBD)** is the main focus of the city. A large, flat rectangle, with wide blocks laid out in a grid pattern, it has a lively and cosmopolitan atmosphere, and is easy to get around on foot. The main north–south artery is bustling **Swanston Street**, site of the State Library of Victoria and the QV shopping development. The most important east–west streets are **Collins** and **Bourke**.

The **east side** of the city from Swanston Street contains an attractive architectural legacy from the goldrush era, with many of the city's finest civic buildings, including the mammoth **Parliament House** and the magnificent cathedrals of **St Patrick** and **St Paul**. At the eastern edge of the district, the fashionable shops and cafés of the "**Paris End**" of Collins Street offer style and culture of a more contemporary kind, as does atmospheric **Chinatown**, still home to the longest established of the city's many ethnic communities.

The **west side** of Swanston Street, the other half of the CBD, is home to bustling **Bourke Street Mall**, a pedestrian-only strip flanked by shops, department stores and the Neoclassical General Post Office. The area is also the location of a large and fascinating network of arcades and passageways, teeming with stylish boutiques, antique shops and innumerable cafés

and restaurants. West of Bourke Street is Melbourne's latest suburb, the **Docklands** development, with a plethora of restaurants, bars and public art lining the waterside, while to the north, **Queen Victoria Market** has been pulling in punters for over 130 years.

Bordering the city's principal axis, the **Yarra River**, are many of Melbourne's glitziest new buildings. These make up the **river district**, which includes Melbourne's tallest building, the **Eureka Tower**, the enormous leisure complexes of **Southgate** and the **Crown Casino**, the **Victorian Arts Centre** with its distinctive spire, and the adjacent **National Gallery of Victoria**. Opposite here, beautifully tended Yarra Park – with

> Melbourne prides itself on being a place that knows how to live well

its iconic **MCG** stadium – and the **Royal Botanic Gardens** present a therapeutic respite from the pace of city life. On the riverfront, relative newcomer **Federation Square** forms a bold link between the CBD and the Yarra. Further south, the bayside suburbs of **South Melbourne** and **Albert Park** are worth visiting for their food markets, delis, upmarket stores and elegant nineteenth-century streetscapes.

Rubbing shoulders just north of the CBD, the inner suburbs of **Carlton** and **Fitzroy** are at the heart of Melbourne's vibrant Italian and alternative communities. To the east, **Richmond** is famed for its Greek and Vietnamese eateries, as well as its bargain shopping, while over the last decade **Collingwood** has gone from industrial no-go area to up-and-coming suburb, with an abundance of cafés and restaurants. South of the CBD, the main thoroughfare is St Kilda Road, a busy, tree-lined boulevard that runs past the exclusive, style-conscious suburbs of **South Yarra**, **Prahran** and **Toorak** before reaching the seafront at vibrant **St Kilda**, the perfect place for kicking back over coffee and newspapers. Beyond these, the city's sprawling outer suburbs hold fewer points of interest, although **Williamstown**, on a promontory southwest of the city, warrants a trip for its maritime leanings and lively

Fitzroy vintage

weekend coffee trade. Further afield, in the northeastern suburbs of Bulleen and Eltham, the artist retreats of the **Museum of Modern Art at Heide** and **Montsalvat** showcase the legacy of bohemian creativity.

Outside Melbourne, Victoria offers a wide range of sights and attractions, from outstanding national parks and volcanic hotsprings to historic homesteads and award-winning wineries, all of which are easily accessible by public transport or car, and make rewarding day- or weekend-trips.

Heading for the coast you'll find **Phillip Island**, famous for its penguins, and the bucolic backdrops and beach resorts of the **Bellarine** and **Mornington peninsulas**, the latter including Wilson's Promontory, a magnificent national park. Inland, the scenic **Dandenong Ranges** and the prestigious wineries of the **Yarra Valley** are convenient escapes from the urban bustle, while the salubrious spa towns of **Daylesford** and **Hepburn Springs** and the grandiose architecture of the former goldmining town of **Ballarat** – Victoria's largest inland city – offer reminders of the area's nineteenth-century heritage. Heading west you'll encounter **Geelong**, the gateway to the coast and further on the magnificent **Great Ocean Road**, which winds 300km along some of Australia's most spectacular coastal scenery.

When to go

A feature of Melbourne's climate is its changeability, particularly during spring and summer when dramatic falls in temperature sometimes occur within a few minutes. In general the city's weather is warm to hot in summer (Dec–Feb), mild in autumn (March–May), cold and damp in winter (June–Aug), and cool in spring (Sept–Nov). January and February usually see the best weather, with clear blue skies tempting locals and visitors alike to enjoy some outdoor eating and drinking, though extreme hot spells –

◄ Cycling along the Yarra

Ice creams at Albert Park

when temperatures can climb into the forties – and hiked-up prices and crowded beaches are the downside. Wintery June and July, when night frosts sometimes occur, are not entirely unpleasant, and are a great time to check out the inner-city pubs with roaring fires, or enjoy some of the excellent galleries and museums.

Average daily temperatures and monthly rainfall

	Jan	Feb	Mar	Apr	May	Jun	Jul	Aug	Sep	Oct	Nov	Dec
Melbourne												
Max/min (°F)	79/59	79/60	75/57	70/53	63/50	57/44	57/44	59/44	63/48	68/50	71/53	75/57
Max/min (°C)	26/15	26/16	24/14	21/12	17/10	14/7	14/7	15/7	17/9	20/10	22/12	24/14
Rainfall (mm)	48	50	54	59	58	50	48	50	58	67	59	58

20

things not to miss

It's not possible to see everything that Melbourne has to offer in one visit, and we don't suggest you try. What follows is a selective taste of the city's highlights, from outstanding museums and cosmopolitan bars to beautiful parks and unforgettable road-trips, arranged in five colour-coded categories. All highlights have a page reference to take you straight into the Guide, where you can find out more.

01 **The Great Ocean Road** Page **173** • Renowned coastal highway famous for its jaw-dropping scenery and picturesque seaside communities.

02 Yarra river cruise Page **61** • Take a leisurely cruise down the Yarra for a wonderful view of Melbourne from the water.

04 Melbourne Cup Page **153** • One of the top sporting events in the Australian calendar, the Melbourne Cup horse race held in November is also a revered Australian tradition.

03 Docklands Page **55** • Melbourne's up-and-coming new waterfront precinct features buzzing cafés and restaurants, and some of the most conspicuous buildings and public art in the city – including the graceful Webb Bridge.

05 Melbourne's cafés See *Foodies' Melbourne* colour section • Experience Melbourne's passion for coffee at one of its ubiquitous cafés.

06 Melbourne Cricket Ground Page **67** • Scream your heart out watching the footy or cricket at the venerable MCG.

07 Melbourne nightlife Page **126** • From sleek clubs and cutting-edge bars to traditional boozers, there are plenty of options for a great night out in Melbourne.

08 Melbourne Museum Page **75** • Excellent museum complex, characterized by cutting-edge design and a variety of exhibition spaces including a towering indoor rainforest.

09 Eureka Tower Page **59** • Get a bird's eye view of the city from the tallest viewing platform in the southern hemisphere and its gravity defying "skywalk".

11 Melbourne's arcades and laneways Page 53 • Australia's most extensive network of arcades and lanes is crammed with stores selling everything from funky glassware to edgy clothing, while cosy cafés provide the perfect pit stop.

10 Phillip Island Penguins Page **185** • Beat a path to the hugely popular Penguin Parade to see hundreds of these cute aquatic birds emerge from the surf and waddle ashore.

12 Wilsons Promontory National Park Page **189** • Magnificent national park with plenty of camping spots and some of Victoria's finest surfing beaches, wetlands and bushwalks.

13 **French Island** Page **188** • The pristine landscapes of this undeveloped island are home to a rich diversity of wildlife – including the country's largest population of koalas.

14 **Queen Victoria Market** Page **49** • Melbourne's busiest market was established over 130 years ago and sells everything from fresh fruit and veg, seafood and cheeses to shoes, bags, bed linen and jewellery.

15 **Chapel Street** Page **87** • With its wall-to-wall boutiques and plenty of cool cafés, exclusive Chapel Street is the place to come to see and be seen.

16 **Chinatown** Page **44** • Small and atmospheric, Melbourne's Chinatown is the real deal, complete with cheap eateries, languid tea parlours and garish souvenir shops.

17 **City Circle Tram** Page **27** • Hop-on, hop-off free tram service circuiting the CBD and passing some of Melbourne's major attractions.

18 **National Gallery of Victoria** Page **62** • The redeveloped NGV on St Kilda Road contains the most comprehensive collection of international art in Australia, including the world's largest stained-glass ceiling.

19 Royal Botanic Gardens Page **65** • Established in 1846, the Royal Botanic Gardens are an inviting oasis amid the clamour and bustle of Melbourne.

20 Federation Square Page **67** • Wander the galleries and museums at Federation Square, an ambitious 21st-century public monument in the heart of the city.

Basics

Basics

Getting there

Unless you're travelling interstate by road or train, you are most likely to arrive in Melbourne by plane.

Melbourne's **Tullamarine Airport** – the second busiest in Australia – services all the major international airlines, while Melbourne's **Avalon Airport** caters solely for flights from no-frills airline **Jetstar**. Airfares depend on the season, with the weeks around Christmas generally being the busiest and most expensive time to travel. The cheapest deals are usually from April to mid-June. Prices rise again from mid-June to mid-August coinciding with the peak European holiday period.

Flights from the UK and Ireland

The quickest way to get to Melbourne from the UK is to fly direct with British Airways or Qantas from London Heathrow, with a **flying time** of around 21 hours from regional airports at Aberdeen, Edinburgh, Glasgow, Manchester and Newcastle, while Singapore Airlines has flights from Manchester to Singapore that connect with onward flights to Melbourne. Plenty of other airlines have indirect flights to Melbourne (involving at least one change of plane), taking longer but costing significantly less. There are no direct flights from Ireland.

The cheapest published scheduled **fares** from the UK start at around £650 return during low season; but if you fly with one of the major airlines such as Qantas or BA this will more than likely be around £800, rising to well over £1000 at peak periods. To stand a chance of getting one of the cheaper tickets at peak times, aim to book anything up to six months in advance. Flying from Ireland involves a stop in London or Europe with fares starting at around €1400 in low season, increasing to around €1900 over Christmas.

Flights from the US and Canada

Most flights from the US and Canada go via Los Angeles, from which there are plenty of one-stop services to Melbourne, usually routed via Sydney. The **flying time** to Melbourne, excluding stopovers, is approximately fifteen hours from Los Angeles; twenty hours from New York or Chicago. From Canada, flying time from Vancouver to Melbourne is approximately eighteen hours; from Toronto or Montréal it's about twenty.

Fares are highest from December to February and lowest from April to August. Typical scheduled fares to Melbourne from the west coast of the US are around US$1500/2100 (low/high season); from the east coast US$1600/2200. From Vancouver, expect to pay CAN$1800/2200 (low/high season); CAN$1900/2700 from Montréal or Toronto. Prices depend upon how far in advance you purchase your tickets, as well as how many seats are available on a particular flight.

Flights from New Zealand and South Africa

There's a good choice of flights to Melbourne from **New Zealand**: routes are busy and competition is fierce, especially since the introduction of cheap no-frills airlines such as Jetstar, Virgin Blue and its sister operator Pacific Blue which have brought the prices down even more (check the websites for the latest deals). It's a relatively short hop across the Tasman Sea, with a **flying time** from Auckland to Melbourne of around three and a half hours. **Fares** depend on how much flexibility you want; many of the cheapest deals are hedged with restrictions – typically, they must be booked at least fourteen days in advance, with a maximum stay of thirty days. Return tickets with the major airlines cost NZ$500–800 for a thirty-day ticket, and rise in price by several hundred dollars for longer stays of up to six months. Flying at peak times (primarily Dec to mid-Jan) can also add substantially to the price.

Six steps to a better kind of travel

At Rough Guides we are passionately committed to travel. We feel strongly that only through travelling do we truly come to understand the world we live in and the people we share it with – plus tourism has brought a great deal of **benefit** to developing economies around the world over the last few decades. But the extraordinary growth in tourism has also damaged some places irreparably, and of course **climate change** is exacerbated by most forms of transport, especially flying. This means that now more than ever it's important to **travel thoughtfully** and **responsibly**, with respect for the cultures you're visiting – not only to derive the most benefit from your trip but also to preserve the best bits of the planet for everyone to enjoy. At Rough Guides we feel there are six main areas in which you can make a difference:

- Consider what you're contributing to the **local economy**, and how much the services you use do the same, whether it's through employing local workers and guides or sourcing locally grown produce and local services.
- Consider the **environment** on holiday as well as at home. Water is scarce in many developing destinations, and the biodiversity of local flora and fauna can be adversely affected by tourism. Try to patronize businesses that take account of this.
- Travel with a purpose, not just to tick off experiences. Consider **spending longer** in a place, and getting to know it and its people.
- Give thought to how often you **fly**. Try to avoid short hops by air and more harmful night flights.
- Consider **alternatives to flying**, travelling instead by bus, train, boat and even by bike or on foot where possible.
- Make your trips **"climate neutral"** via a reputable carbon offset scheme. All Rough Guide flights are offset, and every year we donate money to a variety of charities devoted to combating the effects of climate change.

Package deals can be a hassle-free way of getting a taste of Melbourne. There's a huge variety of holidays and tours to Australia available in New Zealand; call any of the travel agents listed below. Subsidiaries of airlines such as Air New Zealand and Qantas package short city-breaks (flight and accommodation) and fly-drive deals for little more than the cost of the regular airfare.

Flying from **South Africa** the flight time is just over thirteen hours and usually involves a stopover in Sydney or Perth. The main carriers are Qantas and South Africa Airways with fares around R7800 during low season and R11,600 during high season.

RTW and Circle Pacific tickets

Making one or more **stopovers** en route is one way of breaking up the long flight to Australia. You'll usually have to pay a supplement, although these are sometimes included in the price of the ticket. Alternatively,

round-the-world (**RTW**) tickets and a **Circle Pacific**, which has stop-offs in Australia and New Zealand from North America, offer a good way of including Australia as part of a longer journey. The routing permutations are endless, but fares normally reflect the length of the route chosen and the number of stops to be made; London–Bangkok–Melbourne–Auckland–Fiji–Los Angeles–London, for example, would cost around £800. A typical Circle Pacific itinerary from Los Angeles via Hong Kong, Bangkok, Singapore, Cairns and Melbourne costs about US$1600.

Flights from the rest of Australia

Flying from major cities in Australia your choice of airlines is between Jetstar, Qantas, Regional Express, Skywest, Tiger Airways and Virgin Blue. Flight times are relatively short and you can usually find excellent deals from the relevant airlines' websites, though they usually come with restrictions (for example a very limited baggage allowance) and are non-refundable. Flights to Melbourne take around an hour and a quarter from Adelaide; an hour and a half from Sydney; three and a half hours from Perth; around four and a half hours from Darwin; three and a half hours from Cairns; and two and a half hours from Brisbane.

Buses, trains and driving

All the major long-distance **bus** companies run services to Melbourne, either one-way or as part of a hop-on-hop-off route taking in other cities and towns along the way. The main operators are Greyhound Australia and Firefly Express, with journey times roughly 11 hours Adelaide to Melbourne and 12 hours Sydney to Melbourne. Tickets cost around $70 one-way from Sydney and $60 from Adelaide.

If you're **driving** these journey times can usually be cut by a few hours if you're travelling as part of a group and take it in turns, keeping to the highways; the **distance** from Sydney to Melbourne is approximately 1000km, and 730km from Adelaide.

It's also possible to get to Melbourne from regional Victoria by **train** via the state's rail network V/Line, which runs a network of services into the city. Travelling interstate by rail is time consuming and more expensive. Your options are limited to two networks: the XPT which runs from Brisbane via Sydney and is operated by Countrylink; and The Overland from Adelaide, which is run by Great Southern Rail. You can view timetables and buy tickets for both of these journeys via the Rail Australia website (see p.23).

Ferry

The *Spirit of Tasmania* operates nightly between Station Pier in Port Melbourne and Devonport in **Tasmania**. During the summer additional day sailings are also available. The journey takes around eleven hours with low-season fares starting from $132 one-way for a day passenger, $158 for a recliner and $235 for a cabin; cars are $65 extra.

Airlines, agents and operators

Many airlines and travel websites offer the opportunity to book your tickets online,

cutting out the costs of agents and middlemen; these are worth going for, as long as you don't mind the inflexibility of non-refundable, non-changeable deals.

Online booking

Ⓦ **www.expedia.co.uk** (in UK), Ⓦ **www.expedia .com** (in US), Ⓦ **www.expedia.ca** (in Canada)
Ⓦ **www.lastminute.com** (in UK)
Ⓦ **www.opodo.co.uk** (in UK)
Ⓦ **www.orbitz.com** (in US)
Ⓦ **www.travelocity.co.uk** (in UK), Ⓦ **www .travelocity.com** (in US), Ⓦ **www.travelocity.ca** (in Canada), Ⓦ **www.travelocity.co.nz** (in New Zealand)
Ⓦ **www.travelonline.co.za** (in South Africa)
Ⓦ **www.zuji.com.au** (in Australia)

Airlines

Aerolineas Argentinas US ☎1-800/333-0276, Canada ☎1-800/688-0008, UK ☎0800/096 9747, New Zealand ☎09/379 3675, Australia ☎02/9234 9000; Ⓦwww.aerolineas.com.
Air Canada Canada ☎1-888/247-2262, UK ☎0871/220 1111, Republic of Ireland ☎01/679 3958, Australia ☎1300/655 767, New Zealand ☎0508/747 767; Ⓦwww.aircanada.com.
Air China US ☎1-800-9828/802, Canada ☎416-581/8833, UK ☎020/7744 0800, Australia ☎02/9232 7277; Ⓦwww.airchina.com.
Air New Zealand New Zealand ☎0800/737000, Australia ☎0800 132 476, UK ☎0800/028 4149, Republic of Ireland ☎1800/551 447, USA ☎1800-262/1234, Canada ☎1800-663/5494; Ⓦwww .airnz.co.nz.
Air Pacific US & Canada ☎1-800/227-4446, Australia ☎1800 230 150, New Zealand ☎0800/800178, UK ☎020/6264 283; Ⓦwww .airpacific.com.
American Airlines US ☎1-800/433-7300, UK ☎020/7365 0777, Republic of Ireland ☎01/602 0550, Australia ☎1800 673 486, New Zealand ☎0800/445 442; Ⓦwww.aa.com.
Austrian Airlines US & Canada ☎1-800/843-0002, UK ☎0870/124 2625, Republic of Ireland ☎1800/509 142, Australia ☎1800 642 438 or 02/9200 4800; Ⓦwww.aua.com.
British Airways US & Canada ☎1-800/AIRWAYS, UK ☎0844/493 0787, Republic of Ireland ☎1890/626 747, Australia ☎1300 767 177, New Zealand ☎09/966 9777, South Africa ☎114/418 600; Ⓦwww.ba.com.
Cathay Pacific US ☎1-800/233-2742, Canada ☎1-800/2686-868, UK ☎020/8834 8888, Australia

⏱13 17 47, New Zealand ⏱09/379 0861, South Africa ⏱11/700 8900; ⊛www.cathaypacific.com.
Emirates US & Canada ⏱1-800/777-3999, UK ⏱0844/800 2777, Australia ⏱1300 303 777, New Zealand ⏱05/0836 4728, South Africa ⏱0861/364 728; ⊛www.emirates.com.
Garuda Indonesia US ⏱1-212/279-0756, Canada ⏱1-416/924-3175, UK ⏱020/7467 8661, Australia ⏱1300 365 330 or 02/9334 9900, New Zealand ⏱09/3661862; ⊛www.garuda-indonesia.com.
JAL (Japan Air Lines) US & Canada ⏱1-800/525-3663, UK ⏱0845/774 7700, Republic of Ireland ⏱01/408 3757, Australia ⏱1300 525 287 or 02/9272 1111, New Zealand ⏱0800/525 747 or 09/379 9906, South Africa ⏱11/214 2560; ⊛www.jal.com.
Jetstar Australia ⏱13 15 38, ⊛www.jetstar.com.au.
KLM (Royal Dutch Airlines) US & Canada ⏱1-800/225-2525, UK ⏱0870/507 4074, Republic of Ireland ⏱1850/747 400, Australia ⏱1300/392 192, New Zealand ⏱09/921 6040, South Africa ⏱0860/247 747; ⊛www.klm.com.
Korean Air US & Canada ⏱1-800/438-5000, UK ⏱0800/413 000, Republic of Ireland ⏱01/799 7990, Australia ⏱02/9262 6000, New Zealand ⏱09/914 2000; ⊛www.koreanair.com.
Malaysia Airlines US ⏱1-800/5529-264, UK ⏱0871/423 9090, Republic of Ireland ⏱01/6761 561, Australia ⏱13 26 27, New Zealand ⏱0800/777 747, South Africa ⏱11-8809 614; ⊛www.malaysiaairlines.com.
Pacific Blue Australia ⏱13 16 45, New Zealand ⏱0800/670 000, outside New Zealand ⏱07/3295 2284; ⊛www.flypacificblue.com.
Qantas Airways US & Canada ⏱1-800/227-4500, UK ⏱0845/774 7767, Republic of Ireland ⏱01/407 3278, Australia ⏱13 13 13, New Zealand ⏱0800/808 767 or 09/357 8900, South Africa ⏱11/441 8550; ⊛www.qantas.com.
Regional Express Australia ⏱13 17 13, ⊛www.rex.com.au.
Singapore Airlines US ⏱1-800/742-3333, Canada ⏱1-800/663-3046, UK ⏱0844/800 2380, Republic of Ireland ⏱01/671 0722, Australia ⏱13 10 11, New Zealand ⏱0800/808 909, South Africa ⏱11/880 8560 or 11/880 8566; ⊛www.singaporeair.com.
Skywest Australia ⏱1300 660 088, ⊛www.skywest.com.au.
South African Airways South Africa ⏱11/978 1111, US & Canada ⏱1-800/722-9675, UK ⏱0870/747 1111, Australia ⏱1300 435 972, New Zealand ⏱09/977 2237; ⊛www.flysaa.com.
Thai Airways US ⏱1-212/949-8424, UK ⏱0870/606 0911, Australia ⏱1300 651 960, New Zealand ⏱09/377 3886, South Africa ⏱11/268 2580; ⊛www.thaiair.com.
Tiger Airways Australia ⏱03/9335 3033, ⊛www.tigerairways.com.
United Airlines US ⏱1-800/864-8331, UK ⏱0845/844 4777, Australia ⏱13 17 77; ⊛www.united.com.
Virgin Blue Australia ⏱13 67 89, New Zealand ⏱0800/670 000, ⊛www.virginblue.com.au.

Agents and operators

AAT Kings Australia ⏱1300 556 100, New Zealand ⏱0800/500 146; ⊛www.aatkings.com. Long-established Australian coach-tour operator that offers a wide selection of escorted and independent one-day tours from Melbourne.
Abercrombie and Kent US ⏱1-800/554-7016, ⊛www.abercrombiekent.com. Eight to 21-day high-end tours, ranging from basic trips (including Sydney, Melbourne and the Great Barrier Reef) to more extensive ones (including Tasmania and the Outback). Also specializes in family tours and customized itineraries.
Air Brokers International US ⏱1-800/883-3273, ⊛www.airbrokers.com. Consolidator and specialist in round-the-world and Circle Pacific tickets.
ATS Tours US ⏱1-888/781 5170, ⊛www.atstours.com. Huge Australian and New Zealand specialist; dive deals, fly-drives, city stopovers, rail/bus passes, motel vouchers and other add-ons.
Australia Travel Centre Republic of Ireland ⏱01/804 7100, ⊛www.australia.ie. Specialists in long-haul flights.
Austravel UK ⏱0844/873 0977, Republic of Ireland ⏱01/642 7009; ⊛www.austravel.com. Specialists for flights and tours to Australia. Issues ETAs (see p.24) and traditional visas for an administration fee of £20.
Contiki Australia ⏱1300/CONTIKI, ⊛www.contiki.com. Big-group, countrywide bus and 4WD tours for fun-loving 18- to 35-year-olds. All transport and most meals covered; plenty of additional excursions (climbing, diving, etc) at extra cost.
ebookers UK ⏱0871/223 5000, Republic of Ireland ⏱01/431 1311; ⊛www.ebookers.com. Low fares on an extensive selection of scheduled flights and package deals.
Flightcentre UK ⏱0870/499 0040, US ⏱1-866/967-5351, Canada ⏱1-877/967-5302, Australia ⏱13 31 33, NZ ⏱0800/243 544; ⊛www.flightcentre.com. Rock-bottom fares.
Holiday Shoppe New Zealand ⏱0800/866 654, ⊛www.holidayshoppe.co.nz. Great deals on flights, hotels and holidays.
North South Travel UK ⏱01245/608 291, ⊛www.northsouthtravel.co.uk. Friendly, competitive travel agency, offering discounted fares worldwide.

Local tour operators

With Melbourne as a base, a wide variety of **tours** can be made to the interior of Victoria or both east and west along the coast. Popular destinations – both as day-trips and one-way tours – are to the Grampians, Phillip Island and the Mornington Peninsula, and along the Great Ocean Road. For longer trips, you could consider several two- to four-day bushwalking excursions offered by a number of operators. Tour operators include **Autopia Tours** (☎9419 8878, ⓦwww.autopiatours.com.au); **Echidna Walkabout** (☎9646 8249, ⓦwww.echidnawalkabout.com.au); **Let's Go Bush** (☎9640 0826, ⓦwww .letsgobush.com.au); **Wayward Bus** (☎1300/653 510, ⓦwww .waywardbus.com.au); and **Wildlife Tours Australia** (☎1300 661 730, ⓦwww.wildlifetours.com.au).

Profits are used to support projects in the developing world, especially the promotion of sustainable tourism. **STA Travel** US ☎1-800/781-4040, UK ☎0871/2300 040, Australia ☎13 47 82, New Zealand ☎0800/474 400, South Africa ☎0861/781 781; ⓦwww.statravel.com. Worldwide specialists in independent travel; also student IDs, travel insurance, car rental, rail passes, and more. Good discounts for students and under-26s.

Swain Australia Tours US ☎1-800/227-9246, ⓦwww.swainaustralia.com. Excellent range of customized tours to meet individual travel needs and budgets, including around Victoria, the Great Ocean Road and Phillip Island.
Trailfinders UK ☎0845/058 5858, Republic of Ireland ☎01/677 7888; ⓦwww.trailfinders.com. One of the best-informed and most efficient agents for independent travellers.
Travel Bag UK ☎0800/804 8911, ⓦwww .travelbag.co.uk. Specialists in RTW tickets and long-haul flights, with good deals to be had on leading airlines.
Travel Cuts US ☎1-800/592-CUTS, Canada ☎1-866/246-9762; ⓦwww.travelcuts.com. Popular, long-established student-travel organization, with worldwide offers.
World Travel Centre Republic of Ireland ☎01/416 7007, ⓦwww.worldtravel.ie. Excellent fares.

Bus, rail and ferry contacts

Countrylink ☎13 22 32, ⓦwww.countrylink.info.
Firefly Express ☎1300 730 740, ⓦwww .fireflyexpress.com.au.
Great Southern Rail ☎13 21 47, ⓦwww.gsr .com.au.
Greyhound Australia ☎1300 473 946, ⓦwww .greyhound.com.au.
Premier Motor Service ☎13 34 10, ⓦwww .premierms.com.au.
Rail Australia ⓦwww.railaustralia.com.au.
Spirit of Tasmania ☎1800 634 906, ⓦwww .spiritoftasmania.com.au
V/Line ☎13 61 96, ⓦwww.vline.com.au.

Walking tours of Melbourne

A number of companies offer **walking tours** of the city ranging from architectural walks taking in historical buildings to discovering the city's tucked away alleys. **Melbourne's Golden Mile Heritage Trail** ($20; ☎9928 0000, ⓦwww.visitvictoria .com.au) explores the city's heritage buildings and streets and tells the Melbourne story from the gold rush to "Marvellous Melbourne" era. Tours begin at Federation Square and take in many prominent buildings. The popular **Hidden Secrets Lanes and Arcades Tour** ($115, including lunch and goodie bag; ☎9329 9665, ⓦwww .hiddensecretstours.com) takes in the city's many historic alleys and shopping arcades, and offers people the chance to do a bit of shopping along the way from the laneways, many specialty shops. Alternatively the **Melbourne Visitors Centre** at Federation Square has devised a series of **self-guided walks**, including Secret Gardens, On the Waterfront and Arcades and Lanes; free maps are available from the centre. The **National Trust** (☎9656 9800, ⓦwww.nattrust.com.au) and **White Hat Tours** (☎9329 6055, ⓦwww.whitehat.com.au) also offer a range of walks. See also the **Aboriginal Heritage Walk** on p.65.

Entry requirements

All visitors to Australia require a visa or Electronic Travel Authority (ETA) and a valid passport, except New Zealanders, who need only a passport and are issued with a visa on arrival. You can get visa application forms from Australian High Commissions, embassies or consulates listed below.

The easiest option for nationals of the UK, Ireland, the US, Canada, Malaysia, Japan, Singapore, Hong Kong, South Korea and most European countries who intend to stay for less than three months is to get an **ETA**. These are valid for a year for stays of up to three months and can be applied for online at ⓦwww.eta.immi.gov.au for $20, or through travel agents and airlines for a small fee at the same time you book your flight. Citizens of other countries and visitors who intend to stay longer than three months should apply for a **tourist visa** which costs $100, and can be lodged in person or by post to the embassy or consulate, or online at ⓦwww.immi.gov.au. If you think you may stay longer than three months, it's best to apply for the longer visa before departure as extensions once you get to Australia cost $215. You may be asked to show proof that you have sufficient funds – at least $1000 per month – to support yourself during your stay. Once issued, a visa usually allows multiple entries so long as your passport remains valid.

To **extend** your visa in Melbourne, contact the Department of Immigration and Multicultural Affairs at Casselden Place, 2 Lonsdale St (Mon–Fri 9am–4pm, closes 1.30pm Wed; ☎13 18 81). Make sure you apply at least a month before your visa expires, as the process can take some time.

Citizens of the UK, Ireland, Canada, Taiwan, Japan, Korea, Hong Kong and participating European countries, aged between 18 and 30, can apply for a **working holiday visa**, which grants a twelve-month stay and allows the holder to work for up to six months with the same employer. You'll need to apply in your home country several months in advance and be able to show evidence of sufficient funds. Working visas cost $195. For further information, visit the Department of Immigration and Multicultural and Indigenous Affairs website above or contact your local embassy or consulate (see below).

Customs and quarantine

Prior to landing in Australia you'll be handed a passenger card to fill out, as well as Customs and Agriculture declaration forms. Australia has strict **quarantine laws** to protect native flora and fauna, and to prevent the introduction of exotic pests and diseases. You must declare all goods of animal or plant origin, and you can't bring fruit, vegetables or fresh and packaged food into the country. As well as drugs and firearms, Australian customs officials are strict about steroids, pornographic material, protected wildlife and associated products. If you've been snacking on the flight, throw any leftovers in the amnesty quarantine bins available in the arrival area or on the way to the luggage collection bay.

The **duty-free allowance** (for over-18s only) on entry is $900 worth of goods, 2.25 litres of alcohol and 250 cigarettes/250g of tobacco.

To find out more about specific goods that are prohibited in Australia before you travel, visit the Australian Customs Service website ⓦwww.customs.gov.au.

Australian embassies and consulates abroad

Canada Australian High Commission, Suite 710, 50 O'Connor St, Ottawa, ON K1P 6L2 ☎613/236-0841, ⓦwww.ahc-ottawa.org.
Malaysia Australian High Commission, 6 Jalan Yap Kwan Seng, Kuala Lumpur ☎2146 5555, ⓦwww .australia.org.my.

Netherlands Australian Embassy, Carnegielaan 4, 2517 KH The Hague ☏070/310 8200, ⓦwww .australian-embassy.nl.

New Zealand Australian Consulate, 72–76 Hobson St, Thorndon, Wellington ☏04/473 6411, ⓦwww .australia.org.nz.

Republic of Ireland Australian Embassy, 7th Floor, Fitzwilton House, Wilton Terrace, Dublin 2 ☏01/ 664 5300, ⓦwww.ireland.embassy.gov.au.

Singapore Australian High Commission, 25 Napier Rd, Singapore ☏065/6836 4100, ⓦwww .singapore.embassy.gov.au.

South Africa Australian High Commission, 292 Orient St, Arcadia, Pretoria ☏12/423 6000, ⓦwww.australia.co.za.

Thailand Australian Embassy, 37 South Sathorn Rd, Bangkok ☏02/344 6300, ⓦwww.austembassy .or.th.

UK Australian High Commission, Australia House, Strand, London WC2B 4LA ☏020/7379 4334, ⓦwww.australia.org.uk.

US Australian Embassy, 1601 Massachusetts Ave NW, Washington, DC 20036-2273 ☏202/797-3000, ⓦwww.usa.embassy.gov.au.

Arrival

Arriving in Melbourne by plane, bus or train poses no problems: most international carriers fly into Melbourne Airport which is connected to the city by bus. The station for long-distance buses and trains is conveniently located in the city centre and well serviced by public transport. Coming by car from Geelong and the Great Ocean Road you'll enter the city over the West Gate Bridge; from the east coast you can either travel inland along the Hume Highway which in turn becomes Sydney Road in north Melbourne, or the coastal route along Princes Highway which eventually becomes Dandenong Road on its approach to the city.

By air

Melbourne's main **airport** (Tullamarine Airport; ☏9297 1600, ⓦwww.melbourne airport.com.au) is located 25km northwest of the city – about a 30-minute drive, depending on traffic. Australia's second busiest airport, it is open 24 hours and services all the major international airlines. The airport's international terminal has baggage lockers (24hr; $10–14), foreign exchange desk, and various ATMs. There is also a travellers' information desks on the ground floor, which can help you with accommodation.

The **Skybus Super Shuttle** ($16 one-way, $26 return; ☏9335 2811, ⓦwww.skybus .com.au) runs daily every fifteen minutes between 6am and 9.30pm, and every 30 minutes to 1 hour outside these times, from the Qantas domestic terminal at Terminal 1 and the Virgin Blue at Terminal 3 to Southern Cross Station on Spencer Street in the city centre. The journey takes approximately twenty minutes and the buses are adapted for mobility-impaired passengers. Tickets can be purchased from Southern Cross Station or the airport departure points. Skybus runs a free hotel connection service (Mon–Fri 6am–9.30pm, Sat & Sun 7.30am–5.30pm, ☏9600 1711; for hotel pick-ups, it's advisable to book a day in advance).

A **taxi** from the airport costs around $40–45 to the city centre, $60 to St Kilda. **Car rental** desks are located in the short-term car park opposite the airport and in the domestic terminals.

If you're flying into Melbourne on Jetstar you may arrive at **Avalon Airport** (☏5227 9100, ⓦwww.avalonairport.com.au), located on the Princes Highway 55km from Melbourne. Sunbus (☏9689 6888,

The Melbourne and Victoria area phone code is 03.

Ⓦ www.sunbusaustralia.com.au) connects with all Jetstar arrivals to Melbourne's Southern Cross Station (one-way $22) and as well as various suburbs and towns in the area if pre-booked 48 hours in advance (one-way $32). The journey to the CBD takes about fifty minutes depending on the time of day. See the airport website for more details.

By bus and train

Regional **V/Line train** services arrive at Southern Cross Station on Spencer Street. **Long-distance buses** arrive at the adjacent Coach Terminal, which also has offices for last-minute tickets. The station is on the City Loop train network as well as various tram routes in and out of the city.

Getting around

Melbourne has an efficient public transport system of trains, trams and buses, making getting around simple and convenient. The city also has plenty of licensed taxis. Outside Melbourne, bus and train services reach all major cities and most towns (see p.23 for contacts). Alternatively, a network of good roads make it easy to reach your destination by car, motorbike or bicycle.

Melbourne's public transport network called **Metlink**, operates Monday to Thursday from 5am until midnight, until 1am on Friday and Saturday, and Sunday from 7am until 11pm, supplemented in the early hours of Saturday and Sunday by Night-Rider buses (see opposite). For public transport information, routes, timetables and fares, call ☏13 16 38 or visit Ⓦ www .metlinkmelbourne.com.au.

Travel passes

A range of tickets valid on all trains, trams and buses is available. The metropolitan area is divided into two zones: zone 1 covers the city area and zone 2 the outer suburbs. Unless you're going on a day-trip to the outer suburbs, you can get anywhere you need to, including St Kilda and William-stown, on a **zone 1 ticket**, which costs $3.50 ($5.50 for zones 1 & 2) and is valid for unlimited travel within the zone for two hours (or all night if bought after 7pm) on any form of transport. A **daily** ticket ($6.50 for zone 1; $10.10 for zones 1 & 2) is better value if you're making several trips, while for longer stays a **weekly** ticket or a ticket that buys you ten 2-hour trips (both costing $28 for zone 1; $47.40 for zones 1 & 2) is

even more economical. The **Sunday Saver** ($2.90) allows unlimited travel for the whole day in zones 1 and 2. The **City Saver** ($2.60) is valid for a single trip on a tram, train or bus between any two stations within the City Saver area (the CBD and out to Richmond, Jolimont and North Melbourne).

You need to **validate** your ticket in a machine every time you board a new vehicle or enter a train platform; those bought on board a tram are automatically validated for that journey only. Two-hour and day tickets are available from **vending machines** found at train stations, on board trams (machines accept coins only), from the **Metlink Shop** at the Melbourne Town Hall, near the corner of Swanston and Little Collins streets (Mon–Fri 9am–5.30pm, Sat 9am–1pm), the **Melbourne Information Centre** at Federation Square and other selected shops displaying the Metcard symbol (most news-agents, some milk bars and pharmacies). You can't buy tickets from tram drivers, but you can buy them from bus drivers (there are no machines on board).

Make sure you buy a ticket – Melbourne transport staff will slap you a maximum penalty of $500 if you don't have one.

By tram

Although not particularly quick, Melbourne's **trams** give the city a distinctive character and provide a scenic way to explore the city and inner suburbs: the **City Circle** is particularly convenient and free (see box, below) Travelling along most of the city's major thoroughfares and extending out into the suburbs, trams run down the centre of the road, and stops are signposted; passengers can board trams from the side of the road and from central islands in the CBD. These stops often have a map with route numbers and times – the route number is displayed at the front of the tram. Although motorists are prohibited from passing trams that are stationary at stops, always look left to see if there are any vehicles approaching. See the **colour map** at the back of the book for the main tram routes.

By train

Melbourne's **train system** is the fastest way to reach suburban destinations. Flinders Street Station, on the corner of Flinders and Swanston streets, is the hub of Melbourne's train system, and all trains begin or end their journey there. Melbourne also has an underground train system, known as the City Loop, with five stations servicing the CBD: Southern Cross, Flagstaff, Melbourne Central, Parliament and Flinders Street. See the colour map at the end of this book for the main routes. There are also sixteen different train lines servicing the outer suburbs – these lines are all linked to bus and tram services.

You can pick up train route maps at any City Loop station. Trains and train stations are fully accessible for people using wheelchairs or with limited mobility, and there are lifts at all City Loop stations. New trains have a Passenger Emergency Intercom system that can be used to contact train staff (emergency use only), and all stations have a red emergency button – when pushed, a central operator can see the platform on a monitor via closed circuit television (CCTV). If the train is deserted, sit in the front carriage nearest the driver.

By bus

Melbourne's **bus** service supplements the tram and train networks. Probably the most useful are the special after-midnight **Night-Rider** buses, which are run by private transport operators and travel on nine routes to the outer suburbs (Belgrave, Dandenong, Eltham, Frankston, Croydon, Epping, Craigieburn, Melton and Werribee, among others) with a valid Metcard. Buses run hourly between 12.30am and 4.30am on Saturday and Sunday mornings, or after major events such as the Australian Grand Prix and New Year's Eve. NightRider buses depart from the City Square (in front of the *Westin Hotel*) on Swanston Street.

By taxi

Melbourne **taxis** are reasonably numerous and easy to spot – they are uniformly yellow. Cab ranks are clearly signposted at central locations like major hotels in the CBD, or

---

Melbourne's vintage trams

Some of Melbourne's trams are vintage wooden vehicles dating back to the 1930s. The vintage burgundy **City Circle** tram is a free service that runs in a loop around the CBD along Flinders, Spring and La Trobe streets, as well as Harbour Esplanade daily, every ten minutes from 10am to 6pm, continuing until 9pm Thursday to Saturday during the summer.

The Colonial Tramcar Restaurant (☏ 9696 4000, ⊛ www.tramrestaurant.com.au) is a converted 1927 tram offering traditional silver service as you trundle around Melbourne. Operating daily from Normandy Road near Crown Casino in South Melbourne, the restaurant offers a three-course early dinner (5.45–7.15pm; $70) and a five-course dinner (Mon–Thurs & Sun 8.35–11.30pm; $115; Fri & Sat $130), plus a four-course lunch (Sun 1–3pm & other days subject to demand; $75); all drinks are included. Make reservations as early as possible – Friday and Saturday evenings can be booked up two months in advance.

busy spots such as Flinders and Spencer Street stations. You can also hail a taxi in the street if the roof light is illuminated, or book by telephone. In general, taxi meters are clearly visible so you can keep check of your fare. Fares begin with a $3.20 flagfall, and there's an additional $1.53 for every kilometre. Cabs also attract surcharges from midnight to 5am, for using the CityLink (see below), for airport pick-ups and for phone bookings. Note that you have to pay for your trip upfront for journeys taken between 10pm and 5am.

Finding a taxi late at night is difficult, especially at weekends, so if you know you'll need one, book it. Phone bookings start from $2 depending on the number of passengers. Melbourne's major taxi companies include Arrow (☎13 22 11); Embassy Taxis (☎13 17 55); Silver Top Taxis (☎13 10 08); and Yellow Cabs (☎13 CABS). Yellow Cabs and Silver Top Taxis also coordinate and despatch wheelchair-accessible taxis.

By bike

Cycling is extremely popular in Melbourne, with a number of designated bicycle tracks that start in the city and extend to the outer suburbs. The visitors centre at Federation Square has cycling **maps** or you can print them off from ◍www.vicroads.vic.gov.au. There are 24 urban routes in and around Melbourne, including the popular 35-kilometre Main Yarra Trail. Bicycles can be carried free on trains but you are expected to avoid carrying them through rush hours (Mon–Fri 7–9.30am & 4–6.30pm). It is compulsory to wear a helmet when cycling. For more information about cycling in Victoria visit ◍www.bv.com au.

Bikes can be **rented** from Borsari Cycles, 193 Lygon St, Carlton (☎9347 4100); Hire a Bicycle, Federation Wharf (☎9654 2762); or St Kilda Cycles, 150 Barkly St, St Kilda (☎9534 3074). Prices are around $35 per day.

By car

In Australia, driving is on the left-hand side of the road and seatbelts are compulsory. A **driver's licence** from home will suffice for up to three months in Australia, as long as it has photo ID and it's for the same class of vehicle you intend to drive. If you're staying more than three months, you'll need to get a Victorian licence; you can be fined if you don't have your licence with you when you're driving. In Melbourne, the **speed limit** ranges from 40kmph in metropolitan shopping strips and school zones to 100kmph outside built-up areas and 110 kmph on some sections of freeway.

Whatever you do, don't drink alcohol and drive – random breath tests are common, even in rural areas.

Melbourne is a relatively easy city to drive in due to its wide thoroughfares and simple well-signposted grid plan. Really, the only thing you have to watch out for is the trams, which share the roads with cars. You can only overtake them on the left and have to stop and wait behind them while passengers are getting off, as they usually step directly off the tram into the road. This can take some time, especially on Friday and Saturday nights and during the Christmas season (there's no need to stop, however, if there's a central pedestrian island). For more information on road rules and driving safely in Melbourne, contact VicRoads (Mon–Fri 8.30am–5pm, Sat 8.30am–2pm; ☎13 11 71, ◍www.vicroads.vic.gov.au).

A peculiar road rule has been developed to accommodate trams at major intersections in the city centre known as the **hook turn**: when turning right, you pull over to the left-hand lane (leaving the tram tracks clear for trams) and wait for the lights to change to amber before turning. Overhead signs indicate when this rule applies.

The city's three major freeways – the West Gate, Monash and the Tullamarine – are linked by **CityLink** (☎13 26 29, ◍www .citylink.com.au), a 22-kilometre tollway, which is recognizable by blue and yellow signs. Twenty-four hour passes can be purchased to travel on the CityLink before you travel (or up to three days afterwards if you accidentally find yourself on it), and cost $11.40. It starts from your first trip on the tollway. Motorbikes travel for free. You can buy passes from post offices, newsagents or direct from CityLink using a credit card.

Parking is often hard to find in the city centre, even though there are over 10,000 metered spaces and 42,500 off-street car spaces. Coin-operated meters are the norm; for parking lots, expect to pay around $6 an hour, or $30 daily.

Melbourne has a plethora of local and international **car rental** firms, offering a variety of deals and a wide range of cars. Multinational operators such as Hertz, Avis, Budget, Europcar and Thrifty have offices in Melbourne, although local firms almost always offer better value, with "rent-a-bomb" agencies offering good deals from as little as $25 a day; however, these places often have restrictions on how far away from Melbourne you're allowed to go and usually require a minimum rental of at least two days. In general, a city-based rental agency will supply new cars for around $50 a day with unlimited kilometres.

Car and campervan rental companies

Apollo Motorhome Holidays ☎1800 777 779, www.apollocamper.com.au.
Avis UK ☎0844/581 8181, Republic of Ireland ☎021/428 1111, US ☎1-800/331-1212, Canada ☎1-800/879-2847, Australia ☎13 63 33, New Zealand ☎0800/655 111, South Africa ☎11/923 3660; www.avis.com.
Backpacker Campervans ☎1800 670 232, www.backpackercampervans.com.
Britz Australia ☎1800 331 454, www.britz .com.au
Budget UK ☎0870/156 5656, US ☎1-800/527-0700, Canada ☎1-800/268-8900, Australia ☎1300/362 848, New Zealand ☎0800/283 438; www.budget.com.
Europcar UK ☎0845/758 5375, Republic of Ireland ☎01/614 2800, US & Canada ☎1-877/940 6900, Australia ☎1300 131 390; www.europcar .com.
Hertz UK ☎0870/040 9000, Republic of Ireland ☎01/870 5777, US & Canada ☎1-800/654-3131, Australia ☎13 30 39, New Zealand ☎0800/654 321, South Africa ☎21/935 4800; www.hertz .com.
Kea Campers ☎1800 252 555, www .keacampers.com.
Maui ☎1300 363 800, www.maui-rentals.com.
Rent-A-Bomb ☎13 15 53, www.rentabomb .com.au.
Thrifty UK ☎01494/751 540, Republic of Ireland ☎1800/515 800, US & Canada ☎1-800/847-4389, Australia ☎1300 367 227, New Zealand ☎0800/737 070; www.thrifty.com.

The media

Although most newspaper, radio and TV headquarters are based in Sydney, Melbourne produces two daily newspapers and a wide range of media and services.

Newspapers and magazines

Melbourne's premier daily broadsheet is *The Age* (www.theage.com.au), which began operation in 1854. The city's other daily, the tabloid *Herald Sun* (www.heraldsun.news. com.au), has the highest readership. Both Melbourne dailies have more populist, multi-section Sunday versions, the *Sunday Age* and the *Sun Herald Sun*. *The Age* is the paper to buy to find out what's on in Melbourne, especially Tuesday's "Epicure",

which focuses on the city's bar, restaurant and wine scene, and Friday's "EG", an entertainment supplement that includes gig listings and film, art and music reviews. Other specials include Thursday's "Green Guide", a review of the week's TV, latest DVDs and computer games. There are employment and rental sections daily, but the big Saturday edition is the best for these. For a gushy mix of entertainment, sport and gossip, Melbourne's *MX*, a free newspaper geared to commuters, is available each afternoon from Monday to Friday; you'll find it on railway platforms and outside stations. There are also two national newspapers available – the *Australian Financial Review* and *The Australian*.

The *Guardian Weekly* and the *International Herald Tribune* are the most widely available international papers. The State Library of Victoria on Swanston Street (see p.45) keeps a selection of domestic and overseas newspapers. You can also find a good selection of international newspapers at McGills Newsagency, 187 Elizabeth St, in the city, and Borders on Chapel Street (see p.160).

Magazines to look out for include *Beat* and *Inpress*, two free and informative indie music magazines.

Radio

Melbourne has a host of commercial and community **radio stations**. The best are on the government-funded Australian Broadcasting Corporation's (ABC) various local and national stations, all of which can be listened to online at ⓦwww.abc.net.au/streaming. **Radio National** (621 AM) offers a popular mix of arty intellectual topics and **3LO** (774 FM), intelligent talkback radio. **News Radio** (1026 AM), has 24-hour local and international news, current affairs, sports, science and finance, and also airs programmes from a diverse range of foreign radio networks including the BBC World Service, the US's National Public Radio (NPR) and Germany's Radio Deutsche Welle. **ABC Classic FM** (105.9 FM) specializes in classical music; and **3JJJ** ("Triple J"; 107.5 FM) supports local bands and alternative rock. **Nova** (100.3 FM) is another popular station playing new music to 20–30 year-olds. Self-supporting community radio stations, such as **3RRR** (102.7 FM) and **PBS** (106.7 FM), are Melbourne's "underground" alternatives, playing a regular diet of funk, reggae, death metal, techno, house and esoterica. Melbourne's gay and lesbian radio station is **Joy** (94.9 FM).

TV

Australian **television** isn't particularly exciting unless you're into sport. It is extremely commercialized, and films can run for hours because of the number of advertising breaks. Programmes include sport, current affairs, sitcoms (including a number of US imports), real-life and reality game shows and various cop and doc dramas.

Australia's major commercial stations are Channel 7, Channel 9 and Channel 10, while government-sponsored ABC provides the commercial-free Channel 2. Another government-sponsored station is the multicultural Special Broadcasting Service (SBS) on Channel 28.

Travel essentials

Costs

Australia is well set up for budget and independent travellers, offering plenty of low-end accommodation and eating options, and with a student, YHA or backpackers' card you can get discounts on travel, nightlife and entertainment.

Prices in Melbourne are pretty much on a par with Europe or North America. The absolute minimum **daily budget** is around $75 a day for food, board and transport if you stay in hostels, travel on buses and eat and drink frugally. On the other hand, if you're staying in hotels or B&Bs, and eating out regularly, reckon on $115; extras such as clubbing, car rental and tours will all add to your costs.

A goods and services tax (GST) is a broad-based tax of 10 percent on most goods and services such as accommodation, day tours, guides, food, transport (including coach, rail and cruise) and other tourism services within Australia. Visitors can claim back GST through the Tourist Refund Scheme (TRS) when they clear customs at the airport (goods need to be worn or taken with you in hand luggage), providing individual receipts exceed $300 and they were purchased within 30 days.

Although **tipping** is not as widely ingrained as it is in the US or parts of Europe, it is becoming more wide-spread and is always welcomed. Usually 10 percent will suffice for good service, or you might leave the change in a café. For taxi fares, rounding up the fare to the nearest dollar is sufficient. Note that on public holidays cafés and restaurants may add a surcharge of ten percent onto your bill.

Crime and personal safety

Melbourne scores highly for personal safety, but that doesn't mean you should throw caution to the wind. Observe the same precautions with your safety and posses-sions as you would in any other country or at home: avoid badly lit areas at night, keep friends and family informed about where you're travelling to and when you expect to return, and keep items of value in a safe place. Importantly, talk to other travellers about their experiences and get their advice. On Friday and Saturday nights in the city drunk males may pose problems. Train stations are equipped with CCTV cameras – as are many of the busier areas of the city centre. You should also be careful with belongings along most major strips, including the Crown Casino promenade, Spencer Street and Russell Street, a prime area for theft and muggings. Outside the city centre, the popular beachfront suburb and red-light district of St Kilda is still a little rough around the edges so it's wise to be careful at night, particularly in backstreets around Grey, Greeves and Barkly streets.

You're more likely to fall victim to a fellow traveller or an opportunist crime: **theft** is not unusual in hostels and so many provide lockable boxes; if you leave valuables lying around, or on view in cars, you can expect them to be stolen.

If you have any problems, or need to report a theft (for insurance purposes) or any other crime, you can call or drop in at **Victoria Police** station at 637 Flinders St, City (☎9247 6491) or a local police station. For **emergencies**, dial ☎000 for police, ambulance or fire service.

Electricity

Australia's electrical supply runs on 240V, 50 Hz, with three-pronged plugs the norm. Most hotels have provision for AC 110V. British appliances will require an adaptor while North American devices will also need a transformer, available at most leading large hotels or hardware and electrical stores.

Health

The national healthcare scheme, **Medicare**, offers a reciprocal arrangement – free essential healthcare – for citizens of the UK, Ireland, New Zealand, Italy, Malta, Finland, the Netherlands, Norway and Sweden. This free treatment is limited to public hospitals and casualty departments; at GPs, upon presentation of a **Medicare Card** you either pay up front (about $40 minimum) with two-thirds of your fee reimbursed by Medicare, or fill in a bulk bill form and the doctor bills Medicare directly (you don't pay anything). Citizens of New Zealand and Ireland are entitled to free hospital care but will not be issued with a Medicare card and are not entitled to non-hospital care. To apply for a card take your passport along with National Health documents of your country into any Medicare Centre. Ambulance call-outs and dental treatment are not covered on Medicare. You do not need any vaccina-tions to enter Australia.

Major **hospitals** include the Alfred Hospital, Commercial Road, Prahran (☎9076 2000); Royal Children's Hospital, Flemington Road, Parkville (☎9345 5522); Royal Melbourne Hospital, Grattan Street, Parkville (☎9342 7000); and St Vincent's Hospital, Victoria Parade, Fitzroy (☎9288 2211). For first-aid kits and travel health advice contact the Travellers Medical and Vaccination Centre (TMVC), 2nd Floor, 393 Little Bourke St (☎9602 5788).

Insurance

You'd do well to take out an **insurance policy** before travelling to cover against theft, loss and illness or injury. Before paying for a new policy, however, it's worth checking whether you are already covered: some all-risks home insurance policies may cover your possessions when overseas, and many private medical schemes include cover when abroad. In Canada, provincial health plans usually provide partial cover for medical mishaps overseas, while holders of official student/teacher/youth cards in Canada and the US are entitled to meagre accident coverage and hospital inpatient benefits. Students will often find that their student health coverage extends during the vacations and for one term beyond the date of last enrolment.

After checking out the possibilities above, you might want to contact a specialist travel insurance company, or consider the travel insurance deal Rough Guides offer. A typical travel insurance policy usually provides cover for the loss of baggage, tickets and – up to a certain limit – cash or cheques, as well as cancellation or curtailment of your journey. Most of them exclude so-called dangerous sports unless an extra premium is paid: in Australia this can mean anything from scuba diving and surfing to trekking, though probably not kayaking or jeep safaris. Many policies can be chopped and changed to exclude coverage you don't need – for example, sickness and accident benefits can often be excluded or included at will. If you need to make a claim, you should keep receipts for medicines and medical treatment, and in the event you have anything stolen, you must obtain an official statement from the police.

Internet

Public **internet access** is widespread across Australia and keeping in touch online is easy, fast and cheap in Melbourne. Most hostels have internet access, and usually charge around $3–5 per hour; internet cafés offer similar rates. Most local libraries provide free access – usually limited to one hour per day – while public kiosks in some laundries (see above) and larger shopping malls will have you online for a small fee.

The chain Global Gossip has an office (Mon–Sat 9am–11pm, Sun 9am–10pm; ☎9663 0511, ⓦwww.globalgossip.com) in the city at 440 Elizabeth St. Melbourne is also a wireless internet hotspot. Popular access points are the Jam Factory and the Como Centre, both in South Yarra (see p.87), Hudsons Coffee outlets, including one on the corner of Bourke and King streets, and the Crown Entertainment Complex (see p.63).

Laundry

Most hostels and hotels have their own **laundry** facilities, usually coin-operated machines. Commercial laundries include City Edge Laundrette, 39 Errol St, North Melbourne (daily 6am–11pm); My Beautiful Laundrette, 153 Brunswick St, Fitzroy (daily 6.30am–9.30pm); The Soap Opera Laundry & Cafe, 128 Bridport St, Albert Park (daily 7.30am–10pm); and Blessington Street Launderette, 22 Blessington St, St Kilda (daily 7.30am–9pm). Machines cost $3–6 per wash and driers $1 for 6–10min.

Living in Australia

The availability of working visas makes Australia a magnet for budget and independent travellers. Once you've got your visa (see p.24), there are plenty of opportunities **for finding a job**. Melbourne has a number of employment agencies matching people with a variety of roles – from banking and financial positions to call centre work, nannying, nursing and catering. Seasonal and harvest work, in particular, is very popular with travellers across Victoria, especially in the peak season between November and April. On arrival in Melbourne, register with a few agencies to ensure you get access to a good spread of the jobs on offer. Before you start work, open a bank account and get a **Tax File Number** (TFN), available from the Australian Taxation Office (ⓦwww.ato.gov.au); if you don't have a TFN, you'll be slugged a tax rate of 46.5 percent.

Australia-wide online employment websites include JobSearch (ⓦjobsearch.gov.au) and Seek (ⓦwww.seek.com.au). The Saturday editions of *The Age* and *Herald Sun* newspapers also feature comprehensive job listings, while the online versions have jobs searchable by type and location, resume builders, and tips and advice. Some Melbourne hostels have in-house employment agencies, while backpacker travel centres have a job notice board displaying current jobs. For something different, you can sign up to do voluntary work on organic farms – try Willing Workers on Organic Farms (WWOOF) at ⓦwww.wwoof.com.au, which offers everything from animal care to gardening and permaculture.

Melbourne is often referred to as "Australia's student city" and is a major destination for overseas students. **Studying** in Melbourne and Victoria offers value for money as living expenses and tuition costs are less than in the UK and US. Australia's academic year runs from February to December, with applications for many tertiary courses closing the previous October. Most universities provide on-campus accommodation, and are equipped to help students find a place to live. If you're a full-time student you qualify for a range of concessions, including discounted travel and cut-price cinema tickets.

For details on educational opportunities in Melbourne and Victoria, links to Victorian institutions and comprehensive information about studying and living in Victoria, visit the Study in Melbourne website at ⓦwww .studymelbourne.com.au.

Mail

Post offices are generally open Monday to Friday 9am to 5pm. Melbourne's General Post Office at 250 Elizabeth St keeps longer hours: Monday to Friday 8.30am to 5.30pm and Saturday 9am to 5pm. There are red post boxes dotted throughout the city. **Stamps** are sold at newsagents and Australia Post shops costing $0.55 for a postcard or small letter (130mm x 240mm) within Australia; $1.35 to the US, Canada, South Africa and Europe; letters (weighing up to 50g) start at $2.05 to the US, Canada, South Africa and Europe.

A **Poste Restante** service is available at the General Post Office; you'll need a passport or other ID to collect your mail, which is kept for just one month.

Maps

To help you navigate your way around the centre of Melbourne, the maps in this book should be sufficient. Alternatively the Metlink issue **free urban maps** of the city and the suburbs, available from the visitors centre at Federation Square as well as cafés and hostels. If you plan on staying in Melbourne for a while, you might like to buy something more comprehensive; Melbourne's best street directory is *Melway* ($52.95), available from bookshops and newsagents. If you've rented a car, make sure the rental company has provided a Melbourne street directory before you head off.

The best place to buy maps in Melbourne is Mapland, 372 Little Bourke St (Mon–Thurs 9am–5.30pm, Fri 9am–6pm, Sat 9.30am–5pm; ☎9670 4383, ⓦwww.mapland.com .au). Victoria's motoring organization, the Royal Automobile Club of Victoria (RACV), 438 Little Collins St, City (Mon–Fri 9am–5pm, Sat 10am–1pm), publishes road maps of Melbourne and the state. The maps are free to members of associated overseas motoring organizations.

Money

The currency is the **Australian dollar** (sometimes referred to as buck), which is divided into 100 cents. The colourful plastic notes are available in denominations of $100, $50, $20, $10 and $5, while coins come in values of $2, $1, 50¢, 20¢, 10¢ and 5¢. There are no 1¢ or 2¢ coins so an irregular bill will be rounded up or down, for instance $1.98 will be rounded up to $2.

At the time of writing the Australian dollar has an **exchange rate** of AUS$2.05 for £1; AUS$1.40 for US$1; and AUS$1.85 for €1.

The major banks (Australia's "big four") are the National Australia Bank (ⓦwww.national .com.au), the Commonwealth (ⓦwww .commbank.com.au), Westpac (ⓦwww .westpac.com.au), and ANZ (ⓦwww.anz .com.au); their head branches, all with foreign currency counters, are in the CBD along Bourke and Collins streets. **ATM**s are usually located outside banks but also in front of shops, are often open 24 hours and allow international access for cards in the Cirrus-Maestro network (including Visa and Mastercard). The daily withdrawal limit is usually $1000. **Foreign exchange** booths can be found in both the domestic and international airport terminals, and throughout the city centre, mainly along Swanston Street, near Flinders Street Station. Australia Post outlets also act as Commonwealth and Australia Bank agents and allow you to withdraw and exchange cash. Most retailers offer EFTPOS (Electronic Funds Transfer at Point of Sale) facilities which allow you to pay directly for goods like a debit card and withdraw cash as well.

Youth and student ID cards soon pay for themselves in savings. Full-time students are eligible for the International Student ID Card (ISIC; ⓦwww.isiccard.com), which entitles the bearer to special air, rail and bus fares and discounts at museums, theatres and other attractions. The card costs £9; US$22; or $18 in Australia itself. If you're no longer a student, but are 26 or younger, you still qualify for the International Youth Travel Card, which costs the same price and carries the same benefits, while teachers qualify for the International Teacher Card (same price and some of the benefits). All these cards are available from the website or branches of STA Travel.

Opening hours and public holidays

Business hours are generally Monday to Friday 9am to 5pm, with shops and services usually open Monday to Saturday 9am to 5.30pm, and until 7pm or 9pm on Thursday and Friday nights. The major retailers and shopping malls in the city and suburban areas are also open on Sunday between noon and 5pm, and big supermarkets generally open seven days from 8am until 9pm, though some close around 5pm on Sunday. There are several 24-hour convenience stores/supermarkets in the inner city and suburbs, and an all-night Coles supermarket on the corner of Elizabeth and Flinders streets. Melbourne's **banking hours** are generally Monday to Thursday 9.30am to 4pm and Friday 9.30am to 5pm.

Tourist attractions such as museums, galleries and historic monuments are usually open between 10am and 5pm, and during school holidays and public holidays. All close on Christmas Day and Good Friday, as do virtually all banks, post offices and businesses, but otherwise specific opening hours are given throughout this Guide.

Phones

Local calls from a **payphone** cost a flat rate of 50¢, unless you're phoning a mobile telephone (number beginning in 04) then the call is timed. Newsagents, post office and some backpacker hostels sell **phonecards** which can be used to phone home at a discounted rate. If you're staying a while you might want to buy a **pre-paid mobile phone**, available from network providers such as Vodafone, Optus and Telstra.

The prefix ☎1800 indicates a toll-free number, while ☎13 or 1300 are charged at

Public and school holidays

When a **public holiday** falls on a Saturday or Sunday, the following Monday is taken as holiday. Most businesses such as post offices and banks will close and public transport is limited, though many bars, restaurants and cafés stay open. National holidays are listed below.

The school year is divided into four terms with one long six-week holiday from mid-December to end January and three more fortnights spread through the year. You can roughly depend on **holidays** being around Easter, late June to early July and mid-September to early October. Prices rise during these periods, accommodation gets booked up and attractions are generally a lot busier.

New Year's Day January 1
Australia Day January 26
Easter (Good Friday and Easter Monday) Early April
Labour Day First or second Monday in March
Anzac Day April 25
Queen's Birthday Second Monday in June
Melbourne Cup Day First Tuesday in November
Christmas Day December 25
Boxing Day December 26

Calling home from Australia

The **international access code** for Australia is ☎0011. Note that the initial zero is omitted from the area or city code when dialling the UK, the Republic of Ireland and New Zealand from abroad.

To call **New Zealand**: international access code + 64 + city code.

To call the **Republic of Ireland**: international access code + 353 + city code.

To call **South Africa**: international access code + 27 + city code.

To call the **UK**: international access code + 44 + city code.

To call the **US and Canada**: international access code + 1 + area code.

local rate; these numbers can only be dialled within Australia.

The **area code** for Melbourne and Victoria is 03, but when dialling within the state there's no need to include the code. To **call Australia** from home dial the international access code + 61 + city code, omitting the initial zero.

Time

Melbourne follows Eastern Standard Time (EST), half an hour ahead of South Australia and the Northern Territory, two hours ahead of Western Australia, ten hours ahead of Greenwich Mean Time (GMT) and fifteen hours ahead of US Eastern Standard Time. Clocks are put forward one hour in October and back again in March for daylight savings.

Tourist information

Information on Melbourne and Victoria is easy to get hold of, either online at the Australian Tourist Commission website ⓦ www.australia.com or Tourism Victoria's ⓦ www.visitmelbourne.com and ⓦwww .visitvictoria.com, or, after arrival, from the excellent **Visitor Information Centre** in Federation Square, corner of Flinders and Swanston streets (daily 9am–6pm; ⓦwww .thatsmelbourne.com.au/touristinforma-tion). The centre has information on events, advice on the best things to see and do, multilingual facilities, internet access, and an accommodation and tour booking service. There are free pamphlets galore, although some attract a small charge. There's also a volunteer-staffed **visitor information booth** at Bourke St Mall (Mon–Sat 9am–5pm, Sun 10am–4pm).

The Visitor Information Centre is the starting point for the **Melbourne Greeter Service** (☎0401 993 101), a free half-day walking orientation of the city. Visitors are matched with volunteer "greeters" according to language, age and interests. The service, which is available daily, needs to be booked at least a week in advance.

Outside Melbourne, regional Visitor Information Centres are thick on the ground – look out for the distinctive blue and yellow "i" sign. Providing reliable information on attractions, activities and events, the centres can also help you make reservations for accommodation or sightseeing tours, or give up-to-the-minute advice on travel in the area.

For information on **national parks** and conservation areas in Victoria, contact Parks Victoria (☎13 19 63, ⓦwww.parkweb.vic .gov.au).

Tourist offices and government sites

Australian Department of Foreign Affairs
ⓦ www.dfat.gov.au, ⓦ www.smartraveller.gov.au.
British Foreign & Commonwealth Office
ⓦ www.fco.gov.uk/en.
Canadian Department of Foreign Affairs
ⓦ www.dfait-maeci.gc.ca.
Irish Department of Foreign Affairs ⓦwww .foreignaffairs.gov.ie.
New Zealand Ministry of Foreign Affairs
ⓦ www.mft.govt.nz.
US State Department ⓦwww.travel.state.gov.

Travellers with disabilities

The **Travellers Aid Society** (ⓦwww .travellersaid.org.au) provides information for the disabled; they have two offices, one at

35

Southern Cross Station (under Bourke Street Bridge), the other at Flinders Street Station (between platform 9 & 10, within the ticket area).They both offer assistance and internet facilities. The **Melbourne Mobility Centre** located on level 1 of Federation Square car park (Mon–Fri 9am–6pm, Sat & Sun 10am–4pm; ☎9650 6499) rents mobility equipment and provides information and maps for getting around Melbourne. Other resources include ⓦwww.disability.vic.gov.au; ⓦwww .accessibility.com.au and ⓦwww.paraquad .asn.au. Assistance is available at metropolitan, suburban, country and interstate stations, while relevant information for people with disabilities can be obtained by calling the Met Transport Information Centre on ☎13 16 38. Trams are progressively being replaced with low-floor wheelchair-accessible models, and all trains are wheelchair-accessible from the front carriage. The Melbourne City Council produces a **free mobility map** of the CBD showing accessible routes, transport and toilets in the city centre, available from the front desk of the Melbourne Town Hall, or you can download a copy from ⓦwww.melbourne.vic.gov.au. Also look out for the Vic Venue Guide, which provides details on a range of disability access provisions at arts and entertainment venues – for more information, contact **Arts Access** (☎9699 8299; ⓦwww.artsaccess .com.au). For wheelchair-accessible taxis, see p.28.

The City

The City

The east side

The east side impressively captures the "Marvellous Melbourne" era which followed the discovery of gold in 1851. Bounded by Swanston, Flinders, Spring and Victoria streets, the area is replete with grand nineteenth-century buildings, buzzes with designer shops and elegant cafés, and is the focal point of much of Melbourne's cultural and political life.

Many of Melbourne's best-known buildings were constructed in the three decades after gold was discovered, notably the imposing **Parliament House** on Spring Street, book-ended by small and tranquil gardens to the north and south, and the handsome **Old Treasury Building** nearby – now home to the **City Museum**. Melbourne's short but prosperous history is also reflected in two magnificent nineteenth-century cathedrals, Catholic **St Patrick's** and Anglican **St Paul's**, built to administer spiritual salvation to a rapidly expanding and increasingly diverse population, while to the north is arguably the most interesting of all the city's historic sights, the **Old Melbourne Gaol**, which captures in grisly detail the fates of some of the early city's less fortunate souls. The east side also holds plenty of contemporary diversions, from the well-heeled boutiques and cafés at the **"Paris End"** of **Collins Street** to the restaurants and stores of **Chinatown**, home to the large Chinese community that established itself in Melbourne in the 1880s and which – later augmented by waves of postwar Greek and Italian immigrants – has done much to give the east side precincts their cosmopolitan accent. The most recent addition to the area, the **QV** retail complex more than lives up to the splendour of its surroundings, its busy laneways home to cafés, shops and many of the best fashion boutiques in the city.

Flinders Street Station and around

Located in the heart of the city on the corner of Flinders Street and St Kilda Road, the Neoclassical **Flinders Street Station** (1910) is the traditional gateway to the city for the 100,000-plus commuters who pass through it every day. The station's imposing bulk, complete with dome and clock tower, is reasonably eye-friendly, while the entrance acts as a landmark-cum-meeting place (Ava Gardner and Gregory Peck had a gloriously prolonged goodbye here in the film *On the Beach*), where people gather under the famous clocks, each of which indicates the next scheduled departure on a different suburban line.

Opposite the station, on the corner of Swanston and Flinders streets, **St Paul's Cathedral** (Mon–Fri 8am–6pm, Sat 9am–5pm, Sun 8am–7pm; Evensong Tues–Fri 5.10pm, Sun 6pm) rises resplendent, after a recent multimillion-dollar restoration. It was built between 1880 and 1891 on the site where the colony's

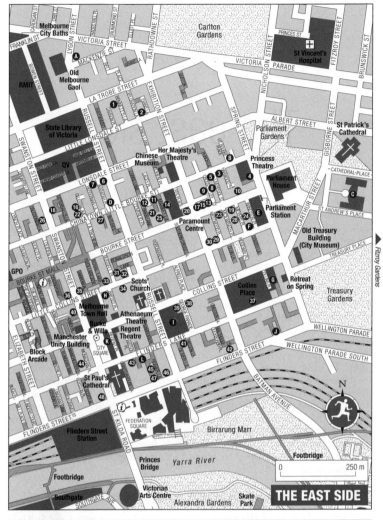

THE EAST SIDE

ACCOMMODATION		CAFÉS & RESTAURANTS				PUBS, BARS & CLUBS			
Adelphi	L	Bamboo House	5	Pellegrini's		Bridie O'Reilly's	29	Purple Emerald	43
City Centre Budget	F	Becco	9	Espresso Bar	13	Cookie	18	Spleen	19
City Limits Motel	B	Café L'Incontro	35	Punch Lane	3	The Croft Institute	21	Troika	2
Exford	D	ezard	L	Shark Fin House	12	Ding Dong Lounge	14	Young &	
Grand Hyatt	I	Fifteen	39	Stalactites	6	The Elephant		Jackson's	48
Hotel Lindrum	J	Flower Drum	25	Supper Inn	16	and Wheelbarrow	20		
Park Hyatt	C	Gopals	36	Tsindos	7	Gin Palace	31	LIVE MUSIC VENUES	
Hotel Sofitel	G	Grossi Florentino	17	Verve Boutique	34	Hairy Canary	33	Bennetts Lane	1
Victoria Hall	A	Il Bacaro	32	West Lake	27	Loop	28	Ding Dong Lounge	14
Victoria	H	Il Solito Posto	38	Yu-u	41	Lounge Upstairs	26	The Forum Theatre	46
Westin	K	Kenzan	37			Madame Brussels	23	Hi Fi Bar	
Windsor	E	Kun Ming Restaurant	22			Melbourne Supper Club	4	and Ballroom	40
		Lounge Downstairs	26			Meyers Place	24	Manchester Lane	44
		Mask of China	11			Misty	45	Palace Theatre	10
		MoVida	47			New Gold Mountain	8	Pony	30
		Nudel Bar	15			Phoenix	42		

first settlers had held ecumenical services in a tent pitched under a gum tree, to a Gothic Revival design by English architect William Butterfield – who never actually visited Australia. The cathedral has the highest spire in the world after England's Salisbury Cathedral, while inside, intricate tiled floors compete with carved woodwork, magnificent stained-glass windows and a beautiful pulpit bearing a representation of the head of Nellie Cain, daughter of lay canon William Cain, chairman of the committee which organized the building of the church, who died at a young age.

Running up from the cathedral is central Melbourne's main north–south axis, **Swanston Street**, a drab and grotty stretch of low-rent shops, souvenir outlets and fast-food joints that gets progressively studenty the further north you head towards the State Library of Victoria (see p.45). If you need a drink, head to the historic **Young & Jackson's** pub on the corner of Swanston and Flinders streets, which has been a boozer since 1861. Upstairs in *Chloe's Bar*, patrons drink pots under the portrait of *Chloe*, a full-length nude painted by her lover, French artist Jules Lefebvre. The painting may seem tame today, but it drew thin-lipped disapproval from Melbourne society when it arrived from France in the 1880s. So much so that when it went on show at the National Gallery of Victoria, it caused a public outcry and was taken down after only a few weeks. The painting was bought by the hotel in 1908, installed in the public bar, and has now become an affectionately regarded Melbourne icon.

Melbourne Town Hall

Two blocks north of the cathedral is another civic icon: the late 19th-century **Melbourne Town Hall** (free guided tours Mon–Fri 11am & 1pm; ☎9658 9658). It is best known as the place where Australia's most famous soprano, Dame Nellie Melba, made her debut in 1884, but it has also played host to everything from public debates and waltzes to poultry shows and wrestling. Here the Queen sipped tea in the stately Melbourne Room in 1954; ten years later, the Beatles waved to their adoring fans from the balcony; and in 1997, Germaine Greer kicked off the annual Melbourne Writers' Festival by launching a stinging attack against "penetration culture" (old-fogey Melburnians are still recovering). Today the Town Hall is a major corporate gala and wedding venue, and can only be seen on a **tour**, when you can roam through rooms mired in syrupy nostalgia, and observe the grand organ, the largest in the southern hemisphere. There's also an excellent collection of rustic paintings by early Melbourne artists Tom Roberts and George Folingsby.

Across Collins Street, the *Westin Hotel* (see p.104) squats over **City Square**, a beleaguered space formed during the 1960s by clearing a number of nineteenth-century buildings in order to create what was hoped to be an appealing and welcoming public square. Today it's nothing more than a desperately small strip of dusty land, having been surpassed by Federation Square (see p.67), further south. On the corner is a forty-ton statue of bewhiskered *Burke and Wills*, two of Australia's best-known explorers who perished on a transcontinental expedition in 1860. The statue was roundly scorned when it was first unveiled, largely because it was felt the artist has made the hapless pair too "heroic". Also worth a look from here is the **Manchester Unity Building** (1932), on the corner of Collins and Swanston streets. Melbourne was in the depths of the Depression at the time, and the project was intended to provide work for the unemployed. It rose at the astonishing rate of a storey per week, to become the tallest building in the city.

The "Paris End"

From City Square, **Collins Street** rises up past the pompous **Athenaeum Theatre**, housing a cosy library with a good selection of biographies and detective fiction as well as a small section on theatre and plays, and continues to Gothic Revival **Scots' Church**, famous mainly as the place where Dame Nellie Melba first sang in the choir. Further up, I.M. Pei's *Hotel Sofitel* dominates the upper part of the street. Though known as the "Paris End" (or "Top End"), there's nothing especially Parisian about this end of Collins Street: alongside the exclusive boutiques and cafés, the imposing corporate buildings with vacuous 1980s-style foyers, are famous for hosting hundreds of doctors and dentists.

At no. 101 is one of Melbourne's more daring modern commercial buildings, inventively combining erotic sculptures with freestanding columns, while nearby **Collins Place** houses the fifty-storey *Sofitel* and below ground the arthouse Kino cinema (see p.144). Opposite, at no. 36, is one of Australia's last bastions of male chauvinism, the snooty, gentlemen-only **Melbourne Club** (1858).

At the top of Collins Street, on the junction with Spring and Macarthur streets, the superb **Old Treasury Building** is emblematic of Melbourne's goldrush prosperity, combining elegance with unbridled opulence in its graceful balconies and high-ceilinged rooms. Completed in 1862 to a design by John James Clark, who was just 19 at the time, the building was built to store the city's gold. Today it houses the **City Museum** (Mon–Fri 9am–5pm, Sat & Sun 10am–4pm; $8.50 ☎9651 2233, ⓦwww.citymuseummelbourne .org), which has exhibitions on the social and architectural history of Melbourne on themes such as *Making Melbourne*, *Growing up in the Old Treasury* and *Built on Gold*, an audio-visual presentation shown in the gold-vaults deep in the basement.

Adjoining the building are the small **Treasury Gardens**, planted with European trees, such as elms, plane trees and Canary Island palms, and packed most weekdays with office workers. Also within the gardens is a bronze-relief memorial to former US President J.F. Kennedy. At night, the gardens are overrun with possums scrounging for food.

Fitzroy Gardens

A stone's throw east, **Fitzroy Gardens** stand on what was a swamp until the 1860s, when the land was reclaimed and turned into a garden laid out in the shape of the Union Jack – a jingoistic conceit happily later abandoned in favour of a more free-flowing design. Named after Sir Charles Augustus Fitzroy, Governor of New South Wales (1846–1851) and Governor-General of the Australian Colonies (1851–1855), they are best appreciated on weekdays, as weekends tend to attract cavalcades of bridal parties having their photographs taken. Hidden among the trees is the twee red-brick, creeper-covered **Captain Cook's Cottage** (daily 9am–5pm; $4.50), family home of Captain James Cook, the English navigator who first "discovered" the east coast of Australia. Purchased for £800 in 1933 by Russell Grimwade, a wealthy Melbourne businessman, it was shipped over piece by piece from its original location in Great Ayton, North Yorkshire, and presented as a gift to the state of Victoria for its 1934 centenary.

Grimwade wanted to set up the cottage in front of the State Library of Victoria, but the idea "of a whole pile of rubbish cluttering up the lawn" was poo-pooed. Other locations were suggested – including the St Kilda foreshore

– until its present position was agreed. Period fittings attempt to re-create the atmosphere of eighteenth-century England, reinforced by worthy displays about the explorer himself. The only link with the cottage and its original inhabitants is the stone inscription "JCG 1755" for Cook's parent James and Grace above the main doorway.

Nearby is a small **conservatory** (daily 7am–5pm; free) whose flower displays change throughout the year. Elsewhere in the gardens a tacky fenced-off model **Tudor village** continues the olde-worlde theme. Created by 77-year-old Edgar Wilson from England, the "village" was presented to the people of Melbourne in 1948 in appreciation of food sent to Britain during World War II. The model apes typical Tudor Kent villages, complete with thatched cottages, school, hotel, barns, church, streets plus an incongruous scale model of the house in which William Shakespeare lived in Warwickshire. Opposite, the **Fairies' Tree** – an old gum tree sculpted with fairies, dwarfs, gnomes and koalas – is popular with visitors of all ages.

Parliament House and around

Returning to the Old Treasury Building and heading up Spring Street brings you to **Eastern Hill**, the site selected by Charles La Trobe, Victoria's first governor, for the state's new parliament building in 1854. Oozing authority at its summit is the colossal **Parliament House** (free 50min tours Mon–Fri 10am, 11am, noon, 2pm, 3pm & 3.45pm on days when parliament is not sitting; ☏ 9651 8568 for dates), built in stages between 1856 and 1930 on a grassy knoll known as Lovers' Lane. Following the federation of Australia's six colonies in 1901, the first Federal Parliament of Australia took over the building, forcing the Victorian Government to find alternative accommodation in the Royal Exhibition Building (see p.75), where it remained until 1927. The Federal Parliament then shifted to Canberra, allowing the Victorian Government to reclaim its original home.

Through the main doors a vestibule leads into the elaborate Queen's Hall, used mainly for formal state functions, while doors to the right and left connect with the chambers of the Legislative Council and Legislative Assembly. If parliament is sitting, don't miss **Question Time** (2pm; arrive early to claim a seat), when you can sit in the Public Gallery and – depending on the subject of the debate – listen either to the members' heated exchanges or count the number who have fallen asleep.

Opposite Parliament House, the immaculately preserved **Windsor Hotel** began life as the *Grand Hotel* in 1883, before being taken over three years later by future Victorian premier James Munro, who established his moral credentials by immediately declaring the establishment teetotal. Check out the palatial interior, its rooms resonating with the hum of well-bred conversation, or indulge in a posh afternoon tea (Mon–Fri 3–5pm; $45; Sat & Sun $65) of pastries and sandwiches in the hotel's restaurant, *111 Spring Street*. Just north on the same side of the street, the **Princess Theatre** is a sparky piece of nineteenth-century chic which opened in 1886 and was transformed a year later into one of Melbourne's most extravagant buildings in recognition of Queen Victoria's Golden Jubilee Year. Designed by William Pitt, the Princess is arguably Australia's most lavish theatre, its flamboyant exterior topped off by a gilded trumpeting angel and its interior housing the latest hi-tech stage equipment. Legend has it that the theatre is haunted by the ghost of one Frederick Baker ("Federici") who had a heart attack and died while playing Mephistopheles in the opera *Faust*. The café is named in his honour.

To the northeast looms Catholic **St Patrick's Cathedral** (daily 8am–5pm), designed by William Wardell, the architect responsible for some of Melbourne's finest nineteenth-century churches. A more modest church stood on the site until 1850, when the Reverend J.A. Goold, Bishop of Melbourne, decided it was too small for the city's burgeoning population and had it demolished. Its replacement was still under construction when, in 1858, the ambitious Goold declared that a still grander cathedral was required, to be constructed on the proceeds of Victoria's booming pastoral industries. Work proceeded slowly, however, and was frequently suspended as labour vanished to the goldfields. Finally consecrated in 1897, the cathedral has some of the city's finest stained-glass windows, while the beautifully proportioned interior is graced by an eagle-shaped brass lectern.

Chinatown

Back towards the city centre, Melbourne's small but lively **Chinatown** revolves around the section of Little Bourke Street between Swanston and Exhibition streets. Australia's oldest permanent Chinese settlement, the area began as a few boarding houses in the 1850s, when the goldrush began to attract prospectors from the Pearl River Delta near Hong Kong. The area grew as gold petered out and Chinese fortune-seekers returned from the backbreaking work of prospecting to settle in the city. Spruced up in 1974 as a tourist attraction, Chinatown retains a low-rise, narrow-laned, nineteenth-century character, with atmospheric cafés, restaurants and shops selling everything from Chinese bric-a-brac to dried mushrooms. Hong Kong actor and director Jackie Chan made good use of the location, shooting several madcap scenes here for his Cantonese-language flick *Mr Nice Guy*, in which he played the part of a Melbourne TV chef.

Established in 1985 in an old warehouse on Cohen Place, the **Chinese Museum** (daily 10am–5pm; $7.50; ☎ 9662 2888, ⓦ www.chinesemuseum.com .au) traces the experience of Chinese immigrants in Australia during the mid-nineteenth century, especially their role in the development of Melbourne during the goldrush. The museum is worth a visit for the 92-metre-long Dai Loong dragon alone, paraded each Chinese New Year and during the Moomba Festival (see p.146). There's also a good collection of antiques and artefacts relating to Chinatown's social history, together with an exhibition gallery showcasing Chinese costumes and musical instruments. The museum organizes two-hour **guided tours** of the building and Chinatown ($18, or $34 including lunch); these require a minimum of four people, and should be booked two or three days in advance.

QV

Bounded by Swanston, Lonsdale, Russell and Little Lonsdale streets, the vast complex known as the **QV building** was built in 2004 to a tune of $600 million on the site of the former Queen Victoria Women's Hospital – Victoria's first women's hospital. It comprises a food court with cheap eats, bars, edgy fashion boutiques, residential apartments and the slick corporate headquarters of global mining giant BHP Billiton. The original hospital, a smart brick building designed by the ubiquitous John James Clarke (of Old Treasury fame – see p.42), looks a bit like a comfortably settled older house that's had a glassy modern shopping mall built around it.

A series of laneways and arcades traverses the complex, designed to extend the network north of the city, and named to reflect the site's medical history: one of the busiest, **Albert Coates Lane** (named after a World War I stretcher-bearer, who became a leading surgeon at the hospital), runs east from Swanston Street above the intersection with Lonsdale Street and showcases stores from top local and overseas designers including Christensen Copenhagen, Cactus Jam, Guess, Hugo Boss and Wayne Cooper.

State Library of Victoria

A blink away just north of here at 328 Swanston St is the **State Library of Victoria** (Mon–Thurs 10am–9pm, Fri–Sun 10am–6pm; free introductory tours Mon–Fri 2pm; ☎8664 7000, ⓦwww.slv.vic.gov.au). Australia's first public library and one of Victoria's grandest civic monuments, the "people's university" was founded by Anglo-Irish judge and philanthropist Sir Redmond Barry, most famous for being the man who sentenced Ned Kelly to hang (see box, p.46). The library opened in 1856, although construction of the portico, dome and reading room, modelled on the reading room of the British Museum, weren't finished until 1913. The library houses a trove of paintings and rare and antiquarian books and newspapers, along with material such as the diaries of founding fathers Charles La Trobe and John Pascoe Fawkner (see p.228); the deed of land purchase by John Batman from the Dugitalla Aborigines; Ned Kelly's armour and the famous rage-filled Jerilderie letter which inspired Peter Carey's Booker Prize-winning novel *The True History of the Kelly Gang* (see p.235); and a leaf of the Gutenberg Bible, the first major work printed using moveable type in 1455. There's also a Chess Room featuring chess-related literature and a number of game tables. At the entrance of the library is a statue of Sir Redmond, and beyond, Petrus Spronks' *Architectural Fragment*, one of Melbourne's more famous and friendlier public sculptures. Refurbishment has returned the building to its former grandeur, complemented by state-of-the-art storage facilities and information services.

Melbourne is home to a large Greek community and **Lonsdale Street**, running along the south side of the State Library, is its heart, a place where you can linger in cake shops and grocery stores, take in the New Age instrumentals of Yanni blasted from doorway speakers or watch the old men playing "tavli" in the outdoor cafes. There are also restaurants such as *Stalactites* and *Tsindos* (p.114) serving tzatziki, souvlaki and traditional Greek coffee and cakes.

RMIT

If it's contemporary architecture you're after the **Royal Melbourne Institute of Technology** (RMIT), just across La Trobe Street, is a scene-stealer that mixes the shock of the new with the style and proportion of the old. Consisting of the shell of a Victorian building embellished with striking modern facades, architectural surprises include Building 8, with a playful combination of colour, shapes and perforations, and Storey Hall, with a pick'n'mix facade of livid green and purple patterns, loosely arranged according to the principles of chaos theory. The interest continues inside Storey Hall, with terrific installations, including an auditorium in which the original Victorian fittings have been immersed in great panels of pink, purple, green and white. Downstairs there's a minimalist gallery, *First Site* (Tues–Fri 11am–5pm, Sat 1–5pm; free), which shows new works by students. There is also a subterranean café.

Ned Kelly

Notorious bushranger, national hero and potent symbol of freedom and resistance to authority, **Ned Kelly** was hanged at Melbourne Gaol in 1880. It was the final curtain in one of the most colourful and controversial careers in Australia's history. Kelly was born in December 1854, near the town of Beveridge in Victoria. When he was 12, his Irish father John "Red" Kelly, an ex-convict, died of dropsy, forcing Kelly to leave school and become the family breadwinner. Soon after, his mother Ellen, a woman of frontier fire and fortitude, moved the family to a slab hut in the tiny Victorian community of Greta to be near her own family, the Quinns, who were squatters. Greta was something of a lawless outpost, and the young Kelly was soon in constant trouble with the police, who considered the whole family troublemakers.

Having served a brief apprenticeship with the infamous bushranger, Harry Power, Kelly formed a gang (Kelly, his brother Dan and mates Joe Byrne and Steve Hart) in 1878 and they fled to the countryside, roaming and living off their wits. At the time, bushrangers stole livestock to cash in on high meat prices; horses for transport; and gold as it was transported from the diggings. They robbed banks, businesses and private houses, and they lived in the bush, where many were born, hiding from a Victorian police force depleted in numbers from an exodus of officers to the goldfields.

One day, hearing that Dan had turned up at his mother's, a policeman set out, drunk and without a warrant, to arrest him. A scuffle ensued and the unsteady constable fell to the floor, hitting his head and allowing Dan to escape. The following day, warrants were issued for the arrest of Ned (who was in New South Wales at the time) and Dan for attempted murder, and their mother was sentenced to three years' imprisonment. From this point on, the Kelly gang's crime spree accelerated and, following the death of three constables in a shoot-out at Stringybark Creek, in east Victoria, the biggest manhunt in Australia's history began, with a £1000 reward offered for the gang's apprehension. On December 9, 1878, they robbed the bank at Euroa in Victoria's northeast, taking £2000, before moving on to Jerilderie in New South Wales, where Kelly dictated a now famous letter to bushranger Joe Byrne justifying his actions (see p.45).

After a year on the run, the gang formulated a grand plan: they executed Aaron Sherritt, a police informer, in Sebastopol, thus attracting a train-bound posse from nearby Beechworth. It was planned to derail this train at Glenrowan with as much bloodshed as possible, before moving on to rob the bank at Benalla and barter hostages for the release of Kelly's mother. In the event, having already sabotaged the tracks, the gang commandeered the *Glenrowan Inn* and, in a moment of drunken candour, Kelly detailed his ambush to a schoolteacher who escaped, managing to save the special train.

As the armed troopers approached the inn, the gang prepared for their last stand. In a back room, the clanking sounds of Kelly donning his home-made iron armour, which has since become his motif, could be heard. The armour weighed ninety pounds. Police surrounded the hotel and at 3am opened fire. When the smoke had cleared, Dan Kelly, Joe Byrne and Steve Hart lay dead. Incredibly, Ned escaped to the bush, but returned to the inn at sunrise hoping to rescue his brother. Seeing Kelly appear out of the morning mist, the police aimed low, where Kelly was vulnerable, taking out his legs in a volley of bullets. The inn was torched, while Ned himself was taken alive, tried by the same judge who had incarcerated his mother, and sentenced to hang.

Public sympathies lay strongly with Ned Kelly, and a crowd of five thousand gathered outside Melbourne Gaol on November 11, 1880 for his execution, believing that the 25-year-old bushranger would "die game". True to form, his last words are said to have been "Such is life".

Today, Ned Kelly is indelibly stamped on the nation's psyche – part villain, part folk hero, but also a man whose courage and defiance is uniquely Australian.

Immediately north is the congenial red-brick building of the **Melbourne City Baths**, constructed in 1860 so that the great unwashed could scrub themselves here rather than in Port Phillip Bay or the typhoid-stricken River Yarra. It was a time when "germ theory", which argued that contagious diseases came from individuals rather than the environment, added impetus to the prevailing obsession with cleanliness. After winning a contract to redevelop the baths in 1901, John James Clark, who also designed the Old Treasury Building and many other great Melbourne landmarks, arrived at the present style, with its distinctive "blood and bandages" red-brick and cream facade, and the new baths were opened in 1904. Over the years, the heritage-listed building has survived numerous fires, termites and rising damp to play a leading role in Melbourne's social history, a place where Melburnians could wash, swim, gossip and work out. In one of the terrazzo-floored cubicles, you can still bathe in a grand claw-foot hot tub shipped over from England in the nineteenth century ($5.10), swim in the thirty-metre men's pool or fifteen-metre women's pool (the pools were segregated until 1947), relax in inviting lounges and open-air terraces, work out in a belly dancing or yoga class, or sweat it out in a sauna (see p.153).

Old Melbourne Gaol

Behind the RMIT on Russell Street, the massive **Old Melbourne Gaol** (daily 9.30am–5pm; $20; guided "Hangman's Night Tour" four times a week: April–Oct 7.30pm, Nov–March 8.30pm; $30; advance bookings through Ticketmaster on ☎ 13 28 49; ☎ 8663 7228, ⊛ www.oldmelbournegaol.com.au) is the city's most popular historic sight, largely on account of its associations with Victorian bushranger Ned Kelly, who was hanged here on November 11, 1880. Opened in 1854, the jail was modelled on Pentonville Prison in London, with high-ceilinged brick cells and observation towers to prevent escape. Melbourne's general state of lawlessness during the goldrushes caused such overcrowding that the jail was continually expanded – later additions include the thick outer wall where, in 1880, thousands gathered to hear that Kelly had been executed. A mix of condemned men and women (there was no segregation until 1864), remand, short-sentence prisoners and "lunatics" (often, in fact, drunks) were housed here – long-term prisoners were incarcerated in hulks moored at Williamstown, or at the Pentridge Stockade. The jail was recommended for closure in 1870 due to overcrowding, but it wasn't until 1929 that it was shut for good, although it later served as a detention barracks for AWOL soldiers during World War II. Much has been torn down since its closure, but the entrance and outer wall still survive, and it's worth walking round the outside of the building to take a look at the formidable arched brick portal on Franklin Street

The gruesome collection of death masks on show in the tiny cells bears witness to the nineteenth-century obsession with phrenology, a branch of science which studied how people's characters were related to the size and shape of their skulls. Accompanying the masks are compelling case histories of the murderers and their victims. Most fascinating are the women: Martha Needle, who poisoned her husband and daughters (among others) with arsenic, and young Martha Knorr, the notorious "baby farmer". Advertising herself as a "kind motherly person, willing to adopt a child", she received a few dollars per child, who she then killed and buried in her backyard. The jail serves up other macabre memorabilia, including the beam from which Kelly was hanged, a scaffold in working order, various nooses, and a triangle on

▲ Old Melbourne Gaol

which malcontents were strapped to receive lashes with a cat-o'-nine-tails. Perhaps the ultimate rite of visitor passage is the "Art of Hanging", an interpretive display about hanging in the 1800s that's part educational tool and part setting for a medieval snuff movie.

The west side

The land on the banks of the River Yarra now occupied by the **west side** of the city was for centuries a favoured hunting ground for the local Aboriginal people, who caught eels from the marshy lagoons. In 1835 it was selected by former bushranger John Batman (see p.228) as the site for a new pastoral settlement, and "bought" from the locals for £200-worth of knives, tools and other trinkets. The river provided early settlers with easy access to the sea and soon docks were constructed, marshlands drained, and slaughterhouses and gasworks introduced. Development only really took off, however, when vast numbers of fortune-seekers began to pour in during the goldrush of the 1850s. Bounded by Swanston Street to the east and Victoria Street to the north and stretching west beyond Spencer Street to the new Docklands development, this is the commercial heart of the city, and the hub of its sea and rail transport.

Much has changed since the area's heyday, and it now has few obvious attractions, save for the vertiginous **Rialto Towers** – recently demoted from being the tallest building in Melbourne by the Eureka Tower (see p.59) – and the multicultural melee of the **Queen Victoria Market** to the north. Here and there, however, you'll find goldrush architecture, glorious gardens, interesting museums and the giant **Etihad Stadium** sports venue (until recently known as the Telstra Dome), while hidden in a fascinating network of historical arcades, laneways and passageways are some of the city's finest cafés and speciality shops. What's more, the evolution of Melbourne's cityscape has been given new impetus with the recently redeveloped **Docklands area**, a thriving waterfront precinct due for completion in 2015 which has slowly risen from what was once a desolate eyesore, and includes the revitalization of Southern Cross Station while providing a convenient gateway to both the Etihad Stadium and surrounding area.

Queen Victoria Market

On the corner of Victoria and Elizabeth streets, the **Queen Victoria Market** (Tues & Thurs 6am–2pm, Fri 6am–5pm, Sat 6am–3pm, Sun 9am–4pm; Nov–Feb same hours plus night market Wed 5.30–10.30pm; guided Foodies' Tour Tues & Thurs–Sat 10am; $30; Style Addict tour Sun 11am; $35; ⓦwww.qvm .com.au) is at once historic landmark, popular shopping destination and much-loved city institution. Built on the site of Melbourne's first cemetery, the market was officially opened in 1878. Its huge, decorative sheds and high-roofed halls – regarded as temporary when first built – remain, fronted along Victoria Street by restored shops, their original porticoes supported by decorative iron posts.

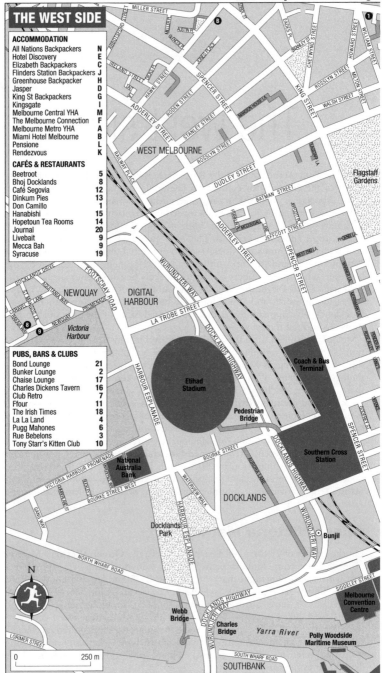

THE WEST SIDE

ACCOMMODATION
All Nations Backpackers	N
Hotel Discovery	E
Elizabeth Backpackers	C
Flinders Station Backpackers	J
Greenhouse Backpacker	H
Jasper	D
King St Backpackers	G
Kingsgate	I
Melbourne Central YHA	M
The Melbourne Connection	F
Melbourne Metro YHA	A
Miami Hotel Melbourne	B
Pensione	L
Rendezvous	K

CAFÉS & RESTAURANTS
Beetroot	5
Bhoj Docklands	8
Café Segovia	12
Dinkum Pies	13
Don Camillo	1
Hanabishi	15
Hopetoun Tea Rooms	14
Journal	20
Livebait	9
Mecca Bah	9
Syracuse	19

PUBS, BARS & CLUBS
Bond Lounge	21
Bunker Lounge	2
Chaise Lounge	17
Charles Dickens Tavern	16
Club Retro	7
Ffour	11
The Irish Times	18
La La Land	4
Pugg Mahones	6
Rue Bebelons	3
Tony Starr's Kitten Club	10

Comic's Lounge

WEST MELBOURNE

Flagstaff Gardens

NEWQUAY

DIGITAL HARBOUR

Victoria Harbour

LA TROBE STREET

Etihad Stadium

Coach & Bus Terminal

Pedestrian Bridge

Southern Cross Station

BOURKE STREET

National Australia Bank

DOCKLANDS

Docklands Park

Bunjil

NORTH WHARF ROAD

N

Webb Bridge

Charles Bridge

Yarra River

Polly Woodside Maritime Museum

Melbourne Convention Centre

SOUTHBANK

0   250 m

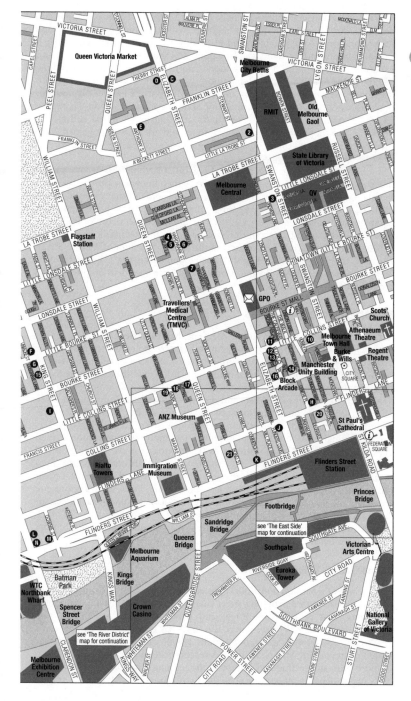

Queen Victoria Market

Melbourne City Baths

VICTORIA STREET

THERRY STREET ⒟ ⒞

FRANKLIN STREET

RMIT

Old Melbourne Gaol

⒠

ANTHONY'S LA

A BECKETT STREET

LITTLE LA TROBE ST

❷

LA TROBE STREET

State Library of Victoria

FRANKLIN STREET

Flagstaff Station

Melbourne Central

❸

QV

LITTLE LONSDALE ST

LONSDALE STREET

LA TROBE STREET

LITTLE LONSDALE STREET

LONSDALE STREET

⒡

⒢

⒖

⓪

⒤

⒋ ⒌ ⒍

❼

Travellers' Medical Centre (TMVC)

CHINATOWN LITTLE BOURKE ST

BOURKE STREET

GPO

BOURKE ST MALL

ⓘ

Scots' Church

Athenaeum Theatre

⓫

⓬

⓭

⒚ ⒙ ⒘

⒗

⓮

Block Arcade

LITTLE COLLINS STREET

Melbourne Town Hall

Burke & Wills

CITY SQUARE

Regent Theatre

Manchester Unity Building

ANZ Museum

⒣

⓴

St Paul's Cathedral

⒥

⒦

FLINDERS STREET

FEDERATION SQUARE

ⓘ-1

COLLINS STREET

Rialto Towers

Immigration Museum

㉑

Flinders Street Station

FLINDERS STREET

Princes Bridge

Footbridge

see 'The East Side' map for continuation

FLINDERS STREET

⒧

⒩

⒨

Melbourne Aquarium

Queens Bridge

Sandridge Bridge

Southgate

Victorian Arts Centre

RIVERSIDE QUAY

Eureka Tower

SOUTHGATE AVE.

CITY ROAD

Batman Park

WTC Northbank Wharf

Kings Bridge

Spencer Street Bridge

Crown Casino

KINGS WAY

WHITEMAN STREET

QUEENSBRIDGE STREET

FRESHWATER PL

COOK ST

SOUTHBANK BOULEVARD

National Gallery of Victoria

see 'The River District' map for continuation

CLARENDON ST

KINGSWAY

WHITEMAN ST

CITY ROAD

POWER ST

FAWKNER STREET

KAVANAGH STREET

STURT STREET

DODDS ST

Melbourne Exhibition Centre

Although quaint and tourist-friendly, Queen Victoria Market is raucous and down-to-earth place, and a stroll through the market, housing nearly a thousand stalls selling fresh fruit, veg, meat and seafood, as well general merchandise such as leather goods and souvenirs, can be a good deal more fun than loafing around exclusive designer shops. There are food- and deli- halls – great for sampling Middle Eastern, Italian, Asian and seafood dishes – while vans outside sell hot dogs, pies and ice cream. Saturday mornings Melbourne's foodies turn out for their groceries; Sunday is for clothing and shoe shopping; while on Wednesday nights in summer there are street musicians, jugglers, alfresco eating and drinking, and shopping for jewellery, clothing and art. As well as guided tours the market also runs a number of cooking classes – check the website for the latest program.

Southeast of Queen Victoria Market, **Flagstaff Gardens** also occupy part of the land once used as Melbourne's cemetery – then known as Burial Hill – and retain a Gothic monument marking the graves of some of the town's pioneers. In 1840, an observatory incorporating a flagstaff and signal house was built, complete with a cannon which was fired to announce the arrival of important vessels in Port Phillip Bay. From this vantage point, the townsfolk would watch as passengers were ferried up the Yarra to the wharf at the foot of William Street. Attesting to its historical and horticultural significance, the Flagstaff Gardens joined the Treasury, Royal Botanic, Carlton and Fitzroy gardens on the heritage protection register in 2004.

Melbourne Central

A couple of blocks east of Flagstaff Gardens, **Melbourne Central** shopping complex was opened in 1991. Unfortunately, the complex turned into a huge urban mistake, draining the life from important city streets, killing off several laneways (see box, opposite) and destroying many public spaces. In an attempt to recapture some of the atmosphere of the streets it destroyed, today's complex features through-streets and recreated alleys and a minotauran maze of over 300 shops and food outlets. Below the centre is the Melbourne Central underground train station, which has over 20 million travellers passing through it each year. The complex's ingenious 20-storey cone-shaped glass dome encloses **Coop's shot tower**, a factory for the manufacture of shot, built on this site in 1889. Entry to the tower and its small museum (free) is via the RM Williams store on the first floor. Opposite the tower is a giant fob watch weighing two tons that lets loose every hour with a grotesque rendition of *Waltzing Matilda* accompanied by a mechanical marionette of Australian animals. Avoid the complex at midday, when there's a jam of office workers, students from the nearby RMIT, and commuters surfacing from the train station below.

Bourke Street Mall

The corner of Swanston and Bourke streets marks the start of **Bourke Street Mall**, a pedestrianized shopping street that is Melbourne's bustling retail hub. Extending west to Elizabeth Street and packed daily with shoppers, city workers, buskers and *Big Issue* sellers, the street has been closed to traffic since 1972, although it's still accessed by trams which can make for some rather anarchic interactions with pedestrians. A recent spruce-up has seen the addition of more trees and seating and improved the lighting. The major draws are the city's major department stores (including David Jones and Myer – see p.164),

Melbourne's laneways

Honeycombing the area bordered by Swanston, Queen, Lonsdale and Flinders streets is one of the city's highlights – a large and labyrinthine network of arcades and passageways, perfect for serendipitous exploring. Once the haunt of gangsters and prostitutes, in recent years Melbourne's **laneways** have undergone a major renaissance and are now full of life, though part of the charm is that the bars, cafés, galleries, tarot readers, watchmakers and pie shops still remain hidden treasures, often only known to locals and inner-city workers.

These days the laneways play host to a range of public artworks and installations, ranging from graphic works by graffiti artists to weather-sensitive instruments that are "played" by the wind. For more **information** about Melbourne's laneways and how they came to be named, pick up a free copy of *Melbourne's Streets and Lanes*, available from the Royal Historical Society of Victoria at 239 A'Beckett St.

Some of the most interesting laneways are:

Block Place (Little Collins St, between Swanston and Elizabeth sts). Narrow, dimly lit warren with umpteen restaurants and cafés – some little more than holes in the wall – catering mainly to the lunchtime trade.

Centre Place (Flinder's Lane, between Swanston and Elizabeth sts). Tiny eat-street where cheap hole-in-the-wall takeaways, sandwich shops and coffee shops vie for trade.

Degraves Street (Flinders Lane, between Swanston and Elizabeth sts). Cosmopolitan walkway throbbing with office workers at lunchtime and after 5pm. The tables down the middle are great for people-watching and provide a nice European touch.

Hardware Street (Bourke St, between Queen and Elizabeth sts). Home to the excellent Beetroot (see p.115), and the Discurio music shop (see p.161). Ranged around the street are hair and beauty salons, skateboard and ski stores. In summer, the laid-back bustle, colourful awnings and footpath tables give the street a bit of a Mediterranean feel.

Mitre Place (Off Bank Place, which runs south from Little Collins St). Surrounded by the late nineteenth-century heritage buildings of Bank Place, which includes the members-only Savage Club and law chambers, this small alley was once the favoured rendezvous of bohemian types and prominent locals such as Sir Redmond Barry and Tom Roberts, who came to drink in the Mitre Tavern established in 1868.

along with sundry food and clothing shops and an entrance to the lovely old Royal Arcade (see p.54).

The mall's western end is dominated by the **General Post Office** (GPO), a solid Neoclassical porticoed pile with a distinctive clock tower. So important was this building in its heyday that that all road distances from Melbourne were measured from the GPO. No longer a post office, today the interior of this grand old icon contains a luxury retail precinct (see p.164), while its broad bluestone steps are a popular spot to perch with a coffee, or to sit and watch performances during the Melbourne International Comedy Festival (see p.148).

The Block and arcades

The area south between Bourke Street Mall and Collins Street – known as **The Block** – was made fashionable in the 1890s by the aristocracy who came here to promenade or ride about in their carriages (referred to as "doing the block"). It's still a draw for dedicated boulevardiers, lured by exclusive shops and cappuccino.

Running off Elizabeth Street (there are other entrances at Little Collins St and Bourke Street Mall), the **Royal Arcade**, Melbourne's oldest, was opened in 1869 to connect Collins and Bourke streets. It's worth taking a look to see the haphazard mix of cafés and secondhand shops flanking the sunlit passageways. Perched at the arcade's entrance on Little Collins Street is a clock with two creepy, larger-than-life wooden figures – Gog and Magog, two mythological Ancient Britons – who strike the time each hour.

Across Little Collins Street and through the busy thoroughfare, Block Place gives access to Melbourne's most illustrious arcade. Constructed in 1891 in emulation of Milan's Galleria Vittorio Emmanuele, the heritage-listed **Block Arcade** features intricate mosaic-tiled flooring, a large glass-domed roof and an eye-catching selection of shops and cafés. You can take a spin through the arcade's ground floor and upper rooms on a heritage **tour** (Tues & Thurs 1pm; $9; ☎9654 5244), which starts from the historic *Hopetoun Tea Rooms* (see p.115) and winds up at 3pm over free afternoon tea at the *Pickwick Restaurant* at the *Charles Dickens Tavern* (see p.128).

West along Collins Street

Leaving the Block and heading south down Elizabeth Street brings you back to **Collins Street**. West of here, at the intersection with Queen Street, the old **English, Scottish and Australian Bank** (1887), designed by William Wardell and often referred to as the Gothic Bank, houses a sumptuous banking chamber, as well as the aptly named Cathedral Room. Below street level, the small but delightful **ANZ Banking Museum** (Mon–Fri 10am–3pm; free) spotlights the history of Melbourne's wealth during the goldrush era, and has displays of weights, scales, safes and adding machines, as well as an interactive display illustrating the history of Australian banking which includes a collection of old money boxes.

Another aspect of Australia's history is captured in the evocative **Immigration Museum** (daily 10am–5pm; $8; ☎9927, 2700, ⓦwww.museumvictoria .com.au), situated on the corner of Flinders and William streets in the Old

▲ Tribute Garden at the Immigration Museum

Customs House. Inside, a poignant collection of stories, images and displays includes dolls brought by children from their home countries, and a detailed cross-section of a ship used to transport immigrants to Australia. In the museum's **Tribute Garden**, a film of water flows over polished granite on which are engraved the names of migrants to Victoria, symbolizing the long passage over the seas. The museum is also the first stop on the Golden Mile Heritage Walk (see p.23).

Rialto Towers and around

On Collins Street, between King and William streets, the **Rialto Block** juxtaposes stylish nineteenth-century buildings, born out of the easy times of the 1880s land boom, and sleek modern office blocks, including **Rialto Towers**. In the 1980s, the block was at the centre of a vituperous controversy caused in part by the planned demolition of several historic buildings. After protracted discussions, the heritage properties were spared, and construction of the towers began. Completed in 1986, Rialto Towers was Melbourne's tallest building, until the Eureka Tower opened in 2006 (see p.59).

At 235m, the skyscraper is still hairily high, covered with more than 13,000 windows reflecting a glassy, gridded city. You can take an elevator ride to the **observation deck** on the 55th floor (daily 10am–10pm; $14.50; ☎9629 8222, ⓦwww.melbournedeck.com.au) for a warts-and-all view of the city.

The **West End**, hugging the edges of the CBD around the Rialto Towers, is where Melbourne was first settled, and where the city's earliest industrial and commercial interests began. Its proximity to the Yarra meant it was the principal gateway to town: in the wake of the goldrush, the area heaved with merchant stores, seedy hotels, pawnshops and brothels. It's now rather drab and unkempt, consisting mostly of run-down warehouses and wool stores from the 1850s – forlorn reminders of what happened when Melbourne expanded to the east – and newer office blocks of should-be-outlawed dreariness.

Docklands

Further downstream, on what was once the city's old **dock** area, is Melbourne's newest suburb, **Docklands**; a large-scale commercial, residential and leisure development that's slowly rising to the west of Southern Cross Station. Of all the city's new developments this is likely to have the biggest impact on the look and feel of Melbourne: if all goes to plan, when it is completed in 2015, this area is expected to house 20,000 residents and and attract more than 20 million visitors a year.

For now, the pleasant if somewhat sterile residential and leisure precinct, **NewQuay**, on Victoria Harbour, is studded with restaurants and bars and at weekends gets swamped with people looking to while away the time before kick-off at the Etihad Stadium (see p.156). Nearby, the Victoria Harbour precinct features the **National Australia Bank's** head-turning twin-tower headquarters, its multicoloured panels Meccanoed together into a giant Rubik's cube. Asserting Melbourne's cutting-edge credentials, **Digital Harbour** is a $300 million technology-based Silicon Valley in miniature, home to the award-winning building 1010 LaTrobe Street, along with film and television studios.

Docklands also features some of the most conspicuous **public art** in Melbourne. You can take a self-guided tour of 29 artists' works (download a **map** from the website ⓦwww.docklands.com.au) including *Cow Up A Tree*, or the slinky Webb Bridge, a pedestrian and cycle link to Southbank, whose outline was inspired by the fishing traps used by Melbourne's original inhabitants. Perhaps most visually intriguing of them all is a remarkable 25-metre-high timber and aluminium eagle sculpture known as **Bunjil**. Marking the gateway to the Docklands at the southern end of Wurundjeri Way, the sculpture is inspired by the eaglehawk, totem animal of the Aboriginal Wurundjeri, who believe that it created all living things from the land.

Immediately behind Southern Cross Station is the **Etihad Stadium** (formerly the Telstra Dome) on Wurunndjeri Way, a 52,000-seater venue with a giant sliding roof that's used for soccer, cricket and rugby union matches, as well as major music concerts and performances. The venue offers behind the scenes **tours** of the stadium (Mon–Fri 11am, 1pm & 3pm; $14; ☎8625 7277).

Docklands is linked to the rest of the CBD by various trains and trams including the free City Circle tram (see p.27). In addition to pedestrian links and a web of designated cycling paths, a weekend 45-minute ferry service operates November to April connecting Docklands to the CBD at NewQuay, stopping at various central locations en route.

The river district, South Melbourne and Albert Park

Nowhere in the last decade has the giddy transformation of Melbourne's urban spaces been more apparent than in the **river district**, the area on either side of the Yarra from the Docklands in the west to the Melbourne Cricket Ground (MCG) in the east. The building boom – driven by a demand for inner-city accommodation and offices – has been on a scale not seen since the goldrush and "Marvellous Melbourne" era. As the city centre becomes ever more congested, development has swept towards and embraced the river, and the vast waterways of the Docklands are fast becoming Melbourne's next major commercial, residential and entertainment precinct, doubling the size of the CBD. Many of the city's cache of cultural spaces have been given fantastic facelifts by

City under threat

Natural disasters figure prominently in the development of Melbourne. In 1891, a "great flood" occurred after the city was pelted with exceptionally heavy rains over two days and nights. At one point, the Yarra rose by 14m and **flooding** was rampant. Over 3000 people, mostly living in the inner-city suburbs of Richmond and Colling-wood, were evacuated from their homes, while two enormous lakes were formed on either side of Chapel Street in South Yarra. According to *The Age* newspaper of the time, the flood "rose so rapidly in the night that one resident reported plunging his arm into water as he stretched, awaking to the real danger of being drowned in his bed". In 1934, **storms** caused widespread destruction throughout the city, destroying houses, commercial and industrial buildings and private mansions. The economic loss was devastating, and the human toll was costly – eighteen people drowned and 6000 were left homeless. Thirty-eight years later, in 1972, flash flooding in the CBD resulted in Bourke and Elizabeth streets disappearing underwater. Apart from floods, the threat of **fire** was an ever-present danger. In 1897, a raging inferno ripped through the city. When the flames were finally extinguished, the entire block between Swanston and Elizabeth streets, and Flinders Street and Flinders Lane, was reportedly reduced to rubble.

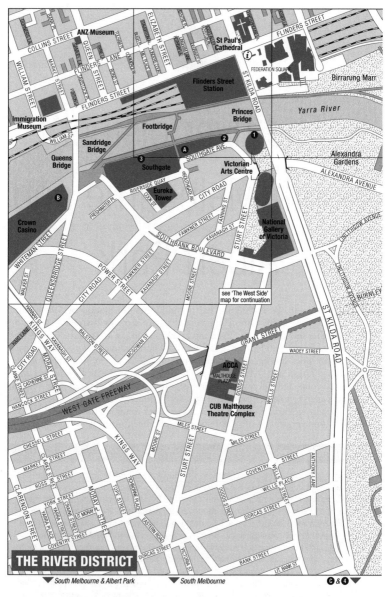

THE RIVER DISTRICT

South Melbourne & Albert Park   South Melbourne   **C** & **4**

forward-thinking governments, while a building frenzy of apartments has attracted thousands of people to move into the area. The river district has consequently undergone a dramatic rebirth and, with the population set to quadruple over the next five years, the revival of its fortunes seems likely to continue.

In contrast, **South Melbourne** and **Albert Park** (see map, p.70) further to the south, are two of Melbourne's oldest suburbs and still manage to retain a

ACCOMMODATION	
Crown Towers	**B**
Langham	**A**
Royce on St Kilda Road	**C**

0 _____ 250 m

CAFÉS & RESTAURANTS	
Blue Train Café	**3**
Dish	**C**
EQ Cafébar	**1**
Koko	**B**
Walter's Wine Bar	**2**

PUBS, BARS & CLUBS	
Belgian Beer Café Bluestone	**4**

pleasant village atmosphere, as well as being home to the popular South Melbourne Market and Albert Park reserve.

The river district's most innovative development is the new 92-storey **Eureka Tower**, named after the site near Ballarat where gold was first discovered in 1851. Finished in 2006 and towering 300m, it is now the tallest building in Melbourne, has its top levels clad in gold, and claims to be the highest residential building in the world. Visitors can get amazing views of the city and beyond from the 88th-floor Skydeck (10am–10pm; $16.50; @www.skydeck.com.au), which features the stomach-churning "skywalk" **The Edge** ($12), a three-metre glass cube that juts out over the city below.

The **Yarra** itself, the lifeblood of early Melbourne, is being progressively reopened to the public and is a popular focus of leisure activities. The majority of the district's attractions are to be found along the south bank and down St Kilda Road. Principal among them is the **Victorian Arts Centre**, home to some of Australia's leading performing-arts companies, while further west along the river are the two enormous leisure complexes of **Southgate** and **Crown Casino**. Nearby, the inventively designed **Melbourne Exhibition Centre** offers a possible clue as to what the city will look like in the future, while across the river the **Melbourne Aquarium** provides a fish-eye view of underwater life. Stretching down St Kilda Road beyond the Arts Centre is the **National Gallery of Victoria** (NGV), a Melbourne landmark containing the most comprehensive collection of international art in Australia. Behind it stands an artfully rusted hillock housing the **Australian Centre for Contemporary Art** (ACCA), and across the road are the expansive parklands and gracious nineteenth-century buildings of **Kings Domain** and the **Royal Botanic Gardens**. On the opposite bank of the river lies the new heart of Melbourne: jazzy **Federation Square** built to celebrate the centenary of the Australian Federation and featuring the **Ian Potter Centre: NGV Australia**, home to an extensive collection of Australian indigenous and non-indigenous art. From here, Melbourne's new parkland of **Birrarung Marr** links Federation Square with the city's sporting precinct, **Yarra Park**, which contains various stadiums, principal among them the legendary Melbourne Cricket Ground.

The Yarra River

Starting out as a series of soaks and swamps at the foot of the Great Dividing Range almost 250 kilometres to the east, and fed by myriad tributaries along the way, the **Yarra River** swells into a broad, brown-stained stretch of water as it silently curves through Melbourne on its way to the sea. Only a few years after the foundation of Melbourne, the Yarra was ripe with effluent from wool washers, bone mills (ground-up bones were used as fertilizer), tanneries, soap makers and other suburban industries, which used the river as a major means of waste disposal. Indeed, so befouled was the waterway that during the nineteenth century it was occasionally seen to "run red with blood", while sharks were known to come as far up the river as Richmond to feed on the blood, offal and dead animals that were deposited in the river. Babies, unwanted by their mothers, were also abandoned along its banks. Typhoid was common, and the river was rightly blamed as a major source of illness.

Tidal movements of up to two metres often menaced the city with floods, a problem which was partly solved in 1888, when the embankments were raised and the river deepened and widened to allow for the upgrading of Melbourne's port facilities. Only three years later, however, the river flooded to a new record, peaking at thirteen metres. It wasn't until 1937, when parts of the river were lined with bluestone to curb erosion and trees were planted to create a flood-buffer zone, that a proper approach to land use was developed to stop the Yarra from bursting its banks.

Long reviled as "the river that flows upside down" (the mud is on the top), the Yarra is now quiet and orderly and, thanks to a number of improvement

Yarra cruises

Cruising on the Yarra has been a popular pastime since Melbourne's earliest days, when steamers plied regularly up and down the river and out to the resorts of Queenscliff and Sorrento. Nowadays the choice of vessels ranges from quaint sailing boats and steamships to gondolas and hi-tech motor launches, and you can go on short trips or longer journeys towards the sea and the bird colonies at Port Phillip Bay and Herring Island.

Melbourne River Cruises ($22 one-way, or combined up- and down-river cruise $29; bookings ☎8610 2600) make regular departures from both Berth 5 at Southgate and from Federation Wharf, below the northern end of Princes Bridge. Their River Gardens Cruise (1hr 15min) will take you upriver past affluent South Yarra and industrial Richmond to Herring Island; the Port and Docklands Cruise (also 1hr 15min) runs downriver past the Crown Casino and the Melbourne Exhibition Centre – and then past shipping channels and docks to the Westgate Bridge.

Bay and River Cruises half-hourly 9am–4.30pm; $15, or $25 return; for recorded information call ☎9517 9444; for bookings ☎9682 9555;) ply the lower section of the Yarra from Southgate's Berth 1 to Williamstown, passing the Crown Casino, the Melbourne Exhibition Centre and Scienceworks (see p000).

projects and stringent anti-pollution legislation, it provides one of the purest water sources available to a city of this size anywhere on earth. It remains an essential part of Melbourne, its banks now dotted with barbecues and beautified by tree-lined boulevards and paths. A **boat cruise** is the best way to see the river (see box, above), but it can also be explored on foot or by bike on the cycle paths which run along both riverbanks. **Bikes** can be rented from Hire a Bicycle (daily 10am–5pm, weather permitting; ☎9654 2762) on the north side of Princes Bridge; prices start from $15 for the first hour (and $5 per hr thereafter) to $35 per day; helmets, locks, maps and backpacks are provided.

Victorian Arts Centre

At the southern end of Princes Bridge is the state's leading performance arts venue, the **Victorian Arts Centre**, home to Opera Australia, the Australian Ballet, the Melbourne Symphony Orchestra and the Melbourne Theatre Company. The centre comprises Hamer Hall, adjacent to the Yarra; the Theatres Building, housing the State Theatre, the Playhouse and Fairfax Studio; and the Sidney Myer Music Bowl (see p.65). The Theatres Building is topped by one of Melbourne's most blatant landmarks – a 162-metre-high lattice spire transformed by night into a powerful rod of blue light.

Linked to each other by walkways, the Theatres Building and the Hamer Hall both house permanent art collections in their gallery spaces which can be viewed on excellent guided tours (Mon–Sat 11am; $15; backstage tour including dressing rooms Sun 12.15pm; $20; ☎9281 8000, ⓦ www.theartscentre.com.au). The centre also houses a Performing Arts Collection research facility covering everything from theatre to rock'n'roll, its exhibits including the schoolboy outfit worn by Angus Young from AC/DC, Dame Edna Everage's spectacles and Kylie's costume collection, including her famous gold hotpants. Viewings are by appointment only, though snapshots of the collection are often displayed in the foyer and gallery spaces, as are splendid temporary exhibitions, normally focusing on the performance schedule. Perhaps the liveliest day to visit the Arts Centre is Sunday. Not only can you go on the Backstage Tour, but there is a good **arts-and-crafts market** held outside on the paved promenade under Princes Bridge.

National Gallery of Victoria: International

Adjacent to the Victoria Arts Centre is the **National Gallery of Victoria: International** (10am–5pm, closed Tues; free; ☎8620 2222, ⓦwww.ngv.vic .gov.au). Designed by Sir Roy Grounds, this resolutely grey slab of 1960s formalism – dubbed the "Kremlin of St Kilda Road" by a former gallery director – was completed in 1968, but underwent a $168 million transformation in 2003 in order to accommodate its growing art collection. While the basic design of the exterior "palazzo" remains, as does the much-loved waterwall entry, works are now split between two sites: the St Kilda Road building houses Australia's largest collection of international art, while Australian art is displayed at the Ian Potter Centre at Federation Square (see p.68).

Inside the Great Hall is the gallery's most famous feature, the world's largest stained-glass ceiling. Designed by artist Leonard French, who was invited by Grounds to make "the biggest ceiling in the world", it consists of hundreds of sculptured pieces of astonishingly vivid red, blue and green glass imported from Belgium and France. Taking five years to produce, French worked on the ceiling as if it was a giant jigsaw, cutting and chiselling each section of glass. To get a closer look at the thick stained glass take a walk along the public passageway on the second level.

Large framed gateways, richly painted colour palettes hanging on the walls, and interconnecting gallery spaces ensure visitors are given open and inviting access to big draws such as Tiepolo's *Banquet of Cleopatra*, arguably Australia's greatest Old Master painting, and a self portrait by Rembrandt. Other artists in the collection include Monet, Bacon, Turner and at least one Canaletto, as well as temporary sculpture, fashion, furniture and glassware exhibits over two levels above.

Twentieth-century artists are well represented in the form of Picasso, Lowry and Hockney, among others. The Federation Courtyard is the gallery's principal gathering place, complete with obligatory café, bookshop, cloakroom and various galleries of antiquities fanning off from it.

Australian Centre for Contemporary Art (ACCA)

Behind the NGV, in the $10 million Malthouse Arts Complex, stands a dramatic sight: the **Australian Centre for Contemporary Art** (ACCA) (Tues–Fri 10am–5pm, Sat & Sun 11am–6pm; free; ☎9697 9999, ⓦwww.accaonline.org .au). The urban equivalent of red-rock Uluru according to some, a "burnt out car body" to others, the building rises from a stark linear landscape clad in nearly one thousand slabs of rust-coloured Corten steel. It was created in 2002 by Wood Marsh Architects to provide a flexible exhibition space for young and emerging local and overseas artists. Also here are the offices and rehearsal spaces of Chunky Move, Victoria's contemporary dance company, and the property and set facilities for the Malthouse Theatre next door.

Taking pride of place in the forecourt of the ACCA is Ron Robertson-Swann's 1980s abstract sculpture **Vault**, cruelly called "Yellow Peril". Misunderstood and much maligned, it is also one of Melbourne's most nomadic public artworks: shunted from site to site, it was originally erected as the crowning glory for the City Square in 1980 where it was likened by one city councillor to a "broken-down barbecue". It was even alleged that sex offenders hid inside, and that its yellow colour encouraged people to urinate. Consequently it was banished to ankle-deep mud next to the Yarra opposite the Crown Casino, where it was used as a crashpad at night by the city's junkies and homeless, before being relocated to the safety and respectability of the ACCA forecourt. At first glance, *Vault* resembles a wall that's collapsed and been hurriedly put back together again, but at close quarters it is an extraordinary fusion of art and engineering. Its author, Robertson-Swann, spent some time as an assistant to Henry Moore while living in London.

Southgate and Crown Casino

On the riverbank opposite Flinders Street Station (to which it is linked by a beautifully engineered pedestrian bridge with grand views of the river), lies **Southgate**, one of the city's smartest food, drink and shopping complexes. Built on former industrial wasteland in the early 1990s, Southgate's three levels fizz with life, especially at lunchtimes and weekends, when it attracts hordes soaking up the views across the river.

West of Southgate, the enormous **Crown Casino** (☎9292 8888, ⓦwww .crowncasino.com.au), stretching across 600m of riverfront, is the indisputable focal point of the Yarra. Australia's largest gambling and entertainment venue, the casino is crammed with over-the-top gaming rooms, bars, nightclubs, cinemas, designer shops, restaurants – including the latest branch of *Nobu* – and the luxury *Crown Towers* hotel. Equally egregious is the five-storey, black-marble atrium, which features a sound-and-light show set amidst a waterworld of fountains and ponds. Outside, the only distinguishing feature, apart from eight granite-columned towers which belch fire at night, is the promenade fountain, which provides a kind of assault course for children dodging the jets of water.

Melbourne Convention and Exhibition Centre and Polly Woodside

Directly across Clarendon Street, the striking **Melbourne Convention and Exhibition Centre** (ⓦwww.mcec.com.au) is a whimsical example of the city's dynamic new architectural style. Opened in 1996 and known locally as "Jeff's Shed" (a reference to Jeff Kennett, the former state premier behind its construction), it was designed by Melbourne's hottest architectural practice, Denton Corker Marshall (DCM), the team behind the distinctive Tullamarine Freeway gateway, the Melbourne Museum (see p.75), the Webb Bridge (see p.55) and just about every other construction project of note in Melbourne during the last ten years. Facing the river is an immense, 450-metre-long glass wall, while the street entrance has one of DCM's signature slicing "blades", which looks something like a ski jump propped up by wafer-thin staves. This area of the river is being furiously regenerated, and at the time of writing, a brand new integrated 5000-seat convention centre was due to open as part of the redeveloped World Trade Centre on the north side, providing trade conventions – from bridal shows and baby expos to motorcycle and fishing fairs – on a much grander scale.

Next to the Melbourne Exhibition Centre, the **Polly Woodside** (ⓦwww .pollywoodside.com.au) in the Maritime Museum is a small barque-rigged sailing ship built in 1885 and described as "the prettiest vessel ever launched in Belfast". After a working life, most of it spent carrying coal and nitrate between Europe and South America, she was acquired by the National Trust in 1968 and added to the Victorian Heritage list in 2007. Undergoing renovation at the time of writing as part of the new Convention Centre development, the *Polly Woodside* has been faithfully restored, and once re-opened you'll be able to climb on board and explore the captain's quarters and storage holds below. Adjoining the ship are historic cargo sheds containing pumping engines and a museum of shipping relics relating to the history of the docks and Port Melbourne.

Melbourne Aquarium

Facing the Crown Casino, on the corner of Flinders and King streets, is **Melbourne Aquarium** (daily 9.30am–6pm; open until 9pm Jan 1–26; adults $31.50, 3–15 yr-olds $18; ☎9923 5999, ⓦwww.melbourneaquarium.com.au), harbouring thousands of creatures from the Southern Ocean. Part of it is taken up by the Oceanarium tank, which rests seven metres below the Yarra, and resembles a fish bowl turned inside out. Visitors stand in a glass room surrounded by over two million litres of water containing over 3000 animals from 150 species such as sharks and stingrays. Elsewhere are habitat areas filled with starfish and eels, mangroves and rockpools, and a floor-to-ceiling coral atoll, while the aquarium's latest development, the Antarctica exhibit, features two of the larger species of penguin, King and Gentoo.

Education-wise, the curved, four-storey building also has a variety of programmes suitable for children of all ages: a hands-on learning centre where children gain a glimpse of life underwater, plus the marine conservation programme, which includes interpretive displays and divers giving underwater presentations, as well as daily feeding sessions and "touch and feel" presentations in the rock pools. The building also contains lecture halls, an amphitheatre, cafés, a shop and a restaurant. And if you want to come nose-to-nose with a shark, the aquarium arranges "Diving With Sharks" experiences. Dives are provided by fully qualified instructors and prices are $150 (certified divers with own equipment), $242 (certified divers without own equipment) and $349 for non-divers (includes pre-dive briefing and practical dive). Bookings are essential on ☎9510 9081 or visit ⓦwww.divingheadquarters.com.au.

▲ Meeting the penguins at the Melbourne Aquarium

Kings Domain

Returning to the Victorian Arts Centre and heading down St Kilda Road brings you to the grassy open spaces of **Kings Domain**. At the northern end of the domain lies the **Sidney Myer Music Bowl**, an outdoor theatre which serves as a music arena for the Victorian Arts Centre. Built in 1958, "the Bowl" hosted everything from symphonies to the Seekers before falling into a state of disrepair. Now returned to its former glory, the Bowl has a futuristic-looking aluminium roof and an underground network of spaces equipped with performers' rooms, changing rooms and public toilets, while out front is fixed seating for over 2000 people and re-configured viewing lawns for thousands more – especially during the summer when a programme of free concerts pulls in the crowds; see ⓦwww.theartscentre.com.au for more details. Further south is the palatial **Government House**, official residence of the Governor of Victoria. The National Trust runs guided **tours** (Mon & Wed; 11am; $15; book in advance on ☎8663 7260) of the formal gardens and several of the rooms, and includes a tour of La Trobe's Cottage – see p.66. Most spectacular is the enormous state ballroom, which includes a throne hung and canopied with velvet, brocade-covered benches and gilded chairs, all brilliantly lit by three massive crystal chandeliers. Every year on Australia Day (Jan 26) the house holds a free **open day**; for more information go to ⓦwww.governor.vic.gov.au.

Immediately south of Government House, before you reach the Royal Botanic Gardens (see below), the **Observatory Gate** precinct includes a number of Italianate buildings (originally built 1861–63) that have been painstakingly restored. The observatory performed a wide range of important functions for the fledgling colony of Victoria, providing scientific data essential for the running of businesses from shipping to farming. Also part of the precinct, the **Visitors Centre** (Mon–Fri 9am–5pm, Sat & Sun 9.30am–5.30pm) has a café (7am–5pm) and garden shop, where you can buy botanical books, maps and brochures. Night tours ($18) which allow visitors to gaze at the stars and planets through huge telescopes start from here, and vary according to the time of year and what planets are passing through our system – see the Royal Botanic Gardens website below for more details. Adjoining the precinct, just inside the gardens' entrance, the **Children's Garden** (see p.170; Wed–Sun 10am–4pm, or daily during school holidays; free) features sculptures from Norman Lindsay's story *The Magic Pudding* (see "Books" on p.236) and is where children are encouraged to explore and learn more about nature in outdoor classrooms.

Heading east of Observatory Gate takes you into the **Royal Botanic Gardens** (daily: April, Sept & Oct 7.30am–6pm; May–Aug 7.30am–5.30pm; Nov–March 7.30am–8.30pm; free; ⓦwww.rbg.vic.gov.au). Established in 1846, the gardens now contain twelve thousand types of plant and over fifty species of bird, not to mention great clumps of big bushy trees, rockeries, waterfalls, flowerbeds and pavilions. Highlights include a **herbarium**, shady walks through native rainforests, a large ornamental lake where you can feed the swans and eels, and various hothouses where exotic cacti and fascinating plants like the carnivorous Pitcher plant thrive. The Terrace Tearooms (daily: April–Sept 9.45am–4pm; Oct–May 9am–5pm) by the lake serves refreshments and Devonshire teas. Various walks explaining the diversity of plant and animal life are available throughout the year – see the website for the latest programme. If you're interested in investigating Melbourne's Aboriginal culture, the **Aboriginal Heritage Walk** (every Thurs & one Sun per month 11am; $18; bookings essential on ☎9252 2429) includes a smoking ceremony, in which permission is asked to enter the traditional lands of the Boonwurrung and Woiwurrung people on which the gardens reside, guided walks (clapsticks and digging sticks in hand) through the native sections of the gardens, explanations of the different uses of plants and trees, and lessons on bush tucker. Every second Saturday of the month, the **Gardens Market** (9am–2pm; Ⓦ www.marketsinthegarden.com .au) is held, where one hundred stallholders sell plants, art, gourmet food and other items.

Directly opposite Observatory Gate, across Birdwood Avenue, is the **Shrine of Remembrance** (daily 10am–5pm; free; Ⓦ www.shrine.org.au), built in 1934 to commemorate those who fought in various conflicts. It's a rather menacingly stolid mass whose architectural style is part classical Greek, part Aztec pyramid. The strangeness continues when a disembodied voice booms out and calls you in to see the symbolic "Ray of Light", a shaft of sunlight that strikes the memorial stone each year at 11am on Remembrance Day (Nov 11) – an effect that's conveniently simulated every thirty minutes by an electric light. The Crypt – the area beneath the shrine – displays the regimental colours of the servicemen who fought in World War I, while directly beneath the Remembrance Stone is the Father and Son statue, a memorial to those fathers who fought in World War I and whose sons went on to fight two decades later. The Hall of Columns features the Changi Flag, a British flag signed by prisoners of war in Changi, Singapore during World War II.

The **visitors' centre**, a large chamber cut into the ground beneath the shrine, features changing exhibitions, and a forty-metre-long **Gallery of Medals**, commemorating the 40,000 Victorians who have served in military and peace-keeping campaigns. In the **Garden of Appreciation**, east of the Shrine, a bronzed statue carrying the words "Homage" and "Remembrance" commemorates the care given to the widows and children of soldiers killed in action, while directly behind the shrine is a solitary Calabrian Pine, germinated from a seed brought by a young soldier who fought at Lone Pine in Gallipoli during World War I. Each year, the shrine attracts over 50,000 visitors on Anzac Day (April 25), who make the very moving early-morning pilgrimage along St Kilda Road and past the Eternal Flame.

Nearby, on the corner of Birdwood Avenue and Dallas Brook Drive, **La Trobe's Cottage** (tours Mon & Wed 11am & 1pm; $10, includes tour of Government House; book in advance on ☏ 8663 7260) was bought in London by Victoria's first lieutenant governor, Charles La Trobe, who had it shipped over to Melbourne in 1839. The remains of the humble prefabricated house were re-erected on the present site in 1998. Small but elegantly furnished, it features the first governor's furniture and possessions, plus historical displays on the early days of the colony.

Circling Kings Domain is "The Tan", a four-kilometre sand and crushed rock path that was once a horse-exercising track and is now a favourite route for joggers.

Yarra Park

Opposite Kings Domain on the north bank of the Yarra (and connected to it by Swan Street Bridge) lies Melbourne's sporting precinct: **Yarra Park**. Within its wide, open spaces are the Melbourne Cricket Ground; Melbourne Park, with venues including the Rod Laver and Hisense arenas (homes of the Australian Open tennis championship); Olympic Park (where the Melbourne Storm rugby league team play their matches); and the Lexus Centre, training ground for Collingwood AFL club.

Melbourne Cricket Ground (MCG)

Taking pride of place in the park is the venerable **Melbourne Cricket Ground** (MCG). Originally built in 1853, but transformed to host the 1956 Olympic Games, the G, as it is affectionately known, is Australia's oldest cricket ground and one of the country's biggest, most popular and most highly-revered stadiums. As well as being the spiritual home of AFL football, the arena accommodates cricket, international soccer and rugby union, rugby league and music concerts.

The present-day MCG has a capacity of 100,000 spectators, boosted by the development of the Northern Stand, which was created for the 2006 Commonwealth Games and houses the **National Sport Museum** (10am–5pm; $15, or $22 combined with a tour), containing various exhibitions on Aussie sports.

Despite potential competition from new venues such as the Etihad Stadium and the Olympic Stadium in Sydney, the MCG's place as an icon among Australia's sporting stadiums is assured – annual pilgrimages to the AFL Grand Final continue to take place there as they have done for decades – while the Boxing Day cricket test match at the MCG has been synonymous with Australian Christmas since 1968. For a greater understanding of the MCG's resonant place in Australia's sporting history, you can take a **tour** (daily from 10am–3pm; $15, or $22 with entry to the Sports Museum; no tours on event days; ℡9657 8879, Ⓦwww.mcg.org.au) of the stands, the coaches' boxes and the ground itself.

Federation Square

Federation Square (Ⓦwww.federationsquare.com.au) lies just across the river from Southgate, opposite Flinders Street Station and St Paul's Cathedral. Opened in late 2002-almost two years after the centenary of federation – it is one of the most ambitious and complex projects ever undertaken in Victoria, involving building across the Flinders Street railway yards, where work was limited to the early hours of the morning so trains would not be disrupted. Conceived as a tribute to the first 100 years of Australian nationhood, the Square – which links the CBD with the Yarra–fuses art, architecture, culture and

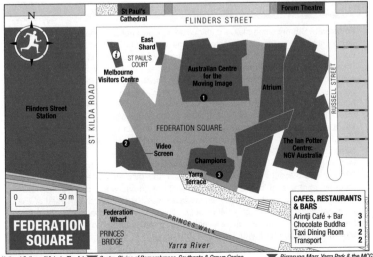

CAFES, RESTAURANTS & BARS
Arintji Café + Bar 3
Chocolate Buddha 1
Taxi Dining Room 2
Transport 2

National Gallery of Victoria, The Arts ▼ Centre, Shrine of Remembrance, Southgate & Crown Casino   ▼ Birrarung Marr, Yarra Park & the MCG

leisure into a distinct public space with crazy paving-style facades of geometric panels.

Former Victorian Premier Jeff Kennett's most costly public monument, it was completed by the Bracks government bearing a price tag of almost $460 million (three times over budget). Often referred to as the city's "new heart", it's also been described by one Melbourne humorist as its "spleen", given that it was "odd, misshapen and nobody's really quite sure what it does". One thing everybody's in agreement about is its size: covering an entire block, it changed the famous grid of streets laid out by Hoddle for the first time in over 150 years (see p.229) by extending the CBD further towards the river. The square includes an expansive plaza of 500,000 sandstone cobblestones from the Kimberleys in Western Australia, from which there are commanding views of Melbourne's riverside and cityscape. There's also a soaring glass and metal Meccano-style structure known as the Atrium, evolved from the same triangular geometry as the building's facades, that connects a couple of galleries, an amphitheatre, the TV studios of multicultural broadcaster SBS, and a number of plaza cafés, bars and restaurants. On the south side of the square is **Champions** (daily 10am–6pm; $9; ☏ 1300 139 407, Ⓦ www.racingmuseum.com.au), a museum and hall of fame showcasing Australia's much-loved sport, horse racing.

Eyeballing the stately bluestone NGV across the river, the **Ian Potter Centre: NGV Australia** (Tues–Sun 10am–5pm, Thurs till 9pm; free; ☏ 8620 2222, Ⓦ www.ngv.vic.gov.au) is the largest building in the square, home to a diverse collection of Australian indigenous and non-indigenous art from the colonial period to the present day. Despite its reputation as the little brother to the NGV (see p.62), the centre has over twenty galleries, with some 70,000 works, of which about 1800 are usually on display (exhibits are regularly rotated), including highly regarded Aboriginal and Torres Strait Islander art such as Emily Kngwarray's Pollock-like *Big Yam Dreaming*. The Heidelberg School (see p.85), which captured the dry colours of the Australian landscape in a non-European style, is represented on the second level by works such as Tom Roberts' *Shearing of the Rams* and Frederick McCubbin's *The Pioneer*. Further eighteenth- and nineteenth-century works can be found in the Joseph Brown Collection, a

---

The case of the missing "shard"

Federation Square's complex and unique design, described by one Melbourne radio commentator as a "rancid lamington", is the result of an international architectural competition won in 1997 by Lab architecture studio of London in association with Bates Smart of Melbourne. The intent of the design, which draws on cutting-edge architecture and engineering, was to create visual harmony, while differentiating between the square's civic, cultural and commercial buildings. Prior to completion, however, the development was embroiled in controversy over the **shards** – large, three-storey glass office towers. The most controversial was the proposed western shard, which was to frame the square's main plaza and act as its entrance, but which would partly obscure the views of St Paul's Cathedral. Under pressure from the National Trust, the Heritage Council of Victoria and vocal members of a sometimes malicious public, Premier Bracks ruled against the building of the western shard, much to the disappointment of the architects and their supporters, who believed its axing went against the spirit of the original design and would provide too much open frontage – something that has long bedevilled the City Square. Instead of the bold, optimistic statement of a giant western shard, there now stands a single-storey building that looks like a fish tank and acts as an entrance to the underground Melbourne Visitor Information Centre.

snapshot of Australian art from colonial times to present day. More confronting contemporary works, installations and special exhibitions are held on the third level, which is also reserved for retrospective and temporary exhibitions (some of which may attract an additional fee). The centre is completed by austere industrial-type spaces that house cafés and bistros, a lecture theatre and a gallery shop that has an impressive stock of art, architecture and design books.

Nearby, the glossy **Australian Centre for the Moving Image** (ACMI) (daily 10am–6pm; ☎8663 2200, ⓦwww.acmi.net.au; some films and exhibitions may attract an entry charge) is a mecca of screen culture charged with the lofty mission of helping visitors understand the moving image in all its forms, from TV to video games. The four-storey complex features two state-of-the-art cinemas and a subterranean screen gallery exhibition space spanning the entire length of Federation Square, and featuring changing exhibitions of screen-based art. ACMI also presents a wide range of programmes ranging from cinema and educational events to hip-hop festivals. The latest development is a free permanent exhibition exploring the last one hundred years of the moving image on the ground floor.

Just west of here, where the controversial western shard was to have stood, is the excellent **Melbourne Visitor Information Centre** which provides information on events, accommodation, transport, entertainment and a travel service for local and overseas visitors. See p.35 for contact details.

Outside, a giant video screen facing into the outdoor plaza from the three-level *Transport* pub (see p.130) features exhibits from ACMI and the Ian Potter Centre, and regularly attracts up to 15,000 people who come to watch major sporting events like the AFL Grand Final and the Australian Open Tennis Championship.

Birrarung Marr

Linking Federation Square to Melbourne's sporting precinct to the east, **Birrarung Marr** (birrarung means "river of mists" and marr is "side") is Melbourne's first new park since the city was originally laid out a hundred years ago. Three times the size of Federation Square, the park forms a continuous green belt to Yarra Park, its wide, open spaces and sculptured terraces designed to host events and festivals throughout the year. Situated on the lower terrace is **ArtPlay** (see p.170), a permanent children's playground with slides and lots of things to scramble over, up and along. They also run various workshops such as storytelling, circus skills and puppetry. Also in the park, on the footbridge linking the river to the city, are Deborah Halpern's colourful *Angel* sculpture and the **Federation Bells**, a permanent installation comprising thirty-nine bells that are struck by computer-controlled hammers each day at 8am, 12.30pm and 5pm.

South Melbourne and Albert Park

Stretching southwest of the river is **South Melbourne**, one of the oldest suburbs in the city. Originally named Emerald Hill, the area features some fine examples of Victoria architecture, including the grand **South Melbourne Town Hall**. In the 1960s it went into decline, as the middle classes moved out and several high-rise housing commission tower blocks were constructed. More recently, however, spurred by the renaissance of nearby Docklands, people have moved back, old houses have been restored and gentrification is in full swing. The area's main shopping street is Clarendon Street with original

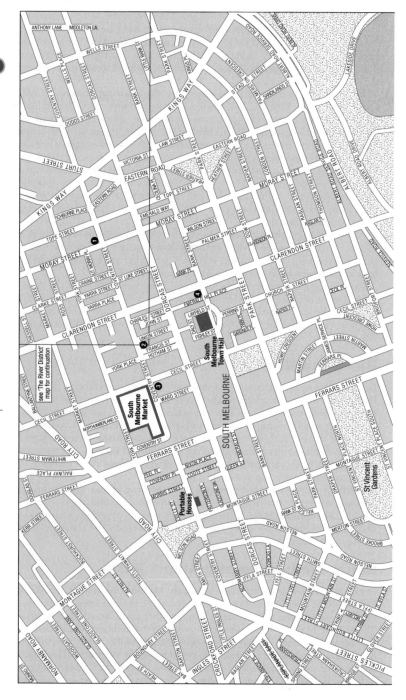

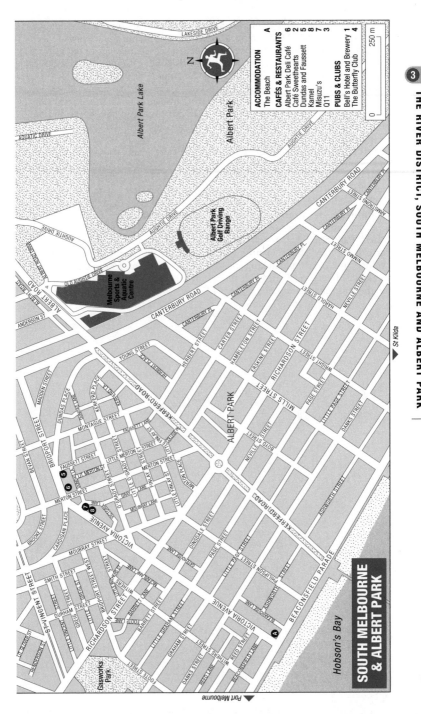

SOUTH MELBOURNE & ALBERT PARK

ACCOMMODATION
The Beach .... A

CAFÉS & RESTAURANTS
Albert Park Deli Café 6
Café Sweethearts 2
Dundas and Faussett 5
Kamel 8
Misuzu's 7
Q11 3

PUBS & CLUBS
Bell's Hotel and Brewery 1
The Butterfly Club 4

0   250 m

Victorian canopies overhanging numerous cafés and bars; and its main focus is the excellent **South Melbourne Market** (see p.166), on the corner of Cecil and Coventry streets. In existence since 1857, it sells all manner of things from homewares and furniture to fresh fruit and seafood. Outside on Cecil Street are a number of places to eat including the famous *South Melbourne dim sum takeaway*, while nearby Coventry Street is lined with cafés and pubs. At no. 399 are three nineteenth-century **portable iron houses**, prefabricated residences that housed civil servants and tradespeople during the goldrush era, and are now preserved by the National Trust (tours first Sunday of the month 1–4pm; $5).

Further south is the exclusive suburb of **Albert Park**, named for its huge and popular 225-hectare park, where the lovely terraced streets and café-lined shopping precincts of Bridport Street and Dundas Place still have the feel of a small village. At the end of Victoria Street there's a narrow strip of sandy beach that continues west to the up-and-coming suburb of **Port Melbourne** and **Station Pier** (tram #109), home to the Tasmanian ferry terminal and a number of good restaurants. In the shadow of St Kilda Road, Albert Park itself has a golf course, excellent aquatic centre (see p.156), barbeques, cafés and a boating lake, and is usually teaming with joggers, cyclists and locals picnicking or playing a game of footy, especially at weekends. Every year in March thousands of people descend upon the park for the Australian Grand Prix (see p.147).

4

Carlton and Fitzroy

With the goldrush of the 1850s, the settlement of Melbourne began to spread outwards, and by the end of the decade prosperous suburbs such as **Carlton** and **Fitzroy** had taken root. Carlton is still an elegant home to the city's thriving middle classes, who stock up on chic clothing and imported European food from the Italian precinct of Lygon Street. Southeast of here is the late nineteenth-century **Royal Exhibition Building**, home of Australia's first parliament, and the award-winning **Melbourne Museum**, which draws on the latest technology to give an insight into Australia's flora, fauna and culture. Flanking Carlton's northwestern reaches, the small enclave of Parkville is home to the **city's university** and the popular **Melbourne Zoo**.

Bordering Carlton to the east, Fitzroy is a vibrant alternative and bohemian area. Its main artery is **Brunswick Street**, included on the historic register of the National Trust, as well as being full of lively eating places, organic food and vintage clothing shops.

Carlton

Carlton lies just north of the city, but in terms of looks and feel it could be a million miles away, the style of life here, that of a café society based around the fashionable trattorias of **Lygon Street**. It was here, in the 1950s, that Melburnians sipped espressos and tasted spaghetti for the first time at spots like *Toto's* (see p.120), opened by the Italian immigrants who flooded into Melbourne in the postwar years. Lygon Street held an unconventional allure in staid Anglo-Saxon Melbourne, attracting the city's intelligentsia, who soon made the bars and pubs in this pretty, kilometre-long strip their home-from-home.

These days, however, Carlton's relevance as an intellectual and culinary milieu is on the wane. Its former bohemians have either left or are older and wealthier, and Lygon Street has gone upmarket, although the encroaching designer stores and tourist restaurants haven't yet completely displaced the arts centres, old-fashioned grocers and bookshops. Carlton's Italian community is still very much evident, despite the demise of the Lygon Street Festa, Australia's oldest street festival. Sustaining the street's heart and soul are a smattering of unpretentious ethnic cafés and restaurants, where students from the nearby university still congregate over tiny cups of bitter existential coffee. And in the Carlton Housing Estate, the high-rise project for low-income Australians between Rathdowne and Lygon streets, live the suburb's new wave of immigrant children – this time more likely to be Somalian or Eritrean than Italian.

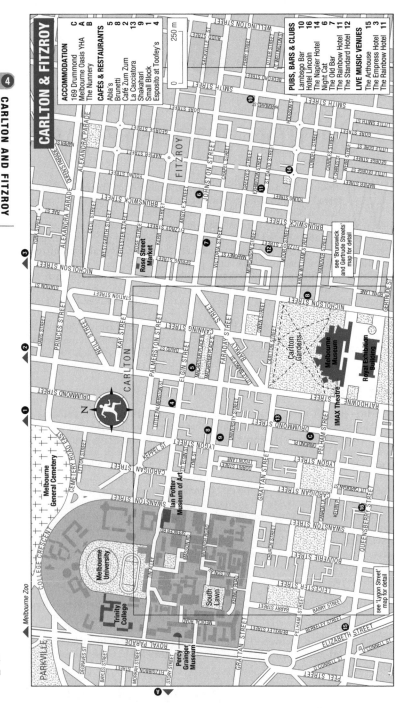

CARLTON & FITZROY

ACCOMMODATION
169 Drummond   C
Melbourne Oasis YHA   A
The Nunnery   B

CAFÉS & RESTAURANTS
Abla's   5
Brunetti   8
Café Zum Zum   2
La Cacciatora   13
Shakahari   9
Small Block   1
Esposito at Toofey's 4

0   250 m

PUBS, BARS & CLUBS
Lambsgo Bar   10
Hotel Lincoln   16
The Napier Hotel   14
Night Cat   6
The Old Bar   7
The Rainbow Hotel   11
The Standard Hotel   12

LIVE MUSIC VENUES
The Arthouse   15
The Empress Hotel   3
The Rainbow Hotel   11

Melbourne Zoo

PARKVILLE

Melbourne General Cemetery

Percy Grainger Museum

Trinity College

Melbourne University

South Lawn

Ian Potter Museum of Art

CARLTON

N

FITZROY

Rose Street Market

Carlton Gardens

Melbourne Museum

Royal Exhibition Building

IMAX Theatre

see 'Brunswick and Gertrude Streets' map for detail

see 'Lygon Street' map for detail

Royal Exhibition Building and Melbourne Museum

At the CBD's northeast corner are the picturesque Carlton Gardens, home to plenty of fossicking possums and one of Melbourne's most significant historic landmarks, the **Royal Exhibition Building** (ⓦmuseumvictoria.com.au/reb), in its prime a perfect symbol of Melbourne's vaulting ambition, with a dome proudly vaunted to be higher than London's St Paul's Cathedral. Conceived by ambitious former London shopkeeper Graham Berry, the building was built by David Mitchell, father of Dame Nellie Melba, for the Melbourne International Exhibition of 1880–81, when everything from steam locomotives to lawnmowers were exhibited. Seven years later, in 1888, over two million people visited the Melbourne Centennial Exhibition held here to mark one hundred years of European settlement in Australia. The Royal Exhibition Building is also where Australia's first parliament sat in 1901 and where the Victorian State Parliament resided from 1901 to 1927. The northern facade and majestic dome were restored to mark the centenary in 2001. Among its other incarnations, the building was used as an emergency hospital during the great flu pandemic of 1919; a barracks and training site during World War II; a sporting venue for the 1956 Melbourne Olympics; and a migrant reception centre in the 1950s.

Exhibition buildings originally covered the whole of the park, but only the magnificent Neoclassical Main Hall remains, although this is still big enough to host the annual Melbourne International Flower and Garden Show (see p.148), plus everything from bridal shows to art fairs. Guided **tours** of the Royal Exhibition Building (Mon–Fri 2pm; $5) can be booked via Melbourne Museum on ☏13 11 02.

Dwarfing the Exhibition Building and, at the same time, giving it a new lease of life, is the mammoth **Melbourne Museum** (daily 10am–5pm; $6; ☏13 11 02, ⓦmelbourne.museum.vic.gov.au). Opened in October 2000, this state-of-the-art museum is in dramatic contrast to its nineteenth-century neighbour, with its geometric forms, vibrant colours, immense blade-like roof and a greenhouse accommodating a lush fern gully flanked by a canopy of dozens of tall forest trees. The museum, whose eight galleries include one especially for kids, also houses a 400-seat amphitheatre, a hall for major touring exhibitions, a study centre and a museum shop. Glass-covered display cabinets are few and far between: instead there is a emphasis on interactive exhibits exploring the way science and technology are shaping the future.

The **Science and Life Gallery** is perhaps the real highlight, exploring the plants and animals inhabiting the southern lands and seas – children, especially, will love the "Bugs Alive!" exhibition. The **Bunjilaka Aboriginal Centre** showcases an extraordinary Aboriginal collection: curving for 30m at the entrance is "Wurreka", a wall of over seventy zinc panels etched with Aboriginal artefacts, shells, plants and fish; while in the "Two Laws" section, traditional paintings depict the outline and anatomy of animals, symbolizing the relationship between external knowledge and "secret" internal knowledge. The **Melbourne Gallery** focuses on the social history of Melbourne, ranging from the (stuffed) legendary racehorse Phar Lap to Luna Park (see p.169). Also of interest is the **Evolution Gallery**, which holds an assortment of dinosaur casts (including the first dinosaur bone found in Australia), and the **Children's Gallery**, where the exhibition gallery "Big Box" is built in the shape of a giant tilted cube painted in brightly coloured squares. One of the most striking exhibits is the **Forest Gallery**, a living, breathing indoor rainforest containing over 8000 plants from more than 120 species, including 25-metre tall gum trees, as well as birds, insects, snakes, lizards and fish.

Also part of the museum is the **IMAX Melbourne**, which boasts the world's biggest movie screen. Up to eight different IMAX films (daily on the hour 10am–10pm; $17.50; ☎9663 5454, Ⓦwww.imaxmelbourne.com.au), ranging from natural wonders to artificial marvels and spacewalks, are projected each day; for 3D action liquid crystal glasses are provided.

Melbourne University

Just west of Lygon Street in the suburb of Parkville, **Melbourne University** is worth a visit for its formidable art collection. This is housed in **The Ian Potter Museum of Art** (Tues–Fri 10am–5pm, Sat & Sun noon–5pm; free; Ⓦwww.art-museum.unimelb.edu.au), near the corner of Elgin and Swanston streets, a small but striking building adorned with muscular Classical statues and containing drawings, archeological exhibits, and nineteenth- and twentieth-century Australian art by the likes of Norman Lindsay and Rupert Bunny. The life of Percy Grainger – composer, linguist, fashion maverick – is captured in the **Grainger Museum** (closed for renovations at the time of writing but usually Mon 10am–12.30pm, Tues–Fri 10am–5pm; free; Ⓦwww .lib.unimelb.edu.au/collections/grainger) at Gate 13, Royal Parade, in the southwestern corner of the university. Grainger designed the museum (which opened in 1938) and stocked it with over 250,000 of his personal effects, including musical instruments and bibles collected from his travels around the world. His provocative and thoroughly interesting life – he favoured clothes made from terry towelling, practiced sadomasochistic sex and was unusually close to his dominant mother, Rose (all major no-nos in the prim and proper Melbourne of the time) – was captured in the film *Passion* by Australian director Peter Duncan. Most bizarre of the university's attractions is the **underground car park** beneath the South Lawn: a Gothic netherworld of

▲ Ian Potter Museum of Art

concrete arches and columns, which was used for the police garage scenes in the film *Mad Max*.

Just north of the university, the **Melbourne General Cemetery** (daily 9am–5pm; ☎9349 3014; entrance College Crescent) was established in 1853 after relocating from the area now occupied by Queen Victoria Market, and is the oldest in the city, although most of its fine examples of funerary architecture have disappeared or fallen apart. Nearly a million people are buried here, including Melbourne founder John Batman, explorers Burke and Wills, and Australian Prime Minister Sir Robert Menzies. There's also a memorial to former Australian Prime Minister Harold Holt (see p.185) who disappeared off the Mornington Peninsula in 1967, engraved simply with the words "He loved the sea." For those who wish to be spooked, the National Trust organizes **full-moon tours** of the cemetery twice a year at Easter and Halloween (2hr; $24; booking essential ☎9656 9800). Alternatively White Hat Tours runs entertaining twice-weekly tours (Wed & Sun 1pm; $15; ☎9329 6055).

Melbourne Zoo

West from the cemetery, the green plenitude of Royal Park is home to the excellent **Melbourne Zoo** (daily 9am–5pm; $23.60; ☎9285 9300, ⓦwww.zoo .org.au/melbournezoo; tram #55 from William St, or train on Upfield or Gowrie lines from Flinders Street Station). The oldest zoo in Australia, it opened in 1862 and several of its original features are still in evidence, including the landscaped gardens with Australian and imported trees, and a few restored Victorian-era cages. An ongoing multi-million dollar revamp has seen the animals rehoused in more sympathetic enclosures, including an **Orang–utan Sanctuary**, featuring a treetop boardwalk, and the Asian Rainforest, part of the award-winning **Trail of the Elephants**, where you can meet the five resident elephants, learn about the life of a "mahout" or elephant keeper, or eat nasi goreng at the Asian food stalls.

The **Australian bush habitat**, densely planted with more than twenty thousand native plants, contains wombats, koalas, echidnas, monitor lizards and cockatoos, while a maze of underground enclosures allows you to observe dozing groups of wombats and includes a small tunnel where you can experience life in a wombat burrow. The dark **Platypus Habitat** is worth a visit to see these notoriously elusive mammals, as is the popular **Gorilla Rainforest**, home to Riga, a Silverback male, and his family. Other highlights include the Butterfly House and the popular meerkats, to the right of the main entrance. For sustenance there's the *Lakeside Bistro* (daily 9am–4.30pm) and the **Meerkat Kiosk** (daily 9am–5pm), as well as plenty of takeaway facilities.

One of the best ways to experience the zoo is to time your visit with an animal handler session or during feeding times. "**Meet the Keeper**" sessions are as follows: giant tortoises (daily 11am), wombats (daily 11.30am), giraffes (daily 11.45pm), elephants (2.30pm), koalas (daily 2.30pm), orang-utans (daily 3pm) and penguins (daily 3.30pm). Free guided tours are available daily from 10am to 3pm. The zoo also runs specialist events such as Behind-the-Scenes and Twilight Tours and the very popular "**Roar 'n' Snore**" sleepover ($185 adults, children 5–12yr $135), where you get to sleep in safari tents in the Historic Elephant enclosure and take an after-dark zoo tour. Dinner, breakfast and snacks are provided, as are tents, but bring your own bedding – for more information call ☏9285 9335.

Fitzroy

Melbourne's first and Australia's smallest suburb, **Fitzroy** has a varied and fluctuating history. In the early years of European settlement it was considered eminently desirable – high, dry and conveniently north of the city. Many colonial buildings remain, and Fitzroy houses some of the city's finest mid-nineteenth-century bluestone buildings (the best, like Royal Terrace, are in Nicholson Street opposite the Royal Exhibition Building, or on Victoria Parade further south). Gradually, however, the area's fortunes declined, and by the turn of the twentieth century Fitzroy was providing land and cheap labour for noxious trades such as tanning and soap- and candle-manufacturing. By the 1930s, Fitzroy had become a slum.

Steadily, the suburb's fortunes were revived: first by the arrival of a mix of European, Middle Eastern and Asian immigrants in the postwar period, later by artists, attracted to Fitzroy's rawness, and young and sophisticated suburbanites who stumbled upon the area, setting the fashion for terrace-style living and louche gentility. For every row of run-down terraces, at least one will have been gutted and stylishly modernized. However, despite the obvious divide between the well-off and the poor, who reside in the suburb's housing commission high-rise estates, Fitzroy still manages to retain a diverse community spirit.

Fitzroy's focal point is **Brunswick Street**, where, in the shadow of Housing Commission high-rises, you can pick up clothes and accessories from funky shops at knock-down prices, eat at the area's abundant ethnic restaurants, drink decaff with artists and actors, bury your head in Aussie "grunge" literature in one of the street's late-night bookshops, or down a stubby at the many bars and live music venues sprinkling the strip. The fires of anti-fashion raging through the area have also left the street full of hotels with "raw" paint jobs and deliberately half-finished decor inside.

Dissecting Brunswick Street to the south is **Gertrude Street** currently experiencing a new lease of life. Once a transient, junkie stronghold it's fast

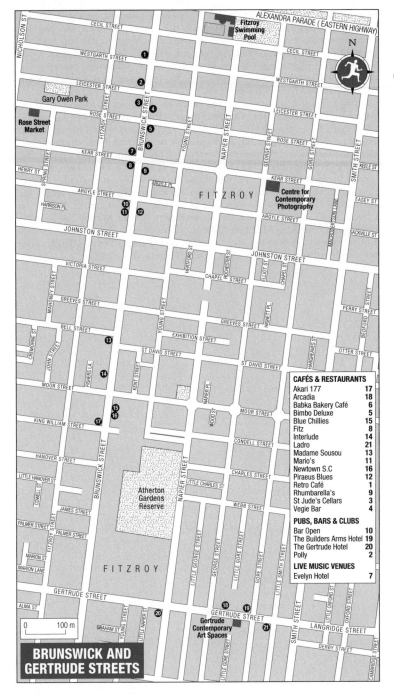

CAFÉS & RESTAURANTS

Akari 177	17
Arcadia	18
Babka Bakery Café	6
Bimbo Deluxe	5
Blue Chillies	15
Fitz	8
Interlude	14
Ladro	21
Madame Sousou	13
Mario's	11
Newtown S.C	16
Piraeus Blues	12
Retro Café	1
Rhumbarella's	9
St Jude's Cellars	3
Vegie Bar	4

PUBS, BARS & CLUBS

Bar Open	10
The Builders Arms Hotel	19
The Gertrude Hotel	20
Polly	2

LIVE MUSIC VENUES

Evelyn Hotel	7

BRUNSWICK AND GERTRUDE STREETS

becoming a chic hub for Melbourne's artistic community, with galleries and performance art spaces. Mixed in with the organic delis, stylish clothing boutiques and art and music shops, is a string of trendy cafés and bars, the chatter of numerous different languages, and a slight whiff of exclusivity.

Running at right angles across Brunswick Street **Johnston Street** is the centre of Melbourne's Spanish community. Along the west of it is a lively stretch of tapas bars and flamenco restaurants.

Fitzroy's fringe-art leanings are embodied in a number of local galleries, in particular the **Centre for Contemporary Photography**, 404 George St (Wed–Sat 11am–6pm; ☎9417 1549, ⓦ www.ccp.org.au), which has up to four gallery spaces showing mostly experimental works from both emerging and established artists, and the popular **Gertrude Contemporary Art Spaces**, 200 Gertrude St (Tues–Fri 11am–5.30pm, Sat 1–5.30pm; ☎9419 3406, ⓦ www .gertrude.org.au), a converted warehouse that is now a state-funded gallery housing three galleries including Studio 12, a space for emerging artists; the latter usually displays works from one of Gertrude's on-site artists. Fitzroy has its own arts-and-crafts market, the **Rose Street Artists Market**, 60 Rose St, held from October to May every Saturday from 11am to 5pm, selling artwork and prints, vintage clothing, silver jewellery and all sorts of ethical designs from soy candles to recycled plastic light shades. There is also a café.

5

Collingwood, Richmond and the east

The last decade has seen the suburbs of **Collingwood** and **Richmond** to the east of the city centre dramatically regenerated and gentrified. Both share a history of blue-collar culture, Irish Catholic-dominated municipal politics and fierce loyalty for their local football teams. Of the two, Collingwood, long the underdog, is now the rising star, a once-dreary industrial area whose revival of fortunes is largely due to an abundance of relatively cheap living space and the café scene that has emerged in its wake along **Smith Street**. Not much further down the road, the **Collingwood Children's Farm** is a popular spot for families and school groups.

More on the tourist route, **Richmond** was once the hilly heart of nineteenth-century Melbourne, and then, after World War II, a lively immigrant quarter. These days people come to shop for bargain food and homeware or for a spot of leisurely boozing. Despite its obvious urbanity, Richmond retains something of a village atmosphere, with a tangle of genteel streets and landmarks like the Dimmeys clock tower and the "Skipping Girl" vinegar sign that have become Melbourne icons.

Even further east is a creative nexus that was once home to some of Australia's greatest visual artists, including the Boyd family home at **Museum of Modern Art at Heide** and **Montsalvat**, the home of architect and painter, Justus Jorgensen. If you prefer your culture a little more popular, don't miss the chance to spot a new plot development on the real-life **Ramsay Street** of Pin Oak Court.

Collingwood

From the very beginning, when the first subdivisions of land were made in 1838–39, **Collingwood** (named after Admiral Lord Collingwood, who led the British fleet to victory at Trafalgar) was a combination of residential and industrial properties. Settlement intensified after the goldrush, as cottages were built to house the workers from the nearby mills and slaughterhouses which were fuelling

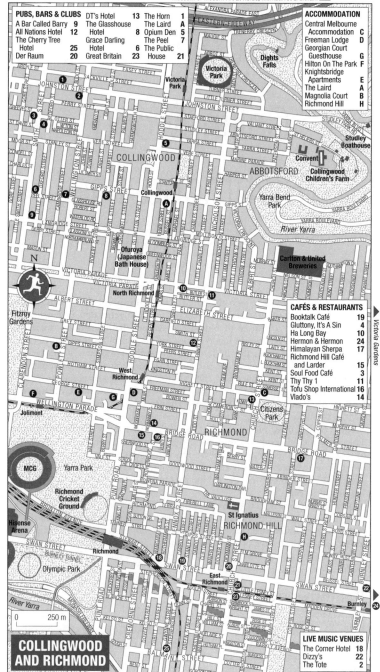

PUBS, BARS & CLUBS

A Bar Called Barry	9
All Nations Hotel	12
The Cherry Tree Hotel	25
Der Raum	20
DT's Hotel	13
The Glasshouse Hotel	8
Grace Darling Hotel	6
Great Britain	23
The Horn	1
The Laird	A
Opium Den	5
The Peel	7
The Public House	21

ACCOMMODATION

Central Melbourne Accommodation	C
Freeman Lodge	D
Georgian Court Guesthouse	G
Hilton On The Park	F
Knightsbridge Apartments	E
The Laird	A
Magnolia Court	B
Richmond Hill	H

CAFÉS & RESTAURANTS

Booktalk Café	19
Gluttony, It's A Sin	4
Ha Long Bay	10
Hermon & Hermon	24
Himalayan Sherpa	17
Richmond Hill Café and Larder	15
Soul Food Café	3
Thy Thy 1	11
Tofu Shop International	16
Vlado's	14

LIVE MUSIC VENUES

The Corner Hotel	18
Dizzy's	22
The Tote	2

COLLINGWOOD AND RICHMOND

0   250 m

the city's growth and polluting the Yarra River in Collingwood's east. The savage depression of the 1890s severely affected the suburb, and it slipped into decline and became a slum area where people subsisted in a miasma of rats and noxious fumes. In the 1950s, Greek, Italian and Lebanese migrants joined the neighbourhood of workers and indigenous people, but in recent years students, artists, a large gay and lesbian community, and a wave of savvy entrepreneurs on the prowl for warehouse space have added to the mix. In 1892, Australia's most famous sporting institution – the Collingwood Football Club – was founded, and still continues to maintain tenacious support and a high level of club membership.

For years Collingwood has had an iffy, after-dark reputation with outsiders, and it still has a seedy undertone, especially in and around **Smith Street**, the main thoroughfare running from Victoria Parade to the south, and marking the boundary with Fitzroy (take tram #86 from Bourke St). Today the street is awash with cafés and restaurants, second-hand shops, discount stores, health food shops, alternative bookshops and gritty nightclubs, while the area to the north of Johnston Street is crammed with clothing and sportswear factory outlets. Local colour is a big part of the ambience, and amid the swathes of untouched and unmodernized nineteenth-century buildings off the main drag you'll find gay-friendly pubs, hole-in-the-wall cafés, and yoga and meditation schools. A few minutes walk east of Smith Street, at 59 Cromwell St, is Australia's first traditional **Ofuroya** (or **Japanese Bath House**; Tues–Fri 11am–10pm, last entry 8pm; Sat & Sun 11am–8pm, last entry 6pm; see p.157), and further east in St Heliers Street, is a restored nineteenth-century **convent**, once a refuge for women and children, that has been converted into an arts and cultural centre, with a bakery and a vegetarian café. Adjacent to the convent, the popular **Collingwood Children's Farm** (see p.169) provides bucolic bliss in the form of paddocks, gardens, rustic buildings and animals, tucked away on a bend of the Yarra River. A **farmers' market** is held here every second and fourth Saturday (8am–1pm; $2). Just east of Collingwood, Abbotsford was once part of the Collingwood municipality, and is now the location for the **Carlton and United Beverages** (CUB) brewery, on the corner of Nelson and Thompson streets. Guided tours of the brewery (Mon–Fri 10am & 2pm; $25; bookings essential ☎9420 6800; tram #109) present the modern face of brewing, from raw materials through the unique filtration and fermentation process to one of Australia's fastest bottling plants, producing over 1.5 million bottles a day. After working up a thirst, visitors are given a complimentary tasting of the famous CUB draught beers, which include Carlton, VB, Fosters and Melbourne Bitter.

Richmond

One of Melbourne's oldest industrial areas, **Richmond** began as a mix of palatial villas, tanneries, wool-washing establishments, brickworks and bars. A municipality in its own right from 1855, the suburb experienced further industrial and residential growth in the 1870s and 1880s, but by the turn of the twentieth century, Richmond's gentility had begun its retreat. The waves of postwar immigration to Australia made a huge impact on Richmond, and with the completion of a high-rise housing project in the 1960s, Italians, Greeks and Vietnamese poured in, signalling full-scale transformation. In recent years, nineteenth-century family cottages have been snapped up by new Richmond bohos pursuing retro-chic and CBD proximity, while the development of riverside parkland has led to a widespread "greening" of the suburb. Indeed, there is no better inner-city area to tackle by foot or bike as Richmond has a fantastic network of walking and cycling tracks fringing the riverbank.

The suburb is bordered to the west by Punt Road, and includes Richmond Hill to the east, with the Yarra River forming a natural eastern and southern boundary. **Richmond Hill** is where most of the shops and restaurants are located, and adorning the highest point is the steeple of St Ignatius, a reminder of the area's early Irish Catholic heritage. This is where you'll find the larger, more palatial brick homes – as opposed to the weatherboard workers' cottages down on the flat.

Three main roads traverse Richmond on their way east from the city: Swan Street, Bridge Road and Victoria Street. **Swan Street** is the most unchanged of Richmond's roads, with a number of solid, sober 19th-century shop facades and verandas, and the clock tower of the former **Dimmey's** store roughly marking the centre of the strip. A mecca for budget shopping since it opened in 1853, the building has now been mooted for redevelopment into a retail and residential complex: to get here take tram #70. A few blocks north, and running parallel to Swan Street, **Bridge Road** (tram #48 and #75) is the place to come for real bargain shopping, and many of Australia's finest fashion designers have factory seconds outlets between Punt Road and Church Street. When you're done hunting knock-down jeans, swimwear,

▲ Sculpture at Heide Museum of Modern Art

trainers, and even surfboards, head off the road to the *All Nations Hotel* (see p.131), 64 Lennox St, a popular local, serving some of the best pub grub in town. Further north, **Victoria Street** or "Little Saigon", forms the boundary between Richmond and the adjacent suburb of Abbotsford, and is the bustling heart of Melbourne's well-established Vietnamese community, a kilometre-long stretch of inexpensive restaurants, supermarkets, grocery stores, butchers' and fishmongers. The traditional Vietnamese soup cafés that line the strip between Hoddle and Church streets serving steaming bowls of *pho* – spicy, aromatic chicken- or beef- broth with noodles and vegetables – are a great place for a delicious, inexpensive lunch. Trams #24 and #109 run here from the city to Victoria Street.

Richmond is also the homeware and design hub of Melbourne, with switched-on shoppers snapping up European and domestic furniture in the showrooms along Bridge Road and Church and Victoria streets, or at Melbourne's branch of furnishing giant IKEA in the Victoria Gardens shopping centre, on the corner of Victoria and Burnley streets. Across the road stands Richmond's famous **Skipping Girl Vinegar** sign, one of the oldest neon signs in Australia. The sign replaces the original one erected atop the old vinegar factory in 1936, but over the years Little Audrey, as she became known, fell into disrepair. Since then the National Trust has started a campaign to restore Audrey to all her neon glory, although the mystery surrounding who the little girl was remains despite various claims.

Eastern suburbs

One of the best ways to explore Melbourne's northeast is by **bicycle** (see p.28 for information on bike rental). A bicycle path runs beside the Yarra all the way from the city centre to Eltham, 24km inland. Starting at Southgate it passes through South Yarra and Toorak before reaching Yarra Bend and Studley parks, with their prime riverside frontage, sandstone escarpments, golf courses, barbecue facilities, boathouses, playing fields, and untouched bushland which is home to many flying foxes. From here there are great views of the city skyline and the massive CUB Brewery. Originally the land was occupied by the Aboriginal Wurundjeri, who used it as a source of fish, eels, freshwater mussels and waterfowl.

After passing Collingwood Children's Farm (see p.83), nestled in the elbow of the river, and then riding under the Johnston Street Bridge, you'll catch a glimpse of Dight's Falls, the remains of Melbourne's first industrial site, a flour mill built by John Dight in 1841. It was also the site for a school set up for Aboriginal boys in 1845, although now closed. Just beyond here is the junction of the Yarra with Merri Creek, a fordable stream that in pre-drought days used to become a mighty torrent in times of flood from where you can continue along the river to Fairfield Boathouse – with old-fashioned skiffs and well-fed ducks – or take a walking track to Kane's Bridge, which leads back to Studley Park Boathouse. Both places have cafés and rent out boats ($22 per hour).

If you're feeling energetic, you can continue on from Fairfield Boathouse to **Banksia Park**. In the late 1880s and 1890s this area was a magnet for a group of artists known as the **Heidelberg School**, who broke with European landscape conventions and charted a distinctive and more naturalistic depiction of local conditions that is said to have captured something truthful about the Australian landscape. For more information, contact the Museum of Modern Art at Heide (see overleaf), which can also provide details on the **Heidelberg Artists Trail** (Ⓦwww.artiststrail.com), a forty-kilometre path of information panels and reproductions located at the sites where Arthur Streeton, Abram Louis Buvelot and Tom Roberts once set up their easels beside the river.

Love Thy Neighbours

Set in Melbourne's eastern suburbs is Pin Oak Court (aka "Ramsay Street"), former address of Kylie, Jason and co from the successful TV soap **Neighbours** (also alma mater of Hollywood darlings Guy Pierce and Russell Crowe). The interior set is closed unless you're on a tour, but you can star-spot in the street location and even catch an upcoming episode being filmed. To get there catch tram #75 from the city to Springvale Road, and make your way to Weeden Drive. There are also several tour companies that will take you onto the set and allow you to meet one of the stars. Ramsay Street Tours (☎9629 5866; tours start from $40) go daily to Pin Oak Court and past other locations. Most days you can get great photos of the houses, but on days when the soap is being filmed, no tours or tourists are allowed into the street. If the drive seems too far then there's always Monday's "Neighbours Night" at the *Elephant and Wheelbarrow* in St Kilda (see p.128) for a chance to play trivia with the stars of today.

Heide Museum of Modern Art

Adjoining Banksia Park, the **Heide Museum of Modern Art** (Tues–Fri 10am–5pm, Sat & Sun noon–5pm; $12; ☎9850 1500, Ⓦwww.heide.com.au) is set in sixteen acres of gardens and parkland at 7 Templestowe Rd in Bulleen. Heide was the home of urbane art patrons John and Sunday Reed, who bought this former dairy farm in 1934; it was also where Australia's second major indigenous art movement – Modernism – took off during the 1930s and 1940s. A volatile collection of artists such as Sidney Nolan, Joy Hester, Albert Tucker, Charles Blackman and Arthur Boyd flourished here with support from the Reeds. The iconographic Ned Kelly series, which was to make Sydney Nolan famous, was painted on Heide's dining table. The property comprises three main buildings: Heide I (the Reeds' original farmhouse), Heide II and Heide III, and has numerous contemporary sculptures including Jeff Thomson's *Cows*, an exquisite Kitchen Garden and an airy courtyard café (Tues–Fri 11am–4pm, Sat & Sun 11am–5pm). The gallery holds a collection of modern Australian art from the 1920s to the 1980s, as well as temporary exhibitions of contemporary art. Heide is well marked off the Eastern Freeway (take the Bulleen Rd turn-off). By public transport, take a Hurstbridge-line train from Flinders Street Station to Heidelberg Station, then bus #291; get off when you see the museum's latest commission *Helmet*, a huge steel sculpture by local artists Tanya Court and Cassandra Chilton.

Montsalvat

Eltham, just east of Heide, cemented its reputation as a crafts centre in 1934 when the painter and architect Justus Jorgensen founded **Montsalvat** (daily 9am–5pm; $10; ☎9439 7712, Ⓦwww.montsalvat.com.au), at 7 Hillcrest Ave, a European-style artists' colony complete with rustic buildings, tranquil gardens, galleries and studios. Built with the help of his students and followers, the colony's eclectic design was inspired by medieval European buildings, with wonderfully quirky results. Jorgensen died before it was completed, and it has deliberately been left unfinished, although he did live long enough to oversee the completion of the mud-brick Great Hall, whose influence is evident in other similar buildings around Eltham. Today the colony is still home to assorted painters, potters and craftspeople, while the galleries and grounds are often used for visual and performing arts, weddings, exhibitions, and jazz and classical concerts, there's also a good café (Tues–Fri 9.30am–4pm, Sat & Sun 8.30am–5pm). You can get to Montsalvat by taking a Hurstbridge-line **train** from Flinders Street Station to Eltham Station, then catch bus #582.

6

South Yarra, Prahran and Toorak

The trio of suburbs southeast of the city centre is one of Melbourne's premier destinations for food, shopping and promenading. Just south of the river, **South Yarra** has long been the haunt of well-heeled and fashion-conscious Melburnians, centred on exclusive **Chapel Street**, lined with painfully cool cafés and label-proud shops. A few hours on the street and you'll be convinced it's the most vacuous plot in the world, but it's hard not to be drawn into the movements of the young and willowy bolting from one boutique or grazing spot to the next. South Yarra's prestigious past is evident in the stately **Como House**, which provides an insight into the luxurious life of a nineteenth-century landowner.

Chapel Street continues south to the less salubrious but infinitely funkier environs of **Prahran**, focusing on switched-on Greville Street and its surrounding market, while further south is the small suburb of Windsor, with a growing number of lively bars and cafés. The gay strip of **Commercial Road** separates South Yarra and Prahran, combining bookshops, gift and clothes stores with gyms, cafés and restaurants. For a real blue-blood experience, head east from Prahran to the rich heart of **Toorak**, home to Melbourne's economic elite and boasting grand homes and even glitzier designer boutiques than South Yarra, but few tourist attractions.

South Yarra

South Yarra is home to Melbourne's smart set, who browse the racks at designer stores, graze at chic hangouts, then head to the nightclubs to work it all off. At the heart of the district is the strip of **Chapel Street** between Toorak and Commercial roads – the so-called "Golden Mile", or "right" end – where myriad shops and restaurants spill onto pavements with white linen napery and full-aproned waiters. At weekends, hotted-up cars and baby-boomers driving 4WDs make this a heavily trafficked strip reverberating with the pound of engine noise and subwoofer bravado.

Halfway down Chapel Street is the **Jam Factory**. Jam-making began here in 1885 and continued until the factory's closure in 1970. Nine years later the building was overhauled and reopened as a shopping centre, and more recently a monster cinema-and-entertainment complex housing a Virgin Megastore, Borders bookshop and a *TGI Friday*.

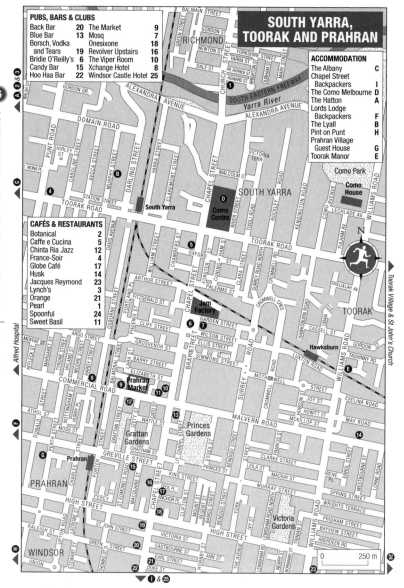

PUBS, BARS & CLUBS

Back Bar	20	The Market	9
Blue Bar	13	Mosq	7
Borsch, Vodka		Onesixone	18
and Tears	19	Revolver Upstairs	16
Bridie O'Reilly's	6	The Viper Room	10
Candy Bar	15	Xchange Hotel	8
Hoo Haa Bar	22	Windsor Castle Hotel	25

SOUTH YARRA, TOORAK AND PRAHRAN

ACCOMMODATION

The Albany	C
Chapel Street	
Backpackers	I
The Como Melbourne	D
The Hatton	A
Lords Lodge	
Backpackers	F
The Lyall	B
Pint on Punt	H
Prahran Village	
Guest House	G
Toorak Manor	E

CAFÉS & RESTAURANTS

Botanical	2
Caffe e Cucina	5
Chinta Ria Jazz	12
France-Soir	4
Globe Café	17
Husk	14
Jacques Reymond	23
Lynch's	3
Orange	21
Pearl	1
Spoonful	24
Sweet Basil	11

Como House

To the north, overlooking the river on the corner of Williams Road and Lechlade Avenue is **Como House** (entry to house by guided tour only May–Aug Wed, Sat & Sun 10am–5pm; Sept–April daily 10am–5pm; $12, gardens $5; for bookings call ☎9827 2500, ⓦwww.comohouse.com.au), a fine example of the kind of townhouse the city's well-to-do nineteenth-century landowners

▲ Como House

liked to build. The site was originally bought by George and Alfred Langhorne in 1837 from the Woiworung Aboriginal people to use as a stock run. Nine years later, a single-storey villa was built on the banks of the Yarra for the barrister Edward Eyre Williams, who named it after Lake Como in Italy, where it is said he proposed to his wife. The house then enjoyed a succession of wealthy owners, including wine merchant John Brown (who added a second storey) and prominent graziers and Melbourne citizens the Armytages, who extended the house by adding a ballroom wing in 1874 and continued to live here until 1959. Now beautifully restored by the National Trust, many of the Armytage family's original furnishings remain intact, while the surrounding landscaped gardens and pine and cypress glades provide ideal spots for a picnic.

Prahran

Chapel Street continues south to **Commercial Road**, renowned for its large gay and lesbian community (see "Gay Melbourne"), then into **Prahran** proper, an area given an interesting dimension by the influx of shopkeepers, students, and emigrants from (in the 1950s) Italy and Greece, and (more recently) Eastern Europe. Prahran's most famous institution is **Prahran Market** (Tues, Thurs & Sat dawn–5pm, Fri dawn–6pm, Sun 10am–3pm), at 163 Commercial Rd. Established on this site in 1881, it is Australia's oldest produce market and today sells all manner of meats, fresh seafood, organic produce, gourmet deli foods and fruit and veg, and also has a number of places to eat.

The further south along Chapel Street you go, the more the fashion boutiques and upmarket cafés give way to secondhand clothing stores, tattooists and fish-and-chip shops. Some prefer this grungey area with its nose-rings and punkish haircuts, while others like the slicker end of Chapel Street to the north.

Just off Chapel Street in the heart of Prahran, **Greville Street**, once the alternative hub of the area, remains a hip strip of bookshops, music and clothing stores and late-night clubs and bars. Weekends in particular see a steady flow of young professionals enjoying the easy-going vibe, the generally fantastic food and spacious bars. Every Sunday the small **Greville Street Market** (noon–5pm) has arts, crafts and secondhand clothes and jewellery on the corner of Grattan Street in Grattan Gardens, a former billabong that's now been landscaped.

Further south across High Street Prahran becomes **Windsor**, a small suburb with a mix of discount shops, ethnic cafés, cheap noodle bars and a burgeoning bar scene, fuelled by students from the nearby campus of Swinburne University.

Toorak

East of South Yarra, **Toorak** is synonymous with money and born-to-rule pedigree. When Melbourne was founded, the wealthy chose to build their homes here, high on the banks of the Yarra, while the cottages of the poor were confined to narrow streets on the flood-prone areas below. During the 1950s and 1960s, old Melbourne money was joined by new, when an influx of European Jews – who arrived penniless in Australia during the 1930s and 1940s – celebrated their hard-earned wealth by moving to Toorak.

Snobbish and conservative, Toorak has little to see or do, apart from wandering around leafy streets of homes with vast gardens and box hedges. On Toorak Road, you can window-shop at the wickedly expensive Toorak Village, a higgledy-piggledy mock-Tudor strip of shops and buildings. Alternatively, pavement-café tables are unrivalled spots for watching Range Rovers and 4WDs (known locally as "Toorak Tractors") idling past. If you're interested in early woodcarvings of Australian flora and fauna, you might want to make a pilgrimage to **St John's Church** (daily 7.30am–5pm), on the corner of Toorak and Orrong roads. Ornamental reliefs of kangaroos, dingos, wattles and ferns can be found on the arm ends and heads of pews on both the north and south side of the church. St John's also occasionally hosts B-list celebrity weddings, usually involving either a local footy star or a scion of Melbourne society.

St Kilda

When the wealthy merchants and legislators of goldrush-era Melbourne sought refuge from the congested and polluted city, they settled upon a green bayside area five kilometres to the southeast. Within a decade the beach suburb of **St Kilda** had become the address of choice for Melbourne's moneyed set. Then, in 1857, Victoria's second train line – running from the city to St Kilda – was opened, and suddenly the suburb's briny pleasures were accessible to the great unwashed. St Kilda's grandeur went to seed as the wealthy took flight to more exclusive areas like South Yarra and Toorak, while in the 1930s its substantial mansions were demolished or left to become a crumbling sea of dosshouses, apartment blocks, dance halls and tacky amusement arcades. Decades later the area became synonymous with drugs, prostitution, and the seamier side of life.

Epitomizing the boom and bust nature of Melbourne's real estate market, St Kilda underwent rejuvenation and renovation in the early 1990s, yet another turnaround in the fortunes of the suburb. Residents finally grasped what fine real estate they had been sitting on, and what kind of fun and fantastic lives they could lead in St Kilda. Property values skyrocketed, shopping and residential complexes sprang up, and trendy cafés and bars seem to open daily. For high-income earners and recreation-seekers intent on partying till dawn several nights a week, St Kilda offers the perfect lifestyle, and is still regarded as *the* place to live or visit for pleasure seeking. Melbourne's most changeable suburb has also seen a new wave of transients – Australia's greatest concentration of backpackers, attracted by the beach and the area's hedonistic reputation, who arrive in their thousands to stay in the suburb's legal and not-so-legal lodges and hostels. While the backpackers may add a certain frisson to St Kilda, many of those who gave the suburb its raffish character – artists, actors, musicians and eccentrics – have been forced out by rising rents and gentrification.

Even so, there's still plenty to explore. Starting in **Fitzroy Street**, with its landmark drinking spots and excellent restaurants and cafés, it is only a short distance to the **Upper Esplanade** and **foreshore**, favourite places for strolling, chatting, seeing and being seen. Continuing, you come to the tourist precinct of Acland Street, noted for its cake shops and sharp cafés, while across Barkly Street and St Kilda Road is the Jewish enclave of East St Kilda, home to the excellent **Jewish Museum of Australia**.

Trains no longer run to St Kilda, but the suburb is easily reached by any of three **tram routes**: #96 from Bourke Street in the city; #16 from Swanston Street; or #112 from Collins Street.

The best time to visit St Kilda is in January and February, when both the fabulous **Midsumma Gay Festival** and the **St Kilda Festival** take place, featuring music, outdoor performances, exhibitions, sporting events and dancing.

No. 96 to City (tram route)

ST KILDA

0 ——————— 250 m

CAFÉS & RESTAURANTS

Bala's Café	15	Jackie O	29
Big Mouth	24	Las Chicas	19
Café Di Stasio	5	Leeroy Expresso	27
Café Racer	30	Melbourne Wine Room	1
Chinta Blues	7	Milktoast	16
Cicciolina	23	Pelican	4
Circa, The Prince	G	Scheherazade	20
Claypots Seafood Bar	28	Soulmama	11
Donovans	22	The Stokehouse	14
The Espy Kitchen	8	Topolinos	3
The Galleon	13	Veludo	25
Il Fornaio	6	Wall Two 80	18
Inkr7	10		

PUBS, BARS & CLUBS

Dog's Bar	12
Doulton Bar	26
The Elephant and Wheelbarrow	B
The Esplanade Hotel	8
The George Public Bar	1
Mink Bar	G
Next Level @ Hotel Barkly	9
Pause	17
The Prince Public Bar	G
Tongue and Groove	2
Veludo	25

LIVE MUSIC VENUES

The Esplanade Hotel	8
The Greyhound Hotel	21
The Prince Bandroom	G

ACCOMMODATION

Annies Bed and Breakfast	A
Base	K
Boutique Hotel Tolarno	E
Charnwood Motor Inn	C
Cosmopolitan	J
Novotel St Kilda	I
Olembia Guesthouse	H
The Prince	G
Ritz for Backpackers	B
St Kilda Coffee Palace	D
Urban St Kilda	F

COMMERCIAL ROAD

QUEEN'S ROAD

BEATRICE AVENUE

MOUBRAY ST

ORRE STREET

ST KILDA ROAD

HIGH STREET

RALEIGH STREET

WINDSOR

GLADSTONE ST

UNION STREET

HENRY STREET

PEEL STREET

ALBERT STREET

DANDENONG ROAD

NELSON ST

WELLINGTON STREET

Albert Park

Albert Park Lake

AUGHTIE DRIVE

UNION ST

ST KILDA JUNCTION

Astor Theatre & Red Stitch Theatre

CANTERBURY ROAD

BEACONSFIELD PARADE

ST KILDA WEST

Old St Kilda Railway Station

George Cinema

Synagogue

Jewish Museum of Australia

ALMA ROAD

CHARNWOOD CRES

Catani Gardens

FITZROY STREET

GREY STREET

WATERLOO CRESCENT

N

ST KILDA ROAD

ARGYLE STREET

Theatreworks

Linden

ST KILDA

INKERMAN STREET

St Kilda Pier

St Kilda Baths

St Kilda Beach

JACKA BOULEVARD

St Kilda Arts & Craft Market

BLANCHE STREET

VALE STREET

CARLISLE STREET

CARLISLE STREET

O'Donnell Gardens

Luna Park

Palais Theatre

Peanut Farm Reserve

BLESSINGTON STREET

St Kilda Botanical Gardens

Port Phillip Bay

St Kilda Marina

Renfrey Gardens

MARINE PARADE

BLESSINGTON STREET

WORDSWORTH STREET

Fitzroy Street

For years, **Fitzroy Street** was the focus of St Kilda's often overblown reputation as Melbourne's epicentre of drugs and sleaze. Recently, however, it has gone decidedly upmarket: most of the pawnshops, hamburger joints and adult bookstores have given way to cafés and bars, although **Grey Street** still attracts its fair share of prostitutes, drug addicts and down-and-outs, and is home to the Sacred Heart Church's welfare centre and popular op shop (charity shop).

On the corner of Grey and Fitzroy streets, the Venetian-style **George Hotel** has been the barometer of St Kilda's fortunes since the days in the nineteenth century when it was one of Australia's finest hotels. Originally known as the *Terminus*, it was renamed the *George* after the *George Hotel* in Ballarat in 1868, when former governor of the Ballarat gaol, Charles Foster, took it over. By the end of the 1940s, the Depression and the two World Wars had taken their toll, but despite the chipped crockery and peeling paint, the hotel's permanent residents clung to the genteel rituals of its glory days. The writer Hal Porter, who worked as the hotel's assistant manager in 1949, described it as "the Titanic that missed the iceberg". By the late 1970s, the *George* had become seriously run down, its floors littered with syringes and its Seaview Ballroom a venue for Melbourne's punk rock explosion – Melbourne's "Prince of Darkness", Nick Cave, used to regularly sing here – hosting nightclubs like *Sedition*. In the 1980s, the *George's* front bar was described by hotel inspectors as "the sleaziest, seamiest, seediest and most sordid hotel in Australia", and each night it was hosed out after a day of boozing, brawling and whoring. Eventually, after years of colourful neglect, the hotel was transformed in the early 1990s into a slick wine bar, pub and restaurant, with adjoining cinema and an apartment complex.

A detour off Fitzroy Street to 270 Canterbury Rd brings you to the former house of retired AFL player and television bad boy **Sam Newman**, which bears the face of pneumatic nymph Pamela Anderson. The extraordinary image, taken from Anderson's famous *Playboy* shoot, covers the entire laminated glass facade of the three-level home, and was constructed initially without council planning.

Back on Fitzroy Street where the road meets the water, the **Catani Gardens** are a palm-fringed expanse of manicured lawns, which look as if they have come straight out of Hollywood casting. Mercifully free of development, it's where many come to escape the showier side of St Kilda with fish and chips and a can or two of VB.

The esplanades and foreshore

Running from the western end of Fitzroy Street, the palm-lined split-level boulevard comprising the **Upper and Lower Esplanades** and its **foreshore** parkland, is the work of a committee set up in 1906 to provide municipal entertainment that did not offend "good taste or sound morals". By Australian standards, the **beach** here is small but beautifully formed, its sweeping crescent of sand framed by gardens and walkways. Melbourne's busiest, the beach can also get suffocatingly thick with bodies, and after hot summer nights, it's often littered with cans, bottles and cigarette butts left behind by boozing revellers. Despite murky water, the swimming here is okay, with not a wave in sight, so it can be a good family beach.

Taking pride of place on the Upper Esplanade is the *Esplanade Hotel* (or "Espy"), a famously beer-soaked corner of the city and one of Australia's best-known band venues, with fantastic views overlooking Port Phillip Bay. Each

▲ Esplanade Market

Sunday, the Upper Esplanade hosts the popular **Esplanade Market** (see p.165), part of the ritual of going to St Kilda that includes taking a look at the beach, feeding your face, browsing a few shops and listening to the buskers.

Across Jacka Boulevard (the Lower Esplanade), **St Kilda Pier** boasts a replica of the first European-style pier pavilion in Australia. The original 1904 building burned down a year before its centenary in 2003. However, following the wishes of local residents, the legendary kiosk was restored to its former glory two years later, with the addition of a new restaurant at the back, and remains a sunny spot for tea and cake. Behind the pavilion, the sheltered breakwater is the unlikely home of a colony of around a thousand **Little Penguins**. The rocky banks where they nest are protected and have been fenced off, but with a little luck you may still catch a glimpse of them coming ashore at dawn or dusk.

Near the base of the pier are the **St Kilda Baths**, which date back to 1931. After decades of deterioration, it was decided to redevelop the historic site in the late 1990s. The result is a vapid complex of a seawater pool, restaurants and various health facilities like a spa and gym available to the public. It's an heroically bad mix of shopping complex and function centre with a Moorish twist, and despite the runaway success of the *Soulmama* restaurant (see p.125), many of the retail spaces remain empty.

Dominating the southern end of the Upper Esplanade, the magnificent art deco **Palais Theatre** has played host to many big name bands including Pink Floyd and Duran Duran. It closed for restoration works in March 2009 for twenty months, part of a controversial project that will see the theatre and the triangle of land that surrounds it much improved or overdeveloped, depending on who you speak to. Nearby is "Mr Moon", a laughing face whose gaping mouth serves as an entrance to St Kilda's most famous icon: **Luna Park** (May to mid Sept Sat & Sun 11am–6pm, or daily during school holidays; mid-Sept to April Fri 7–11pm, Sat 11am–11pm, Sun 11am–6pm, or daily during school holidays; admission free, single rides $8, unlimited rides adults $37.95, 4–12 yr-olds $27.95, 1–3 yr-olds $12.95; ☏1300 888 272, ⓦwww.lunapark.com.au).

When it opened in 1912, the attractions were circus performers, contortionists and "Big Ben", an enormous twelve-year-old boy who weighed almost 350 pounds. Later, during World War I, Luna Park screened propaganda movies and audiences were encouraged to throw objects at images of the Kaiser. Despite a couple of new attractions, there's still nothing too hi-tech about this amusement park: the Scenic Railway (one of the world's oldest operating roller-coasters) runs along wooden trestles and the Ghost Train wouldn't spook a toddler, but that's half the fun. Rides are reasonably priced, ensuring Luna Park is still *the* place for local children's birthday bashes.

Acland Street and around

St Kilda has long had a strong Jewish presence. Following World War II, Central European Jews introduced **Acland Street** to *kugelhšpfs*, Wiener schnitzels and early-morning get-togethers, while Eastern European Jews have added their mark since the collapse of the former Soviet Union, particularly in the section of Carlisle Street east of St Kilda Road. The leafy northern end of Acland Street is predominantly residential, although there are a few cafés and bars. At no. 26, occupying a National Trust-listed mansion, the **Linden Centre for Contemporary Arts** (Tues–Sun 1–6pm; free; ✆9209 6794, ⓦwww .lindenarts.org) is probably the best community gallery in Australia as it offers a studio to new artists and displays the newest contemporary paintings, installations and video art all year round. It also offers a programme of painting and drawing classes – see website for more details.

Once noted for its Jewishness and family-run restaurants, the southern end of Acland Street is now a melange of gift stores, bookshops, cafés, fast-food franchises, bars, florists, and continental cake shops. A single Jewish restaurant remains, the once legendary *Scheherazade* (see p.124), though several other excellent cake shops and eateries are worth checking out. Now a "tourist precinct", the main strip's widened footpaths can become busy at weekends with visitors staring at the strange assortment of buskers.

To escape the throng, head for the **St Kilda Botanical Gardens** – across Barkly Street and up nearby Blessington Street (sunrise–sunset; free) – which include a huge rose garden, a giant chess board, an indigenous plant section, a duck pond and a conservatory.

East St Kilda

As St Kilda has grown in size and popularity, rents in the area have swelled, pushing many of the original Jewish families into the surrounding suburbs. By way of response real-estate agents have craftily invented **East St Kilda** (also called **Balaclava** by those who don't have property there), a grungier alternative to its shiny neighbour. Still distinctively Jewish (some wryly refer to it as the "Bagel Belt"), East St Kilda's appeal owes much to the immigrants – mostly from the Ukraine, Poland and Russia – who arrived here decades ago. Their presence can be immediately seen in the low-rise skyline of worker's cottages or Art Deco flats, dominated by synagogues and Jewish schools, while Saturdays see residents dressed in their best buzzing along to worship. The area also boasts the interesting **Jewish Museum of Australia**.

In recent years, another wave of refugees has moved in: bohemians and hipsters fleeing the rocketing rents and yuppification of St Kilda and Prahran further to the north. On **Carlisle Street**, the main thoroughfare, instead of big chains there are authentic European butchers, Asian grocers, $2 stores, trendy cafés and funky but low-key clothing boutiques. Heading back to St Kilda, on the corner of Carlisle Street and Nepean Highway, the restored **St Kilda Town Hall** (1890) was renovated in the 1960s to include a scaled-down replica of architect Alvar Aalto's scalloped Finlandia Hall in Helsinki, while facing here, the **St Kilda Public Library** is the suburb's popular community hub, featuring an extension in the shape of an open book. The area's only parkland is the pleasant **Alma Park** on Alma Road, while the sprawling **St Kilda cemetery** further east on the same road serves as the final resting place of Australia's second prime minister, Alfred Deakin, and Albert Jacka, the popular former mayor of St Kilda. To get to East St Kilda, take either a Sandringham-line **train** from Flinders Street Station in the city and get off at Balaclava Station, or **tram** #3 or #16 from the city to Carlisle Street.

The Jewish Museum

The best place to find out more about the Australian-Jewish experience is the rewarding **Jewish Museum of Australia** at 26 Alma Rd (Tues–Thurs 10am–4pm, Sun 11am–5pm; $10; ☎9534 0083, ⓦwww.jewishmuseum.com.au). Opened in 1995, exhibitions display thousands of pieces of Judaica with four permanent exhibitions: the Australian Jewish History Gallery, documenting Jewish life in Australia since colonization 200 years ago; the Timeline of Jewish History, tracing the last four thousand years; and Jewish Year and Belief and Ritual, both dedicated to the culture of Judaism, with a focus on festivals and customs. Temporary exhibitions on a wide range of related topics are another feature of the museum. Take tram #67 along St Kilda Road.

Williamstown

U ntil the Yarra was widened in the 1880s to allow for the upgrading of Melbourne's port facilities, **Williamstown** – occupying a peninsula southwest of the city – was Port Phillip Bay's major seaport. Named after British King William IV, it was established in 1835, and was briefly considered the capital of Victoria, seeing scores of vessels unloading convicts, gold-diggers and farmers bound for the open plains of central Victoria. But a lack of fresh water saw Melbourne chosen as the site, and as the new capital's port facilities improved, Williamstown's maritime significance waned. Eventually, a band of industrial suburbs to the west of the centre isolated Williamstown from the city and the small seaside settlement withdrew into itself.

Then, with the opening of the West Gate Bridge near the mouth of the Yarra in 1978, "Willy" became more accessible, and its charms were rediscovered. At weekends it's every bit as frantic as St Kilda or Southgate, yet on weekdays it is just another quiet town. Most visitors beat a path to **Nelson Place**, Williamstown's historic precinct, ringed by stately bluestone buildings, cafés, pubs and galleries. From here it's a short stroll to the picturesque waterfront park of **Commonwealth Reserve** and **Gem Pier**, while further east, **Point Gellibrand** is where convicts from Britain were shipped ashore. There are also three small but excellent rail and maritime museums and some popular beaches. In the adjacent suburb of Spotswood, the **Scienceworks** deserves a visit for its fascinating array of interactive displays and exhibits and the hi-tech planetarium.

Getting to Williamstown

As the crow flies, Williamstown is only 5km southwest of the city. The easiest way to get there is to catch a Williamstown **train** from Flinders Street Station to the end of the line (roughly 30min), from where it's a short walk along Ann Street to Nelson Place. By **boat**, Williamstown is connected to Southgate by the Bay & River Cruises' ferry (see p.61). If you're feeling energetic, you could always **cycle** to Williamstown: the Bay Trail bicycle path runs along the St Kilda foreshore to Port Melbourne and Eastbridge Park (under the West Gate Bridge), from where you can catch a punt (Sat & Sun only 10am–5pm; $3) across the mouth of the Yarra to join up with the track, which then winds through Riverside Park and on to Williamstown, a total of around 10km each way.

Williamstown is also the starting point for the 55-kilometre **Bay West Trail** to Werribee (see p.216), which begins at Scienceworks and finishes at Werribee Park. The route is signposted, or you can pick up a map from the visitors centre at Federation Square.

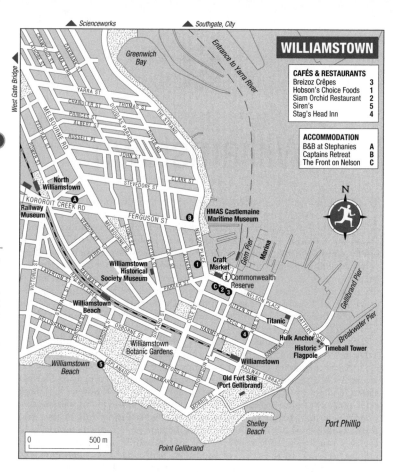

Scienceworks
Southgate, City
West Gate Bridge
WILLIAMSTOWN
CAFÉS & RESTAURANTS
Breizoz Crêpes 3
Hobson's Choice Foods 1
Siam Orchid Restaurant 2
Siren's 5
Stag's Head Inn 4
ACCOMMODATION
B&B at Stephanies A
Captains Retreat B
The Front on Nelson C
N
Greenwich Bay
Entrance to Yarra River
CRAWFORD ST
LATROBE ST
ALMA TERR
OAKBANK ST
YARRA ST
CHANDLER ST
THOMAS ST
PRINCES ST
ALBERT ST
RUSSELL PL
DOUGLAS PARADE
THE STRAND
DOVER RD
MELBOURNE RD
FEDERAL ST
POWER ST
JOHN ST
STEVEDORE ST
CLARK ST
North Williamstown
KOROROIT CREEK RD
Railway Museum
FERGUSON ST
HMAS Castlemaine Maritime Museum
VERDON ST
MELBOURNE RD
LYONS ST
ELECTRA ST
CECIL ST
AITKEN ST
NELSON PLACE
Gem Pier
Marina
Craft Market
PERRY ST
Williamstown Historical Society Museum
Commonwealth Reserve
VICTORIA ST
LAVERTON ST
RAILWAY PL
RAILWAY CRES
PARKER ST
NELSON PLACE
Gellibrand Pier
STEWART ST
Williamstown Beach
AITKEN ST
COLE ST
CECIL ST
ANN ST
Titanic
BATTERY ROAD
Breakwater Pier
GELLIBRAND ST
FORSTER ST
GARDEN ST
OSBORNE ST
GIFFARD ST
HANMER ST
Hulk Anchor
Historic Flagpole
Timeball Tower
KANOWNA ST
Williamstown Botanic Gardens
Williamstown
Williamstown Beach
ESPLANADE
TWYFORD ST
ILLAWARRA ST
THOMPSON ST
RAILWAY TERRACE
Old Fort Site (Port Gellibrand)
MORRIS ST
Shelley Beach
Port Phillip
0 500 m
Point Gellibrand

Around Nelson Place

Ferries berth at **Gem Pier** and, as they pull in, you'd almost think you were coming ashore at a naval shipyard. For years Williamstown has been an important ship-building site and was once the home of the Victorian Navy. The HMAS *Castlemaine*, a decommissioned World War II minesweeper built at the yard, is permanently docked at the pier, and now houses an interesting **maritime museum** (Sat & Sun 11am–5pm; $5). Also here, the tallship *Enterprize*, a replica of the vessel that brought the first settlers to Melbourne, runs a variety of cruises around the bay during the week and at weekends (prices range from $20 for a one hour trip to $245 for an overnight sail; for more information contact ⓣ9397 3477, ⓦwww.enterprize.com.au). For a less watery experience Melbourne Seaplanes offers **scenic flights** from Gem Pier to around Port Phillip Bay and the city from $125 (ⓣ0418 688 388, ⓦwww.seaplane.com.au)

Next to Gem Pier, the small park of **Commonwealth Reserve** affords panoramic views of Melbourne's city skyline and houses a **visitor information centre** (daily 9am–5pm; ⓣ9932 4310), along with a bandstand, a tide-gauge

house and a water fountain donated by a certain Reverend John Wilkinson to deter sailors from hitting the grog. The visitors centre provides maps for a series of **self-guided walks** around Williamstown that take in routes around the seaside, the waterfront, or the town.

Across the park is displayed an anchor from the nineteenth-century British warship HMVS *Nelson*, the first vessel to enter the Williamstown dockyards. On the third Sunday of each month, the popular family-friendly **Williamstown Craft Market** is held in the reserve (10am–4pm), with live music performed on the bandstand. In its heyday the section of **Nelson Place** opposite once had the highest concentration of pubs anywhere in the southern hemisphere (hence the Reverend Wilkinson's water fountain), and today is lined with cafés, restaurants and ice-cream parlours.

Point Gellibrand

A half-hour walk along Nelson Place past the piers, dockyards and storage tanks brings you to **Point Gellibrand**, named after Joseph Tice Gellibrand, a member of Batman's original scouting party who first came ashore here in 1835. Nearby, a copper ball in the convict-built **Timeball Tower** is lowered each day at 1pm – a time-check by which shipmasters used to calibrate their chronometers before taking to sea. Further southwest of the tower are the remains of **Fort Gellibrand**, a former defence battery that saw plenty of mock battles but never fired a shot in anger. Just behind the fort, and below an old railway embankment, mutineering convicts stoned the Inspector-General of Penal Establishments, John Price, to death in 1857. As there was no local morgue, Price was taken to the *Prince of Wales* hotel, on the corner of Nelson Place and Kanowna Street, where his body was laid out. Today the *Prince of Wales* is known as the **Titanic** and lives on as a reconditioned theatre-restaurant that re-enacts the sinking of the famous ocean-liner, offering costume rental, dinner, dancing and the choice of experiencing it in Steerage Passage ($55) or First Class ($79) every Saturday (℡9397 5101, Ⓦwww .titanic.com.au).

In the nineteenth century, convicts were carried by barge ashore from prison hulks moored at sea and employed in chain gangs on public works, including the building of **Breakwater Pier** on the southeastern tip from bluestone extracted from quarries on Point Gellibrand. For a time, Ned Kelly (see box, p.46) languished in a yellow-daubed prison hulk anchored offshore – they were painted yellow to distinguish them from other vessels.

Around the point and beyond the cricket ground, **Williamstown Beach** is one of Melbourne's best bayside swimming spots, while the lush nineteenth-century botanical gardens, just back from the beach, make a good spot for a picnic. Following Giffard Street along the eastern side of the Botanical Gardens as far as Electra Street to no. 5 brings you to the small **William-stown Historical Society Museum** (Sun 2–5pm; $3), a repository for a fine collection of maritime displays and some interesting artefacts from the suburb's early and somewhat grim development from the 1840s, including antique furnishings, detailed models of ships, convict leg irons and paintings of Price's murder. Williamstown's other museum is trainspotter heaven: the **Railway Museum** (Sat & Sun noon–5pm, Wed during school holidays noon–4pm; $6) on Champion Road, which has an impressive collection of beautifully restored steam and diesel engines, and railway carriages. The museum is next to North Williamstown Station, the second-to-last stop on the Williamstown line.

Scienceworks

In the neighbouring suburb of Spotswood, **Scienceworks**, at 2 Booker St (daily 10am–4.30pm; $6, plus $5 each for Planetarium and Lightning Room shows; ☎13 11 02, ⓦwww.museumvictoria.com.au/scienceworks), is an excellent hands-on science and technology museum. Inside the space-age building, set in a desolate wasteland, the tactile displays, exhibits and touring shows are ingenious, fun and highly interactive. Permanent highlights include "Nitty Gritty Super City", an interactive exhibition that allows children to explore a number of roles from construction to steering a ship, and "Sports-works", which lets you work out how sporty or otherwise your body is. The museum also runs free short workshops from woodwork to toy-making. In addition the **Lightning Room** holds electrifying half-hour shows (noon–3pm) explaining the science behind fireworks among other lighting forms and features high-voltage equipment capable of simulating real lightning bolts.

Part of the site consists of the original Spotswood Pumping Station, an unusually attractive industrial complex with working steam pumps. Protected by the National Trust, the station and its pumps helped nineteenth-century Melbourne get rid of its severe stench (satirists of the day called the city "Marvellous Smellbourne"); guided and self-guided tours are available. There's also a state-of-the-art **Planetarium** (45min shows held hourly 11am–3pm), which uses the latest digital technology to re-create the night sky on the domed ceiling. You can recline in comfy chairs and watch a variety of shows taking you on a 3D journey through space and time on themes ranging from "The Search for Life" to "Black Holes". To get to Scienceworks, take a Williamstown- or Werribee-line train from Flinders Street Station to Spotswood Station, from where it's a ten-minute walk. You can also take a ferry from Southgate (see p.61). If you're cycling from the city, Scienceworks is just off the bicycle route west of Riverside Park.

see
p.61

▲ "Sportsworks" at Scienceworks

Listings

Listings

9

Accommodation

M elbourne has a range of accommodation options, from multi-bed hostels, motel chains and cosy B&B establishments to luxury hotels and serviced apartments that allow you to spread out in style and comfort. The only time you're likely to have problems **finding a room** is during major sporting events such as the Grand Prix or the AFL Grand Final (see "Festivals and events"), when rooms are often booked out a long time in advance – it's best at these times to reserve a couple of months ahead. Hostels, particularly those in the CBD and St Kilda, also fill up quickly from December to March, so plan on making a reservation a few weeks in advance.

If you fly in without a reservation, head for the **travellers' information service desk** at Melbourne Airport, located on the ground floor of the international terminal. This provides a free booking service for all types of accommodation throughout the city and suburbs. Bookings can also be made downtown at the **Melbourne Visitor Information Centre** (see p.35) in Federation Square on the corner of Swanston and Flinders streets. Again, there's no booking fee. Gay and lesbian visitors are unlikely to experience more than a sideways look booking into hotels in Melbourne, but for **gay and lesbian accommodation**, see p.140.

When deciding which **area** to stay in, your choice is between the CBD, adjacent inner-city suburbs, and St Kilda. The **city centre** (particularly Collins Street) and the leisure precincts of Southgate and the Crown Casino are the domain of upmarket hotels, while a number of mid-range places cluster around Southern Cross Station, although the area is rather noisy and unattractive. For cheaper rooms, there's plenty of backpacker accommodation, especially along Elizabeth and King streets. **Inner-city suburbs** such as North and East Melbourne, Carlton, Richmond, South Yarra and South Melbourne offer good

---

Accommodation prices

All accommodation listed in this book has been categorized according to the following price codes, which represent the **cheapest rate for a double** or twin room available (excluding special offers) during high season. Note that all accommodation includes GST (Goods and Services Tax, see p.30), and that rates generally increase during the summer months (Dec–March), peak holiday periods such as Christmas and Easter and major sporting and cultural events (see Chapter 15). For **hostels** providing dormitory accommodation, the code represents the per-person charge for a bed.

❶ under $25	❹ $91–130	❼ $221–250
❷ $26–50	❺ $131–180	❽ $251–300
❸ $51–90	❻ $181–220	❾ over $301

alternatives to the CBD in all price ranges, while seaside **St Kilda** ("backpacker central") has perhaps the best-value accommodation in Melbourne, with hostels by the bucketload and plenty of inexpensive hotels, lodges and motels.

For last-minute, **discounted accommodation** you can book through Ⓦwww.wotif.com. For places to stay outside Melbourne, check out Ⓦwww.greatplacestostay.com.au, where you can search for B&Bs, self-contained cottages and boutique hotels, get regional profiles and learn about upcoming events.

Our listings are grouped by **area**, subdivided into **type of accommodation** (hotels and motels, B&Bs, and hostels). The majority are easily accessible by tram, train or bus.

The east side

For locations of the following see the map on p.40.

Hotels

Adelphi Hotel 187 Flinders Lane ☎8080 8888, Ⓦwww.adelphi.com.au. Occupying a converted warehouse, the 34-room Adelphi is a boutique hotel par excellence, with slick service, an even slicker design, and rates starting from $560 a night. The interior is minimalist, walls are hung with contemporary art and photography, and rooms are large. Rounding out the experience is an art bar with several interesting works on display, a sauna, a tiny fitness centre and, most strikingly, a glass-bottomed rooftop pool suspended above the street. In the same building is the superb *ezard* restaurant (see p.113). ❾

Grand Hyatt 123 Collins St ☎9657 1234, Ⓦwww.melbourne.grand.hyatt.com. Fresh from a $40 million makeover this over-the-top hotel has 547 rooms, 18 executive suites and a lobby big enough to land a plane in. Rooms are tasteful and bathrooms are plated with marble. ❽–❾

Hotel Lindrum 26 Flinders St ☎9668 1111, Ⓦwww.hotellindrum.com.au. Named after legendary Australian billiards player Walter Lindrum, this intimate and very expensive five-storey boutique hotel has a reading room with large comfy chairs, an open fireplace and books, and instead of a formal reception you register at the front bar. As well as a billiard table and lots of Lindrum memorabilia, you'll find a back bar with a selection of wines, the classy *felt* restaurant and 59 rooms complete with huge beds, CD player and complimentary in-house movies. Rooms from $425. ❾

Park Hyatt 1 Parliament Sq, off Parliament Place ☎9224 1234, Ⓦwww.melbourne.park.hyatt.com. This opulent bunker for business travellers and Melbourne's junior moguls has deluxe rooms and suites with lush trimmings, such as open fireplaces and spa baths with TV. The service, naturally, is first class. ❽–❾

Hotel Sofitel 25 Collins St ☎9653 0000, Ⓦwww.sofitelmelbourne.com.au. I.M. Pei-designed hotel with marvellous views across Melbourne. Gloriously comfortable rooms, which begin on the 36th floor, as well as a plush bar and a popular restaurant, *Café La* located on level 35. ❽–❾

Victoria Hotel 215 Little Collins St ☎9669 0000, ☎1800 331 147, Ⓦwww.victoriahotel.com.au. Huge, old refurbished hotel dating back to 1880 in an unbeatable central location, with its own café and bar, and a large lobby that retains some of its historic flavour. Rooms – with or without bathrooms – are gradually being updated, though remain rather plain, and come with telephones, heating, fridge and tea- and coffee-making facilities. Covered parking available ($15 per day). ❹–❺

Westin Hotel 205 Collins St ☎9635 2222, Ⓦwww.westin.com.au. Right on City Square, the hideous exterior of this monstrous 262-room hotel hides surprisingly glamorous interiors and rooms notable for their understated elegance, featuring full-length windows, comfy beds and Molten Brown bathroom products. Downstairs the *Martini Bar* (Mon–Sat 5pm–late) is a popular pre-dinner spot. Rooms from $310. ❾

Windsor Hotel 111 Spring St ☎9633 6000, Ⓦwww.thewindsor.com.au. Built in 1883 opposite Parliament House, this grand colonial pile has played host to Sir Laurence Olivier, Vivien Leigh and Muhammad Ali, though these days it attracts a rather more conservative clientele. The prestigious suites are pure nineteenth-century opulence. Service is excellent, and the afternoon tea at the hotel's *111 Spring Street* restaurant is not to be missed. A multi-million dollar heritage-approved restoration is due to start 2009. Rooms from ❻

Budget hotels, motels and hostels

City Centre Budget Hotel 22 Little Collins St ☎9654 5401, 🌐www.citycentrebudgethotel .com.au. Friendly hotel in a good position on a quiet street, 100m from Parliament Station, with a selection of doubles, singles, and family rooms on the first and second floor, all sharing bathrooms. Rooms are clean with laminate flooring, fridge, TV, kettle and fan; other facilities include free internet, a sunroof terrace, heating, basic kitchens, laundry and car parking ($25 per day). No breakfast or lift. ❸

City Limits Motel 20 Little Bourke St ☎9662 2544, ☎1800 808 651, 🌐www.citylimits.com .au. Motel-style units with en-suite bathrooms, kitchenettes with microwave, and the usual mod cons, just around the corner from Parliament Station. Rates include continental breakfast, parking is extra ($15). Rates go up at weekends. ❹–❺

Exford Hotel 199 Russell St ☎9663 2697, 🌐www.exfordhotel.com.au. In an extremely central position above a lively, refurbished pub, this hostel is secure and clean with friendly and helpful staff. Usual amenities, plus a tiny sundeck with barbecue. The four- to ten-bed dorms (women-only on request) are a little scruffy, though doubles are better looking with pine furniture. Shared facilities only. Dorms ❷, rooms ❸

Victoria Hall 380 Russell St ☎9662 3888, 🌐www.victoriahall.com.au. It may look like a multi-storey car park from the outside, but this completely refurbished hostel offers "five-star backpacker" accommodation, with excellent facilities including a games room, a 26-seat movie room, a gym and a rooftop kitchen-dining area. The four- to six-bed dorms have partitions for privacy, private reading lights, and huge lockers, and there are also en-suite doubles and family rooms with TVs. Top value, and great location near the Old Melbourne Gaol. Dorms ❷, doubles ❸

The west side

For locations of the following see the map on pp.50–51.

Hotels

Jasper Hotel 489 Elizabeth St ☎8327 2777, ☎1800 468 359, 🌐www .jasperhotel.com.au. A complete design makeover has raised this YWCA-owned hostel, just across the road from the Queen Victoria Market, to boutique hotel status and its rating to four stars. Cool and contemporary from the outside, spacious and bold inside, with each hallway painted a different colour. The 65 rooms are well appointed and stylishly furnished with queen-size beds, flat-screen TVs and sleek bathrooms, and the hotel also offers in-room treatments and massage. Next door, *Jasper Kitchen* is open for breakfast ($20) and well-priced lunches. ❺

Kingsgate Hotel 131 King St ☎9629 4171, 🌐www.kingsgatehotel.com.au. Huge, refurbished private hotel. The en-suite rooms with colour TV, heating, a/c and telephone are good value, and there are also inexpensive singles and doubles with shared facilities, as well as a few rooms for small groups or families (up to four beds). Facilities include a laundry, a pleasant TV lounge, a bar, restaurant and café. Cheap breakfast. ❹–❻

Pensione Hotel 16 Spencer St ☎9621 3333 or 1800 816 168, 🌐www .pensione.com.au. Refurbished and renamed

▲ Jasper Hotel

(it used to be the *Explorers Inn*) this well-priced boutique hotel close to the Melbourne Exhibition Centre is popular with both cost-cutting business types and travellers. Pleasant and well maintained, it offers a variety of modern en-suite singles, doubles and triples, finished in soft, dark tones, along with a bar, restaurant and rooftop sundeck. Rooms on the ground floor have retained the *Explorers Inn* decor for returning customers, and are slightly cheaper, while some triples (❺) have three single beds so are a viable option for budget travellers. There's also a branch in St Kilda (see p.110). ❹

Rendezvous Hotel 328 Flinders St ☎9250 1888 ⓦwww.rendezvoushotels.com. Located near Flinders Street Station, this elegantly restored 340-room hotel retains an air of timelessness and even comes with its own ballroom; not that you'll find time to use it with the CBD conveniently located on your doorstep. Rooms are understated and tastefully decorated with all mod cons. Breakfast extra. There's also a bar and restaurant, plus a gym and valet parking. ❼

Motels and hostels

All Nations Backpackers Hostel 2 Spencer St ☎9620 1022, ⓦwww.allnations.com.au. Friendly no-frills place offering some of the cheapest beds in the CBD catering primarily to working backpackers, with bar, in-house job centre and clean rooms, plus free breakfast. Regular events include pool competitions, BBQs and soccer friendlies. Dorms ❶, rooms ❸

🏃 **Hotel Discovery 167 Franklin St** ☎9329 7525, ⓦwww.hoteldiscovery.com.au. Happening place with lots of activity and information. Hundreds of beds in a converted former school building brightened up with colour-coordinated paintwork and polished timber. Facilities include an in-house employment agency, travel shop, basement bar and function room, café, internet room and cinema. Self-contained tent accommodation available on the new rooftop terrace with great views of the city. Dorms (female-only available on request) come with between four and sixteen beds, lockers and shared facilities.There are also doubles (some with private bathrooms) and a family room with one double and two single beds. Dorms from ❶, doubles from ❸

Elizabeth Backpackers 490 Elizabeth St ☎9663 1685, ⓦwww.elizabethhostel.com.au. Centrally located above a convenience store, with internet, laundry, kitchens and a cinema room with cable TV. Three- to ten-bed dorms with shared facilities, plus some doubles and a family room. Dorms ❶, doubles ❸

Flinders Station Backpackers 35 Elizabeth St ☎9620 5100, ⓦwww.flindersbackpackers.com.au. Central hostel in a former office block a few hundred metres from Flinders Street Station. Basic twins and doubles with TV, and two en-suite doubles for wheelchair users. Dorms have lockers and four or ten beds (single-sex dorms on request), and there is also an internet café and a bar with terrace. Free when you pay for a week in advance. Dorms ❶, rooms ❸

🏃 **Greenhouse Backpacker 228 Flinders Lane** ☎9639 6400, ⓦwww.friendlygroup.com.au. Superb hostel and location in the heart of the CBD. Clean singles, doubles and dorms, plus a range of free services from employment assistance to luggage storage, and as much tea and coffee as you can drink. Rates include free breakfast and internet. Dorms ❷, rooms ❸

King St Backpackers 197 King St ☎9670 1111, ☎1800 671 115, ⓦwww.kingstreetbackpackers.com.au. Clean and friendly hostel in a refurbished office building. Dorms with wooden floorboards are bright, have a/c and heating and are mainly four- to six-bed (some women-only); each floor has a cosy sitting area with TV. Cheaper sixteen-bed dorms and doubles available. Small kitchen and common room; rates include free breakfast, tea and coffee and internet. Well situated for Southern Cross Station. Dorms ❶, doubles ❸

Melbourne Central YHA 562 Flinders St ☎9621 2523, ⓦwww.yha.com.au. Brand new 208-room hostel occupying a five-storey building in a prime location near to Southern Cross and Flinders Street stations. Facilities include a ground floor bar and café and a roof terrace. Dorms ❷, doubles ❹.

The Melbourne Connection 205 King St ☎9642 4464, ⓦwww.melbourneconnection.com. Small hostel in a convenient location close to Southern Cross Station. Rooms and dorms (4–6 beds) are clean; facilities include laundry, kitchen and lounge with Foxtel TV. Dorms ❶, doubles ❸

Melbourne Metro YHA 78 Howard St ☎9329 8599, 🌐www.yha.com.au. Excellent value, award-winning purpose-built hostel with dorms (4–8 beds), single, double and family rooms. Facilities include a café, rooftop lounge and BBQ area, a huge, well-equipped kitchen and bicycle rental. Take tram #57 from Elizabeth St. Dorms ❷, rooms ❸

Miami Hotel Melbourne 13 Hawke St ☎9321 2444 or 1800 132 333, 🌐www.themiami.com .au. On the edge of the city, not far from the airport – so a good first stop if you are exploring Victoria by car – this motel has a variety of rooms – some with shared facilities, some with private bathrooms, TV, tea- and coffee-making facilities and small fridge. Decor is rather bland but you can't beat the rates. There's also a TV lounge with Foxtel, laundry, and off-street parking. Though it's a bit out of town, there are plenty of good cafés and restaurants nearby on Errol and Victoria sts. ❹–❺

The river district, South Melbourne and Albert Park

The places listed below are marked on the map on p.58, unless otherwise stated.

Hotels

The Beach Accommodation 97 Beaconsfield Parade, Albert Park ☎9690 4642, 🌐www .thebeachaccommodation.com.au. See map, p.70. Budget boutique accommodation above a refurbished pub in a superb location across the road from the beach, and handy for the Tasmanian ferry terminal. Rooms (six-bed dorms and doubles) with shared facilities are clean and basic with pine furniture, lockers and most have sea views. Rates include all-you-can-eat breakfast, tea and coffee, plus there's also a TV room and a guest kitchen. Dorms ❶, doubles ❸.

Crown Towers Hotel Crown Casino, 8 Whiteman St, Southbank ☎9292 6868 or 1800 811 653, 🌐www.crowntowers.com.au. This luxurious five-star hotel in Australia's largest casino is far and away the most opulent place to stay in Melbourne. Combining a central location with over 480 spacious and beautifully appointed rooms, it's the ideal destination for high-rollers and cashed-up travellers, although the glitzy tat surrounding the hotel is a real downer. Rooms from $355 with breakfast an extra $36. ❾

Langham Hotel 1 Southgate Ave ☎ 8696 8888, 🌐www.langhamhotels.com. Large deluxe hotel offering first-class service from the moment the escalators whisk you past the elaborate water feature to the grand lobby above. Rooms are equipped with all the amenities you would expect of a five-star hotel, but it's the location you're paying for – right on Southgate, overlooking the Yarra and the CBD. ❽–❾

Royce on St Kilda Road 379 St Kilda Rd ☎9677 9900 or 1800 820 909, 🌐www.roycehotels .com.au. This stunning, heritage-listed boutique hotel is usefully positioned within walking distance of the CBD, Royal Botanic Gardens, Shrine of Remembrance and Arts Centre. There's a variety of room types available: suites with kitchenette, mezzanined doubles with a ground-level lounge, deluxe spa rooms and rooms with balconies. All have the usual trimmings, plus marble bathrooms and in-house movies to borrow. Food is available at the renowned *Dish* restaurant. ❻–❾

Carlton and Fitzroy

See the map on p.74 unless otherwise stated.

Hotels

Downtowner on Lygon 66 Lygon St, Carlton ☎9663 5555, ☎1800 800 130, 🌐www .downtowner.com.au. See map, p.76. Chain hotel with 98 attractively refurbished room with private bathrooms, some with spas, all with TV, tea- and coffee-making facilities and toaster. There is also a restaurant, a bar and free covered parking. Ideally situated on Lygon St and close to the city. ❺–❻

9

ACCOMMODATION | The river district, South Melbourne and Albert Park • Carlton and Fitzroy

107

Budget hotels, motels and hostels

Lygon Lodge 220 Lygon St, Carlton ☎9663
6633, ☎1800 337 099, ⓦwww.lygonlodge.com.
au. See map, p.76. Good drive-in motel with
40 rooms in a terrific location. Rooms are
clean and attractive, and come with the
usual in-room facilities including a fridge,
while some also have small kitchenettes. ➍
Melbourne Oasis YHA 76 Chapman St, North
Melbourne ☎9328 3595, ⓦwww.yha.com.au.
More intimate than its sister hostel, the
Melbourne Metro YHA, but further away
from the city centre (3km), this hostel has a
leafy garden and a very friendly atmosphere.
Accommodation is mainly in twin-share
rooms (no dorms) with a few singles and a
four-or five-bed family room. There's also a
self-catering kitchen, pancake breakfasts,
free car parking, free DVD rental, swimming
passes, bike rental and personal lockers.

Take tram #59 from Elizabeth St. Dorms ➋,
rooms ➌
The Nunnery 116 Nicholson St, Fitzroy ☎9419
8637, ☎1800 032 635, ⓦwww.nunnery.com.au.
Attractive budget guesthouse, in a former
convent, located in a much sought-after
part of Fitzroy close to Carlton Gardens and
the Melbourne Museum. The three-storeyed
building retains original stained glass
windows and a grand staircase, and has a
range of rooms, all with shared bathroom,
from the high-ceilinged, characterful single
and doubles in the guesthouse to a newer
townhouse which offers slightly more sedate
boutique style accommodation. There are
also several budget dorms and doubles.
Rates include free breakfast as well as tea,
coffee and hot chocolate throughout the
day. There's also a big, cosy TV lounge,
courtyard, internet facilities and a kitchen.
Dorms ➋, rooms ➌–➍

Collingwood, Richmond and the east

For locations of the following see map on p.82.

Hotels, B&Bs and apartments

Georgian Court Guesthouse 21–25 George St,
East Melbourne ☎9419 6353, ⓦwww
.georgiancourt.com.au. Cosy B&B in an
attractive terrace house, with standard
rooms sharing bathrooms, and en-suite
rooms equipped with TV, kettle, fridge and
a/c; all are bright, tastefully furnished and
some have spa baths. Rates include
breakfast and parking. Quiet, but central to
the CBD, MCG and Richmond. ➍–➎
Hilton on the Park 192 Wellington Parade, East
Melbourne ☎9419 2000, ⓦwww.hilton.com.
Towering opposite the MCG, and popular
with football and cricket enthusiasts, facilities here include the Hilton day spa, sauna
and heated outdoor pool. Breakfast and
dinner packages available. Parking $20 per
day. ➑–➒
Knightsbridge Apartments 101 George St, East
Melbourne ☎9419 1333, ⓦwww
.knightsbridgeapartments.com.au. Modern,
serviced, self-catering studio apartments
1km from the centre, on a quiet street off
the east side of Fitzroy Gardens. Laundry
and off-street parking. Family suites come
with either two king beds or four singles.
Excellent value ➍–➏

Magnolia Court Boutique Hotel 101 Powlett St,
East Melbourne ☎9419 4222, ⓦwww
.magnolia-court.com.au. Elegant, family-run
hotel with accommodation in two lovingly
restored old buildings and a newer motel
section, located on a quiet residential street,
a hop, skip and jump from Fitzroy Gardens,
the city, MCG and the Rod Laver Arena in
Melbourne Park. Twenty-six en-suite rooms
all with TV, fridge and kettle, some with a
kitchen, sitting room or balcony. Breakfast
available (extra if staying in cheaper rooms)
in a sunny room overlooking front courtyard
garden. Minimum two-night stay at
weekends. Website has good deals. ➎–➐
Richmond Hill Hotel 353 Church St, Richmond
☎9428 6501, ☎1800 801 618, ⓦwww
.richmondhillhotel.com.au. Friendly hotel with a
variety of simple, clean rooms in a refurbished
old mansion. There are cosy sitting rooms, a
large shared kitchen, laundry, courtyard and
off-street parking. Accommodation consists
of economy singles and doubles (➍) with
balcony and shared bathroom; en-suite
singles, doubles and family rooms (3–4
people); apartments (➐); plus a few budget
rooms (1–6 beds; ➌) with shared facilities.
Prices of all except the budget rooms include
continental breakfast ($9 otherwise). ➎

Budget hotels and hostels

Central Melbourne Accommodation 21 Bromham Place, Richmond ☎9427 9826, ⓦwww.centralaccommodation.net. Small place that runs like a shared house with most guests staying long-term. Four- and six-bed dorms (usually single-sex) along with a few single and double rooms, located close to the main drags of Church St and Bridge Rd. Owners have good employment contacts in the area as well as connections within the TV and radio industry so there are usually free tickets for shows and events up for grabs. Excellent weekly rates. Dorms ❶, doubles ❸

Freeman Lodge 153 Hoddle St, Richmond ☎9421 8038, ⓦwww.freemanlodge.com.au. Part budget guesthouse, part hostel, this place offers small singles, doubles and single-sex dorms with shared bathrooms, as well as a communal kitchen and a pleasant courtyard. Located on hellishly busy Hoddle St so you may want to ask for a room at the back. Dorms ❶, rooms ❸

South Yarra, Prahran and Toorak

For locations of the following see the map on p.88.

Hotels and B&Bs

The Albany Corner of Toorak Rd & Millswyn St, South Yarra ☎9866 4485, ⓦwww.thealbany .com.au. Conveniently located motor hotel across from Fawkner Park, close to the Botanic Gardens. Choose from standard and superior rooms in the 1960s block or a room in the original Victorian mansion. Interiors are bright and modern, plus there's a restaurant and a bar. Rates include breakfast. Good online deals. ❼

The Como Melbourne 630 Chapel St, South Yarra ☎9825 2222 or 1800 033 400, ⓦwww .mirvachotels.com. Stylish hotel that often plays host to visiting celebs and businesspeople. All 107 rooms are gratifyingly spacious, with some facing onto the hotel's Japanese gardens and feature the usual luxury facilities, plus CD players and gigantic bathtubs that come with a complimentary companion – the hotel's signature rubber duck. The *Como's SOBar* is also a good place for a drink. ❽

The Hatton Hotel 65 Park St, South Yarra ☎9868 4800, ⓦwww.hatton.com.au. Modern boutique hotel in a grand Italianate house within walking distance of the Botanic Gardens. Each of its twenty stylish rooms is immaculately and individually styled. Bathrooms are modern with deep bathtubs, and kitchenettes come with real coffee plungers. The hotel's *Front Lounge* doubles as reception and is a pleasant spot for coffee or a glass of wine. ❻–❼

The Lyall Hotel 14 Murphy St, South Yarra ☎9868 8222 or 1800 338 234, ⓦwww .thelyall.com. Discreet, luxury lifestyle bolthole that has understandably featured in Condé Nast Traveller's list of top ten hotels. Has a surprisingly relaxed feel and the suites, which are stylishly fitted out in a contemporary Oriental style, come with all one could ever need and more, including gourmet minibars, steam-free mirrors and heated bathroom floors, as well as separate living area and kitchen, and balcony. When you wish to emerge from your room, indulge in a treatment in its award-winning spa, perch at the *Champagne Bar*, or relax in front of an open fire in one of the mini art galleries. Rooms from $525. ❾

Toorak Manor Boutique Hotel 220 Williams Rd, Toorak ☎9827 2689, ⓦwww.toorakmanor.net. Across the road from Hawksburn train station, this lovely old manor house has eighteen rooms replete with opulent Victoriana. Rooms are homely and all have en-suite shower rooms, TV and tea- and coffee-making facilities. Deluxe rooms are slightly bigger than the standards and there's also a premium room with a small balcony (❼). Downstairs a comfortable drawing room provides complimentary port and Foxtel TV. Continental buffet breakfast and free parking is included in the price. No lift. ❺

Hostels

Chapel Street Backpackers 22 Chapel St, Windsor ☎9533 6855, ⓦwww.csbackpackers .com.au. This friendly hostel close to Albert Park and St Kilda offers small, clean dorms (4–6 beds; women-only available) and en-suite doubles with free buffet breakfast, tea and coffee. Tight security, internet service and 24hr access. To get there, take the Sandringham-line train from Flinders Street Station to Windsor Station; the hostel is across the road. Weekly rates available. Dorms ❷, rooms ❸

Lords Lodge Backpackers 204 Punt Rd, Prahran ☎9510 4273, ⊛www.lordslodge.com .au. Small hostel housed within an old mansion near the bars, cafés and retro shops of groovy Greville St. Basic but scruffy singles and double rooms (all with heating), and medium-sized dorms (some women-only) with fridge and lockers.

Communal kitchen and free tea and coffee. Dorms ❶, rooms ❸

Pint on Punt 42 Punt Rd, Windsor ☎9510 4273/9510 3310, ⊛www.pintonpunt.com.au. Hostel above a refurbished British-style pub within walking distance of Chapel St and St Kilda nightlife. Clean dorms (4–6 beds), twins and doubles, all with shared facilities. Full kitchen, common room and cable TV; cheap pub dinners available and discounts on drinks. Rates include continental breakfast. Take train to Windsor Station (Sandringham line) or tram #3, #5, #16 or #67 from Swanston St to St Kilda Junction. Dorms ❶, rooms ❸

St Kilda

For locations of the following see the map on p.92.

Hotels and B&Bs

Annies Bed and Breakfast 93 Park St ☎9534 8705, ⊛www.anniesbedandbreakfast.com.au. Traditional-style B&B in an old terrace house, with friendly service, delicious break-fasts and all the comforts of home. *Annies* is conveniently located on a quiet road between the Port Phillip Bay beaches and Albert Park Lake that is serviced by tram #112 into the city. ❺

Boutique Hotel Tolarno 42 Fitzroy St ☎9537 0200, ⊛www.hoteltolarno.com.au. Set right in the thick of things on Fitzroy St, occupying a restored building that once housed the Tolarno Gallery. Stylish and bright en-suite bedrooms with 1950s and 60s retro furnishings, original artwork, polished timber floors and all mod cons. Good value for money. ❺

Cosmopolitan Hotel 6 Carlisle St ☎9534 0781 or 1800 333 073, ⊛www.cosmopolitan hotel.com.au. Part of the same boutique hotel chain that owns the *Pensione Hotel* (see p.105), the *Cosmopolitan* occupies a restored building just a pebble's throw from Acland St and the foreshore. Rooms are smart and contemporary with muted decor, luxurious white bedlinen, and all mod cons, Facilities include an informal restaurant, a laundry and a gym. Online deals see rates drop by fifty percent. ❻

Novotel St Kilda 16 The Esplanade ☎9525 5522 or 1300 656 565, ⊛www.novotelstkilda.com. au. This chain hotel with over 200 rooms

may not win many accolades in aesthetics, but it does have a bird's-eye view of the beach and Sunday market, plus heated pool, gym, spa, sauna and restaurant, as well as being convenient for both Acland and Fitzroy sts. Check website for latest offers when rates drop considerably. Rack rates from $320. ❾

Olembia Guesthouse 96 Barkly St ☎9537 1412, ⊛www.olembia.com.au. Old Edwardian building obscured by trees and shrubs provides a peaceful retreat from the bustle of Barkly St. Smallish rustic-looking singles, twins and doubles, with shared facilities only, are spotlessly clean and simple as are the three- to four-bed "dorms" (some women-only). There's also a small kitchen and laundry, plus free tea and coffee, but no breakfast. Its homely drawing room complete with comfy armchairs, resident cat and open fire is a treat in winter. Book in advance. Dorms ❷, rooms ❸

The Prince 2 Acland St ☎9536 1111, ⊛www .theprince.com.au. This forty-room boutique hotel housed within *The Prince* complex is one of Melbourne's most elegant places to lay your head. Minimalist bedrooms include Loewe TVs and DVD players and Bose radios, while bathrooms are stocked with Aesop products. Away from your room you can grab breakfast at *Il Fornaio* (see p.124), relax in the Aurora spa and relaxa-tion centre (see p.157), dine in the elegant *Circa* restaurant (see p.123), drink at *Mink* (see p.133), or dance in the club/band room. With service and facilities this good you may never set foot outside the front door. **❼–❽**

Urban St Kilda 35 Fitzroy St ☎8530 8888, ⓦwww.urbanstkilda.com.au. St Kilda's latest boutique hotel (formerly the *Marquee Hotel*) has a slick contemporary feel, and trendy guest areas replete with the latest sound system and aromatherapy burners. The kind of place that's equates cool with wordplay; its facilities include Jim, the gym. There's also a restaurant. The night owls who flock here will appreciate the double-glazed windows that keep the street noise at bay. Good online deals. **❻–❽**

Motels and hostels

Base 17 Carlisle St ☎8598 6200, ⓦwww.stayatbase.com. This funky St Kilda hostel, rated as one of the best hostels in Australia, is slick and well managed. There are plenty of communal areas including a bar, kitchen and common room, and all rooms have their own bathroom. There's even a girls-only Sanctuary floor (with six- to eight-bed dorms) which provides free champagne of an evening, full-length mirrors and has hair straighteners for rental, all for an extra $6 per night – this is boutique backpacking. Dorms ❷, rooms ❹

Charnwood Motor Inn 3 Charnwood Rd ☎9525 4199 or 1800 010 477, ⓦwww.charnwood motorinn.com. Quiet location off St Kilda Rd, 10min walk from the bars and cafés of Fitzroy St. The fussy rooms are uninspiring but are clean, have private bathrooms and come with TV, toaster, fridge, microwave and tea- and coffee-making facilities. Room-service breakfast from $8. ❹

Ritz for Backpackers 169b Fitzroy St ☎9525 3501 or 1800 670 364, ⓦwww.ritzbackpackers .com. Well-furnished and friendly hostel above the English-style *Elephant and Wheel-barrow* pub (see p.128), and within easy walking distance of restaurants, cafés and milk bars. Rooms are simple and generally clean, and there are two TV lounges, a pool table, dining room, tiny kitchen and internet and laundry facilities, plus free bike rental. Lots of activities and tours and free pancake breakfast. Dorms ❷, rooms ❸

St Kilda Coffee Palace 24 Grey St ☎9534 5283 or 1800 654 098, ⓦwww.coffeepalaceback packers.com.au. Bustling hostel in large and rambling building popular with ravers and revellers. Some of the spacious four- to eight-bed dorms are women-only, and come with en-suite bathrooms. The older part of the building is in need of a makeover, however. Nice rooftop garden, plus good travel shop and work centre. Free pancake breakfast. Dorms ❶, rooms ❸

Williamstown

For locations of the following see the map on p.98.

B&Bs

B&B at Stephanie's 154–160 Ferguson St ☎9397 5587, ⓦwww.stephanies.biz. A comfy, large B&B in a delightful weatherboard house, with antique furniture and original fireplaces, several of whose rooms have a spa bath and a private courtyard. Be sure to get up for the hearty cooked breakfast in the morning. Free parking. ❺–❻

Captains Retreat 2 Ferguson St ☎9397 0352, ⓦwww.captainsretreat.com.au. Set in a Victorian-era homestead, this lovely B&B is conveniently located close to the port and busy Ferguson St. Views of the city and

rooms with period furniture, spa baths, late checkout and a good selection of magazines make this the best spot for even the most decadent of captains to hang their hat. Doubles ❺, with balcony ❻

The Front on Nelson 143 Nelson Place ☎9397 2557, ⓦwww.thefrontonnelson.com.au. Housed on the first floor of a nineteenth-century house, this petite B&B has three tastefully decorated rooms with shared bathroom, polished floorboards and high ceilings. There's also a small breakfast room, a lounge and a leafy courtyard. Ideally located on Nelson's opposite Hobsons Bay. ❺

Eating

Melbourne is a melting pot of cultures, a fact reflected vividly in its restaurants, cafés, bistros and bars. Fashionable, eclectic and eccentric, the city's dining spots offer a dizzying spread of the world's great cuisines.

In the city, you can settle into the genteel surroundings of a nineteenth-century hotel, and take afternoon tea in a starched table-clothed timewarp; watch and be watched in buzzing laneway cafés and bar; or handpick a bottle of Yarra Valley Chardonnay at the latest über-chic hangout. Outside the city centre, world cuisines have spread to **suburbs** such as Fitzroy, South Melbourne, South Yarra, St Kilda, and the Vietnamese enclave of Richmond – affectionately known as "Little Saigon" – which is also a burgeoning location for cheap and cheerful Burmese and Middle Eastern fare. In the past, the Italian eateries of Lygon Street in Carlton were among the city's culinary highlights, and although they've now become something of a tourist trap, there are still a few places worth seeking out. Further out are other specialist eating destinations: Footscray in the west has excellent Vietnamese cuisine; Brighton along the southern coast is renowned for its fine Italian restaurants and cafés; while Box Hill in Melbourne's eastern outer suburbs has some of the city's best Chinese food.

Melbourne also has a number of quality fruit, meat and veg markets, excellent places to stock up for an impromptu picnic or barbeque by the beach.

For a sandwich and coffee at a café you can expect to pay around $10, while for $14–17 you can get a counter meal, such as a steak sandwich and a beer, at a pub or bistro. At restaurants expect to pay anything from $25 – $40 for a main course and a glass of wine while don't expect much change from $100 for three courses at a top restaurant. The cheapest places to eat are food halls in major department stores and Southgate, or Asian restaurants where a plate of noodles or a bowl of Vietnamese *pho* costs around $7. Most restaurants and upmarket cafés offer special **lunchtime** set menus of three courses with wine for about half the cost of an equivalent evening meal. In addition, some Melbourne eateries are **bring your own** (BYO), allowing you to supply your own drink,

Restaurant prices

In the following listings, prices are indicated by the terms:
cheap (under $25)
inexpensive ($25–35)
moderate ($35–50)
expensive ($55–80)
very expensive (over $80).
These refer to the cost of a starter, main course and dessert for one person, excluding drinks.

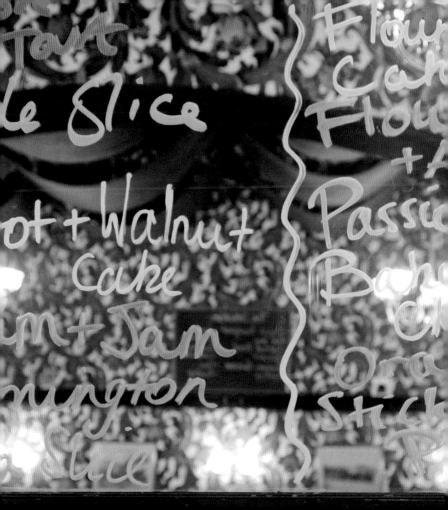

Foodies' Melbourne

Melbourne knows how to eat. The city's reputation as "foodies' capital" is largely influenced by European and Asian immigrants whose dishes and flavours have inspired modern Australian cuisine. Today, Melbourne is full of eateries offering cuisines from all around the world and for all budgets. The ubiquitous Aussie barby is still popular, with markets selling tantalizingly fresh produce, but nowadays you can expect to find langoustines languishing alongside snags, and a fine Shiraz amongst the VB slabs.

Café culture

A well-established café culture pervades the Melburnian psyche. From the 1950s when the first immigrants from **Italy** settled in Melbourne, foremost in the suburb of Carlton, a **European influence** has been imbibed into society. So much so that locals know a thing or two about their coffee, and won't be palmed off with badly made concoctions or – heaven forbid – instant. Even the most humble of milk bars have a coffee-making machine that grinds its own beans.

Reputation spreads fast and where to get the best coffee can be a topic of serious debate, with **well-trained baristas** keenly sought. Cafés of every shape and size can be found throughout the CBD and outer suburbs, from shoeboxes in Block Place to the larger complexes of *Brunetti* (see p.118). The emphasis on inner-city living, combined with a backlash against mega-corporate enterprises like Southgate and the Crown Casino, has seen a **coterie of small cafés** spring up. Human and cosy, these cafés are the perfect accompaniment to the European architectural style and feel of the area. However, there are plenty of places that have stood the test of time, Melbourne institutions that keep customers coming back year after year. Some are loud and bustling, some intimate and little changed for fifty years, but all serve great coffee and food, try: *Pellegrini's Espresso Bar* (p.114), *Mario's* (p.119), *Caffe e Cucina* (p.121) and *The Galleon* (p.124).

To experience the best of Melbourne's café culture, head to Fitzroy and Acland streets in St Kilda (p.122) or Brunswick Street in Fitzroy (p.117), especially at weekends.

Latte at Brunetti's ▲

Pellegrini's Espresso Bar ▼

Award-winning chef restaurants

The rivalry between Melbourne and Sydney is nowhere more evident than in the battle for the title of food capital of Australia. However, the influx of **French and British chefs**, such as Jacques Reymond and Michael Lambie, along with locals such as Maurice Esposito, has helped keep Melbourne firmly placed on the culinary map. What's more, the decision of "celebrity" chefs **Gordon Ramsay** and **Jamie Oliver** (see p.113) to launch their first antipodean restaurants in Melbourne, along with *Nobu Melbourne* opening at the Crown Entertainment Complex, are further gastronomic slaps in Sydney's face.

To get a taste of what these chefs have to offer be prepared to shell out a fair few bucks, especially if you go all-out for the degustation menu.

▲ Jamie Oliver outside Fifteen

▼ Riverbank barbecue

Eating al fresco

With so many good chefs around, and such an abundance of different ingredients it's no wonder that Melburnians love to cook. **Barbecues** in the summer are *de rigueur*, with markets offering the best and freshest selection of seafood, meat and delicatessen items, often cheaper than supermarkets, and many locals are on first-name terms with their butcher or fishmonger. Check out South Melbourne (p.166), Queen Victoria (p.165) and Prahran (p.165) markets for the finest produce, then grab a few tinnys and head to one of the barbecues at Elwood beach or Alexandra Gardens beside the Yarra for a picnic. Alternatively, pick up some take-away from Southgate food hall and watch the boats pass by on the river.

▼ Fruit stall at Victoria Market

Pavement dining ▲

Grossi Florentina ▼

The Stokehouse ▼

Ten great restaurants

▶▶ **Livebait** Spanking fresh seafood. See p.116.
▶▶ **MoVida** Fantastic tapas, lively crack. See p.114.
▶▶ **Himalayan Sherpa** Good value Malaysian. See p.120.
▶▶ **Yu-u** Japanese gem. See p.115.
▶▶ **Ladro** Buzzing pizzeria. See p.119.
▶▶ **Vegie Bar** Popular Brunswick Street hangout. See p.120.
▶▶ **Thy Thy 1** Cheap, cheerful Vietnamese. See p.121.
▶▶ **Café Di Stasio** Exquisite, elegant Italian. See p.123.
▶▶ **Donovans** Excellent food, rustic ambience. See p.124.
▶▶ **Soulmama** Veggie food on the beachfront. See p.125.

Splurge!

▶▶ **Jacques Reymond** The only "Three Hat" restaurant in Victoria. See p.122.
▶▶ **Taxi Dining Room** Fab food and river views. See p.117.
▶▶ **Interlude** Robin Wickens' creative degustation menu explores the science of food and regularly discovers something new. See p.118.
▶▶ **ezard** One of the best hotel restaurants in Melbourne. See p.113.
▶▶ **Grossi Florentino** Fine, venerable Italian restaurant in the city centre. See p.113.
▶▶ **The Stokehouse** Amazing beachfront views and food to match at this St Kilda eatery. See p.125.
▶▶ **Botanical** Confident food amidst bustling surroundings, Paul Wilson's parkside restaurant is a hit with locals. See p.121.
▶▶ **Pearl** Popular Mod Oz restaurant that's just spawned a less formal café. See p.121.
▶▶ **Circa, The Prince** Cool, sophisticated St Kilda restaurant with superb wines. See p.123.

though a corkage fee of $5–7 per person often applies. Most places listed accept payment by **credit card**.

Watch out for *Epicure*, an excellent pullout appearing each Tuesday in *The Age*, which features a lively mix of gossip, news of the comings and goings of chefs, cheap eats, recipes from noted cookbook authors, along with café and restaurant reviews. Two other indispensable **guides** to the city's restaurants are *The Age Cheap Eats* and *The Age Good Food Guide*, which are published annually and available from bookshops and major newsagents.

The east side

The following establishments are marked on the map on p.40.

Bamboo House 47 Little Bourke St ☎9662 1565. Much favoured by businessfolk and politicians, who come to wheeler-deal and point-score over scampi, spicy Sichuan beef and tea-smoked duck, along with dishes from northern China, Mon–Fri noon–3pm & 5.30–11pm, Sat 5.30–11pm, Sun 6–10pm. Moderate to expensive.

Becco 11–25 Crossley St ☎9663 3000. If the uncomplicated Italian food and interesting wine selection in the formal dining area don't whet your appetite, perhaps a quick drink, dessert or late supper at the bar will. Mon–Sat noon–3pm & 6pm–11pm; bar noon–late. Expensive.

Café L'Incontro Corner of Little Collins and Swanston sts ☎9650 9603. The focaccias, burgers and sweets in this smart-looking licensed café play second fiddle to the alfresco setting in a prime location overlooking busy Swanston St. Daily 24hr. Cheap.

ezard 187 Flinders Lane ☎9639 6811. Situated below the *Adelphi Hotel*, this sophisticated, dimly lit place with tables set close together is one of Melbourne's hottest and most seductive eateries. Award-winning chef Teage Ezard's bold Asian-influenced food is not only tasty but looks good too. Mon–Fri noon–2.30pm, Mon–Sat 6–10.30pm. Very expensive.

Fifteen Basement, 115–117 Collins St, enter off George Parade ☎1300 799 415. The latest restaurant to be opened by Fifteen, the charitable foundation set up by celebrity chef Jamie Oliver to train young people from disadvantaged backgrounds as chefs. Italian-inspired food is delivered with aplomb in stylish basement surroundings from a choice of a la carte and degustation menus. Mon–Sat noon–3pm & 6–10.30pm. Expensive.

Flower Drum 17 Market Lane, off Bourke St ☎9662 3655. This capacious restaurant is quite simply the finest Chinese restaurant in Melbourne – if not Australia. Its sophisticated Cantonese cuisine (Peking duck, dumplings, Hainanese pork, *yi-meen* noodles) and discreet service from an army of waiting staff have garnered it a clutch of top awards. An essential Melbourne dining experience. Mon–Sat noon–3pm & 6–10pm, Sun 6–10pm. Expensive to very expensive.

Gopals Level 1, 139 Swanston St ☎9650 1578. Typically wholesome, vegetarian food – curries, salads and cakes – in from the Hare Krishna organization, in a bright and airy room overlooking Swanston St. Even cheaper is their *Crossways Food for Life* at 123 Swanston St (Mon–Sat 11.30am–2.30pm), which has all-you-can-eat lunch deals for next to nothing. Mon–Sat 11.30am–8.30pm. Cheap.

Grossi Florentino 80 Bourke St ☎9662 1811. A Melbourne institution. Downstairs the grill restaurant (moderate) and the adjacent cellar bar (inexpensive), serve home-style pasta dishes, drinks and good coffee, while upstairs is a very pricey and elegant Italian restaurant that's been synonymous with fine dining for many years. Cellar bar Mon–Sat 7.30am–late, restaurant Mon–Fri noon–3pm & 6–11pm, Sat 6–11pm. Inexpensive to expensive.

Il Bacaro 168–170 Little Collins St ☎9654 6778. Classic Italian restaurant with an interesting menu of modern favourites coupled with an intimate ambience. Popular business lunch spot by day and impressive first date venue by night. Mon–Sat noon–midnight. Expensive.

Il Solito Posto Basement, 113 Collins St, enter off George Parade ☎9654 4466. Charming subterranean location, casual rustic atmosphere and fine no-fuss Italian food make for one of Melbourne's best dining experiences. Choose from either the bistro menu or the more formal restaurant menu. Mon–Fri 7.30am–1am, Sat 9am–1am. Moderate to expensive.

Kenzan Lower level, Collins Place, 45 Collins St ☎9654 8933. Epitome of Japanese food and style: known for its excellent sushi and sashimi selection and simple but elegant surroundings beneath the *Hotel Sofitel*. Mon–Fri noon–2.15pm & 6–10pm, Sat & Sun 6–10pm. Moderate to expensive.

Kun Ming Restaurant 212 Little Bourke St ☎9663 1851. Despite recently going all upmarket – the laminate tables have gone, smart waiters and tablecloths have arrived – the food is still some of the tastiest you'll find on this busy Chinatown strip, and the prices remain low. Excellent lunch specials for under $10. Daily 11.30am–3pm & 5.30–10pm. Cheap to inexpensive.

Lounge Downstairs 243 Swanston St ☎9663 2916. Sleek, pleasurable eating spot underneath *Lounge bar* (see p.127) with a surprisingly grown-up menu – spicy tofu and bok choy salad or salt and pepper calamari alongside gourmet pizzas and porterhouse steak – stylishly presented in a retro setting. Mon–Sat 7.30am–late. Inexpensive.

Mask of China 115–117 Little Bourke St ☎9662 2116. Extensive menu and wine list with the emphasis on Southern Chinese-style Chiu Chow dishes of seafood, poultry and fresh produce, along with a great selection of desserts. Service is also good. Try the banquet menu, which changes every few weeks. Mon–Fri & Sun noon–3pm & 6–11pm, Sat 6–11pm. Expensive.

MoVida 1 Hosier Lane ☎9663 3038. Tables are scarce at this popular tapas bar/restaurant but grab a seat at the bar or a place on a couch and soak up the Spanish flavours – don't leave without trying the air-cured wagyu beef with truffle foam and poached egg. Spanish beers and wine complete the vibe. Daily noon–3pm, 5pm–late. Inexpensive to moderate.

Nudel Bar 76 Bourke St ☎9662 9100. Wide-ranging menu serving both Asian and European noodle dishes such as *mee goreng* and pasta with counter seats downstairs for quick meals, and tables upstairs for more leisurely dining. Mon–Sat 11am–late (closes 3pm Mon in winter). Cheap to inexpensive.

Pellegrini's Espresso Bar 66 Bourke St ☎9662 1885. A Melbourne institution, *Pellegrini's* has changed little since it first opened in the

1950s, retaining its chequered floors and mirrored walls. It's just the ticket for platefuls of hearty Italian food (risotto, meatballs, spag bol) presented at the counter bar at lightning speed. Also good for coffee and home-made cakes. Mon–Sat 8am–11.30pm, Sun noon–8pm. Cheap.

Punch Lane 43 Little Bourke St ☎9639 4944. A classy haunt for Melbourne urbanites, this wine bar serves antipasto, tapas and fish, late suppers, cheese plates and has a long wine list – including many by the glass. Comfortable seating in solid red-leather chairs. Mon–Fri noon–11pm, Sat & Sun 5pm–11pm. Moderate.

Shark Fin House 131 Little Bourke St ☎9663 1555. Award-winning *yum cha* specialists located in a converted three-storey warehouse that is the quintessential Chinese eating experience: preposterously loud, closely packed tables, adrenaline-charged waiters and queues of people waiting to be seated. Mon–Fri 11.30am–3pm & 5.30–11pm, Sat & Sun 11am–3pm & 5.30–11pm. Cheap to inexpensive.

Stalactites 177 Lonsdale St ☎9663 3316. Operating for over thirty years the recently spruced-up *Stalactites* serves so-so giros, souvlaki, moussaka and saganaki (traditional deep-fried cheese), all dished up in huge portions in a congenial dining area. Most Melburnians have eaten here at least once in their life. Daily 24hr. Cheap to inexpensive.

Supper Inn 15 Celestial Ave ☎9663 4759. The decor may be dated but the generous Cantonese food is worth the climb up those stairs. The menu is large, with plenty of unusual options, and the kitchen stays open till very, very late, making it a favourite for those in the hospitality trade. Daily 5.30pm–2.30am. Cheap.

Tsindos 197 Lonsdale St ☎9663 3194. Long-established traditional Greek café with all the classics, including moussaka and souvlaki. Leave some space for the incredibly sweet desserts. Mon–Thurs 11.30am–3pm & 5–10pm, Fri 11.30am–3pm & 5–11pm, Sat 5–11pm, Sun 5–10pm. Inexpensive to moderate.

West Lake 189 Little Bourke St ☎9662 2048. This large, noisy and often messy restaurant speeds good *yum cha* and a long list of other Chinese dishes to your table, and soaks up a lot of passing trade due to its location on Chinatown's main thoroughfare. Daily 11am–2am. Inexpensive.

Yu-u 137 Flinders Lane ☏ 9639 7073. Hard to find, due to its small sign – enter via Oliver Lane, through the red steel door – this tiny Japanese-style bar serves delicious, inexpensive meat and rice dishes, sashimi, tempura and miso with quick service.

Popular with those in the know, the place is so hip that the foot you're likely to stand on probably belongs to one of Melbourne's architectural or design elite. Set lunch menu. Bookings advised. Mon–Fri noon–2.15pm & 6–9.30pm, Sat 6–9.30pm. Inexpensive.

The west side

The following establishments are marked on the map on pp.50–51.

Beetroot 123 Hardware St ☏ 9600 0695 This small, but stylish back-alley lunch room offers great sandwiches, fajitas, home-made bakes, stews and pastas. Staff are ultra-friendly and the menu has a vegetarian spin. Mon–Thurs 7.30am–3pm, Fri 7am–3pm. Cheap.

Bhoj Docklands 54 NewQuay Promenade, Docklands ☏ 9600 0884. Nestled in the glitz and glam of Docklands, Bhoj has a stylish timber and tiled interior, a decent wine-list and possibly the best Indian food in Melbourne using only the freshest ingredients. Daily noon–3pm & 5.30–10.30pm. Inexpensive to moderate.

Café Segovia 33 Block Place ☏ 9650 2373. Cute Spanish-style café serving good coffee and modern Australian food that satisfies rather than stupefies. Reportedly one of the first cafés in this now crammed laneway, it remains a firm favourite among inner-city workers. Mon–Sat 7.30am–late, Sun 9am–6pm. Moderate.

Dinkum Pies 29 Block Place ☏ 9654 6792. No-frills canteen-style pie shop that does a roaring trade with suits and city workers at lunchtimes. Grab a seat if you can and browse the quirky reading material on the walls in the form of laminated jokes, sayings and email funnies. Also does quiche, pastries and cakes. Mon–Thurs 7.30am–4.30pm, Fri 7.30am–5pm. Cheap.

Don Camillo 215 Victoria St ☏ 9329 8883. Classic, unspoiled 1950s Italian café with a terrazzo floor and long bar. The walls are covered with photographs of AFL and other sporting stars, many of whom have formed part of the Don's clientele. Take tram #57 from Collins St. Mon–Thurs 7am–3.30pm, Fri 7am–3.30pm & 6pm–late, Sat 7.30am–2.30pm Inexpensive.

Hanabishi 187 King St ☏ 9670 1167. In the middle of slightly seedy King St, this modest establishment serves up some of the city's best Japanese food, including great sushi, crisp tempura and generous udon noodle dishes. Mon–Fri noon–2.30pm & 6pm–10.30pm. Moderate.

Hopetoun Tea Rooms Shop 2, Block Arcade, 282 Collins St ☏ 9650 2777. Food and drink have been served in these elegant surroundings for more than a century. The delicious scones and cakes for which it is famous are now served alongside more exotic treats such as focaccia with pesto and a small selection of warm dishes. They also sell their own brand of tea leaves. Mon–Thurs 9am–5pm, Fri 9am–6pm, Sat 10am–3.30pm. Cheap.

▲ Hopetoun Tea Rooms

Journal 253 Flinders Lane ☏ 9650 4399. Housed within City Library, bookish types and students flock to this savvy, intellectual hangout lured by the seductive glow of Art Deco lamps and large communal tables, perfect for in-depth debates over a glass of red and a plate of bruschetta. Journal

Canteen on level 1 serves good Italian meals and antipasto. Mon–Fri 7am–9pm, Sat 8am–6pm. Inexpensive.

Livebait 55b NewQuay Promenade, Docklands ☎9642 1500. Sparsely designed and unadorned so diners can fully appreciate the impressive panoramic views of the city, Docklands and Bolte Bridge, Livebait's emphasis is on super fresh Mediterranean-style seafood. Daily noon–3pm & 6–11pm. Expensive.

Mecca Bah 55a NewQuay Promenade, Docklands ☎9642 1300. Mouth-watering modern Middle Eastern treats and a killer spot on the harbour (below *Livebait*) make this place a popular choice day or night. On

still days the outdoor deck is perfect for sharing mezze platters and watching the boats cruise by. Daily 11am–11pm. Inexpensive to moderate.

Syracuse 23 Bank Place ☎9670 1777. Situated in a small laneway, Syracuse's bright interior is immediately timeless, from its arched ceiling and large wall mirrors to its bentwood chairs and wood racks stacked with wine bottles. Come for mouthwatering tapas, bacalà crusted blue eye, or rabbit and caper sausages then move on to fantastic cheese plates, amaretto, crème caramel and coffee. Extensive, almost daunting wine list and seductive atmosphere. Mon–Fri 7.30am–11pm, Sat 6pm–late. Moderate to expensive.

The river district, South Melbourne and Albert Park

The following establishments are listed on the map on p.70, unless otherwise stated.

Albert Park Deli Café 129 Dundas Place, Albert Park ☎9699 9597. Lunchtimes and weekends are busy at this Mediterranean deli with locals in the know eager to chow down on freshly made salads, pastas and soups from the counter as well as filling breakfasts. Daily 5.30am–8pm. Cheap to inexpensive.

Arintji Café + Bar Federation Square ☎9663 9900. See map, p.67. Jacques Reymond's wonderful addition to Federation Square offers flavoursome modern Australian food in a bright uptempo setting, with great outdoor seating and patrons rubbernecking at the local celebrities. Open for coffee in the morning. Mon–Sun 10am–late. Moderate–expensive.

Blue Train Café Level 2, Southgate ☎9696 0440. See map, pp.58–59. Attracts a young, hip crowd and dishes out basic meals like wood-fired pizzas, pasta and salad. There's also full bar service, a children's menu and plenty of reading material if you're dining solo. Walls display works from local artists. Daily 7am–late. Cheap to inexpensive.

Café Sweethearts 263 Coventry St, South Melbourne ☎9690 6752. Breakfasts are the order of the day at this sunny corner café, in particular eggs, in a variety of ways. Also does lunches that are a cut above your usual café fare. Mon–Fri 7am–3pm, Sat & Sun 8am–3pm. Cheap to inexpensive.

Chocolate Buddha Federation Square ☎9654 5688. See map, p.67. A busy space inspired by Japanese canteens serving large portions of delicious organic modern Japanese food such as sushi, ramen and *donburi* on light timber tables. The sake-based cocktails will surely kick-start your night – and if they don't, you can always look over the sandstone expanse and watch free movies on Federation Square's big screen. Daily noon–1am. Inexpensive.

Dish 379 St Kilda Rd ☎9677 9933. Hip, cavernous restaurant nestled in the *Royce on St Kilda Road* hotel (see p.107), just past the Shrine of Remembrance. The modern Australian cuisine is expensive and modish, running from salmon fish cakes, risotto and lamb shanks to a reasonable choice of desserts. Mon–Fri 6–10.30am, noon–2.30pm & 6–10.30pm, Sat 6.30am–noon & 6–10.30pm, Sun 6.30am–noon. Moderate to expensive.

Dundas and Faussett Corner or Dundas Place and Fassett St, Albert Park ☎9645 5155. Large, funky café with an extensive menu that includes ubckydes eggs, pasta, foccacia, noodles and laksa. Great if you fancy something different, and the outside tables occupy the best spot on this busy strip. Mon–Fri 6am–9pm, Sat & Sun 6am–5pm. Cheap.

EQ Cafébar Victorian Arts Centre, 100 St Kilda Rd ☎9645 0644. The creation of Dur-Dara (of

Nudel Bar fame – see p.114), this café-bar is a firm favourite with the Arts Centre crowd pre- or post-show. There is a varied selection of snacky, down-to-earth but fantastic Mediterranean-style food such as bread and dips, pasta salads, sausage and mash. Fabulous during the summer when you can sit outside overlooking the Yarra. Daily 8am–late. Moderate.

Kamel 19 Victoria Ave, Albert Park ☎9696 1386. Cosy Middle Eastern restaurant with a delectable menu of mezzes, seafood or grill dishes, There's also a good vegetarian selection. Mon–Thurs 5.30–10pm, Fri–Sun 8am–3pm, 5.30–10pm. Cheap to inexpensive.

Koko Level 3, Crown Casino, Southbank ☎9292 6886. See map, pp.58–59. Once Melbourne's premier Japanese restaurant, Koko has finally undone its top button and feels a lot less exclusive for it. Inhabiting a large and decorative space fitted out with tables, myriad grills, a tranquil water garden and, in one corner, a sushi-sashimi bar perfect for pre-dinner drinks, it's still an excellent – albeit pricey – choice for diners. Daily noon–3pm & 6–11pm. Expensive to very expensive.

Misuzu's 3–7 Victoria Ave, Albert Park ☎9699 9022. Well-priced Japanese cafe-restaurant that's usually packed with locals. Warm and inviting, with pretty lanterns hanging outside, and a dark wood interior, it has a menu that ranges from sushi and sashimi to Japanese curries and tasty noodle soups; the extensive sake menu won't

disappoint either. Daily noon–10pm. Cheap to moderate.

Q11 303 Coventry St, South Melbourne ☎9646 6006. Located across from South Melbourne market, this petite café is well positioned for those in need of a pit-stop. The food doesn't go beyond toasties, brushetta and paninis but the ingredients are locally sourced and the result is delicious and filling. Excellent coffee and cakes too. Cheap.

Taxi Dining Room Level 1, Federation Square ☎9654 8808. See map, p.67. Above *Transport* (see p.130), the high ceilings and open windows of this highly designed eatery give a stunning perspective on the city and the Yarra. In the driving seat is former *Circa* (see p.123) chef Michael Lambie, whose modern Australian/Japanese creations range from nibbly sushi to mains such as roast barramundi with fennel puree and prawn dumplings. delivered by staff wearing zippy cab-driver uniforms. Alternatively you can just grab a beer or sake and watch the city lights blur. Daily noon–11pm. Expensive to very expensive.

Walter's Wine Bar Level 3, Southgate ☎9690 9211. See map, pp.58–59. Long-established restaurant-cum-wine bar, Walter's has been preparing excellent contemporary bistro food for over fifteen years. This, combined with knowledgeable staff, good Australian wines by the glass and superb views across the Yarra to the city make this a popular choice for breakfast, lunch or post-theatre. Mon–Fri 9am–late, Sat & Sun 8am–late. Moderate to expensive.

Carlton and Fitzroy

For locations of the following establishments, see map on p.79 unless otherwise stated.

Abla's 109 Elgin St, Carlton ☎9347 0006. A homely restaurant serving some of the best Lebanese food in town. The twelve-course banquet (compulsory on Thur, Fri & Sat nights) is magnificent. Mon–Wed & Sat 6–11pm Thurs & Fri noon–3pm & 6–11pm. Moderate.

Akari 177 177 Brunswick St, Fitzroy ☎9419 3786. A mainstay on Brunswick St for many years, Akari 177 has a deluge of Japanese-style goodies, with wonderful beef teriyaki, tempura, tofu dishes, sushi and recommended daily specials.

Takeaway menu available. Mon & Sat 6–10.30pm, Tues–Fri noon–3pm & 6–10.30pm. Cheap to inexpensive.

Arcadia 193 Gertrude St, Fitzroy ☎9416 1055. Bright, open café with blackboard specials and delicious hearty fare such as soups, pastas and foccacias. A popular local hangout; take a seat at the large communal table if you're feeling sociable or nab a seat at the front window for a spot of people-watching. Mon–Fri 8am–5pm, Sat & Sun 9am–5pm.

Babka Bakery Café 358 Brunswick St, Fitzroy
℡9416 0091. Part bakery, part café,
Russian-influenced *Babka* serves up simple
fare such as eggs, blinis and borscht. The
decor is unpretentious and simple, with
white walls and large ceiling fans. The
coffee will win over the most discerning
caffeine addict, while one of their delicious
pastries or "shoofly" buns (yeast buns with
currants, eaten with butter), will do wonders
for the soul; feast your eyes on their
selection while waiting for a table. Pick up a
warm loaf of freshly-baked bread on your
way out, or try one of the Babka pies.
Tues–Sun 7am–7pm.

Balzari 130 Lygon St, Carlton ℡9639 9383.
A welcome addition to Lygon Street, this
chic bistro-style eatery serves well-
presented modern Mediterranean/Italian
food and not a margherita pizza in sight.
A $25 set lunch menu (primi, secondi &
dolci) is available weekdays. Tues–Fri
noon–late, Sat & Sun 9.30am–late.
Moderate.

Bimbo Deluxe 376 Brunswick St, Fitzroy ℡9419
8600. An endless procession of super-cheap
and delicious pizzas (only $4 for lunch Mon–
Fri and dinner Sun–Thurs) along with a few
other favourites, keep the diners coming
back again and again, so you may need to
wait for a table. The large, dimly-lit bar out
back keeps the drinkers and pool sharks
happy. DJs play most nights. Daily noon–
3am. Cheap.

Blue Chillies 182 Brunswick St, Fitzroy ℡9417
0071. Modern Malaysian cuisine served in
relaxed and intimate surroundings located
near cool Gertrude St. Locals flock here to
dine on tasty spicy crab rolls, satay chicken
with peanut sauce and excellent laksas.
The banquet menus for four people or
more are good for sampling a bit of everything. Quick service. Daily noon 2.30pm,
6pm–late. Inexpensive to moderate.

Brunetti 194–204 Faraday St, Carlton ℡9347
2801. See map, p.74. This buzzing Carlton
icon has been trading here for over twenty
years when it began as a cake shop. Today
its many shopfronts contain a café, restaurant, panineteca, pasticceria and gelateria.
A steady stream of well-dressed customers
file past an array of display cases filled with
a selection of cholesterol-boosting chocolates, pastries, savouries, biscuits and cakes
to get their daily espresso in the café, or
have pasta and meat dishes in the licensed

restaurant next door (closed Sun for lunch &
dinner). If that doesn't put a smile on your
face then the jovial staff will. Mon–Thurs &
Sun 6.30am–11pm, Fri & Sat 6.30am–
midnight. Moderate.

Café Zum Zum 645 Rathdowne St, Carlton North
℡9348 0455. See map, p.74. This hidden
nook (on the western side of the street)
serves outstanding Middle Eastern food in a
warm and cheerful space. *Sambousik* (fetta
and mint-filled pastries), *ma'anek* sausages
and pumpkin and eggplant tajine will satisfy
even the most ambitious appetite, but try to
leave room for baklava. Tues 6–10pm,
Wed–Sun noon–3pm & 6–10pm.
Inexpensive.

Fitz 347 Brunswick St, Fitzroy ℡9417 5794. *Fitz*
has a deserved reputation for fuelling locals
in stylish surroundings. The decor is modern
and simple, with large windows looking out
onto the street, the European cuisine is feel-
good and down-to-earth – roo burgers,
calamari and gnocchi – while the leafy
outside area is ideal for catching the sun.
Tasty breakfasts served till 4pm, plus daily
specials. Daily 7am–late. Inexpensive.

Interlude 211 Brunswick St, Fitzroy ℡9415
7300, ✆www.interlude.com.au. Fine Modern
Australian cuisine in a stylish and sophisticated setting that appeals to a food-literate
crowd. Choose from entrées such as blue
swimmer crab alongside mains featuring
kangaroo and roast chicken with truffles.
Fixed-price menus (two-courses $75, three
$95), plus an innovative degustation menu
that explores food science from $110 per
person. Lunch specials from $30 for two
courses, including a glass of wine, Mon
6.30pm–late, Tues–Fri noon–3pm,
6.30pm–late, Sat 6.30pm–late. Expensive.

Jimmy Watson's 333 Lygon St, Carlton ℡9347
3985. See map, p.76. Designed by Robin
Boyd in 1962, this place has survived the
vagaries of Melbourne's food and drinking
trends, and still attracts locals, academics,
students and anyone who loves a tipple.
Despite several minor renovations, not much
has changed and that includes its reputation
for pub grub in convivial, atmospheric
surroundings. Formerly a wine salon,
Jimmy's continues to sport a superb list of
Australian vintage wines from the cellar. If
you don't fancy eating, do as the locals do
and pop in for a glass of wine or two at the
bar. Mon 10.30am–6pm, Tues–Sat
10.30am–late. Moderate to expensive.

Ladro 224 Gertrude St, Fitzroy ☎9415 7575.
Excellent, authentic and inspired Italian-style pizzas – arguably the best in town – means Ladro is one of the toughest places to get a seat, but your efforts will be rewarded. Bookings advised. Tues–Sun 6pm–late. Inexpensive to moderate.
La Cacciatora Corner of Grattan & Drummond sts, Carlton ☎9663 6906. See map, p.74. There's no shortage of good pizza places in Carlton, but this off-Lygon St spot is worth singling out from the crowd. They slice up gourmet flavours such as artichoke and sweet potato in either the customary pie, or by the metre in long rectangles for big appetites. Dine in for platefuls of pasta and an authentic Italian atmosphere. Daily noon–3pm & 5–11pm. Inexpensive.
Madame Sousou 231 Brunswick St, Fitzroy ☎9417 0400. Step inside this corner restaurant and you'll feel like you've walked off the rue into a Parisian café. From the posters lining the walls, the large chandeliers and the tightly packed chairs, the atmosphere is elegantly chic and inviting. The menu naturally has a heavy French influence, but also features risotto and gnocchi – with a French twist, of course. Staff are friendly and attentive. A popular spot for coffee, breakfast or dinner. Tues–Sun 9am–late. Moderate.
Mario's 303 Brunswick St, Fitzroy ☎9417 3343. Anyone who wants to get a true feel of Brunswick St should come for brekkie (served until midnight) in this 1950s European-style café with wood counters and tiled floors. They also serve lunch and dinner or you can just have a coffee or a drink. Service is always friendly and efficient. While waiting for a seat (it gets very busy at weekends), you can browse the bookstores down the road. Mon–Wed & Sun 7am–midnight, Thurs–Sat 7am–1am. Inexpensive to moderate.
Newtown S.C 180 Brunswick St, Fitzroy ☎9415 7337. Popular with locals who regularly gather at this cosy café to chat over good coffee and catch up with the staff. The food here is simple (crumpets, cereal, filled baguettes and pide) all prepared at an open-plan gallery kitchen. The experience is much like dropping by a friend's place for coffee. Mon–Fri 8am–5pm, Sat 9am–5pm. Cheap.
Piraeus Blues 310 Brunswick St, Fitzroy ☎9417 0222. Has built a solid reputation for serving flavoursome, homespun cooking such as moussaka, beef rissoles or stuffed peppers with feta and offering a great ever-changing specials board and fish of the day, their charcoal grills are particularly popular too. A must for lovers of Greek food. Mon, Tues & Sat 5pm–1am, Wed–Fri noon–3pm & 5pm–1am, Sun noon–late. Moderate.
Retro Café 413 Brunswick St, Fitzroy ☎9419 9103. Inviting and casual eatery with worn wooden floorboards, a mix of chairs and comfy couches and a plethora of 1970s kitsch. Whether your preferences are for savoury pancakes, pasta dishes or even kangaroo, you'll be guaranteed to leave pleasantly stuffed. Also serves good coffee, cheap muffins and syrupy-sweet desserts. The window seats are a great place to people-watch. Breakfast till 4pm. Daily 7am–11.30pm. Inexpensive to moderate.
Rhumbarella's 342 Brunswick St, Fitzroy ☎9417 5652. Buzzing and vibrant café, *Rhumbarella's* hums to the sound of jazz and conversation. Breakfast until midday – eggs Benedict is a favourite – then anything from focaccia to steak. Vegetarians will be pleased with the large veggie menu. Daily 9am–1am. Cheap to inexpensive.
Shakahari 201–203 Faraday St, Carlton ☎9347 3848. Excellent, well-priced and superbly presented East-meets-West vegetarian favourites such as satays, pasta, curries and laksas, where you can sample delights such as tempura fried avocado rolls or chilli and saffron flavoured lasagne from a menu that changes according to season. Housed within two terraces and entered via a ruby-red corridor this has been Carlton's benchmark in dining for sophisticated lentil-lovers for years. Mon–Thurs noon–3pm & 6–9.30pm, Fri & Sat noon–3pm & 6–10pm, Sun 6–9.30pm. Inexpensive.
Small Block 130 Lygon St, East Brunswick ☎9381 2244. See map, p.74. Fantastic coffee, huge breakfasts and an ever-changing lunch list makes this slightly industrial looking café – stripped concrete floors, large metal signs lining the walls – a favourite for both locals in the know and those wanting to escape the Brunswick St scene. The sunny window seats are great for watching the world go by. Mon–Fri 7.30am–5pm, Sat & Sun 8.30am–5pm. Cheap.

St Jude's Cellars 389 Brunswick St, Fitzroy
☎9419 7411. With a carefully stocked wine shop at the front and large open-plan restaurant out the back, St Jude's raises the bar a notch among Fitzroy's café-laden street, and fills the gap for discerning locals who enjoy fine-dining and a full-bodied shiraz. Emphasis is on grazing in groups of two or more, with staff in crisp white shirts serving a selection of well-presented Modern European dishes from a menu that includes grilled eel and paté on rye bread, rabbit and lentil cottage pie or fish wrapped in vine leaves. Tues–Sun noon–3pm & 6pm–late.

Tiamo 1 303 Lygon St, Carlton ☎9347 5759.
See map, p.76. Family-run Carlton establishment that's been offering classic Italian food and expressos to locals for over thirty years. The food, including old favourites such as lasagne and carbonara, isn't flash but is filling and hearty. Timber tables and walls adorned with 1950s posters, plus the strip's best tiramisu, make this little gem a favourite with students and locals alike. Tiamo 2, next door, offers a slightly more modern approach to its menu, but is still excellent value. Mon–Sat 7am–11pm, Sun 8am–10pm. Cheap to inexpensive.

Esposito at Toofey's 162 Elgin St, Carlton
☎9347 9838. See map, p.74. A magnet for local fishophiles, *Esposito's* extremely fresh seafood dishes are prepared by owner-chef

Maurice Esposito with a modern Italian twist. Start with ravioli of Tasmanian crayfish or risotto with blue swimmer crab and progress to barramundi with lentils or John Dory fillets with calamari spaghetti. There's beef and beer-battered fish too. Mon–Sat noon–3pm & 6–10.30pm, Sun 6–10.30pm. Expensive.

Toto's Pizza House 101 Lygon St, Carlton
☎9347 1630. See map, p.76. Melbourne's first pizzeria, dating from the 1950s, serves decent no-frills pizza towards the city end of Lygon St. Just don't come here looking for an authentic mamma trattoria experience. Daily noon–11pm. Inexpensive.

Trotters 400 Lygon St, Carlton ☎9347 5657.
See map, p.76. Popular for breakfast, *Trotters* is a rustic and sometimes cramped spot where you can plough through big servings of bacon and eggs (till 3pm), home-made cakes, BLTs, steak and good coffee. Mon–Fri 7.30am–10.30pm, Sat 8am–10.30pm, Sun 9.30am–9pm. Cheap to inexpensive.

Vegie Bar 380 Brunswick St, Fitzroy
☎9417 6935. Spacious and vibrant, the *Vegie Bar* is popular and hip rather than hippie. Large portions of simple, fresh food such as lentil burgers, risottos and delicious salads are cooked to order with a range of healthy nibbles for gym bunnies and whippet-thin regulars. Daily 11am–10pm. Cheap to inexpensive.

Collingwood, Richmond and the east

The following establishments are marked on the map on p.82, unless otherwise stated.

Booktalk Café 91 Swan St, Richmond
☎9428 1977. Pop in for great deals on new and second-hand books and discover a fantastic café nestled within. The atmosphere is relaxed and social while the food is wholesome, hearty and cooked daily – choose from dishes such as vegetable frittata, tuna bake, Mediterranean roti, shepherd's pie – and finish up with excellent coffee and cakes. Cheap. Mon–Fri 7.30am–5.30pm, Sat & Sun 8.30am–5.30pm.

Gluttony, It's A Sin 278 Smith St, Collingwood
☎9416 0336. Frequented by locals who come here for great breakfasts, lunches and gluten-free cakes all served in large

portions. Mon–Fri 7am–11pm, Sat & Sun 8am–9.30pm.

Ha Long Bay 82 Victoria St, Richmond ☎9429 3268. If you're searching for a good Vietnamese restaurant on Victoria St then look no further. Ignore the lurid lime walls – you won't be sitting here long enough for them to take effect – and concentrate on choosing something from the long, long list of dishes. Cheap corkage, plus lunch specials for less than $10. Daily 10am–11pm. Cheap to inexpensive.

Himalayan Sherpa 340 Bridge Rd, Richmond ☎9428 1240. Tables are tight and at peak times you may have to shout to hear yourself above the din, but it's a small price to pay for securing a spot at this cosy Nepalese restaurant. Start with a number of small dishes such as *momo* (steamed dumplings with chicken or vegetables), samosas and *pakodas* (vegetable fritters) before moving on to one of the delicious curries: chickpea flavoured with spicy mashed potato or kasaudi chicken (chicken marinated in spices). Bookings advised. Tues–Sun 5.30pm–10.30pm. Cheap to inexpensive.

Pearl 631–633 Church St, Richmond ☎9421 4599. See map, p.88. Slickly designed establishment with loads of natural light and attentive service whose inventive, modern Australian food consistently impresses the appreciative, young crowd. Entrees are strong on seafood – clams, oysters, scallops and crab – while mains are subtly spiced and continue the Asian-inspired theme. The bar has a cheaper, snack-like menu, that is just as interesting. In addition the newly opened café (daily 7am–4pm) at 599 Church St is open for breakfast and offers a well-priced lunch menu. Mon–Fri noon–3pm & 6–10.30pm, Sat & Sun 9am–3pm & 6–10.30pm. Expensive to very expensive.

Richmond Hill Café and Larder 48–50 Bridge Rd, Richmond ☎9421 2808. Exquisite though pricey food served in spacious, bistro-style surroundings. As well as a casual dining area, there's a larder and cheese shop (see p.165). Perfect for breakfast, coffee or a glass of wine while poring over the daily papers. Mon–Thurs & Sun 8.30am–5pm, Fri & Sat 8.30am–6pm. Moderate to expensive.

Soul Food Café 273 Smith St, Collingwood ☎9419 2949. Large vegetarian café serving a pleasing menu of salads, burgers, curry, tagines, rotis and risotto, and pumpkin in many variations – try the pumpkin and feta pie. Things get more intimate towards the back where there's a small bar and a few comfy chairs. Mon–Thurs 8am–9pm, Sat & Sun 9am–6pm.

Thy Thy 1 Level 1, 142 Victoria St, Richmond ☎9429 1104. Climb the stairs to one of the most popular Vietnamese restaurants in Melbourne. The food, which includes crispy spring rolls, noodles and chicken dishes, is basic but great. Daily 8am–10pm. Cheap.

Tofu Shop International 78 Bridge Rd, Richmond ☎9429 6204. A great example of healthy food being really delicious, this tiny place has been going for years, serving consistently good vegetarian meals to eat in or take away. Treat your body to salads, pasta, stews and tofu (all freshly made on the premises), or try the spring rolls or a *soyvlaki* – a massive wrap filled with a choice of salads. Food is ordered according to plate size and prices include dips and ginger. Usually shoulder to shoulder at the counter seats at lunchtimes. Mon–Fri noon–9pm, Sat noon–5pm. Cheap.

Vlado's 61 Bridge Rd, Richmond ☎9428 5833. Sausages, hamburger, liver, steak, you name it – if it has four legs it'll end up on long-established *Vlado's* set-price four-course menu. Heaven for carnivores, the wine list here supports the simple fleshy cuisine. Vegetarians, however, will find it hellish – there's nothing. Mon–Fri noon–3pm & 6–11pm, Sat 6–11pm. Expensive.

South Yarra, Prahran and Toorak

The following establishments are marked on the map on p.88.

Botanical 169 Domain Rd, South Yarra ☎9820 7888. Bright, modern restaurant opposite the Botanic Gardens, whose open kitchen offers a sneak peek at chef Paul Wilson's bold signature dishes. You might start with Tuscan bean soup with rabbit, or sticky pork salad, before choosing from the premium meat menu – the wagyu burger and steak were recently voted Melbourne's best. If your wallet won't stretch to dinner try the superb breakfasts or the tasty grazing menu with wines by the glass available in the adjacent café and seats outside. There's

also a wine shop, and a sleek and sexy bar. Mon–Fri 7am–11pm, Sat & Sun 8am–11pm. Expensive to very expensive.

Caffe e Cucina 581 Chapel St, South Yarra ☎9827 4139. This became the benchmark for Melbourne restaurant/café style when it opened in 1988, and has spawned a score of imitators with its wood panelling, cute little table lamps and a creative menu written up on a central blackboard. Very Italian, dark, and small enough to make a toilet cubicle look spacious, it's staffed by immaculately dressed, theatrically aloof waiters serving sublime al dente pasta, mouthwatering bigne pastries and some of the best coffee in town. Daily 11.30am–10pm. Moderate to expensive.

Chinta Ria Jazz 176 Commercial Rd, Prahran ⊕9510 6520. Consistently good Malaysian hawker fare – the fat Hokkien noodles, roti bread and curry laksa, in particular, are to die for. Takeaway available. Tues–Fri noon–2.30pm & 6–10.30pm, Mon, Sat & Sun 6–10.30pm. Cheap to moderate.

France-Soir 11 Toorak Rd, South Yarra ⊕9866 8569. The food's modest at this French brasserie restaurant but the list of exceptional bottles of French wine, ranks as one of Melbourne's finest. Attracts a mix of local diners, intimate couples and well-heeled tourists. Daily noon–3pm & 6pm–midnight. Expensive.

Globe Café 218 Chapel St, Prahran ⊕9510 8693. Small space crammed with tables serving fabulous breakfasts, great meals and sinful cakes – you're bound to find something here to satisfy. Mon–Fri 8am–late, Sat & Sun 9am–late. Cheap to inexpensive.

Jacques Reymond 78 Williams Rd, Prahran ⊕9525 2178. Jacques Reymond's shrine to fine food brings together eclectic ingredients from Europe, Australia, Asia and the Pacific to startling effect. The space is glamorous and striking, while the menu focuses on small-plate three-, four- or five-course fixed-price menus ($98/125/150) to encourage sampling. There's also a seven-course degustation menu ($150) for the adventurous. Tram #64 from Swanston St. Tues, Wed & Sat 6.30–10pm, Thurs & Fri noon–2pm & 6.30–10pm. Very expensive.

Lynch's 133 Domain Rd, South Yarra ⊕9866 5627. Popular dining place for wealthy locals, who come for the first-class service,

private rooms, old-fashioned food, racy nudes hanging on the walls and the child-free environment. Opposite the Botanic Gardens. Mon–Fri noon–2.30pm & 6.30–10.30pm, Sat 6.30–10.30pm. Expensive to very expensive.

Orange 124–126 Chapel St, Windsor ⊕9529 1644. Popular bistro-style café and bar serving great coffee and decent food. During the day the seats are packed with diners sampling dishes such as beef carpaccio and grilled haloumi as well as more substantial veal and steak dinners (service at peak times can be slow). If the bistro is busy, grab a seat next door at the bar, replete with soft leather booths and wooden counter seating, which gets progressively busier as the night draws on. Outside tables are heated in winter. Daily 7am–late.

Spoonful 543 High St, Prahran ⊕9521 5212. Elegantly informal café that's popular with ladies who lunch and – judging by the reading material being passed round – interior designers. The food is a cut above regular café-fare, expect roast chicken in a white wine sauce or venison terrine, ciabatta and eggs in all variations. Next door, *Teaspoon*, has a small takeaway menu for those in a hurry. Mon–Sat 7.30am–4.30pm. Cheap to inexpensive.

Sweet Basil 209 Commercial Rd, South Yarra ⊕9827 3390. Delicious modern Thai cuisine served in simple, relaxed surroundings ensure that people come back here time after time. Choose from an extensive menu featuring contemporary delights such as pumpkin-flavoured steamed dumplings with chicken, or crispy stir-fried quail as well as more familiar favourites. Excellent vegetarian options too. Tues–Sun 6pm–10pm. Inexpensive to moderate.

St Kilda

The following establishments are marked on the map on p.92.

Bala's Café 1c Shakespeare Grove, St Kilda ⊕9534 6116. Tiny but hugely popular café that's perfect for a quick fuel stop or takeaway. Although the seating at small wooden tables is cramped, the Southeast Asian food is fast and affordable, and includes Malaysian noodles, Thai curries, Indian samosas and cooling lassis. Daily noon–10pm. Cheap.

Big Mouth 168 Acland St, St Kilda ⊕9534 4611. Relaxed and unpretentious, the large, triangular Art Deco restaurant and bar has warm mix 'n' match decor, which includes many original features, and offers great views of the street. The lounge bar upstairs (Mon–Fri 5pm–late, Sat & Sun 10am–late) is a good place to unwind during the week, but there's also a restaurant (daily 5pm–3am) and a

▲ Choosing cakes on Acland Street

lively downstairs café (daily 7am–3am; cheap) serving a variety of excellent café-style fare to a hip local crowd. Cheap to moderate.

Café Di Stasio 31 Fitzroy St, St Kilda ☎9525 3999. Small and understated, softly lit and elegantly authentic, Café Di Stasio serves up a masterful blend of traditional and modern Italian cooking, and remains one of the best Italian restaurants in Melbourne, despite the occasionally temperamental waiters. The two-course lunch menu with a glass of wine is good value at $30. Daily noon–3pm & 6–11pm. Moderate to expensive.

Café Racer 15 Marine Parade, St Kilda ☎9534 9988. Ocean-facing minimalist-look café providing an ideal rendezvous for lycra-clad cyclists in search of turbo-charged snacks – baguettes, quiche, salads and the like – and their next caffeine hit. Daily 6.30am–6pm. Inexpensive.

Chinta Blues 6 Acland St, St Kilda ☎9534 9233. Malaysian restaurant with a blues theme. Fortunately the authentic and reasonably priced dishes more than make up for the daft concept. Start with tender calamari fillets, crispy whitebait or home-made dim sums then progress onto one of the delicious laksas, curries or noodle dishes. Daily noon–2.30pm & 6pm–late. Inexpensive to moderate.

Cicciolina 130 Acland St, St Kilda ☎9525 3333. A sociable atmosphere prevails at the tightly packed tables of this small and always crowded space where they serve high-quality modern Mediterranean food including chilli fishcakes, tuna carpaccio and antipasto. You can't book, so be prepared to wait in the cosy bar out back while cosseting the extensive wine list. Don't forget to leave room for sticky date pudding. Mon–Sat noon–11pm, Sun noon–10pm; bar Mon–Sat 4.30pm–1am, Sun 3.30–11pm. Moderate to expensive.

Circa, The Prince 2 Acland St, St Kilda ☎9536 1122. Part of the multimillion-dollar redevelopment that has transformed this once-grungy pub into a magnificently theat-rical Art Deco treasure, with black drapes, wicker lights, crisp white linens and soft white banquettes. Touted as one of Melbourne's best restaurants, *Circa* serves excellent modern food, has an award-winning wine list, and boasts superb service. Mon–Fri & Sun 7–11am, daily noon–3pm & 6.30pm–late. Very expensive.

Claypots Seafood Bar 213 Barkly St, St Kilda ☎9534 1282. You can't book, so arrive early at this tiny and perpetually busy seafood bar, which offers fabulous blackboard specials, a daily $5 paella hour (timings vary) and claypots that are used to casserole everything from seafood to lamb and tempting veggie combinations. Come summer escape the heat of the open kitchen and head out back to the courtyard. The next door bar, *Tavern and Fair* is open

until 1am. Daily 10am–3pm & 6–10.30pm.
Cheap to moderate.

Donovans 40 Jacka Blvd, St Kilda ☎ 9534 8221.
Originally a 1920s bathing pavilion, Donovans
is now a relaxed beach-house restaurant that
exudes a homely, oaky ambience, complete
with heaving bookshelves, sofas bulging with
cushions and oceanfront views. The menu is
comforting, focusing on grills and seafood,
and it's one of the best places for lounging
around the log fireplace in winter. Daily noon–
late. Expensive.

**The Espy Kitchen Esplanade Hotel, 11 Upper
Esplanade, St Kilda ☎ 9534 0211.** Restaurant
of the iconic Espy (see p.134) that's seen a
few changes in space, decor and menu in
recent years, but the ambience remains as
laid back as ever and there's still no better
place to warm body and soul with excellent
comfort food. On Monday nights $10 will
get you a burger with chips and a pot of
beer, or a choice of four lasagnes on a
Wednesday. Mon–Wed 5–11pm, Thurs
5pm–late, Fri noon–late, Sat & Sun 8am–
late. Inexpensive to moderate.

The Galleon 9 Carlisle St, St Kilda ☎ 9534 8934.
One of St Kilda's long-standing favourites,
The Galleon was around long before the area
was transformed from a run-down and
forgotten beach resort to the funky place it is
today. Large and grungy with lots of formica-
topped tables, it's busy and noisy, the menu
is good, the coffee is above average and the
fried breakfasts are great – the Eggs Benedict
particularly so. Daily 7am–5pm. Cheap.

Il Fornaio 2 Acland St, St Kilda ☎ 9534 2922.
Hip bakery serving excellent breads,
pastries, pastas and coffee to take away or
eat in, and at night more substantial risotto
or pasta mains, plus a few daily specials (in
the evenings you may even get a loaf of
unsold bread to take away with you).
Popular at breakfast time, with seating
outside on the small veranda. Daily
7am–10pm. Cheap to inexpensive.

Inkr7 7 Inkerman St, St Kilda ☎ 9534 6011.
Welcoming lunchtime pitstop with polished
floors, modern art lining the walls and a mix
of seating arrangements; the couch in front
of the fire is particularly nice in colder
months, while the few tables out front are a
suntrap in more clement weather. On the
menu is a range of tasty pides, wraps,
salads and hearty soups, plus delicious
muffins and cakes. Mon–Fri 8am–5pm, Sat
& Sun 9am–5pm. Cheap.

**Las Chicas 203 Carlisle St, Balaclava ☎ 9531
3699.** Bright and bustling café that's almost
too cool for school but thankfully free of all
pretension. On-the-ball staff buzz around its
funky brick interior, delivering huge
sandwiches, breakfasts, excellent cakes and
good coffee to diners who fill every available
space. Daily 7am–5pm. Cheap.

**Leeroy Expresso 191 Acland St, St Kilda ☎ 9525
5166.** Popular with locals who breeze by and
grab a coffee from the window or linger for
longer at one of the wooden tables for more
substantial pides, burgers, and wraps.
Nabbing one of the outside tables for crowd
surveillance is almost de rigeur. Daily 7am–
5pm. Cheap.

**Melbourne Wine Room George Hotel, 125 Fitzroy
St, St Kilda ☎ 9525 5599.** Excellent Victorian
wine list and an innovative Italian menu from
either the bar or the more sophisticated
chandelier-lit dining area out back. Top
service, top setting, top place. Tues–Thurs
3pm–late, Fri–Sun noon–late. Expensive.

🏃 **Milktoast 115 Carlisle St, St Kilda ☎ 9531
3527.** Walking into *Milktoast* is like
dropping by an old aunt's house; staff greet
you warmly and there are old mirrors and
horseshoes hanging on the walls. Then
there's the choice of food; the front counter
literally groans with freshly made pastas and
salads and pides to die for (try the pumpkin,
pea, spinach and fetta salad or olive
tapenade with salami and sun-dried
tomato). From the kitchen there are risottos
along with burgers and excellent breakfasts.
This is one aunty you'll want to visit often.
Mon–Sat 7.30am–5pm. Cheap.

Pelican 16 Fitzroy St, St Kilda ☎ 9525 5847.
Groovy buzzing tapas bar that offers a
menu with more than a few standouts,
perfect for sharing over a bottle of wine
before hitting the clubs. The outdoor timber
deck is a good spot for lazy summer breakfasts. Daily 7.30am–11pm. Cheap to
inexpensive.

**Scheherazade 99 Acland St, St Kilda ☎ 9534
2722.** Hangout for elderly Eastern European
émigrés, Scheherezade was opened by a
Jewish couple in the 1950s and has grown
in popularity to become an Acland St
institution. Famous for its chicken soup
(some swear it has medicinal properties)
and inexpensive mains – tasty chicken
schnitzel, goulash and blintzes, as well as
salmon bagels and eggs, it's also the only
place on Acland St where you can still get a

good bowl of borscht – a great escape from modern-day haute cuisine. Daily 9am–late. Inexpensive.

Soulmama Level 1, St Kilda Sea Baths, 10 Jacka Blvd, St Kilda ☎9525 3338. Large, glam vegetarian open-plan café, serving wholesome food in three bowl sizes, including beetroot in tahini and zesty tofu curries. Great beach views from the open beachfront terrace, couch seating and a formidable drinks list make this the perfect place to hole up for the afternoon with a group of friends. Daily noon–late. Cheap to inexpensive.

The Stokehouse 30 Jacka Blvd, St Kilda ☎9525 5555. Boasting a spectacular beachfront location and views, this converted teahouse is one of the most popular eating spots in Melbourne for those who fancy a splurge by the water. Both the café-bar downstairs (daily noon–late; moderate) serving nibbles, pizza, steak, roast chicken and fish and the stylish restaurant upstairs (bookings recom-mended) are always busy. Although the restaurant menu has a leaning towards seafood, there's always a wide variety of inventive dishes available, from rabbit tortellini to venison fillet. Daily noon–2.30pm & 6–10pm. Expensive to very expensive.

Topolinos 87 Fitzroy St, St Kilda ☎9534 1925. A dimly lit and noisy St Kilda institution, which pumps out pizzas, generous pasta dishes and good cocktails until dawn. Mon–Wed 4pm–late, Thurs–Sun noon–late. Cheap to inexpensive.

Veludo 175 Acland St, St Kilda ☎9534 4456. Street-level restaurant with dark-stained floorboards and a wall feature made out of wine bottles. Good Modern Australian dishes, and brekkies – the Big Fat Pommie Bastard speaks for itself. The open fire is a welcome feature in winter, while the outside tables are perfect for being seen in the summer. There's also a groovy upstairs bar (see p.134). Daily 8am–late. Inexpensive to moderate.

Wall Two 80 Rear, 280 Carlisle St, Balaclava ☎9593 8280. Restored kosher butcher's shop that's one of the coolest cafés in the city, offering simple but delicious food (mostly toasted pides and breakfasts) and good coffee. Inside is a series of small alcoves and a larger space dominated by a wooden communal table, perfect for chit-chat. Check out the takeaway window and cushioned milk crates for seating outside. Daily 6.30am–6pm. Cheap.

Williamstown

Eating establishments are marked on the map on p.98.

Breizoz Crêpes 139 Nelson Place ☎9397 2300. Authentic French creperie that does a delicious selection of sweet crepes and savoury galettes, along with a good range of French apple cider for that true Breton experience. Mon–Fri noon–3pm & 6–10pm, noon–5pm & 6–10pm, Sun 9.30am–9.30pm.

Hobson's Choice Foods 213 Nelson Place ☎9397 1891. Busy café that serves every-thing from eggs, steak and tandoori chicken to croissants and pastries. With seafront views and a breezy atmosphere, this is a popular place for breakfasts and lazy Sun lunches. Daily 7.30am–late. Cheap.

Siam Orchid Restaurant 145 Nelson Place ☎9397 5303. Busy, friendly and comfortable place serving filling, but affordable Thai food in the middle of a very competitive restau-rant strip. Tues–Sun 5–10.30pm. Cheap to inexpensive.

Siren's Beach Dressing Pavilion, The Esplanade ☎9397 7811. Located in a former bathing pavilion, Siren's serves above-average Mediterranean food in its formal restaurant (lunch Tues–Fri & Sun, dinner Tues–Fri & Sat), while the bistro also serves a good spread of light meals and pizzas. Great for grabbing a pot of beer and plate of chips, then heading to the deck for the fantastic beach views. Daily 10.30am–late. Moderate.

Stag's Head Inn Corner of Ann & Cecil sts ☎9397 5303. This friendly backstreet treat is one of the few pubs in the area that retains its tradi-tional pub character, with a formal dining room out the back, pool table, courtyard and live music Thurs–Sun. The menu (kitchen open noon–2.30pm & 6–9pm) does hearty unpretentious pub grub including steaks, bangers and mash, ribs and risotto and a truly intimidating club sandwich. Mon–Sat 11am–midnight, Sun 11am–11pm. Cheap.

Pitts, bars and clubs

Pubs, bars and clubs

Melburnians take their drinking very seriously and their love affair with all things alcoholic is reflected in the city's excellent **pubs and bars** – from places so obscure and cutting-edge you'll only know they exist by word of mouth, to large establishments catering to broader and louder tastes. Over recent years the once staid CBD has undergone a renaissance, with many older watering holes transformed into cool, sophisticated venues, and numerous alley bars popping up in tucked away pockets of the city – often hidden down a dark laneway but usually worth the effort.

In 2007 the government introduced a **smoking ban** in all pubs, bars, restaurants and enclosed spaces. Many establishments responded by adding outside smoking areas, heated with butane lamps in winter.

In general, bars stay **open** to around 1am during the week and 3am at weekends, while some clubs are open until 5am or 7am at the weekend. Some of the more upmarket places also have **dress codes** which are often rigidly enforced.

For online information, visit Ⓦwww.melbournepubs.com, which has a searchable guide to the city's drinking spots; otherwise *The Age Bar Guide* is available from bookshops. If you're interested in finding out how beer is made, Aussie-style, the **Carlton and United Beverages** in Abbotsford runs tours (see p.83).

Melbourne's **club culture** is as vibrant as its bar scene and all but the most resolute party animals will find plenty to keep them entertained, with most dance styles and genres, from house, techno and break-beat to indie and retro, catered for. The hot spots are **Chapel Street** in South Yarra and the **CBD**, but clubs take root anywhere they can, from big commercial nights in the suburbs to obscure experimental sessions in inner-city nooks and crannies. Overseas DJs visit frequently, and local talent keeps the scene thriving. The bigger the night, the more the **cover charge**, though it rarely tops $15 unless there's an international guest. For listings pick up a copy of Melbourne's essential free clubbing **guides** *Beat* and *Inpress* magazines from record shops, bars and fashion outlets. Also look out for posters on billboard sites around town, announcing the next big event.

The east side

For locations of the following see the map on p.40.

Bars and clubs

Cookie Level 1, 252 Swanston St ☎9663 7660.
Quirky but cool first-floor bar-restaurant,

Cookie successfully combines cocktail bar, beer hall and Thai restaurant in a large open space that still manages to feel dark and intimate. Daily noon–late.

The Croft Institute 21–25 Croft Alley, off Paynes Place, off Little Bourke St ☎ 9671 4399. Tucked down the end of a dark lane in Chinatown and spread over three floors, this place, with its notoriously oddball decor, was once a permanent fixture on the bar scene. Today much of the hype has died down but it's still worth a look to see the large collection of laboratory apparatus and hospital-style toilet, and the grass-topped bar. Mon–Thurs 5pm–1am, Fri 5pm–3am, Sat 8pm–3am.

Ding Dong Lounge 18 Market Lane ☎ 9662 1020. Sister bar to the rock 'n' roll hangout in New York but with a modern Australian touch and a varied line-up of local and touring international bands (see "Live Music"). Wed–Sat 7pm–late.

Gin Palace 10 Russell Place, off Little Collins St ☎ 9654 0533. Plush subterranean joint with an upmarket drinks list specializing in cocktails, especially martinis, and lounge music low enough to allow for conversation. Daily 4pm–3am.

Hairy Canary 212 Little Collins St ☎ 9654 2471. This modern, stylish bar is perfect for whiling away an afternoon or nursing a hangover, with an extensive menu available most of the day, plus cocktails and a wide range of local and imported beers and wines. Mon–Fri 7.30am–3am, Sat 9am–3am, Sun 9am–1am.

Loop 23 Meyers Place ☎ 9654 0500. Super-stylish venue and project space that's a big hit with the local intelligentsia and arty types. Apart from screening experimental films and shorts, there's a regular line-up of DJs dropping everything from new wave cuts and 1980s UK electronic pop to disco, techno and funk. Daily 3pm–late.

Lounge Upstairs 243 Swanston St ☎ 9663 2916. Veritable grandaddy of the inner-city scene, with the focus on cool tunes and a beatnik vibe. By day there are drinks and snacks and a chance to kick back and play a few games of pool, but late Wed–Sat the floor is cleared for techno, electro, disco, breakbeat and house club nights. The balcony is a treat on hot summer nights. Fri & Sat entry charge around $15. Mon–Fri 11am–late, Sat & Sun 1pm–late.

Madame Brussels Level 3, 59 Bourke St ☎ 9662 2775. Not knowing quite what awaits you is only half the fun as you ascend the lift to this ever-so kitsch bar. Imagine an indoor tea party on the gardens of Buckingham Palace – complete with astroturf and white wrought-iron garden furniture: camp it most definitely is. Lounge out with jugs of cocktails and fruit punch on the roof terrace, and if it gets chilly grab one of the blankets. Daily noon–late.

Melbourne Supper Club Level 1, 161 Spring St, City ☎ 9654 6300. This convivial upstairs lounge bar opposite Parliament House exudes an air of timeless decadence and attracts a lively mixed crowd. As well as an excellent wine list, the bar offers inexpensive food and deep leather Chesterfields. The perfect place to flop after a night of bar-hopping or post-theatre. Tues–Thurs 5pm–4am, Fri 5pm–6am, Sat 8pm–6am, Sun 8pm–4am, Mon 8pm–4am.

Meyers Place 20 Meyers Place, off Bourke St ☎ 9650 8609. Designed by Melbourne architectural firm Six Degrees, this swish, dimlylit hole-in-the-wall was one of the city's first laneway bars and remains a hit with Melbourne's trendy professionals, who often spill out onto the pavement. The grooviest place to fall down on a Friday night. Tues & Thurs 5pm–late, Fri & Sat 4pm–4am.

Misty 3–5 Hosier Lane, off Flinders St ☎ 9663 9202. On Melbourne's coolometer, *Misty* can't be beat. Most nights it is filled with students and assorted artists bathing in the soft glow of the bar's mood lighting – it changes colour and tone; just pull up a stool, pretend you're an architect, and you'll fit right in. Mystifyingly hard to find down a graffiti-covered alley, so look out for the gleaming light box at the entrance. Tues–Thurs 5pm–1am, Fri 5pm–3am, Sat 6pm–3am.

New Gold Mountain Level 1 & 2, 21 Liverpool St ☎ 9650 8859. Hidden behind an unassuming door and bereft of signage, this recently opened bar mixes colonial-era glamour with opium den chic. Upstairs the plush red Poppy Room offers table service. If you really like the place you can ask for a "keep bottle" which is stored behind the bar for your next visit. Mon–Fri 5pm–late, Sat 6pm–3pm, Sun 8pm–2am.

Phoenix 82 Flinders St ☎ 9650 4976. Funky and friendly bar covering four levels, from subterranean dance floor (DJs Fri & Sat) to the "quieter" top-floor lounge area. There are plenty of places to lose yourself here, while better-than-average bar food make it a popular haunt for the post-work crowd. Mon–Fri noon–late, Sat 5pm–late.

PUBS, BARS AND CLUBS | The east side

Purple Emerald 191 Flinders Lane ℡9650 7753. Funky space that often has live jazz-funk bands. The open-plan seating means it never feels too crowded. Mon–Fri 2pm–late, Sat 7.30pm–3am.

Spleen 41 Bourke St ℡9650 2400. A warren of a place, aimed at precocious party animals that fills up rapidly at weekends with folk warming up for a big night or having a drink after the movies. Features a varied programme of entertainment (no cover charge) from comedy to live music. Mon–Fri 4pm–3am, Sat & Sun 5pm–late.

Troika 106 Little Lonsdale St ℡9663 0221. Inner-city crowd meets suburban trendies and creative types in a relaxed, casual atmosphere with a selection of local and imported beers that will satisfy the most

discerning punter. Don't forget to do the "eye test" before you leave to gauge how much you've had to drink. Tues–Fri 4pm–late, Sat 5pm–late.

Pubs

Young & Jackson's Corner of Swanston & Flinders sts ℡9650 3884. Victoria's oldest and most famous boozer (see p.41) has a congenial café/bar area, plus two central bars and is a great place to start drinking your way around town. In winter, a boisterous footy crowd usually descends after matches. If you're looking for something more intimate, head upstairs to *Chloe's Bar*, whose stylish surroundings are tantalisingly comfortable. Daily 10am–late.

Irish and English Pubs

The list below covers just some of the Irish and English theme pubs that have sprouted across Melbourne – each offering atmosphere and entertainment, as well as cheap pub tucker that's a long way from fish fingers and baked beans on toast.

Bridie O'Reilly's 62 Little Collins St, City (east side) ℡9650 0840. See map, p.40. Above-average theme pub sporting lots of Emerald Isle gewgaws, and attracting hordes of customers with hearty, humungous dishes such as stew, steak, bangers and mash, and beef and Guinness pie. Cute upstairs seating area. Also at Chapel St, South Yarra (see map, p.88) and Sydney Rd, Brunswick. Daily 11.30am–late.

Charles Dickens Tavern 290 Collins St, City (west side) ℡9654 1821. See map, p.50. Cosy basement pub for homesick Brits, with bitter and Guinness on tap, pint glasses, and live soccer and rugby on a big-screen TV. Also rustles up excellent bar food at non-rip-off prices, with a more expensive sit-down restaurant to the side. Daily 10am–late.

The Irish Times 427 Little Collins St, City (west side) ℡9642 1699. See map, p.50. Striving to provide a real taste of Dublin, *The Irish Times* has simple, comfy decor, Australian/Irish cuisine and shows live sport on its TV screens. Mon–Thurs noon–midnight, Fri noon–3am, Sat 5.30pm–3am.

Pugg Mahones 106–112 Hardware Lane, City (west side) ℡9810 0060. See map, p.50. Irish theme pub with a great weekend party atmosphere fuelled by live music Mon, Fri & Sat, cheap drinks specials and the ubiquitous match crowds. Also on Elgin St, Carlton. Daily 11am–late.

The Elephant and Wheelbarrow 94–96 Bourke St, City (east side) ℡9639 8444. See map, p.40. English theme pub with timber booths, a log fire in winter, and photographs of the Beatles and Big Ben on the wall. The food is simple, wholesome and inexpensive. Its St Kilda sister pub (169 Fitzroy St ℡9534 7888; see map, p.92) has a Monday night "Meet the Neighbours", when stars of the Australian soap play trivia games, hand out prizes and generally rub shoulders with the punters. Daily 11am–late.

The west side

For locations of the following see the map on pp.50–51.

Bars and clubs

Bond Lounge 24 Bond St, off Flinders Lane ☎9629 9844. Sleek and roomy downstairs lounge bar, with an award-winning space-age design, and very high cool factor, where you can relax in a dark corner, and rub shoulders with beautiful media and fashion industry-types. Thurs 4pm–1am, Fri 4pm–3am, Sat 9pm–5am.

Bunker Lounge 407 Swanston St ☎9650 5099. The dimly lit stairs down to this basement bar set the tone of this hidden den, though once inside friendly staff, generous sofas and (most nights) local DJs await. Choose from daily bar specials of wine, beer and cocktails or order a shisha pipe and chill out in one of the booths. Mon–Fri 1pm–late, Sat 8pm–late.

Chaise Lounge 105 Queen St ☎9670 6120. Underground bar filled with opulent antique furnishings that's reminiscent of a resplendent boudoir – cushioned chaise longues aplenty and a soft warm glow of candles and table lamps. Popular after-work spot with drinks specials and an extensive list of cocktails and beers. DJs (Thurs–Sat) play a mix of house, soul, funk and up-tempo numbers to keep the crowds happy. Free entry before 10.30pm. Wed & Thurs 4pm–late, Fri 4pm–3am, Sat 9pm–3am.

Club Retro (Niagara Hotel) 383 Lonsdale St ☎9670 6575. Unpretentious club taking up two floors of the Niagara Hotel that's been pulling in the punters for over ten years. The 1970's style dancefloor is usually packed

from 11pm with people dancing to hits from 1970s through to the 1990s – great for perfecting your karaoke act. Entry $15. Fri & Sat 10pm–5am.

Ffour Level 2, 322 Little Collins St ☎9650 4494 Constructivist-inspired decor, a different music roster each night, and 2-4-1 drinks specials make this a popular hideout for after-work drinks and gaggles of party people. Wed 9pm–3am, Thurs–Sat 10pm–late.

La La Land level 1, corner of Hardware Lane & Little Lonsdale St ☎9670 5011. Resembling a 1970's lounge with a choice of warm-coloured velour couches, chairs, stools and cushions to sink into. DJs spin cool lounge-inspired sounds after 10pm. Mon–Thurs 5pm–late, Fri 1pm–late, Sat & Sun 7pm–late.

Rue Bebelons 267 Little Lonsdale St ☎9663 1700. So laid-back that the bar staff flip the vinyl in between serving drinks, this small and dimly lit place has friendly service and a simple but reasonably priced selection of beers and rolls. Mon 9am–8pm, Tues–Fri 9am–3am, Sat 11am–3am, Sun 1–11pm.

Tony Starr's Kitten Club Level 1, 267 Little Collins St ☎9650 2448. Definitely one for the ladies. Sit back in the sexy Love Lounge and work your way through the 100-strong cocktail list with concoctions such as the fabulously named Tina's Thai Tranny Trouble, or check out the music and cabaret nights at the sleek and stylish Galaxy Space with its 1950s/1960s-inspired interior. Good food too. Mon–Wed 4pm–11pm, Thurs 4pm–1am, Fri & Sat 4pm–3am.

The river district, South Melbourne and Albert Park

For locations of the following see the map on pp.58–59 unless otherwise stated.

Bars and clubs

Belgian Beer Café Bluestone 557 St Kilda Rd ☎9529 2899. Sprawl on the lawn with Belgian fries and mayonnaise or tuck into a bowl of mussels, meatballs or pork sausages inside this handsome nineteenth-century building housed within the grounds of Vision Australia. Five draught Belgian beers plus a large range of bottled beers served by super-efficient bar

staff. Large beer garden plus live music on Sun afternoons. Tram #16 from the city. Daily 11am–late.

The Butterfly Club 204 Bank St, South Melbourne ☎9690 2000, ⊛ www.thebutterfly club.com. See map, p.70. A dash of artsy cocktail bar mixed with a cabaret salon, the Butterfly Club is one of Melbourne's more camp environments. Keep an eye out for exotic Madame Sin and her merry band of mistresses. Nightly cabaret shows cost $15–25. Wed–Sun 5pm–late.

Transport Federation Square ☎ 9654 8808. See map, p.67. Enormous pub complex with a staggering range of beers (over 100) and good local wines on offer. Noisy and fun with DJs and live music most nights, it attracts a mixed crowd of suits, tourists and film school students. Daily 11am–late.

Bell's Hotel and Brewery 157 Moray St, South Melbourne ☎ 9690 4511. See map, p.70. Busy corner pub with four bars and a microbrewery that produces a range of award-winning brews; the Hell's Bell's (at six percent) is not to be trifled with. Great pub grub too. Mon–Sat 11am–late, Sun 11am–5pm.

Carlton and Fitzroy

For locations of the following see the map on p.74, unless otherwise stated.

Bars and clubs

Bar Open 317 Brunswick St, Fitzroy ☎ 9415 9601. See map, p.79. Cosy little bar attracting a chilled-out arty crowd who come to listen to live music most nights of the week. It is especially popular at weekends, when music of a more folksy or roots bent spills out into the rear courtyard. During the winter grab a couch and hole up in front of the open. No cover charge. Mon–Sat 1pm–3am, Sun 1pm–2am.

Carlton Yacht Club Bar 298 Lygon St, Carlton ☎ 9347 7080. See map, p.76. Decidedly landlocked, but seafaring kitsch, well-priced cocktails, a good beer list and tapas have this bar firmly moored as a favourite in local hearts. Mon–Wed & Sun 5pm–1am, Thurs–Sat 5pm–3am.

Lambsgo Bar 135 Greeves St, Fitzroy ☎ 8415 0511. Tucked just off Smith St within a lovely bluestone house, this is a paradise for beer lovers. Choose from one of 100 or so beers from around the world then find a pew in the warren of cubby-hole bars. Mon–Wed 5pm–late, Thurs–Sat 4pm–late, Sun 4–11pm.

Night Cat 141 Johnston St, Fitzroy ☎ 9417 0090. Nearly fifteen years since it opened, this retro-opulent venue still maintains a lived-in charm. Plenty of dimlylit tables and lounges for slouching, plus a large dance floor if you're taken by the live music, which ranges from swinging jazz and up-tempo Latin to hip hop, funk and reggae. Salsa lessons every Thurs & Sun from 7.30pm. Live Cuban band every Sun. Thurs–Sun 9pm–3am.

The Old Bar 74 Johnston St, Fitzroy ☎ 9417 4155. Lived-in bar that's popular with those in the know. There's an eclectic weekly schedule of live music, DJs, quiz nights, comedy and the odd cult movie; plus $10 jugs. Cover charge may apply some nights. Daily 4pm–4am.

Polly 401 Brunswick St, Fitzroy ☎ 9417 0880. See map, p.79. Bespectacled student types descend on this opulent velvet and rococo joint to colonize the large central bar, and finger through the comprehensive but pricey cocktail list. Smart dress code applies. Mon–Thurs & Sun 5pm–1am, Fri & Sat 5pm–3am.

Pubs

The Builders Arms Hotel 211 Gertrude St, Fitzroy ☎ 9419 0818. See map, p.79. Hip without being exclusive, *The Builders Arms* is more trendy bar than local pub with its bold colours, chill-out areas and funky lighting, especially at the weekend when a live DJ set pulls in the punters. The swanky dining room out the back dishes up Modern Australian/ Middle Eastern cuisine (Mon–Thurs from 6pm, Fri & Sat noon–3pm, Sun 2–9pm), and there's a barbeque every Sunday. Mon–Thurs 6pm–10pm, Fri–Sun noon–late.

The Gertrude Hotel 148 Gertrude St, Fitzroy ☎ 9419 2823. See map, p.79. This is the closest thing you'll get to a local pub on Gertrude St; brown leather couches, open fire, funky beer garden and multicuisine menu (daily noon–3pm, 5.30–10pm). It also puts on nightly specials such as Tuesday's $10 parma (chicken parmigiana) and pasta and "wing" Wednesday. Mon–Sat noon–1am, Sun noon–11pm.

The Hotel Lincoln 91 Cardigan St, Carlton ☎ 9437 4666. Friendly, traditional corner pub just off Lygon St renowned for its excellent food and laid-back ambience. The vibrantly red front bar is a great place to chill out with

a glass of wine and has a well-priced bar menu. There's also a fine dining restaurant out the back (Mon–Fri noon–2.30pm & 6–9pm, Sat 6–9pm). Mon–Thurs noon–11pm, Fri noon–midnight, Sat 5.30pm–midnight.
The Napier Hotel 210 Napier St, Fitzroy ☎9419 4240. Small, eclectic pub with friendly

▲ The Napier Hotel

service and several beers on tap. The cosy lounge with pool table and roaring fire is perfect for a winter's day, as is the small outside area during warmer months. There's also down-to-earth grub at reasonable prices – try the enormous Bogan Burger, a chicken schnitzel, steak, egg and potato cake – plus the kitchen keeps long hours. Mon–Thurs 3–11pm, Fri 1pm–1am, Sat 1pm–1am, Sun 1–11pm.
The Rainbow Hotel 27 St David St, Fitzroy ☎9419 4193. Cosy little boozer under new management featuring free live music from local bands (see p.138). Although crowded at weekends, the bar is comfortable and relaxing, and the bands aren't so loud as to spoil conversation, there's also a beer garden. Daily noon–1am.
The Standard Hotel 293 Fitzroy St, Fitzroy ☎9419 4793. Fitzroy's quintessential local, frequented by regulars and feeling a world apart from the Brunswick St crowd, with a large landscaped beer garden and a decent pub menu to boot. Students and locals alike come here to soak up the authentic pub feel. Mon & Tues 3pm–11pm, Wed–Sun noon–11pm.

Collingwood, Richmond and the east

For locations of the following see the map on p.82.

Bars and clubs

A Bar Called Barry 64 Smith St, Collingwood ☎8415 1464. Barry (to his mates) has become a Collingwood institution thanks to its large indoor space, mezzanined dance-floor and resident DJs playing a mix of indie (Thurs), 80s retro and cheesy pop (Fri), RnB and chart hits (Sat) – the kind of place where DJs take requests. Free entry. Thurs–Sat 9pm–5am.
Der Raum 438 Church St, Richmond ☎9428 0055. Small and intimate bar that prides itself on only using the best spirits from around the world and no post-mixed syrups or cordials, just fresh juices. You won't find any cream cocktails here; only sophisticated mixology. Tues–Sat 5.30pm–1am.
The Horn 20 Johnston St, Collingwood ☎9417 4670. African music lounge that rambles through three rooms out the back of a converted house and plays host to live jazz, African, ska and reggae bands most nights.

There's also a kitchen serving cheap Ethiopian food, with a good selection of veggie options too. Wed–Fri 7pm–late, Sat & Sun 2pm–late.

Pubs

All Nations Hotel 64 Lennox St, Richmond ☎9428 1564. Traditional and largely unchanged Melbourne pub, complete with horseshoe bar, a "snug", and a hugely popular dining room out back serving great Modern Australian food (lunch & dinner daily) and a courtyard. Daily noon–11pm.
🏃 **The Cherry Tree Hotel 53 Balmain St, Richmond** ☎9428 5743. Hidden away in the backstreets of Richmond and surrounded by ad agencies, this unpretentious gem of a pub sees a steady stream of locals and media bods alike – especially on a Friday afternoon. There's a spacious front bar replete with soft brown leather couches and a curved long bar, plus a contemporary

bistro out the back. Worth seeking out. Mon–Wed noon–midnight, Thurs–Sat noon–1am.

Grace Darling Hotel 114 Smith St, Collingwood ☎9416 0055. With its extensive pub menu, nightly specials and open fires this attractive bluestone pub is a great place to while away the hours. Footy fans will be interested to know this was the first meeting place of Collingwood Football Club back in 1892. Mon noon–9pm, Tues–Fri noon–11pm, Fri & Sat noon–midnight, Sun 2–9.30pm.

Great Britain 477 Church St, Richmond ☎9429 5066. Grungy, lived-in pub with comfy couches, pool tables and a beer garden for

hot summer nights, there's also a basement bar for weekend DJ sessions. Possibly the only pub you can get a pint of PISS – the pub's homebrewed beer – on tap. Or try PISS weak, the light brew. Mon–Thurs & Sun 4pm–midnight, Fri 4pm–3am, Sat noon–3am.

The Public House 433 Church St, Richmond ☎9421 0187. Ultra chic but with a remarkably relaxed vibe, *The Public* also has an excellent bar menu and bistro-style seating upstairs if you fancy some food with your drinks. On warm nights head upstairs to the roof terrace, which is heated in winter. Mon–Thurs & Sun noon–midnight, Fri & Sat noon–2am.

South Yarra, Prahran and Toorak

For locations of the following see the map on p.88.

Bars and clubs

Back Bar 67 Green St, Windsor ☎9529 7899. Opulent lounge bar that's reminiscent of a grand manor drawing room. The off-street red lounge bar has rich furnishings, soft cushioned couches, gilt mirrors and a roaring log fire in winter, while upstairs the gold lounge offers much the same but in, you guessed it, gold, with DJs spinning house and upbeat tunes at weekends till the small hours. Renowned for its relaxed, friendly vibe and excellent cocktail list – at least 60 to choose from – you won't want to leave. Tues–Sun 5pm–late.

Blue Bar 330 Chapel St, Prahran ☎9529 6499. Other places may come and go but this lively bar remains a Chapel St institution that spills out onto the street at weekends, with groovers checking each other out while sipping mineral water. Good range of local and imported beers, as well as decent pizzas to line your stomach. DJs most nights. Mon–Wed & Sun noon–1am, Thurs–Sat noon–3am.

Borsch, Vodka and Tears 173 Chapel St, Prahran ☎6530 2694. Wonderfully intimate vodka bar and café with over 100 vodkas on offer and a range of Polish and Russian faves on the menu such as blintzes, pierogi, sausages and goulash. Mon–Wed 8.30am–1am, Thurs & Fri 8.30am–3am, Sat 9.30am–3am, Sun 9.30am–midnight.

Candy Bar 162 Greville St, Prahran ☎9529 6566. Funky and spacious and attracting a twenty-something, party-going crowd – you won't find teenagers in fluoro T-shirts here – the *Candy Bar* is a good place to head for some solid drinking and dancing. Dress up, however, or you may have trouble getting past the fashion police at the door. Also a popular café by day with diners sitting on comfy sofas under mirror balls. $5 cover charge at weekends. Mon–Fri noon–late, Sat & Sun 10am–late.

Hoo Haa Bar 105 Chapel St, Windsor ☎9529 6900. Hidden away behind an unassuming door off busy Chapel St, this first-floor bar is quite a find (if indeed you can find it). Chill out in the spacious bar or courtyard, or tuck in to hearty Italian-influenced fare from the kitchen. DJs Thurs–Sun. Tues–Thurs 4pm–1am, Fri & Sat 4pm–2am, Sun noon–1am.

Mosq 2/60 Bray St, South Yarra ☎9533 2181. Cosy Moroccan-themed bar furnished with day-beds, cushions and hanging lamps. A great place to stop by during the week (it's closed for functions at weekends) for tapas, shisha and cocktails – the blueberry lychee martinis are excellent. Mon–Thurs 5pm–midnight.

Onesixone Level 1, 161 High St, Prahran ☎9533 8433. One of the coolest clubs south of the river and a veritable 1970s den – shagpile carpet, volumes of vinyl and gold walls as far as the eye can see. Cover charge $10 to $15. Thurs–Sun 9pm–late.

Revolver Upstairs 229 Chapel St, Prahran
℡ 9521 5985, Ⓦ www.revolverupstairs.com.au. Revolver has established itself as a popular venue with Melbourne's drinking and partying crowd. Live bands and cult electronic beat DJs and artists create a cool vibe most nights (modest cover charge). You can grab a snack in the Thai restaurant, lounge around with a drink in the spacious main area, or chill out in the back room where the DJs play. Entry from $5–10. Tues–Thurs 5pm–3am, Fri 5pm through to Sat noon, non-stop DJs, Sat 5pm–late.

The Viper Room 373 Chapel St, South Yarra
℡ 9827 1771. A young, body-conscious crowd, progressive trance, big beats and hard techno. Glam every Sat plays a mix of house, electro and RnB. Fri & Sat 10pm–7am.

Pubs

Windsor Castle Hotel 89 Albert St, Windsor
℡ 9525 0239. Tucked away in a residential area of Windsor, the revamped take on pub-grub classics, velour seating and the open fire and beer garden make this a great place to stop for a while. Check out the pink elephants on the lime green roof. Mon–Thurs 3–11pm, Fri & Sat noon–1am, Sun noon–11pm.

St Kilda

For locations of the following see the map on p.92.

Bars and clubs

Dog's Bar 54 Acland St, St Kilda ℡ 8534 3000. One of the first bars in St Kilda, and as popular as ever, even if its distressed paint finish and fake cracks are beginning to look more genuine with every year. Terrific wine list, over 15 bottled beers and good tucker. The wrought-iron terrace out front is the perfect place for eyeballing passers-by, especially on a sunny afternoon. Mon–Fri noon–1am, Sat & Sun 10am–1am.

Doulton Bar 202 Barkly St, St Kilda ℡ 9534 2200. Part of the *Village Belle Hotel*. Ignore the front bar and head for the old-fashioned *Doulton Bar* – via a discreet door next to the bottle shop – for a relaxing oasis away from the St Kilda crowds, with a one-way window overlooking the street. Sun–Wed 1pm–1am, Thurs–Sat 1pm–3am.

The George Public Bar 127 Fitzroy St, St Kilda ℡ 9534 8822. Long-established underground bar with an upbeat design in contrast to its wine bar (see p.124). Favoured by locals, travellers and artists, it has a large range of beers on tap, a pool table, free live music on Saturday 4–7pm and Sun 6–10pm, and a trivia night every Mon. The service is friendly and the kitchen is open until around 10pm, serving a wide range of snacks and good-value meals ($10 deals Mon–Thurs). Mon–Thurs 4pm–2am, Fri & Sat noon–3am, Sun noon–1am.

Mink Bar The Prince St Kilda, 2b Acland St ℡ 9536 1199. Carved out of the remade part of *The Prince St Kilda*, this subterranean space has back-lit refrigerated shelves stacked high with an astonishing array of vodkas in a variety of flavours. There are also private booths for intimate chats. A great place for convivial quaffing and mellowing, as long as you are dressed smartly enough to make it past the door staff. Daily 6pm–late.

Next Level @ Hotel Barkly 109 Barkly St, St Kilda ℡ 9525 3354. Located on the fourth floor of the popular Hotel Barkly, the Next Level offers more than a brew with a view. Stylish, modern space with soft white couches, floor-to-ceiling windows and a balcony that affords amazing views over St Kilda, along with cool vibes to match. Downstairs, the public bar with regular pub hours is the laid-back brother, but just as pleasing to the eye. Fri 6pm–late & Sun 4pm–late.

Pause 268 Carlisle St, Balaclava ℡ 9537 0511. Moorish-themed decor, fab cocktails, and a great Moroccan-influenced bar menu with mezzes to share and friendly local feel. Mon–Fri 4pm–1am, Sat & Sun noon–1am.

Tongue and Groove 16 Grey St, St Kilda ℡ 9534 9205. With a nightly programme of club nights from indie to retro, a deafening sound system, cheap drinks and a late close, this is a popular place with backpackers from the nearby hostels. Moderate cover charge $2–5. Daily 9pm–5am.

Veludo 175 Acland St, St Kilda ☎9534 4456. A magnet for St Kilda's fashionable crowd, *Veludo* sports a bar upstairs, its exposed brick walls and cool lighting lending it a funky warehouse feel. Spacious and stylish, it really gathers steam at the weekends. Downstairs there is a smart restaurant (see p.125). Mon–Fri 5pm–2am, Sat & Sun 3pm–3am.

Pubs

The Esplanade Hotel 11 Upper Esplanade, St Kilda ☎9534 0211. Famous for its beachside views, this hotel is the epicentre of St Kilda's drinking scene and shouldn't be missed. Bands play every night and there are inexpensive meals from *The Espy Kitchen* (see p.124), plus pool tables and pinball machines. Mon–Thurs & Sun noon–2am, Fri & Sat noon–3am.

The Prince Public Bar 29 Fitzroy St, St Kilda ☎9536 1177. Defiantly no-frills, the downstairs public bar at *The Prince of Wales* is the antithesis of the *Mink Bar* (see p.133) and exudes an air of stubborn resistance in the face of St Kilda's freewheeling gentrification. Frequented in equal parts by colourful local personalities and desperadoes, this hotel is not for the faint-hearted, especially on match days. Mon–Wed noon–2am, Thurs–Sun noon–3am.

Live music

M elbourne has arguably the best live **music scene** in Australia. Every night of the week scores of bands play at venues around the city, covering everything from grunge rock and retro to blues, jazz, folk and avante-garde. Despite an inner-city culture of gentrification which threatened some of the city's best rock venues, replacing PA systems with pokies (slot machines) and DJ booths, as well as an increase in noise complaints that forced many places to cancel loud bands, Melbourne's music scene has remained healthy and remarkably resilient. The city has the largest concentration of live music venues in Australia.

With a little inside knowledge, you can catch one of the bigger and more expensive touring acts for next to nothing at one of the "secret shows" that abound at the city's smaller venues. Label-wise, the seminal Melbourne-based Mushroom Records (see box, below) was responsible for launching the vocal talents of both indie and mainstream singers such as Kylie Minogue and Peter Andre onto an unsuspecting world.

Melbourne music

The city's **rock and pop** heritage is a rich one. During the 1970s and 1980s, Melbourne spewed forth numerous high-calibre bands like the Skyhooks, Daddy Cool, the Sports, incendiary punk-blues outfit The Birthday Party and sweaty pub-rock stalwarts Hunters and Collectors, while Powderfinger, The Cat Empire and the AC/DC-inspired Jet all got their start on the local live music scene before breaking into the charts.

Until its sale in 1998, **Mushroom Records** was the largest independent record label in Australia, handling over four hundred local artists, with over eight thousand releases and sales of more than eight million. The label was founded in 1972 by Michael Gudinski, an ambitious 19-year-old who quickly rose to become the most successful entrepreneur in the Australian music industry. His encouragement of domestic talent spawned a whole swag of memorable pop songs, including Split Enz's "I Got You" (their album True Colours was the label's first international hit), Skyhooks' "Living in the '70s", Paul Kelly's "Before Too Long" and Kylie Minogue's "I Should Be So Lucky". Gudinski's patronage of Australian music gave exposure to Melbourne-based acts the Sports, Black Sorrows and Hunters and Collectors, while others such as Nick Cave and Peter Andre also graced the Mushroom roster, delivering several no. 1 UK hits and contributing substantial revenue to the label's coffers.

Twenty-six years of Mushroom Records ended when Gudinski flogged his remaining stake to News Limited for $40 million. As a last hurrah, Gudinski staged a mammoth "Concert of the Century" at the MCG, where groups ground their way through past Mushroom songs to over 70,000 dewy-eyed fans.

Comprehensive gig listings of bands and venues can be found in the free *Beat* and *Inpress* magazines, available from cafés, record shops and fashion boutiques in the inner city, or the "EG" insert in the Friday edition of *The Age*. Probably the best listings, however, are found in the *Herald Sun*, Melbourne's other daily, which has an excellent liftout called "Hit" every Thursday. You can also tune into one of Melbourne's community radio stations, such as 3RRR (102.7 FM) or 3PBS (106.7 FM), and there's a good gig guide available on Triple J radio's website (Ⓦtriplej.yourevents.com.au).

For larger events you may need to **book in advance** through Ticketmaster (Ⓣ13 61 00, Ⓦwww.ticketmaster.com.au) or Ticketek (Ⓣ13 28 49, Ⓦpremier .ticketek.com.au), or at music stores (see p.166). At pubs and smaller venues you can pay at the door; entry to gigs ranges from about $12 to $50 depending on the calibre of the band.

In summer, Melbourne hosts a number of outdoor **music festivals**, including the groovy Good Vibrations (see p.147) and the national and international line-up of Big Day Out (see p.146).

The city is also blessed with a fine **classical music** scene. The Melbourne Symphony Orchestra gives regular performances at the Melbourne Concert Hall in the Victorian Arts Centre (see p.61) and the Melbourne Town Hall (see p.41). Opera Australia (Ⓦwww.opera-australia.org.au) has productions during the season (March–May & Nov–Dec) at the State Theatre in the Arts Centre, while chamber music can be heard at Hamer Hall and Melbourne Town Hall. Expect to pay $40–90 for classical music performances, $60–150 for opera; tickets can be obtained from Ticketmaster or Ⓦwww.mytickets.com.au.

Indie and mainstream rock

City Centre

See the map on p.40.

Ding Dong Lounge Level 1, 18 Market Lane Ⓣ**9662 1020.** The kind of bar The Strokes would feel right at home in – full of cool rock 'n' roll types, with padded booths lining the walls and beer taps shaped like guitar necks. Plays host to international and local bands (cover charge applies). Once they've finished expect a soundtrack of loud, classy rock favourites or regular DJs playing more dancy tunes. Wed–Sat 7pm–late.

The Forum Theatre 154 Flinders St, City Ⓣ**9299 9700,** Ⓦ**www.marrinerstheatres.com.au.** Opposite Federation Square, this grand old theatre with its distinctive copper-domed clock and grandiose interior opened in 1929 and today is the place for popular touring big-name international live bands.

The Hi Fi Bar and Ballroom 125 Swanston St Ⓣ**9654 7617,** Ⓦ**www.thehifi.com.au.** Reason- ably spacious underground space with two bars on different levels where you can view acts in relative comfort, as well as an overheated mosh-pit below. A mainstay venue for high-profile local and international indie-rock bands such as The Fratellis and The Kooks.

Palace Theatre 20–30 Bourke St Ⓣ**9650 0180,** Ⓦ**www.palace.com.au.** Recently relocated from its St Kilda location, the *Palace* has taken over the former *Metro* nightclub and re-established the place as a venue for big-name international indie and rock bands, as well as lesser known acts. Renovations have restored much of the theatre to its former glory including retaining a number of its Art Deco features.

Pony 68 Little Collins St Ⓣ**9662 1026.** "Shout 'til you're a little horse". Small and grungy place that plays host to indie, punk and rock bands from around 9pm, and DJs to finish the night off. Thurs 5pm–5am, Fri 5pm–7am, Sat 8pm–7am.

Carlton and Fitzroy

The Arthouse Corner of Elizabeth & Queensberry sts, Carlton Ⓣ**9347 3917,** Ⓦ**www .thearthouse.com.** See map, p.74. A bit of a dive, with punk and metal bands six nights of the week aimed squarely at those who like their music at ear-bleeding volumes. Despite its hardcore credentials, poetry readings and and comedy are also held here every Mon. Open 4pm.

The Empress Hotel 714 Nicholson St, North Fitzroy ☎9489 8605, ⓦwww.theempress hotel.com.au. See map, p.74. A mecca for Melbourne's emerging bands, featuring anything from electronica to folk and rock, with a friendly, low-key atmosphere, cheap meals and occasional screenings of cult films. Modest cover charge from $5. To reach North Fitzroy, take tram #96.

Evelyn Hotel 351 Brunswick St, Fitzroy ☎9419 5500. See map, p.79. Stalwart of the Fitzroy scene, the cave-like Evelyn is a good introduction to Melbourne's alt-rock bands, who play here nightly (cover charge of $10–25 usually applies). Good beer garden.

Collingwood and Richmond

See the map on p.82.

The Corner Hotel 57 Swan St, Richmond ☎9427 9198, ⓦwww.cornerhotel.com. Typical live music venue: dark and grungy hotel complete with sticky carpet and two bars (one on the roof) showcasing local and international bands, mostly of a geetar-toting indie-rock persuasion. Tickets $12–50.

▲ Live music at the Tote Hotel

The Tote 71 Johnston St (corner of Johnston and Wellington sts), Collingwood ☎9419 5320, ⓦwww.thetotehotel.com. Classic Melbourne rock 'n' roll venue, with sharp-tongued staff, stained carpet and plastic beer glasses. Home to Melbourne's punk and hardcore scene, with nightly bands that will blow your socks off. If you've ever owned a Ramones record, this is the place for you. Even the jukebox selection is cool. Entry $4–14.

Prahran

See the map on p.88.

Revolver 229 Chapel St, Prahran ☎9521 5985, ⓦwww.revolverupstairs.com.au. Catering mainly to a garage, punk and hard rock crowd, Revolver has bands Wed–Sat, and also doubles as a nightclub (see p.133). Always something going on and plenty of room to dance.

St Kilda

See the map on p.92.

The Esplanade Hotel 11 Upper Esplanade, St Kilda ☎9534 0211, ⓦwww.espy.com.au. Long-established fixture in Melbourne's pub-rock and drinking scene, attracting both established and fledgling acts. Bands nightly, either free in the front bar, or with a nominal cover charge in the Gershwin Room at the rear. No frills, but iconic – playing at the Espy is almost a rite of passage – and hugely enjoyable.

The Greyhound Hotel 1 Brighton Rd, St Kilda ☎9534 4189, ⓦwww.greyhoundhotel.com.au. A bit seedy, but still a good place to see established local artists as well as younger bands strutting their stuff. Bands nightly, with an emphasis on stripped-down rock 'n' roll, competing with great drag shows on Saturday nights and karaoke on Sunday night. There's usually a cover charge ($10–12).

The Prince Bandroom 29 Fitzroy St ☎9536 1168, ⓦwww.princebandroom.com.au. This historic live music venue that's part of the *Prince Public Bar* (see p.134) has been going for over fifty years. Generally haunted by Melbourne and overseas band rats, it also attracts international DJs and hip-hop acts. Touring artists such as Coldplay often use the venue for "secret shows". Tickets $25–75).

Blues and folk

City Centre

Manchester Lane 36 Manchester Lane, off Flinders Lane ⊤9663 0630, ⓦwww .manchesterlane.com.au. See map, p.40. Popular purpose-built, split-level, amphitheatre-style venue that has a small dance floor, comfy tables and booths, plus a good range of predominantly local acts playing a range of genres from folk and jazz to acoustic, funk and swing. Open daily for food and drinks, with music from 8pm; cover charge $10–15.

Fitzroy

The Rainbow Hotel 27 St David St, Fitzroy ⊤9419 4193. See map, p.74. Comfy, intimate pub (see p.131) with a mellow atmosphere and interesting crowd, not to mention a good selection of live blues, jazz, funk and roots from local bands four or five nights a week, including Saturday. No cover charge.

Jazz

City Centre

Bennetts Lane 25 Bennetts Lane, off Little Lonsdale St ⊤9663 2856, ⓦwww .bennettslane.com. See map, p.40. One of Melbourne's more interesting jazz venues, Bennett's Lane has recently been expanded to include a larger back room to complement the original cramped, archetypal 1950s-style cellar. Most nights feature high-quality local and touring acts, which play to knowledgeable and appreciative audiences. Open daily from 8.30pm. Entry is from $12.

Richmond

Dizzy's 381 Burnley St, Richmond ⊤9428 1233, ⓦwww.dizzys.com.au. See map, p.82. Dizzy's blasts out contemporary jazz courtesy of local, national and international acts. Comprising a main bar that hosts bands nightly (8pm Tues–Thurs, 9pm Fri & Sat), and breakfast sessions (11am Sun). Bar snacks and food available, plus Sun brunch menu. Tues–Thurs 5.30–11pm, Sat 5.30pm–12.30am, Sun 11am–3pm. Free jam sessions Fri & Sat 5.30pm to 8pm, after which a cover charge of $8–16 applies.

Gay Melbourne

A
ttitudes to gays, lesbians and transgendered people in Australia are among the most relaxed in the world. With one of the highest official populations of same-sex couples in the world, it's hardly surprising that Melbourne is so gay-friendly. Pockets of gay and lesbian life exist all over inner-city Melbourne, especially along **Commercial Road**, which bisects the suburbs of Prahran and South Yarra and houses nightclubs, bookstores, boutiques, cafés and gymnasiums. Saturday morning at **Prahran Market** is the time to people-watch, while **Smith Street** in Collingwood also offers a large eclectic range of gay-oriented eateries, retail outlets and night-spots. There are **gay beaches** at South Melbourne, at the end of Kerford Road (known as "Screech Beach"), and at Port Melbourne, near the sand dunes, while the beaches at Elwood and St Kilda are also popular.

Festivals to watch out for are the fabulous **Midsumma Festival** (early Feb, see p.146), which has a wide range of sporting, artistic and theatrical events, as well as a Pride March, in multiple venues throughout the city; and the **Melbourne Queer Film and Video Festival** (mid-March; ⓦwww.melbournequeerfilm .com.au). Out of town there's the **ChillOut Festival** (ⓦwww.chilloutfestival .com.au) held in Daylesford (see p.204) every March, three days of partying, including market stalls, dog shows and tug of war events.

Melbourne Community Voice (MCV), a free weekly **gay and lesbian newspaper**, is available locally at gay and lesbian venues, bookshops and gay-friendly businesses, where you will also find free interstate newspapers and guides to sights and activities. Melbourne's best **gay bookshop**, Hares and Hyenas (ⓣ9495 6589, ⓦwww.hares-hyenas.com.au), is at 63 Johnston St,

Gay organizations and support groups

Melbourne is blessed with a dazzling variety of gay and lesbian organizations, support services and businesses, the most important of which are listed below. Everything else, from gay vets to lesbian psychologists, can be found in the ALSO Directory (see below).

ALSO Foundation Level 8, 225 Bourke St, City (ⓣ9660 3900, ⓦwww.also.org.au). Organizes events and publishes the ALSO Directory of businesses and community groups, free from community outlets.

Gay and Lesbian Switchboard Victoria (Mon, Tues & Thurs 6–10pm, Wed 2–10pm, Fri, Sat & Sun 6–9pm; ⓣ9663 2939, ⓦwww.switchboard.org.au) for counselling, referral and information.

Women's Information and Referral Exchange Queen Victoria Women's Centre, 210 Lonsdale St, City (WIRE; Mon–Fri 9am–5pm; ⓣ1300 134 130, ⓦwww.wire.org.au). Information about lesbian groups, referral to female doctors, solicitors, and the like.

Fitzroy. It also has an online bookshop and book review magazine covering lesbian, bisexual, transgender, gay, feminist and homosexual literature.

Other good sources of **information** are Gay and Lesbian Tourism Australia (Ⓦwww.galta.com.au); Tourism Victoria (Ⓦwww.visitvictoria.com); and *Over the Rainbow*, a guide to the law for lesbians and gay men in Victoria (available from Victoria Legal Aid; Ⓦwww.over-the-rainbow.org); or you can tune into Joy Melbourne 94.9 FM, Australia's only full-time queer radio station. Alternatively, check out the organizations and groups listed below.

Entry to pubs and clubs in the following listings is free most nights of the week, although a door charge (no more than $15) may apply at the weekend.

Accommodation

For more accommodation possibilities, check out **Gay Share** (Ⓦwww .gayshare.com.au), which arranges house shares for gays and lesbians, or visit the Gay and Lesbian Accommodation website at Ⓦwww.galavic.com for places to stay around Victoria.

169 Drummond 169 Drummond St, Carlton ☎9663 3081, Ⓦwww.169drummond.com.au. See map, p.74 Carlton & Fitzroy. Discreet B&B in a two-storey refurbished Victorian terrace house. Fours rooms with ensuite. ❺

The Laird 149 Gipps St, Abbotsford ☎9417 2832, Ⓦwww.lairdhotel.com. See map, p.82 Collingwood & Richmond. One of Melbourne's oldest gay hotels (see opposite), *The Laird* has large, comfortable rooms upstairs, some with en suite, for gay

men only. Rates include continental breakfast. The service is especially helpful with tips on nightspots and local eateries. ❹

Prahran Village Guest House 39 Perth St, Prahran ☎9533 6559 Ⓦwww.guestlink.com .au. See map, p.88 South Yarra, Toorak & Prahran. Private boutique B&B close to the bars and cafés of Chapel St and Commercial Rd, with four en-suite rooms in tasteful neutral tones and modern bathrooms. ❻

Cafés

Jackie O 204 Barkly St, St Kilda ☎9537 0377. See map, p.92 St Kilda. St Kilda's first recognized gay café, Jackie O quickly rose to become the most popular place to be gay (and be seen) in Melbourne. Nowadays it's frequented by gay and straight alike,

attracted by its food – especially the breakfasts – cocktails, retro decor and relaxed atmosphere, while the view along Acland St is well worth the price of a drink from the bar. Daily 7.30am–late.

Pubs, bars and clubs

Many venues in Melbourne are not exclusively gay or straight but are home to an easy-going mixed crowd, some hosting exclusively gay and lesbian nights, such as GirlBar (Ⓦwww.girlbar.com.au) held once a month at the *Prince of Wales* (see p.134).

DT's Hotel 164 Church St, Richmond ☎9428 5724. See map, p.82 Collingwood & Richmond. Friendly pub that attracts a mixed-gay crowd and hosts drag shows every Sat as well as other gay-themed events from barbeques to pool competitions.

Daily happy hour drinks specials and music. Tues–Sat 4pm–late, Sun 2pm–11pm.

The Glasshouse Hotel 51 Gipps St, Collingwood ☎9419 4748. See map, p.82 Collingwood & Richmond. Stylishly revamped hotel with a relaxed and friendly vibe that's popular with

Melbourne's pool-playing lesbians and their admirers. Good, inexpensive meals, and a regular programme of live music, DJs and cabaret. Wed, Thurs & Sun 5pm–late, Fri & Sat 5pm–5am.

The Laird 149 Gipps St, Abbotsford ☎ 9417 2832. See map, p.82 Collingwood & Richmond. Operating for over thirty years, Melbourne's sole men-only pub attracts a mainly leather crowd, and has three bars, DJs, a beer garden and pool room. Regular events include leather and bear parties. The atmosphere is relaxed and welcoming, and accommodation is also available (see opposite). Mon–Thurs 5pm–1am, Fri & Sat 5pm–3am, Sun 5pm–midnmight.

The Market 143 Commercial Rd, South Yarra ☎ 9826 0933. See map, p.88 South Yarra, Toorak & Prahran Dance club for men only with DJs playing mainly house and dancers on stage. Fri 10pm–8am & Sat 10pm–11am.

Opium Den 176 Hoddle St, Collingwood ☎ 9417 2696. See map, p.82 Collingwood & Richmond. Popular venue hosting drag queens and kings, cabaret and trans shows. Attracts a mixed crowd most nights, while Saturday is girls-only featuring girl DJs and shows. Lotus Night every Wednesday is the hotel's longest running night for Asian men, with shows and DJs. A modest cover charge usually applies. Wed–Sun 9pm–late.

The Peel Corner of Peel & Wellington sts, Collingwood ☎ 9419 4762. See map, p.82 Collingwood & Richmond Busy, gay venue with a dance floor, pumping grooves, and lots of disco lights. No cover charge. Thurs–Sat 9pm–dawn.

Xchange Hotel 119 Commercial Rd, South Yarra ☎ 9867 5144. See map, p.88 South Yarra, Toorak & Prahran. Men-only drinking and dancing spot with chill-out bar and large video screens. Drag shows Wed–Sun. Mon, Thurs & Sun 4pm–late, Fri & Sat 2pm–3am.

⑬

GAY MELBOURNE | Pubs, bars and clubs

14

Theatre, comedy and cinema

M elbourne's standing as the centre of Australian **theatre** has been recognized since 1871, when visiting English novelist Anthony Trollope remarked on the city's excellent venues and variety of performances. Nowadays, you can see a host of quality productions most nights of the week, from big musicals to experimental drama. And, judging by box-office returns, they're generally well supported. **Tickets** can be booked through Ticketmaster (☎13 61 00, ⓦ www.ticketmaster.com.au) and Ticketek Victoria (☎13 28 49, ⓦ premier.ticketek.com.au), while Half-Tix (Mon 10am–2pm, Tues–Thurs 11am–6pm, Fri 11am–6.30pm, Sat 10am–4pm; ☎9650 9420), in the Melbourne Town Hall, has discounted tickets (cash only) on the day of performance. A highlight of the city's theatrical year is the **Melbourne Arts Festival** (see p.49), which runs for a couple of weeks in late October.

Melbourne is still the heart of Australian **comedy**, with regular performances by home-grown and overseas comedians in pubs and clubs. A definite highlight is the **Melbourne International Comedy Festival** (see p.148) in late April, when more than a thousand comics converge on the city.

There are plenty of mainstream **cinemas** in Melbourne, mostly in and around Bourke Street, as well as a number of plush arthouses. Tickets are usually cheaper on Tuesdays and, in some places, Mondays too. The centrepiece of Melbourne movie life is the annual **Melbourne International Film Festival** (see p.148), which runs for two weeks from late July in venues like ACMI, Kino and the Forum, showcasing hundreds of local and international releases.

For theatre, comedy and cinema **listings**, check *The Age* (especially Friday's comprehensive arts and entertainment guide, "EG") and "Hit", the Thursday supplement of the *Herald Sun*.

Theatre

Athenaeum Theatre 188 Collins St, City ☎9650 1500, ⓦ www.melbourneathenaeum.org.au. See map, p.40. Built in 1842, the Athenaeum Theatre stages everything from Shakespearean drama to comedy and fringe performances.

CUB Malthouse 113 Sturt St, South Melbourne ☎9685 5111, ⓦ www.malthousetheatre.com.au. See map, p.58. Former brewery now transformed into state-of-the-art performance-and-gallery complex. Contains the small 200-seater Beckett Theatre, the larger

▲ Foyer, Como cinema

Merlyn Theatre and the Tower Room. The resident company – the Malthouse Theatre – produce contemporary Australian plays. To get there, take tram #1 from Swanston St or St Kilda Rd.

Her Majesty's Theatre 219 Exhibition St, City ☎8643 3300, ⊛www.hmt.com.au. See map, p.40. Fabulously ornate theatre built in 1886. Now features popular productions like *Chicago* and *Billy Elliot*.

La Mama 205 Faraday St, Carlton ☎9347 6948, ⊛www.lamama.com.au. See map, p.76. A Carlton institution for over forty years, La Mama hosts low-budget, innovative works by local playwrights. Ticket prices are probably the cheapest in town.

Playhouse Theatre Victorian Arts Centre, 100 St Kilda Rd, City ☎9281 8000, ⊛www .theartscentre.com.au. See map, p.58. One of the Victorian Arts Centre's Theatre Buildings, the Playhouse offers a wide-ranging choice of programmes, from musical comedy to Shakespeare, as well as plays by the renowned and very popular Melbourne Theatre Company, whose work is usually performed at the smaller Fairfax Studio. The centre's other main theatre, the 2000-plus seat State Theatre puts on large-scale Broadway musicals and opera.

Princess Theatre 163 Spring St, City ☎9299 9800, ⊛www.marrinerstheatres.com.au. See map, p.40. Established at the height of the goldrush, this small, exquisitely restored theatre is one of the city's best-loved venues, and stages musicals such as *Guys and Dolls* and other mainstream theatrical productions.

Red Stitch Actors Theatre Rear 2, Chapel St, St Kilda ☎9533 8083, ⊛www.redstitch.net. See map, p.92. Set up by a group of local actors, this theatre specializes in performing cutting-edge works by Melbourne play-wrights. Opposite the Astor Theatre (see p.144).

Regent Theatre 191 Collins St, City ☎9299 9500, ⊛www.marrinerstheatres.com.au. See map, p.40. Opened in 1929, this mammoth, lavishly restored theatre (by the same people who bought the Princess Theatre) presents razzle-dazzle West End/Broadway produc-tions like *Wicked* and *Showboat*.

Theatreworks 14 Acland St, St Kilda ☎9534 3388, ⊛www.theatreworks.org.au. See map, p.92. Cutting-edge Australian plays in a reasonably large, wooden-floored space that was formerly a church hall.

Comedy

**The Comedy Club The Athenaeum Theatre,
188 Collins St, City** ☎9650 6668, Ⓦwww
.thecomedyclub.com.au. See map, p.40.
Rattling the rafters in this historic theatre,
The Comedy Club is considered the home of
Australia's comedy and offers a decent
dinner and show deal (from $47) with local
stars from the comic circuit, and international
stars, too, making regular appearances.

**The Comic's Lounge 26 Errol St, North
Melbourne** ☎9348 9488, Ⓦwww
.thecomicslounge.com.au. See map, p.50.
This out-of-the-way club (tram #57 from
Elizabeth St) has big laughs six nights a
week with local funny men from TV and
radio matching wits with the odd touring
comic. Tickets $10–20, with meal packages
also available.

Cinema

**Astor Theatre Corner of Chapel St and Dandenong
Rd, St Kilda** ☎9510 1414, Ⓦwww.astor-theatre
.com.au. See map, p.92. Built in 1936, the
Astor's fabulous Art Deco architecture,
popular front steps and divine choc-top ice
creams have made it a favourite meeting
place for film buffs. It shows a mix of classics,
recent releases and cheesy double bills.
**Australian Centre for the Moving Image (ACMI)
Federation Square** ☎8663 2583, Ⓦwww.acmi
.net.au. See map, p.67. Swish Fed Square
venue (see p.69) with two large screens
showing a varied schedule of screenings
and events.
**Cinema Nova Lygon Court Plaza, 380 Lygon St,
Carlton** ☎9347 5331, Ⓦwww.cinemanova.com
.au. See map, p.76. Labyrinthine theatre
specializing in arthouse and European films.
Other popular events held at the cinema
include Script Alive, where actors read an

unproduced screenplay, and Cry-Baby film
sessions for parents and babies.
  IMAX Rathdowne St, Carlton ☎9663 5454,
Ⓦwww.imaxmelbourne.com.au. See map,
p.76. Part of the Melbourne Museum
complex (see p.75), the IMAX has gigantic
screens and film reels so big they require a
fork-lift to move them. Shows both 2-D and
3-D films, mostly documentaries on
inaccessible places or anything involving a
tyrannosaurus rex, but also the occasional
mainstream film specially made in large
format.
Kino lower level, Collins Place, City ☎9650
2100. See map, p.40. Sophisticated and
civilized complex beneath the Collins Place
atrium showing new – predominantly
arthouse – releases for the city's cinephiles.
Moonlight Cinema Royal Botanic Gardens
Ⓦwww.moonlight.com.au. See map, p.58.

No laughing matter

Melbourne has long been regarded as the home of Australian comedy. During the
1970s, a comedy cabaret scene developed around small theatre-restaurants such as
The Flying Trapeze and *The Comedy Café*, later evolving into a healthy stand-up
circuit in the 1980s at venues such as *The Last Laugh* and the *Prince Patrick Hotel*,
which drew passionate and loyal followers and launched myriad careers. Founded in
1987 by Barry Humphries and Peter Cook, the **Melbourne International Comedy
Festival** (see p.148), which has grown to become one of the world's top three
comedy events alongside those in Montreal and Edinburgh, usually attracts nearly
two thousand national and international comics. Some of Melbourne's **comedy
stalwarts** include Greg Fleet, a wonderfully surreal stand-up comic who gained
enormous exposure in the long-running TV show *Neighbours*; Anthony Morgan,
whose tear-streaming comic timing and deadpan delivery have made him one of
Australia's most adored performers; and fully fledged "national treasure" Rod
Quantock. The festival continues to launch stand-up careers including that of
Brisbane's likeable Josh Thomas who won the festival's RAW Comedy Competition
in 2005 aged 17, the youngest ever winner, as well as Best Newcomer in 2007.

Cinema buffs can swap popcorn for picnic baskets each year from Nov/Dec to early March when arthouse, cult and classic films are projected, weather permitting, onto a big outdoor screen on the central lawn of the Royal Botanic Gardens. Don't forget to take another layer of clothing, a rug and, most importantly, insect repellent. Movies begin when the sun goes down, but gates open at 7pm.

Palace Como Como Centre, South Yarra ☎9827 7533, ⊛www.palacetheatres.com.au. See map, p.88. Boutique, four-cinema complex with a gorgeous plush bar area within the Como Centre. It screens international arthouse releases and hosts the Italian and Greek film festivals.

Palace George 135 Fitzroy St, St Kilda ☎9534 6922, ⊛www.palacetheatres.com.au. See map, p.92. Three screens showing crossover mainstream and alternative releases with an edge. The recently renovated bar and foyer does excellent choc-top ice creams.

Village Jam Factory, 500 Chapel St, South Yarra ☎1300 555 400, ⊛www.villagecimeas .com.au. See map, p.88. Sprawling multiplex containing two movie houses: the multiscreen cinema shows a steady stream of blockbusters, while the opulent Cinema Europa screens the latest international arthouse films, some mainstream films and has a bar. Big, roomy seats at both cinemas.

⑭

15

Festivals and events

M elbourne is renowned for its multitude of **festivals and events**, which bring together an array of Australian and international talent to collaborate on major exhibitions, performing arts productions and sporting spectaculars – from the high-octane excitement of Formula One motor racing to touring the markets with a well-known chef as part of the Melbourne Food and Wine Festival. Melbourne also boasts an enviable range of venues and arenas to host these events – all within walking distance or a short tram ride from the city.

The following are the major festivals only; for one-offs or smaller goings-on, pick up a copy of *Melbourne Events* – available from hotels or the Melbourne Visitor Information Centre – which lists monthly happenings throughout the city, or visit the **City of Melbourne** and **Tourism Victoria** websites at Ⓦ www.thatsmelbourne.com.au and Ⓦ www.visitvictoria.com, respectively. For most festivals, **tickets** can be obtained through the booking offices of Ticketmaster (Ⓣ 13 61 00, Ⓦ www.ticketmaster.com.au), Ticketek (Ⓣ 13 28 49, Ⓦ premier.ticketek.com.au), Half Tix at Melbourne Town Hall (Mon 10am–2pm, Tues–Thurs 11am–6pm, Fri 11am–6.30pm, Sat 10am–4pm), or at the venue itself.

January

Summadayze Jan 1 It wouldn't New Year's Day without a massive hangover and Summadayze. This popular outdoor music event held at the Sidney Myer Music Bowl attracts an impressive line-up of international DJs and bands from the world of dance. Past headliners include Underworld and Groove Armada. Ⓦ www.summadayze.com.

Australian Open Tennis Championship Mid-Jan to end Jan The year's first Grand Slam attracts hordes of zinc-creamed tennis fans to see the best players in international tennis compete for two weeks at Melbourne Park. Ⓦ www.australianopen.com.

Midsumma Mid-Jan to early Feb Politically supported month-long gay and lesbian festival celebrating local, national and international queer talent and transgender art in all its finery. Some of the bigger events

include the opening Carnival Day and nighttime T-Dance, the Love Boat Cruise and Pride March, but there are also myriad smaller events in venues around the city. Ⓦ www.midsumma.org.au.

Big Day Out Late Jan Held at Flemington Racecourse, this event lines up an astonishing array of bands and DJs – past visitors include the likes of the Dandy Warhols, Metallica, Silverchair, Bjork, The Strokes and Aphex Twin. Apart from music, there are also skating shows, carnival rides and dance and techno rooms. Bring a hat and sunscreen. Ⓦ www .bigdayout.com.

Chinese New Year Late Jan/early Feb Melbourne's Chinatown hosts a packed programme of festivities, featuring music, dance, cultural performances, food, and an appearance by Dai Loong, the world's longest ceremonial dragon. The celebrations kick off at noon on new Year's Eve and finish around 6pm New Year's Day, expect lots of fire crackers and all things red. ⓦwww.melbournechinesenewyear.com.au.

February

Tropfest One Sun in Feb The Sidney Myer Music Bowl screens live from Sydney the sixteen short films chosen from over 800 entries as part of Tropfest. Films last no longer than seven minutes and all must incorporate that year's chosen theme. Gates open at 3pm and entrance is free. ⓦwww.tropfest.com.

Good Vibrations Early Feb This one-day outdoor music event at the Sidney Myer Music Bowl incorporates live stages and DJ areas, complemented by a chillout area. Recent line-ups have included Kanye West, Moloko and Blackalicious, as well as DJ sets from Gilles Peterson. A wide variety of food and drink options add to the experience. ⓦwww.jammusic.com.au /goodvibrationsfestival.

St Kilda Festival Early Feb Grown from a Sunday-only event to a week-long music, arts and culture extravaganza, climaxing with a street party of tinnitis-inducing live bands and fireworks along St Kilda's foreshore, the Esplanade and Acland St. The festival's "something-for-everyone" approach means you can expect dusk cinema screenings, street performances, art exhibitions and carnival rides, not to mention huge crowds. ⓦwww.stkildafestival.com.au.

March

Australian Grand Prix One Sun in March Formula 1 mania takes over Melbourne for four noisy days, with action centred on the purpose-built Albert Park race track in South Melbourne. As well as the high-adrenalin 58-lap race, which takes place on Sunday, off track entertainment includes air displays, rides, go-karting and glamour in the form of the pit girls. ⓦwww.grandprix.com.au.

Melbourne Food and Wine Festival Early March Australia's premier food-and-wine event, held over sixteen days at various venues in Melbourne and regional Victoria, showcasing specially prepared dishes by some of the city's finest chefs and excellent wines from around the state. Highlights include the "World's Longest Lunch" and guided tours of Melbourne's best-known eating streets. ⓦwww.melbournefoodandwine.com.au.

Taste of Chapel Early March A fortnight of food tastings, fashion shows and "long lunch" events held around Chapel St. ⓦwww.chapelstreet.com.au.

Melbourne Moomba Festival Early March One of Australia's largest – and longest running – outdoor festivals, focusing on the Yarra, the adjacent Alexandra Gardens and Docklands, with a mixture of free cultural and sporting events like water-skiing, dragon-boat racing and night parades. Don't miss the "Birdman Rally" in which various flying contraptions assemble at Princes Bridge and attempt to defy gravity. ⓦwww.melbournemoombafestival.com.au.

Melbourne Queer Film and Video Festival Mid-March A highlight of queer Melbourne's arts and culture calendar, with Australian and international features, documentaries, shorts, and experimental works screened at ACMI. ⓦwww.mqff.com.au.

Brunswick Music Festival Mid-March Ten-day world, folk and roots music and community events in and around Brunswick, with a pumping street party along Sydney Rd the main act. ⓦwww.brunswickmusicfestival.com.au.

Melbourne Fashion Festival Mid-March Sponsored by L'Oréal, this week-long fashion festival pushes mainstream and emerging Australian design. Catwalk shows, intimate salon presentations, business seminars, installations and exhibitions and, of course, heaps of absolutely fabulous parties, darling. ⓦwww.lmff.com.au.

April

Melbourne International Comedy Festival
Throughout April Leading laughathon that runs throughout the month attracting more than a thousand home-grown and overseas comics. Action is based around the Melbourne Town Hall, but there are programmes in over fifty other city venues, spanning stand-up comedy, plays, film, TV and street theatre. Ⓦ www.comedyfestival.com.au.
Melbourne International Flower and Garden Show Early April Held within the Royal Exhibition Building and Carlton Gardens, this is Australia's largest and most prestigious horticultural and outdoors lifestyle event, with hundreds of floral and landscape displays taking place over the five days. Ⓦ www.melbflowershow.com.au.
Melbourne Jazz Festival Late April Six days of Jazz held at various theatres and smaller Jazz venues around town, with performances from overseas and home-grown acts. Ⓦ www.melbournejazz.com.

May

Next Wave Festival Mid May to end May Biennial festival – the next one is in 2010 – featuring cutting-edge multimedia, visual arts and writing, created and performed by emerging Australian artists aged 16–30, in various venues around the city, but also as far afield as Geelong. Ⓦ www.nextwave .org.au.

St Kilda Film Festival Late May St Kilda's Palais Theatre and George Cinema are the usual venues for this small but good six-day survey of contemporary Australian short films and videos, with a spotlight on emerging film-makers and new media. There is also an industry open day for budding film makers. Ⓦ www.stkildafilmfestival.com.au.

July

Melbourne International Film Festival July–Aug Hugely popular event held over nineteen days with a big focus on Australian, cult and arty films, plus a multimedia component highlighting the latest in film technology. Hundreds of films from a variety of countries are shown, while a who's who of local and overseas film-makers attend to talk about their work. Venues city-wide include the Forum Theatre, Greater Union and the Australian Centre for the Moving Image (ACMI). Ⓦ www.melbournefilmfestival.com.au.

August

Melbourne Writers' Festival Late Aug Hundreds of Australian and overseas writers converge on Melbourne for ten days, where they get completely plastered, forget their hotel keys, wangle deals with publishers and, when sober, give talks and lectures to members of the book-loving public. Activities centre on Federation Square except for the keynote address which takes place at the Melbourne Town Hall. Ⓦ www.mwf.com.au.

September

Asian Food Festival Month-long showcase of Asian food at various venues around town celebrating and promoting Melbourne's Asian culture and cuisine. Events include food tours, cooking classes using a huge golden wok, celebrity dinners, travel competitions, banquets and more. Ⓦ www.asianfoodfestival.com.au.
Royal Melbourne Show Mid-Sep Eleven-day agricultural bonanza at the Royal Melbourne Showgrounds, featuring sheep-shearing, dog and horse shows and performing pigs.

Rides, baked potatoes and candyfloss compete with contests featuring everything from Jersey-Holstein cows to wood-choppers. Popular attractions include the horse breed demonstrations and the animal nurseries. ⓦ www.royalshow.com.au.

AFL Grand Final Last weekend in Sep Close to 100,000 people pack the MCG to watch the final between the two best teams in the AFL, while worldwide untold millions catch the game via cable TV. Tickets to the "G" are like gold dust so find a screen in a pub or join the crowds at Federation Square and soak up the atmosphere. ⓦ www.afl .com.au.

Melbourne Fringe Festival Late Sep Kicks off usually the last week in Sep for three weeks, starting with the outrageous Brunswick St parade and all-day party, and ending in a raucous gathering of feral types in an inner-city venue. Other debauched events typically include street raves, saucy plays, slam poetry, spoken word performances and watching people having their bodies pierced. ⓦ www .melbournefringe.com.au.

October

Australian Motorcycle Grand Prix Held over one weekend on Phillip Island, this is one of the last races of the World Championship and a popular pilgrimage for all motorbike enthusiasts. ⓦ bikes.grandprix.com.au.

Spring Racing Carnival Early Oct to mid-Nov Fifty days of metropolitan racing and country meets, parties, balls and the most extraordinary displays of hats – from oversized ensembles with lots of every-thing to chic and beautifully crafted millinery creations – that culminate in the running of the famous Melbourne Cup at Flemington. ⓦ www.springracingcarnival .com.au.

Melbourne International Arts Festival Mid-Oct. One of Australia's pre-eminent annual arts events, the seventeen-day festival has a cast of thousands drawn from the fields of music, multimedia, opera, dance and theatre. Ticketed and free performances are held both indoors at various venues and on Melbourne's streets. ⓦ www.melbournefestival.com.au.

November

Lygon Street Festa Mid-Nov Founded in 1978, Australia's oldest street festival was master-minded by the traders and restaurateurs of Carlton's cappuccino belt. Crowd favourites include the waiters' race, the pizza-throwing competition, *bocce* (bowls), fencing and ballroom dancing Italian-style. Carlton Business Association.

December

Boxing Day Cricket Test Dec 26 One of the most keenly awaited matches on the cricket calendar, the Boxing Day Test pits Australia against whichever cricketing nation is touring the country at the time, and ensures a sell-out crowd at the MCG. Tickets can be bought through Ticketmaster. ⓦ www .mcg.org.au.

⑮

FESTIVALS AND EVENTS | October • November • December

16

Sport and activities

The acknowledged **sporting capital** of Australia, Melbourne was the birthplace of Test cricket and Australian Rules football, and is today home to a string of major events including the AFL Grand Final, the Australian Grand Prix, the Australian Tennis Open, the Melbourne Cup and a number of important golf tournaments. Its leading position has been enhanced by the opening of major sporting facilities such as **Etihad Stadium** (formerly the Telstra Dome) and the **Hisense Arena**, while the famous and much-loved **Melbourne Cricket Ground** (MCG) continues to draw mammoth crowds. Visitors can watch a range of spectator sports, including Australian Football League (Aussie Rules), basketball, cricket, rugby union and football (soccer). In addition to its regular calendar of sporting events, Melbourne offers a number of **recreational sports**, with cycling, rollerblading, swimming, surfing and sailing all widely enjoyed.

You can catch live big-screen sport at a number of CBD and inner-city drinking spots, including the Crown Casino (see p.63) and the *Charles Dickens Tavern* (see p.128). For **tickets** to most sporting events, book through Ticketek Victoria (☏13 28 49, Ⓦwww.premier.ticketek.com.au), or Ticketmaster (☏13 61 00, Ⓦwww.ticketmaster.com.au).

Australian Football League (AFL)

The **Australian Football League** ("Aussie Rules", or simply "the footy") is a Melbourne institution. Originally contested by the city's suburban teams, the AFL has now grown into a national league, with teams from Melbourne, Adelaide, Perth, Sydney and Brisbane playing games each weekend from March to September, culminating in the AFL Grand Final at the MCG on the last Saturday in September. Victoria has ten of the sixteen AFL teams – Geelong and Hawthorn are two of the most successful – and consequently hosts the majority of games. See Ⓦwww.afl.com.au for more information.

Games are played at the **Etihad Stadium** (any train to Spencer Street Station, or tram #96 along Spencer Street or down Bourke Street) and the MCG (tram #75 along Wellington Parade, or the Epping line train from Flinders Street Station to Jolimont Station). **Tickets** can be bought from the grounds or through the ticket outlets above, with prices ranging from $21 to $44. Availability is generally good (fans are not segregated), but for big matches it pays to book tickets as early as possible.

The rules of Rules

To those unfamiliar with the game, **Australian Football** may seem bizarre, but once you've experienced it live and understand a few basic rules, it soon begins to make sense. The game was originally conceived as a winter fitness routine for Melbourne's cricketers, which is why it's played on a cricket oval. At each end of the oval are two upright posts, with another two (shorter) posts on either side of these. Each team is made up of eighteen players (plus four reserves or interchange players) who run around in incredibly tight shorts attempting to kick the football – in size and shape somewhere between a rugby ball and an American football – between the posts. A goal (worth six points) is when the ball is kicked through the two inner posts; a "behind" (worth one point) is when the ball passes between the two outer posts.

The game has four quarters of twenty minutes each. There are no offside rules, and players can run with the ball, although they must bounce it every 15m. A tackle can only be made below the shoulders and above the knees, but there's plenty of scope in the rules for a legal "bump" with the hip or shoulder which, when done correctly, produces an intensely violent level of body contact. If a player catches a ball which has travelled over 10m before it bounces, it's called a mark and he's awarded a free kick. This produces the game's trademark signature: a player leaping for a mark or "speccie", often high enough to rest his knees or feet on an opponent's shoulders. An incredible seven umpires (don't call them "refs") officiate – two goal umpires, two boundary umpires and three main umpires on the field. Umpires are traditionally booed whenever they run onto the ground and throughout the game, but the animosity from the one-eyed, scarf-waving fans is mostly good-natured, an element of the game that's evident from the number of children and women who go to barrack their teams on just as fervently as the men.

Basketball

There are over 600,000 registered **basketball** players in Australia, and games with Melbourne's two teams – the Melbourne Tigers and the South Dragons – enjoying considerable support. The city's main basketball venue is the Hisense Arena (☎9286 1600), in Yarra Park near the MCG; it's easily accessible by tram #75 along Wellington Parade (which runs along the southeastern corner of Fitzroy Gardens), or the Epping line train from Flinders Street Station to Jolimont Station. Tickets can be obtained through Ticketek (see opposite), and the season runs from October to April. For more information go to Ⓦ www.nbl.com.au.

Cricket

When the footy season is over, the **cricket** begins. The MCG hosts all the major games, such as the Boxing Day Test match and four-day Sheffield Shield matches involving the Victorian state team, plus limited-overs matches involving state and national teams (usually held between Dec and Feb), which regularly attract huge crowds. Check the Victorian Cricket Association website Ⓦ www.cricketvictoria .com.au for fixtures and ticket information. Tickets cost $30–60.

Cycling

Melbourne has an extensive network of quality **cycling tracks**. Popular routes include the Yarra riverside track from Southbank to Eltham and beyond (see p.85), the Bay Trail from Port Melbourne to Brighton, the Capital City Trail which starts at Southbank and follows a loop around the city to Docklands, and the Maribyrnong River Trail from Footscray Road to Brimbank Park. For more on these trails and others around Melbourne and the outer suburbs, including downloadable maps, visit Bicycle Victoria at Ⓦ www.bv.com.au.

A refreshing alternative to cycling in amid Melbourne's urban sprawl is the network of rural and suburban **railtrails**, abandoned railway tracks converted into paths for cycling, rollerblading, horse riding or walking. Over 500km of rail lines have now been reclaimed across Victoria, with public access trails in Melbourne, the Yarra Valley, the Dandenong Ranges, and Mornington Peninsula and Phillip Island, among other regions. For more information, see Bicycle Victoria or visit Ⓦ www.railtrails.org.au.

One of the best ways to see the city is to participate in **Around the Bay in a Day**. Run each year in October, the whole route circumnavigates Port Phillip Bay and totals 250km, though you can opt to do the route as smaller 210km, 100km, 80km and 50km rides. For more information, or to register online visit the Bicycle Victoria website. For details of **bike rental**, see p.28. Alternatively, many Melbourne hostels rent out bikes. Wearing a **helmet** is compulsory in Victoria, and you must have front and rear **lights** on your bike for night riding. During off-peak periods bikes can be carried free on **trains**.

Diving

Diving in Victoria, with its wrecks, reefs and drifts, is every bit as good as diving in Australia's more illustrious northern states. A particularly good spot is **Port Phillip Heads**, which forms the narrow entrance to Port Phillip Bay. Here, you can dive the "Yellow Submarine", a J-class submarine, scuttled outside the heads in the 1920s. Port Phillip Bay itself also has some great dives – **Popes Eye** and **Portsea Hole**, the most popular dives in Victoria, are both renowned for their vast array of marine life. Other popular diving sites are found along the **Great Ocean Road**, where there are dozens of turn-of-the-twentieth-century wrecks waiting to be explored. **Dive centres** providing boat and shore dives along Victoria's coastline are scattered in and around Melbourne. For the best dive access, base yourself in the beachfront towns of Portsea, Sorrento or Queenscliff. Courses are conducted at numerous dive centres if you want to learn or become more advanced. Visit Dive Victoria (Ⓦ www.divevictoria.com .au) for more information.

Golf

Melbourne is one of the worlds' great golf meccas, with excellent sandbelt courses in the city's southeastern suburbs, a favourable climate and a strong golfing heritage. There are no fewer than seventy **golf courses** throughout metropolitan Melbourne. Although some are members-only with waiting lists several years long, there are a dozens of public courses. Typical green fees are around $25 for an eighteen-hole round, but check in advance. One of the best and most accessible courses is the Albert Park Public Golf Course on Queens Road (daily 6.30am–sunset; ☏ 9510 5588; tram #96 from Bourke St), which has an eighteen-hole course, a driving range with 65 tee-off bays and four target greens, and experts on hand to fix your technique. Other good courses include the nine-hole Royal Park Public Golf Course, The Avenue, Parkville (℡9387 3585; tram #55 from William St), near Melbourne Zoo, and the eighteen-hole Yarra Bend Golf Course (℡9481 3729). Most have pro shops where you can rent clubs and buggies, or book lessons. Beyond the city, you can try some of the newer pay-as-you-play courses on the Mornington and Bellarine peninsulas. For more information on where to play visit the Victorian Golf Association on Ⓦwww.golfvic.org.au.

Gyms and fitness centres

Melbourne has plenty of **gyms and fitness centres**. Gym fees are around $19 per session for aerobics, weights or circuits. The Melbourne City Baths, at 420 Swanston St (Mon–Thurs 6am–10pm, Fri 6am–8.30pm, Sat & Sun 8am–6pm; ℡9663 5888) has excellent facilities, including a large gym, massage room, pools (including a thirty-metre heated indoor pool), floor and water aerobics classes, and saunas and spas. A swim costs $5.10, or $10.95 including a spa and sauna; use of the gym is $18.95 and a class is $16.50; both include use of the pool, sauna and spa. Other centres include Carlton Baths YMCA, 248 Rathdowne St, Carlton (℡9347 3677, Ⓦwww.carltonbaths.ymca.org.au; tram #1).

Horse and greyhound racing

Horse racing is a popular spectator sport in Australia, especially during the Spring Racing Carnival, which runs from October to mid-November. The centrepiece is the 3.2-kilometre **Melbourne Cup**, arguably the top event in the country's entire sporting calendar (see box, below). Melbourne's other metropolitan racecourses are the Caulfield Racecourse, Station Street, Caulfield (℡9257 7200); the Sandown Racecourse, 591–659 Princess Highway, Springvale (℡9518 1362); and the Moonee Valley Racecourse, McPherson Street, Moonee

---

Melbourne Cup

On the first Tuesday in November, the nation stops for one of the world's most famous horse races – the **Melbourne Cup** (Ⓦwww.melbournecup.com). The celebrated highlight of the Spring Racing Carnival, "Cup Day" (a Victorian public holiday) is a festive occasion, with racegoers enjoying champagne and canapés as they flaunt their finest outfits, hats and costumes. If they're not actually at the event, Australians gather around television sets or radios to watch or listen to the calling of the race, and over three-quarters of the country place a bet. Indeed, visiting American writer Mark Twain was so transfixed he wrote: "Cup Day is supreme; it has no rival. I can call to mind no specialised annual day, in any country, whose approach fires the whole land with a conflagration of conversation and preparation and anticipation and jubilation."

The home of the event is the Flemington Racecourse, Epsom Road, Flemington (℡1300 727 575; tram #57 from Elizabeth St), where up to 100,000 people gather to watch the race. Owners, trainers and jockeys from as far afield as Ireland, Hong Kong, Dubai and the USA come to compete in the event, which began in 1861 and has been run every year since. Tickets to the event start at $60 for general admission and must be booked in advance; contact Ticketmaster (℡1300 136 122, Ⓦwww.ticketmaster.com.au).

Ponds (☎ 1300 797 959), which also has night racing. For a racing calendar go to 🅦 www.racingvictoria.net.au.

If you fancy a flutter on the dogs, there's **greyhound racing** at the Sandown Greyhound Racing Club on Lightwood Road, Springvale (☎ 9546 9511; take the Dandenong line from Spencer St Station to Sandown Park Station). For information on race meets at other city locations or throughout the state, contact the Melbourne Greyhound Racing Association (☎ 8329 1100, 🅦 www .grv.org.au). When betting at the tote at trackside, "call out" your picks to the operator at the counter (who then gives you a ticket), rather than filling out a betting slip.

Hot-air ballooning

One of the more unique ways of seeing Melbourne is to take a flight in a **hot-air balloon**. Balloon Sunrise (☎ 9730 2422, 🅦 www.hotairballooning.com.au) operates one-hour flights over the city for $345 per person, taking in sights such as the Royal Botanic Gardens and the MCG, and finishing with a champagne breakfast at the Langham Hotel. Flights are subject to weather conditions, and bookings are essential. Global Ballooning (☎ 9428 5703, 🅦 www.globalballooning.com.au) offers a similar experience for $350, starting and finishing at the Hilton on the Park.

Motor sports

The **Australian Grand Prix** (🅦 www.grandprix.com.au), the opening race of the Formula One World Championship season, is held over four days each year in March at Albert Park (free trams operate from the city to the track). Over 300,000 fans and feted guests attend Australia's largest corporate event, which, apart from the main race, includes celebrity challenges, V8 supercar shows, air displays, live bands and hospitality on tap in the many marquee tents. Falling revenues recently led Melbourne's future of hosting the race to be thrown into doubt. Suggestions included holding a night race to encourage a wider television audience overseas, and even moving the race back to Adelaide (where it was held between 1985 and 1995) but in 2008 the city secured a new contract to keep the Grand Prix in Melbourne until 2015, with the race to start at 5pm instead of the customary 2pm.

Tickets can be bought through Ticketmaster (☎ 13 61 00, 🅦 www.ticketmaster .com.au). For general admission, expect to pay around $55–95 (depending on the day) for a one-day ticket, $150 for a four-day ticket, or between $350 and $550 for a grandstand seat. Away from the track, you can catch the action on the big screen at Federation Square, where car displays, grid girls, interactive activities, giveaways, bands and video DJs add to the mix.

Melbourne's other major motor-sports event, the **Australian Motorcycle Grand Prix** (🅦 www.ebikes.grandprix.com.au), is held at the Phillip Island Racing Circuit over three days in early October.

Rollerblading

Rollerblading is all the rage in summer, especially along St Kilda's bayside bike tracks. Skates and equipment can be rented from Rock'n N Roll'n, suite

3, 22 Fitzroy St, St Kilda (Mon–Fri 11am–6pm, Sat & Sun 10am–6pm; ⓣ9525 3434). $10 for the first hour, then $5 for subsequent hours; or $25 for 24 hours.

Rugby

Both rugby league and union have tradtionally received little support in Melbourne. **Rugby union** has experienced slow growth in the city, which now has 19 clubs, including championship-winning teams Melbourne Rugby Club and Harlequins. For more information go to Ⓦwww.rugby.com.au. **Rugby league** took off in the city only in 1998 with the creation of a new city team, Melbourne Storm (Ⓦwww.melbournestorm.com.au). Formed the previous year as part of the National Rugby League's push to nationalize the code, the Storm is the only Melbourne team in the NRL, and regularly draws healthy crowds to their home ground at Olympic Park.

Both union and league are played from April to September. International matches involving both codes are played at Etihad Stadium.

Sailing

There are a number of **sailing** schools dotted around the bayside suburbs. The Royal Melbourne Yacht Squadron, Pier Road, St Kilda (ⓣ9534 0227, Ⓦwww .rmys.com.au) offers learning-to-sail courses for $230, and its website has links to other yachting clubs around Melbourne. One of Melbourne's more scenic sailing spots is on the Yarra at Boathouse Road, Kew, where Studley Park Boathouse (ⓣ9853 1972, Ⓦwww.studleyboathouse.com.au) rents out boats for from $15 per half-hour, $28 per hour, as well as canoes and kayaks.

▲ Surfing along the Great Ocean Road

Soccer

Soccer is well supported in Melbourne, especially by the city's Italian, Greek and Croatian communities. There are eight teams that complete in the national A League (see Ⓦ www.footballfedvic.com.au for more details), including Melbourne Victory (Ⓦ www.melbournevictory.com.au) which draws the most crowds. The season runs from October to May playing at the Etihad Stadium and Olympic Park. Admission is around $20.

Surfing

Some of Victoria's more popular **surfing** spots include Phillip Island, Mornington Peninsula, Torquay and nearby Bells Beach, along the Great Ocean Road, which hosts the international Rip Curl Pro (Ⓦ www.ripcurl.com.au) each Easter for professional surfers (expect to pay around $11 to enter the Bells Beach Surfing Recreation Reserve to catch a glimpse of the action in the water). For daily surf reports, log on to the website Ⓦ www.coastalwatch.com. Surfing schools are also plentiful along the Great Ocean Road and on the Mornington Peninsula. In most cases, equipment is provided. For more information go to Ⓦ www.surfingaustralia.com.

Swimming

Swimming is popular over the hot summer months, when Melburnians pack the metropolitan **beaches** at Port Melbourne, Middle Park, St Kilda and Elwood, and the beaches further afield at Brighton, Sandringham and Mentone (all accessible by public transport). Surf lifesavers patrol Victoria's most popular beaches at weekends and public holidays during the summer months from November to March (always swim between the red and yellow striped flags).

Pools include the cavernous Melbourne Sports and Aquatic Centre (see also p.168), on Aughtie Drive, Albert Park (leisure pool Mon–Fri 6am–10pm, Sat & Sun 7am–8pm; indoor and outdoor fifty-metre pools Mon–Fri 5.30am–10pm, Sat & Sun 7am–8pm; $6; ☎ 9926 1555; tram #96 from Bourke St); the open-air Fitzroy Pool, corner of Alexander Parade and Young St, Fitzroy (Mon–Thurs 6am–9pm, Fri 6am–8pm, Sat & Sun 8am–6pm; $4.20; ☎ 9205 5180; tram #112 from Collins St); and the St Kilda Baths (see p.94; $12; Mon–Thurs 5.30am–9.45pm, Fri 5.30am–8.45pm, Sat & Sun 8am–8pm; ☎ 9525 4888), a seawater alternative to the chlorine pools and recreation centres.

Tennis

The highlight of Melbourne's **tennis** season is the annual Australian Open (Ⓦ www.australianopen.com), one of the world's four grand slam tennis events, which takes place over two weeks from January to February at the Rod Laver and Hisense arenas in Melbourne Park, next to the MCG. Tickets range from $29 to $99 (bookings through Ticketek, see p.150; a box office operates in the foyer Mon–Fri 9am–5pm; tram #75 along Wellington Parade, or the Epping line train from Flinders St Station to Jolimont Station). If you want a knock about, the Rod Laver Arena has 22 outdoor and seven indoor public courts (Mon–Fri 7am–11pm, Sat & Sun 9am–6pm; bookings ☎ 9286 1244). Rates are $26–34 per

In recent years, Melbourne's hotels have invested enormous sums of money into **spas** and **well-being centres**. Many of them have expanded their repertoire to include walk-in treatments promoting both physical and mental health, unisex packages, juice bars, even restaurant facilities offering food designed to keep patrons lean and healthy. Below is a selection of some of Melbourne's best places for pampering, healing and well-being. If you're looking to rejuvenate outside Melbourne, visit the sublime Hepburn Spa Resort in Hepburn Springs (p.206), Queenscliff Day Spa (p.222), Peninsula Hot Springs on the Mornington Peninsula (p.183) or Werribee Park Mansion and Spa (p.217).

Aurora The Prince St Kilda, 2 Acland St, St Kilda ☎9536 1130, ⓦwww .aurorasparetreat.com. Housed in The Prince complex, the hip Aurora, reputedly Australia's largest spa retreat, offers 22 treatment rooms and a courtyard where you can work on your tan. Specialized treatments include the "kitya karnu" signature treatment (desert salts and oils are rubbed all over your body in a steam room), body care, water therapies (rain shower room, steam room, geisha tub), skincare, exfoliation, nutrition and well-being activities, and range in duration from one hour to retreats of up to five days. Between treatments you can sip herbal tea or graze on vegetarian morsels prepared by staff at *Circa* (see p.123). Come prepared to relax. Mon & Fri 8.30am–8pm, Tues–Thurs 8.30am–9pm, Sat 8.30–6pm, Sun 9am–6pm.

Crown Spa Crown Towers, Level 3, 8 Whiteman St ☎9292 6182, ⓦwww .crowntowers.com.au. Huge, opulent spa that has everything from massages and saunas to body wraps, facials, hair and beauty make-overs, including Australia's most expensive facial, the $800 Pearl of Beauty Facial. Spa daily 8am–8pm.

Ofuroya 59 Cromwell St, Collingwood ☎9419 0268, ⓦwww.japanesebathhouse .com. If you've been partying or working hard, this traditional Japanese bath house is the solution. Guests can indulge in segregated hot tubs (bathing is done naked), saunas and cooling shower, then wrap up in plush cotton robes and lounge around drinking green tea, Japanese beer or sake, or have a shiatsu massage. Allow at least two hours. Bookings essential. Tues–Fri 11am–10pm, Sat & Sun 11am–8pm; last booking accepted two hours prior to closing. Bath and sauna $26.

Retreat on Spring 49 Spring St, City (east side) ☎9650 6261, ⓦwww.retreatonspring .com.au. Housed in a Nonda Katsilidis-designed building, Retreat spans three levels of hedonistic delight. With holistic spa, Aveda treatments and Philippe Starck bath fittings, not to mention a cocktail-style juice bar menu and nail salon, you're bound to come out glowing with satisfaction and feeling suitably refreshed. Recommended is the "Himalayan Rejuvenation Treatment" – involving steam inhalation and massage. Mon & Tues 10am–6pm, Wed & Thurs 10am–8pm, Fri 10am–7pm, Sat 9.30am–6pm, Sun 10am–5pm.

hour for an outdoor court, $34–40 per hour for an indoor court. Other public courts include the Albert Park Tennis Centre, Hockey Drive, Albert Park (☎9593 8188), the East Melbourne Tennis Centre, corner of Simpson and Albert sts, East Melbourne (☎9417 6511), and the Fawkner Park Tennis Centre in Fawkner Park on 65 Toorak Rd West, South Yarra (☎9820 0611).

Tenpin bowling

During the week, you'll find young and old rolling in style at **bowling alleys** around town. Open late, alleys attract a hip clientele keen to slip on retro footwear, slurp cocktails and, er, bowl. You can even get in a bit of pre-clubbing action with regular DJ nights, or party on at one of the private rooms. One of Melbourne's most popular places is King Pin at the Crown Entertainment Complex, 8 Whiteman St, Southbank (daily 10am–late; ☎1300 132 695, ⓦwww.kingpinbowling.com.au). This stylish bowling lounge offers a fully licensed bar, music, disco lighting, pool tables and sports telecasts; there's also a branch at Victoria Gardens in Richmond. Another good bowling venue is Strike Bowling Bar, 325 Chapel St (Mon–Fri noon–late, Sat & Sun 10am–late; ☎1300 787 453, ⓦwww.strikebowlingbar.com.au), an architect-designed space, with luxe banquets, loud music and low lighting. When your arm is no longer willing, check out the bar, which has an extensive drinks list and an assortment of smart eats. There's also a pool hall, karaoke and interactive games, as well as a branch at the QV in the city. For both venues, expect to pay between \$22 and \$34 for two games including shoe hire – phone to ask about their cheap deals.

Shopping

Melbourne's eclectic **shopping** scene accurately reflects the preoccupations of its lifestyle-conscious citizens, from the chic boutiques of Collins Street and South Yarra to the ethnic foodstalls of the Queen Victoria Market.

Shopping hours are generally 9am to 5.30pm, with late-night shopping till around 9pm on Thursday and Friday evenings. Many shops are open seven days a week, especially in suburban areas such as Carlton, Fitzroy, South Yarra and St Kilda. Shopping hours are also extended by up to two hours during daylight-saving months (Oct–March).

For **clothing** some good, middle-of-the-road Australian brand names are Country Road, David Lawrence, Jag, Rivers, Sportsgirl and Witchery. At the higher end of fashion look out for designer names such as Alannah Hill, Lisa Ho, Collette Dinnigan, Carla Zampatti and Saba. Some streets or precincts have clusters of shops of a particular type, making it possible to go clothes hunting by district.

Bargain hunters should make a beeline for the suburb of Richmond (especially Bridge Rd and Church St; trams #48, #70 or #75 from Flinders St), a clearance centre for some of Australia's most popular designers, or look out for **stocktake sales** during January and July. Smith Street in Collingwood (tram #86) has a cornucopia of discount stores and factory outlets tucked among its street cafés and take-away restaurants. Annual copies of *The Bargain Shopper's Guide to Melbourne* ($9.95) and *Pamms Guide to Discount Melbourne* ($23.95) are available from leading newsagents and bookshops.

The best places for **window shopping** are Chapel Street and Fitzroy's Brunswick Street (tram #112); the latter is also a good place to pick up **vintage** and second-hand clothes, while both places are ideal for a spot of people-watching at one of the many cafés. For **homeware** check out Richmond's Bridge Road or Johnston Street between Collingwood and Abbotsford. Finally, a visit to one of Melbourne's lively and eclectically stocked **markets** is a must, whether you're after cheap food produce at South Melbourne or crafts at Victoria Arts Centre's Sunday market.

Tours to various factories and warehouses can be arranged through Shopping Spree Tours ($75, including lunch; departing daily except Sunday, ☎9596 6600, ⓦwww.shoppingspree.com.au) and Melbourne Shopping Tours ($28; monthly; ☎1300 867 467, ⓦwww.melbourneshoppingtours.com.au). For retail outlets specializing in the more unusual or exotic, pick up a deck of *Shopping Secrets Melbourne* cards ($9.95), available at most bookshops.

Many stores offer "**lay-by**", which allows you to pay for something over a period of time while they hold onto it for you, handy if you don't want to pay for an expensive item with a credit card or perhaps haven't got enough money to buy it outright.

Books and maps

City Centre

Borders Shop 106, Melbourne Central ☎9663 8909. The city branch of this huge chain carries all the genres from crime to travel, plus magazines and stationery. Also stores in South Yarra, Lygon St, Carlton and Chadstone Shopping Centre (see p.164). Mon, Tues, Sat & Sun 10am–7pm, Wed 10am–8pm, Thurs & Fri 10am–9pm.

Foreign Language Bookshop Lower level, 259 Collins St ☎9654 2883, ⓦwww.languages.com .au. One of Australia's largest selections of travel guides and maps, plus dictionaries and learning kits for over seventy languages. Mon–Thurs 9am–6pm, Fri 9am–7pm, Sat 10am–5.30pm.

Haunted Bookshop 15 McKillop St, off Bourke St ☎9670 2585, ⓦwww.haunted.com.au. Decked out with dim lighting and red velour, this is Australia's leading occult, paranormal and mystical bookshop – titles range from lycanthropy and vampirism to spellcraft and demonology. The shop also organizes the two-hour "Haunted Melbourne Ghost Tour" (Sat 8.30pm; $20), which takes you to some of Melbourne's spookier haunts. Mon–Fri 11am–5.30pm.

Kill City Basement, 119 Swanston St ☎9663 3741. The store for all those with a fixation on hard-boiled characters and true crime. Titles by Elmore Leonard, James Ellroy, Carl Hiaasen, Robert Cray and Patricia Highsmith, plus other genres too. Mon–Thurs 10am–6pm, Fri 10am–7pm, Sat & Sun 11am–6pm.

Mapland 372 Little Bourke St ☎9670 4383, ⓦwww.mapland.com.au. Travel guide and map specialist, plus globes, compasses, GPS products, marine charts and travel accessories like money-belts. Mon–Thurs 9am–5.30pm, Fri 9am–6pm, Sat 10am–5pm.

Carlton and Fitzroy

Brunswick Street Bookstore 305 Brunswick St Fitzroy ☎9416 1030, ⓦwww.brunswick streetbookstore.com Renowned for its huge range of art and design titles, you can also dip into all the latest fiction at this well-stocked store right in the heart of Brunswick St. In the light-filled room upstairs it's easy to spend hours browsing

through magnificent books on subjects ranging from Le Corbusier to Japanese Manga. Daily 10am–11pm.

Polyester Books 330 Brunswick St, Fitzroy ☎9419 5223, ⓦwww.polyester.com.au. Controversial store that's been denounced for its racy and offbeat titles. Among the popular culture, Satanism and conspiracy theory genres, drug titles, adult comics and magazines are works by literary outlaws William Burroughs, Jean Genet, the Marquis de Sade and Adolf Hitler. Has a good music biography section. Mon–Thurs 10am–8pm, Fri & Sat 10am–9pm, Sun 11am–8pm.

Readings 309 Lygon St, Carlton ☎9347 6633, ⓦwww.readings.com.au. Shelves of history, food and wine, literary and children's books dominate this Carlton institution. There's also enough cultural theory detritus to stone a dozen academics, and a music section bulging with jazz, classical and world music CDs. Other branches in Hawthorn, Malvern, Port Melbourne and St Kilda. Mon–Sat 9am–11pm, Sun 10am–11pm.

Travellers Bookstore 294 Smith St, Collingwood ☎9417 4179, ⓦwww.travellersbookstore.com .au. The owner knows her stuff, having worked in the industry for years and traipsed her way around the globe many times over. A vast collection of guides, phrasebooks, maps and travel accessories. Mon–Sat 10am–6pm.

South Yarra

Borders The Jam Factory, 500 Chapel St, South Yarra ☎9824 2299, ⓦwww.borders.com.au. Melbourne's first mega-bookstore crams over 200,000 books, CDs, DVDs, magazines and daily newspapers onto its shelves. Also has loads of discounts, a coffee shop, children's playing area and regular in-store events like cooking demonstrations, live music and author signings. Daily 10am–11pm.

St Kilda and Albert Park

The Avenue Bookstore 127 Dundas Place, Albert Park ☎9690 2227, ⓦwww .avenuebookstore.com.au. The stock in this shop is almost overwhelming – both in subject range and sheer quantity – and the

staff really know their stuff. In particular, the store boasts a very comprehensive travel guidebook section. Daily 9am–7pm.
Readings 112 Acland St, St Kilda ☎ **9525 3852,** ⓦ **www.readings.com.au.** Everything from the latest bodice-ripper to the most obscure items of esoterica, plus a comprehensive music catalogue and a well-stocked kid's section. Good selection of design and architecture tomes too. Daily 10am–10pm.

Williamstown

Seagulls Bookshop 141 Nelson Place, Williamstown ☎ **9397 1728.** This very browsable independent bookstore stocks a small range of books about Australia, particularly guidebooks, and has a dedicated children's section at the back. They also specialize in maritime books. Mon–Fri 10am–6pm, Sat & Sun 10am–5pm.

Clothes, shoes and jewellery

City Centre

Alice Euphemia Shop 6, Cathedral Arcade, 37 Swanston St ☎ **9650 4300,** ⓦ **www .aliceeuphemia.com.** Edgy mix of up-and-coming, unconventional local designs and established Australian labels for women, plus hand-finished one-off scarves, stylish accessories such as precious jewellery and leather, and screen-printed T-shirts and bags. Mon–Thurs & Sat 10am–6pm, Fri 10am–7pm, Sun noon–5pm.
Chiodo Basement, 114 Russell St ☎ **9663 0044,** ⓦ **www.chiodo.net.au.** Clean lines and an elegant interior design are echoed in Chiodo's stylish, bright garments. You'll also find Comme des Garçons fragrances and other assorted treats such as sunglasses and locally crafted jewellery. Mon–Thurs 10am–6pm, Fri 10am–7pm, Sat 10am–5.30pm, Sun noon–5pm.
Christine 181 Flinders Lane ☎ **9654 2011.** A cornucopia of expensive accessories from fabulous bags and scarves to gorgeous shoes, jewellery, trinkets and perfume. Mon & Sat 10am–5pm, Tues–Fri 10am–6pm.
Cose Ipanema 113 Collins St ☎ **9650 3457.** Fashion frontliner harbouring super-chic labels like Issey Miyake, Yohji Yamamoto, Armani Collezione, Jean-Paul Gaultier, Dries Van Noten and Dolce & Gabbana. Their sales often provoke a buying frenzy as the usually expensive labels are sold at bargain prices. Mon–Thurs 9.30am–6pm, Fri 9.30am–7pm, Sat 10am–5pm, Sun noon–4pm.
e.g.etal 185 Little Collins St ☎ **9663 4334,** ⓦ **www.egetal.com.au.** Designer gold- and silversmiths showcase their art – both functional and decorative – in this little shop in the heart of boutique land. Spend money

here on something small but beautiful. Mon–Thurs 10am–6pm, Fri 10am–7pm, Sat 10am–5pm.
Gallery Funaki 4 Crossley St ☎ **9662 9446.** Small and stylish gallery showcasing contemporary jewellery by renowned international and local artists. Regular exhibitions. Commission works available. Tues–Fri 11am–5pm, Sat 11am–4pm.
Genki Shop 5, Cathedral Arcade, 37 Swanston St ☎ **9650 6366,** ⓦ **www.genki.com.au.** Japanese for "happy, healthy and feeling fine", Genki is a store for quirky Melburnians, stocking hard-to-find Japanese, European and US streetwear, especially home-brand T-shirts for "It girls". There's also lots of inspired frippery like sequinned purses, polaroid cameras and other assorted knick-knacks from around the world. Mon–Thurs 11am–6pm, Fri 11am–7pm, Sat 11am–6pm, Sun noon–5pm.
Kozminsky 421 Bourke St ☎ **9670 1277,** ⓦ **www.kozminsky.com.au.** Esteemed antique and twentieth-century jewellery firm housed in an elegant former stock and station agent's premises. The art gallery upstairs shows works by Mila Schoen, Jeremy Park and Bryan Westwood, among others. Mon–Fri 10am–5.30pm, Sat 11am–4pm.
Lisa Ho Shop F19, Level 1, GPO ☎ **9650 1399,** ⓦ **www.lisaho.com.** City branch showcasing the latest collection from Australian designer, Lisa Ho, who's responsible for draping many a celebrity's back and bum, and is known for her romantic dresses, classic-cut trousers and gorgeous fabrics. Another store at Chadstone Shopping Centre (see p.164).
Makers Mark 464 Collins St ☎ **9621 2488,** ⓦ **www.makersmark.com.au.** Makers Mark showcases the crop of the country's top

SHOPPING | Clothes, shoes and jewellery

jewellery designers, with exhibitions featuring everything from fancy opera rings to handcrafted pens. Another branch at 88 Collins St. Mon–Thurs 10am–6pm, Fri 10am–7pm, Sat 10am–5pm, Sun noon–4pm.

Mooks 296 Swanston St, QV ☎9650 3525, ⓦwww.mooks.com. Covetable streetwear and accessories, including beanies, trucker caps, backpacks, quirky T-shirts and ziphood sweats. Also at Chadstone Shopping Centre (see p.164). Mon–Thurs 10am–7pm, Fri 10am–9pm, Sun 10am–6pm, Sun 11am–5.30pm.

Scanlan & Theodore 285 Little Collins St ☎9650 6195, ⓦwww.scanlantheodore.com.au. Women's clothing from Melbourne duo Fiona Scanlan and Gary Theodore, who specialize in contemporary classics in simple shades cut from couture-grade fabrics. A second branch on Chapel St, South Yarra. Mon–Thurs 10am–6pm, Fri 10am–8pm, Sat 10am–5.30pm, Sun noon–5pm.

Zambesi 167 Flinders Lane ☎9654 4299, ⓦwww.zambesi.co.nz. Prestigious and stylish store showcasing cutting-edge designs of New Zealand labels Zambesi and Nom.D, with a solid range of other imports on board, including Belgian label Martin Margiela. Mon–Fri 10am–6pm, Sat 10am–5pm, Sun noon–4pm.

Fitzroy

Clear It 188 Brunswick St, Fitzroy ☎9415 1339. A women's clothing clearance outlet for Aussie labels Allanah Hill, Dangerfield and Revival, plus accessories. Head upstairs for fabrics and samples from a few seasons ago. Mon–Thurs & Sat 10am–6pm, Fri 10am–7pm, Sun 11am–6pm.

Dangerfield 289 Brunswick St, Fitzroy ☎9416 2032, ⓦwww.dangerfield.com.au. Reasonably priced rock chick and punk boy streetwear, including crotch-clutching jeans, US workwear and jewellery for guys and girls. Has another four city locations and stores plus one in Greville St, Prahran and Chapel St, South Yarra. Mon–Thurs & Sat 10am–6pm, Fri 10am–8pm, Sun 11am–6pm.

Douglas & Hope 181 Brunswick St, Fitzroy ☎9417 0662, ⓦwww.douglasandhope.com.au. Using antique silk kimonos, as well as modern cotton reproductions of old design patterns, Douglas & Hope produce exquisite

quilted bedding, soft furnishings and cushions, every item an original. Women's clothing and jewellery by Karen Walker and their own Immune label are also stocked, alongside candles, ceramics and soaps. Also in Block Arcade in the city. Mon–Sat 11am–6pm, Sun noon–5pm.

Hunter Gatherer 274 Brunswick St, Fitzroy ☎9415 7371, ⓦwww.huntergatherer.com.au. Considered one of the best vintage clothing and accessories stores in Melbourne with all profits going back to the Brotherhood of St Laurence charity. Also features its own vintage inspired label for men, women and children. There's another store at 82a Acland St, St Kilda. Daily 10.15am–5.45pm.

▲ Hunter Gatherer

Kinki Gerlinki 360 Brunswick Street, Fitzroy ☎9495 6059. Good for medium-priced, off-the-wall women's fashion and accessories, whipped up by some of Asia's best young designers. Cardigans in riotous colours and handbags fashioned from goat hair are among the treats. Mon–Thurs & Sat 10am–6pm, Fri 10am–87pm, Sun 11am–6pm.

South Yarra

Alannah Hill 533 Chapel St, South Yarra ☎9826 2755, ⓦwww.alannahhill.com.au. Boudoir chic store stocking overtly girly but extremely wearable clothes from Tasmanian-born Hill, plus a small selection of accessories such as scarves, bags and jewellery. A good place to pick up pretty blouses for work. Mon–Thurs & Sat 10am–6pm, Fri 10am–8pm, Sun 11am–6pm.

Collette Dinnigan 553 Chapel St, South Yarra ☏ 9827 2111, ⓦ www.collettedinnigan.com.au. Intricate, opulent and expensive fare from the New Zealand-born, Sydney-based, Paris-feted designer extraordinaire. Mon–Fri 10am–6pm, Sat 10am–5pm, Sun noon–5pm.

Country Road Corner of Chapel St & Toorak Rd, South Yarra ☏ 9824 0133, ⓦ www.countryroad .com.au. Flagship store offering a small but considered selection of home wares, plus good basic clothing, shoes and accessories for men and women as well as children's clothing. Mon–Thurs 10am–6pm, Fri 10am–8pm, Sat 10am–5.30pm, Sun 11am–5pm.

Dinosaur Designs 562 Chapel St, South Yarra ☏ 9827 2600, ⓦ www.dinosaurdesigns.com.au. Chunky Flintstone-like resin and sterling silver jewellery, crockery and glassware, all designed and handmade in Australia. Affordable. Mon–Sat 10am–6pm, Sun noon–5pm.

Marcs Shop 2, 576–584 Chapel St, South Yarra ☏ 9826 4906. Huge range of understated but modern men's and women's wear, including T-shirts, button-downs, jeans, suits, knits and shoes. Mon–Thurs 10am–6pm, Fri 10am–8pm, Sat 10am–5.30pm, Sun 11am–5pm.

St Kilda

Hudson 229 Carlisle St, Balaclava ☏ 9525 8066. Coolest kid on the block, Hudson is leading the retail revival of Balaclava's bagel belt. Arty types stock up on Japanese talking watches, kooky handmade knitted toys, exclusive US and UK street labels and fresh local talent. Keep an eye out for regular kick-arse art exhibitions. Daily 10.30/11am–5.30pm

Crafts, gifts and beauty products

Aesop 268 Flinders St, City ☏ 9663 0862, ⓦ www.aesop.net.au. Quality skin and hair products derived from botanical extracts and essential oils which smell divine and come packaged in simple UV-resistant brown bottles and jars. Mon–Sat 10am–6pm, Sun noon–5pm.

Craft Victoria Basement, 31 Flinders Lane, City ☏ 9650 7775, ⓦ www.craftvic.asn.au. Contemporary jewellery, ceramics, woodcraft, glass, textiles and other objects by Australian designers. Regular exhibitions. Tues–Sat 10am–5pm.

Kleins Perfumery 313 Brunswick St, Fitzroy ☏ 9416 1221. Luscious-smelling boutique with over sixty product lines including Aesop, L'Occitane, Burt's Bees, Jurlique, Diptyque and Crabtree and Evelyn. From perfumes to scented candles, soaps, oils and body products, it's a veritable lolly shop for the adult scent enthusiast. Mon–Thurs & Sat 9am–6.30pm, Fri 9am–9pm, Sun 10am–6pm.

Napoleon Perdis Level 1, Como Centre, South Yarra ☏ 9569 7111, ⓦ www.napoleonperdis .com. Concept store from make-up artist to the stars, Napoleon Perdis, stocking his own range of professional make-up products, including brushes, and a sideline in nail and body products. One-hour make-up lessons cost $95, plus one-day workshops available. Mon–Wed 9am–5.30pm, Thurs & Fri 9am–9pm, Sat 9am–5pm, Sun 10am–5pm.

R.G. Madden 269 Coventry St, South Melbourne ☏ 9696 4933, ⓦ www.rgmadden.com.au. The jewel in the Coventry St homewares hub, R.G. Madden offers up a superb assortment of design classics – from Alessi kettles and Starck lemon squeezers to chunky doorstops and spiky Dish Doctors by Australian style guru Marc Newson. Other branches are at 597 Church St, Richmond, 333 Drummond St, Carlton and 349 Little Bourke St in the City. Mon–Fri 9.30am–5pm, Sat 10am–5pm, Sun 11am–4pm.

⑰

SHOPPING | Crafts, gifts and beauty products

Department stores and shopping malls

Chadstone Shopping Centre 1341 Dandenong Rd, Chadstone ☎ 9563 3355, ⓦ www .chadstoneshopping.com.au. Take the Cranbourne or Pakenham train line to Hughesdale or Oakleigh stations, then a bus to get to one of Australia's first shopping malls. The huge American-style Chadstone Shopping Centre is filled with major brand retailers, Australian designers and specialty shops. You'll also find cafés, cinemas and plenty of diversions for the kids. Mon–Wed 10am–5.30pm, Thurs & Fri 9am–9pm, Sat 9am–5pm, Sun 10am–5pm.

David Jones Bourke St Mall ☎ 9643 2222, ⓦ www.davidjones.com.au. Australia's oldest retailer with stores either side of Bourke Street Mall. Renowned for its domestic and international designer range, beauty section and food hall. Mon–Wed 9.30am–6pm, Thurs 9.30am–7pm, Fri 9.30am–9pm, Sat 9am–7pm, Sun 10am–6pm.

GPO Corner of Bourke & Elizabeth Sts ⓦ www .melbournesgpo.com. The grand old general post office site has been refurbished and now offers dozens of retail outlets, many exclusive to the centre, including Mandarina Duck, Georg Jensen, Ben Sherman, Mimco, Belinda Seper and Karen Millen. Mon–Thurs & Sat 10am–6pm, Fri 10am–8pm, Sun 11am–5pm.

Melbourne Central Corner or Latrobe & Swanston sts ☎ 9922 1100, ⓦ www.melbournecentral .au. Re-launching itself as a one-stop sartorial shop, the "Central" is a shadow of the former centre that once housed Japanese store Diamaru, but it still has myriad shops including Witchery, De Cjuba, the Marcs, RM Williams, G-Star, General Pants Co and plenty of others. Mon–Thurs & Sat 10am– 6pm, Fri 10am–9pm, Sun 10am–5pm.

Myer Bourke St Mall ☎ 9661 1111, ⓦ www .myer.com.au. Upmarket store spread over six floors across almost two blocks with perfumes, lipsticks, jewellery, home wares, electrical goods, local and imported fashion, books, records, a giant sporting emporium, and an Apple store. Mon–Wed, Sat 9am– 6pm, Thurs 9am–7pm, Fri 9am–9pm, Sun 10am–6pm.

QV Corner of Swanston & Lonsdale sts ☎ 9658 0100, ⓦ www.qv.com.au. The old Queen Victoria Hospital once occupied this site, which is now a huge complex of laneways and shops, cafés, bars and restaurants. Pitched as a gritty urban precinct, stores include Cactus Jam, Kam Otto, Zimmer- mann, Wayne Cooper, Dizingof and Chris- tensen Copenhagen. Mon–Wed & Sat 10am–6pm, Thurs 10am–7pm, Fri 10am– 9pm, Sun 10am–5pm.

Shop and eat

Make no mistake, Melburnians love their shopping. They also love their food, so what better way to combine the two than to create a retail experience in which to graze while you shop.

Hermon & Hermon 556 Swan St, Richmond ☎ 9427 0599. Speciality furniture and homewares store – lots of dark timber and Japanese Zen-style designs – with a great café serving bruschettas and cakes that attracts a mixed crowd of shoppers, workers and locals. Mon–Fri 8am–5pm, Sat 10am–5pm, Sun noon–5pm.

Husk 557 Malvern Rd, Toorak ☎ 9827 2700. Beautiful, restful space which combines elegant items such as Moroccan glassware, jewellery, ceramics and designer clothes for women, men and children (both at Albert Park store) including Easton Pearson, Hoss Intropia, Kate Sylvester, Vixen and more, with a wonderful courtyard café serving its own range of home-made herbal teas, authentic Bedouin coffee, hearty soups and cakes. Mon–Thurs & Sat 9am–5.30pm, Fri 9am–6.30pm, Sun 10am–5pm. Also at 123 Dundas Place, Albert Park and 176 Collins St in the City.

Verve Boutique 177 Little Collins St, City ☎ 9639 5886. Amid the designer clothing and accessories are tables and stools where you can drink excellent coffee and eat mouthwatering foccacias, soups and sticky cakes. After stuffing your face simply begin your spree. Mon–Fri 7.30am–5pm, Sat 8.30am–5pm.

Food and drink

Haigh's 7 & 8 Block Arcade, 282 Collins St ☎9654 7673, ✉www.haighschocolates.com.au. The oldest family-owned chocolate manufacturer in the country sells award-winning premium chocolates. Also stores at 191 Swanston Walk and 26 Collins St. Mon–Thurs 8.30am–6pm, Fri 8.30am–7pm, Sat 9am–5pm, Sun 11am–5pm.

Jock's Ice Cream & Sorbets 83 Victoria Ave, Albert Park ☎9686 3838. Jock Main's ice creams are worth crossing town for, with a great spread of unusual flavours such as date, pumpkin or baked apple. Mon–Thurs noon–8pm, Fri & Sat noon–10.30pm, Sun noon–9pm.

King and Godfrey 293 Lygon St, Carlton ☎9347 1619. Established in 1870, this Carlton landmark is a deli-cum-café, with Italian pasta, cheeses, breads, salamis and other cured meats, sweets, biscuits and crackers, and a superb stock of wine, beer and spirits. Mon–Sat 9am–9pm, Sun 11am–6pm.

Richmond Hill Café and Larder 48 Bridge Rd, Richmond ☎9421 2808, ✉www.rhcl.com.au. Good though pricey selection of groceries including bread, preserves, savouries, sweets and magnificent cheeses plus produce from its own range, as well as gourmet hampers. Mon–Thurs & Sun 8.30am–5pm, Fri & Sat 8.30am–6pm.

Simon Johnson 12–14 St David St, Fitzroy ☎9486 9456, ✉www.simonjohnson.com.au. Food merchant with top-quality produce, including oils, vinegars, chocolates and a great cheese room. Mon–Fri 10am–6pm, Sat 9am–5pm. The store at 471 Toorak Rd (☎9826 2588) in Toorak is open the same times plus Sunday from 10am–4pm.

Markets

Camberwell Market Station St car park, Camberwell ☎1300 367 712, ✉www .sundaymarket.com.au. A Melbourne institution for over twenty years, this "trash and treasure" early-morning market is set in a car park that metamorphoses into a sea of trestle tables and racks buried under second-hand clothing, furniture, watches, records, cards, stuffed toys, curios – you name it. There are over 350 regular stalls, and spaces can be hired for around $50. To get there, take tram #72 from Flinders St. Sun 6.30am–12.30pm.

Chapel St Bazaar 217 Chapel St, Prahran ☎9510 9841. An Aladdin's cave of around eighty dealers' stalls displaying antiques and collectibles ranging from Coca-Cola memorabilia to Royal Doulton china. Eclectic, to say the least – if you're looking for an Art Deco ashtray or a plastic punch set this is the place to come. Daily 10am–6pm.

Esplanade Market Upper Esplanade, St Kilda ☎9534 0066. St Kilda's most popular weekly fixture, featuring works from nearly 200 artists, combining the heady aromas of fresh produce with the musty whiff of second-hand clothing and century-old fittings. Sun 10am–5pm.

Prahran Market Commercial Rd, Prahran ☎8290 8220. Excellent, upmarket food emporium selling fish, meat, fruit, vegetables, and with a delicatessen for the gourmand, and the store The Essential Ingredient, which sells local and imported spices, oils, pastas, pastes, dry goods, cookbooks and kitchenware, as well as offering cooking classes. Tues, Thurs & Sat dawn–5pm, Fri dawn–6pm, Sun 10am–3pm.

Queen Victoria Market Corner of Victoria & Elizabeth sts ☎9320 5822. The place to go for fresh fruit and vegetables, meat, poultry, fish, deli goods and other fine things to eat. It's also an arts and crafts market that's been a major draw for locals and tourists for years, though these days you have to do a little rummaging before you find a bargain. Paintings, jewellery, leatherwork and didgeridoos are just some of the goods on offer. Clothing and shoes stalls abound on Sun. Tues & Thurs 6am–2pm, Fri 6am–5pm, Sat 6am–3pm, Sun 9am–4pm; also night market Nov–Feb Wed 5.30–10.30pm.

South Melbourne Market Corner of Cecil & Coventry sts, South Melbourne ☎9209 6295. Established over 140 years ago, Melbourne's second-oldest market is one of the city's most popular and sells a huge range of fresh fruit and vegetables, seafood, meat, delicatessen goods, clothes, furniture and household items. Cecil St has some fantastic

⑰

SHOPPING | Food and drink • Markets

eateries serving everything from crepes to tapas –and you shouldn't leave without trying the famous South Melbourne dimmies, delicious dim sums to take away, though be prepared to queue. Tram #96 from the City. Wed 8am–4pm, Fri 8am–6pm, Sat & Sun 8am–4pm.

Victorian Arts Centre Market Victorian Arts Centre Undercroft, 100 St Kilda Rd ☎9281 8000, ⓦ www.theartscentre.com.au. Over 150 stalls selling handmade arts and crafts direct from the artist or designer. Artwork, wood carvings, ceramics, textiles and jewellery. Sunday 10am–5pm.

Music

Basement Discs 24 Block Place, off Little Collins St, City ☎9654 1110, ⓦ www.basementdiscs .com.au. Discreet underground space with an exhilarating range of jazz and blues, inviting sofas and listening stations. There is also a huge selection of magazine back copies to browse. Mon–Thurs 10am–6pm, Fri 10am–8pm, Sat 10am–6pm, Sun 11am–5pm.

Discurio 113 Hardware St ☎9600 1488, ⓦ www.discurio.com.au. Having relocated from Elizabeth St to Hardware St (its fourth move in recent years), Discurio has finally settled down, continuing with its broad range of jazz, opera, soul, classical, world music and movie soundtracks in another sleek environment. You can also grab the latest issue of *Songlines* to go with your Coltrane. Mon–Thurs 10am–6pm, Fri 10am–7pm, Sat 10am–5pm.

Northside Records 236 Gertrude St, Fitzroy ☎9417 7557, ⓦ www.northsiderecords.com.au. Choice inner-city music store specializing in

cool funk, the latest hip-hop, jazz, electronica and Latin music on CD and vinyl. Mon–Wed 10am–6pm, Thurs & Fri 11am–7pm, Sat 11am–5pm, Sun 1–5pm.

Profile Music 128 Greville St, Prahran ☎9510 1133, ⓦ www.profilemusic.com.au. Aimed at boys and girls who love their beats phat and furious, this store is also where Melbourne and Australia's foremost DJs come to shop for their vinyl – from house and electronica to disco and rare groove, with a couple of turntables and headphones for trying before you buy. Hours are flaky at best, so ring in advance. Mon & Tues noon–6pm, Wed–Fri noon–7pm, Sat 11am–6pm.

Record Collector's Corner 240 Swanston St ☎9663 3442. Mecca for DJs hunting vintage vinyl as well as collectors seeking out rare Japanese import CDs. This is a specialist store with a good range of well-priced old and new CDs and records. Mon–Thurs 10am–7pm, Fri 10am–10pm, Sat & Sun 11am–5pm.

Kids' Melbourne

M elbourne has a wide range of **activities for children**: splashing about at the Melbourne Sports and Aquatic Centre, feeding the animals at Collingwood Children's Farm, or checking out the exhibits at the Melbourne Aquarium and the Scienceworks museum. Other childproof diversions include indoor play centres and recreational areas such as St Kilda beach and foreshore, as well as the major parks, most of which have playgrounds. Heading out of town you're spoilt for choice, from the Koala Conservation Centre and Penguin Parade on Phillip Island (see p.185) or the Enchanted Maze on the Mornington Peninsula (see p.183), to a ride on the Puffing Billy steam railway through the Dandenongs (see p.193).

Children are generally welcome in Melbourne's cafés and restaurants, especially in the ethnic places. Most also provide child-sized portions and "babycinos", a child's cappuccino of milk froth sprinkled with chocolate. A couple of good places for babycinos are *Mario's* (see p.119) and *Tiamo* (see p.120), in Fitzroy and Carlton respectively; they also have highchairs and do small servings.

You can plan your days by scouring *Melbourne's Child* (Ⓦ www.melbournes child.com.au) and *Aussie Kids*, free monthly magazines both available from the visitors centre and libraries.

Children can also rent bikes and rollerblades (see chapter 16), and there's much to amuse tots at the numerous festivals (see chapter 15); highlights include the carnival rides at the St Kilda Festival and watching parading animals at the Royal Melbourne Show.

Indoor

Australian Centre for the Moving Image (ACMI) Federation Square, corner of Flinders & Swanston sts, West Side ☎ 8663 2200, Ⓦ www.acmi.net.au. ACMI has loads of special screenings for kids, regular cartoon festivals and Japanese animation.

Victoria's school holidays

Summer Five to six weeks, beginning roughly five days before Christmas to the last week in January.
Autumn Two weeks, from early April to mid-April (incorporating Easter).
Winter Two weeks, normally from the end of June to the second week in July.
Spring Two weeks, beginning late September.

In general, private schools break up earlier and come back later than state schools. Precise annual school term dates can be found at the Victoria Department of Education and Early Childhood website (Ⓦ www.education.vic.gov.au).

Bernard's Magic Shop 211 Elizabeth St, West Side ☎ 9670 9270, ⓦ www.bernards.com.au. Chock-a-block with puzzles, tricks, practical jokes and games, plus silly glasses, jumbo tongues, masks, costumes and plenty of copies of that perennial children's favourite, *Teach Yourself Rope Magic*.

Eureka Skydeck Eureka Tower, River District ☎ 9693 8888, ⓦ www.skydeck.com.au. View Melbourne 88 storeys up from the highest viewing platform in the Southern Hemisphere. For those with nerves of steel there's also "The Edge" ($12; 4–16yrs $8), a three-metre glass cube that protrudes out 300m above the ground. Daily 10am–10pm; $16.50; 4–16yrs $9.

IMAX Theatre Rathdowne St, Carlton ☎ 9663 5454, ⓦ www.imaxmelbourne.com.au. Adjoining the Melbourne Museum (see p.75), IMAX has big comfy seats in which to enjoy 2-D and 3-D films (usually lasting 45–60min) on a giant screen. Films screened every hour daily 10am–10pm; $17.50, 3–15 years $12.50.

Melbourne Aquarium Corner of Flinders & King sts, West Side ☎ 9923 5999, ⓦ www .melbourneaquarium.com.au. Harbouring thousands of creatures from the Southern Ocean, the Melbourne Aquarium also comprises a hands-on learning centre where children gain a glimpse of life under-water, as well as daily feeding sessions, "touch and feel" presentations, cafés and a shop. Daily 9.30am–6pm; $26.50, 5–15yrs $16.

Melbourne Museum Carlton Gardens, Carlton ☎ 13 11 02, ⓦ www.melbourne.museum.vic.gov .au. Tram #86. State-of-the-art museum over many levels housing several superb galleries and spaces, including "Bugs Alive!" and the Children's Gallery aimed at 3–8 year-olds, where the exhibition gallery, "Big Box", is built in the shape of a giant tilted cube painted in brightly coloured squares and features the exhibition "1,2,3 Grow". Also check out the Forest Gallery, a living, breathing indoor rainforest containing over 8000 plants, as well as birds, insects, snakes, lizards and fish. Daily 10am–5pm; $6; under 16s free.

Melbourne Sports and Aquatic Centre Aughtie Drive, Albert Park ☎ 9926 1555, ⓦ www.msac .com.au. Tram #96. Part sporting facility, part fun park and host to a number of major sporting events, the centre has a pool for every occasion: a wave and toddlers' pool, a fifty-metre pool, a 25-metre lap pool and a twenty-metre multipurpose pool. Childcare is available (Mon–Fri 9am–noon; ☎ 9926 1533; $5.70/90min), and the centre also runs excellent day-long school-holiday programmes, including "Planet Sport", for 5- to 12-year-olds ($36/day) with games, sports and arts and crafts activities, and "Splashout" (11am–4pm; adult $8, children $6), with water slides and inflatables. General opening hours Mon–Fri 6am–10pm, Sat & Sun 7am–8pm; phone for specific pool times; $6, 3–15yrs $4.50.

Scienceworks 2 Booker St, Spotswood ☎ 13 11 02, ⓦ museumvictoria.com.au/scienceworks.

Child-care facilities

Child care in Melbourne is often in high demand and usually involves long waiting lists. If you plan on staying in Melbourne a while it's a good idea to put your child's name down at a centre as soon as possible to ensure a place. The places listed below require advance bookings of at least two weeks. In addition, the council-run Melbourne City Child Care, 104 A'Beckett St, City (☎ 9329 9561), offers occasional care for children up to five years (9am–1pm $42; 1–4.30pm $36.50; 9am–4.30pm $78), which you must book seven days in advance. Melbourne council has a list of child care centres on its website ⓦ www.melbourne.vic.gov.au.

East Melbourne Child Care Co-operative Operates two sites: Powlett Reserve, corner of Grey & Simpson streets, East Melbourne ☎ 9419 4301; and Yarra Park, 27 Berry St, East Melbourne ☎ 9428 0896. Children 3–5 years. Mon–Fri 7.30am–6pm; $67 full day, $310 weekly. ⓦ www.emcc.org.au

Sunkids Children's Centre Level 4, 544 Collins St ☎ 9614 3011. Children up to 5 years. Mon–Fri 7am–7pm; $92.50 full day or $462.50 weekly; plus a $60 non-refundable application fee. ⓦ www.sunkids.com.au

▲ Collingwood Children's Farm

Learn about science and technology through a series of interactive exhibitions on topics ranging from sport to waterways pollution. There's also a digital planetarium, lightning shows and plenty of hands-on activities, as well as school-holiday programmes on the human mind and body, and touring exhibitions. Daily 10am–4.30pm; Scienceworks only adults $6, under-16s free; Planetarium and Lightning shows adult $5, children $3.50. Williamstown or Werribee lines from Flinders Street Station to Spotswood Station.

Outdoor

CERES Cafe 8 Lee St, East Brunswick ☎9387 2609, ⓦ www.ceres.org.au. An environmentally sustainable farm where local parents gather to let their kids range free. Organic and vegetarian snacks include spinach and cheese pides, sausage rolls, samosas, muffins and sticky cakes, all made on the premises, using ingredients mostly from the café gardens; babycinos are also available. The shop sells home-made produce such as jams and chutneys, plus there's an organic market Wed & Sat 9am–1pm. Mon–Sat 8.30am–5pm, Sun 9.30am–5pm. Tram #96.
Collingwood Children's Farm St Heliers St, Abbotsford ☎9417 5806, ⓦ www.farm.org.au. Tucked on the banks of the Yarra, this small working farm allows kids to feed piglets, lambs, chooks and goats, help with farm chores, have a go at milking a cow (10am & 4pm) or do a farm tour and learn about plants and animals. There's also a farm café (free entry). Family days (first Sun of the month) include hay and pony rides, a barbeque and themed events ranging from cheese tasting to sheep shearing. Every second and fourth Sat of the month there's a farmers' market (8am–1pm; adults $2; children free, includes entry to the farm) offering a selection of local produce. Daily 9am–5pm; adult $8, child $4. Epping line from Flinders Street Station to Victoria Park Station.
Luna Park 18 Lower Esplanade, St Kilda ☎1300 888 272, ⓦ www.lunapark.com.au. Old-fashioned roller-coaster, ferris wheel and ghost-train rides, plus harum-scarum attractions like the "Pharoah's Curse" and "Shock Drop", which will have you hanging on for dear life. Lots of rides for young children too. Wandering around is free, but you pay $8 ($6 children) for individual rides, or $37.95 ($27.95) for unlimited rides.

Art and play at Birrarung Marr

In addition to its many family-friendly attractions, the city of Melbourne created **ArtPlay**, an enterprising programme of events for children aged five to twelve years, aimed to increase families' engagement in city life by fostering creativity and imagination within the confines of **Birrarung Marr** (see p.69) on the northern banks of the Yarra River, adjacent to Federation Square. As the name suggests, ArtPlay offers a range of weekend and holiday workshops, where children are encouraged to take part in arts activities, both individually and collaboratively, and to romp around in a variety of indoor and outdoor play, exhibition and performance spaces. For programme information and weekend and holiday workshops call ☎9664 7900 or visit ⓦ www.artplay.com.au.

May–mid Sept Sat & Sun 11am–6pm, or daily during school holidays; mid Sept–April Fri 7–11pm, Sat 11am–11pm, Sun 11am–6pm, or daily during school holidays.

Melbourne Zoo Elliot Ave, Parkville ☎9285 9300, ⓦ www.zoo.org.au/melbournezoo. Apart from watching monkeys scratching their privates, children can line up for daily meet-the-keeper sessions: giant tortoises (daily 11am), wombats (daily 11.30am), giraffes (daily 11.45pm), elephants (2.30pm), koalas (daily 2.30pm), orang-utans (daily 3pm) and penguins (daily 3.30pm); or sleep over on a Roar 'n' Snore experience (Sept–May adult $185; child $135). Other highlights include the elephant and gorilla rainforests, and a treetop boardwalk in the Orang-utan sanctuary. Daily 9am–5pm; $23.60, 4–15yrs $11.80, under-4s free. Tram #55.

Royal Botanic Gardens Birdwood Ave, South Yarra. As well as the main park where young ones can feed the swans or wander along winding leafy paths, there's also the educational Children's Garden (Wed–Sun 10am–4pm, or daily during school holidays; free) featuring a number of different areas to explore and hide such as the bamboo forest, a plant tunnel, the gorge, the ruin garden featuring a rock grotto and the

wetlands area. Daily: April, Sept & Oct 7.30am–6pm; May–Aug 7.30am–5.30pm; Nov–March 7.30am–8.30pm.

St Kilda Adventure Playground Neptune Place, off Neptune St, St Kilda ☎9209 6348. Hidden away, this huge playground has a flying fox, trampolines, a wooden maze, slides and a giant ship, as well as cubbyhouses, a castle with a drawbridge, a kitchen for adults and a barbeque area. What more could the kids want? Mon–Wed & Fri 3.30–5.30pm, Thurs 10am–5.30pm, Sat & Sun 10am–5pm, or daily 11am–5pm during school holidays; free. Tram #16.

Werribee Open Range Zoo K Rd, Werribee ☎9731 9600, ⓦ www.zoo.org.au. Great place for watching a bunch of African wildlife (rhinos, hippos, zebras and giraffes) cavorting in a natural environment. Highlights include a bus safari (first at 10.30am, last at 3.30pm), the thirty-minute Volcanic Plains Walking Trail, or for the older children a "Slumber Safari" (adults $270; 12–17 year-olds $260), where you get to camp overnight and awake to the sights and sounds of the savannah. See also p.217. Daily 9am–5pm; $23.60, 4–15yrs $11.80, under-4s free. Werribee line from Flinders Street Station to Werribee Station.

Beyond the City

Beyond the City

The Great Ocean Road

Regarded as one of the world's great coastal journeys, the **Great Ocean Road** stretches from Torquay, 20km south of Geelong (see p.218), to just before Warrnambool almost 300km to the west. The road snakes along the rugged Victorian coast past innumerable coves, cliffs, scenic lookouts, waterfalls, rainforests and shipwrecks, and there are opportunities aplenty en route for bushwalking, swimming, surfing, fishing and whale-watching. When construction began in 1919, the route was intended as a memorial to those who fell in World War I. As the Great Depression took hold it also became a source of much-needed work for thousands of unemployed ex-servicemen who were equipped with little more than picks and shovels. After years of difficult and sometimes dangerous work, the Great Ocean Road was finally completed in 1932.

One of the most visited stretches of the route is the **Port Campbell National Park**, where the coastline, buffeted by wild seas and fierce winds, has been sculpted over millions of years to form a series of striking natural features. You can also wander the boardwalks and paths at the **Twelve Apostles**, remarkable limestone rock stacks rising from the ocean, and marvel at **London Bridge**, another amazing rock formation not to be missed. The **Great Otway National Park**, stretching from Torquay to Princetown and taking in the Otway mountain ranges inland, offers fantastic walking opportunities through lush rainforest.

Along with striking ocean views, the Great Ocean Road boasts a number of laid-back towns and villages on the water's edge: the resort town of **Torquay** is widely regarded as Australia's surfing capital, while buzzing restaurants and cafés dot the picturesque beachfront towns of **Lorne** and **Apollo Bay**. **Warrnambool** in the far west, is a prime whale-watching destination.

Getting around

To get the most out of touring the Great Ocean Road it's best to have your own **car** (see p.29 for rental companies). Alternatively, V/Line runs a **bus** service along the Great Ocean Road from Geelong to Apollo Bay, stopping at Torquay, Anglesea, Lorne and other points along the way (Mon–Fri three times daily, Sat & Sun twice daily; 2hr 30min; $13 one way). On Monday, Wednesday and Thursday the bus continues on to Warrnambool. There's also a **train** service between Melbourne's Southern Cross and Warrnambool (Mon–Sat three daily, Sun twice daily; $35.30 peak/$24.70 off-peak one way), a journey of just over three hours, though as the line cuts across the peninsula, you won't see anything of the coast. For further details, contact V/Line on ☎13 61 96, or see ⓦ www.vline.com.au.

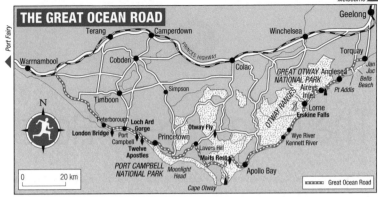

THE GREAT OCEAN ROAD

Geelong

Terang   Camperdown   Winchelsea

Port Fairy

Warrnambool   Cobden   Colac   Torquay

Jan Juc
Bells Beach

GREAT OTWAY
NATIONAL PARK   Anglesea
Aireys   Pt Addis
Inlet

Simpson

OTWAY RANGES

Timboon

N

Lorne
Erskine Falls

Peterborough   Loch Ard
Gorge   Otway Fly

London Bridge   Port
Campbell   Princetown   Wye River
Kennett River

Twelve
Apostles   Lavers Hill

Maits Rest

PORT CAMPBELL
NATIONAL PARK   Moonlight
Head   Apollo Bay

0   20 km

Cape Otway

▪▪▪▪▪ Great Ocean Road

In addition, a number of companies offer one-way **tours** down the Great Ocean Road, either on its own or as part of a longer trip: Oz Experience (℡1300 300 028, Ⓦwww.ozexperience.com) does a three-day tour between Melbourne and Adelaide, taking in the Great Ocean Road and the Grampians for $325, including accommodation; Wayward Bus (℡1300 653 510, Ⓦwww .waywardbus.com.au) offers a similar tour for $395, inclusive of meals and accommodation. See also the box in Basics on p.23. A good resource for helping plan your itinerary is the website Ⓦwww.greatoceanroad.org, which allows you to take a virtual tour.

Torquay

Gateway to the Great Ocean Road, **TORQUAY** is a nirvana for surf-seekers and those looking for a barefoot existence within reach of the beach. **Surfing** is big business here, which is hardly surprising given that some of the biggest surfing names had their beginnings in this southern coastal town. Teenage surfers from the 1960s and "hippy drop-outs" sick of braving the winter water, have grown up to become millionaire owners of locally based global wetsuit and surfwear brands like Rip Curl and Quiksilver (Billabong, Oakley and Reef are also on show here), while behind the ritzy shopfronts lining the Surfcoast Highway, newer surf and accessory labels are taking hold in the town's industrial estates. Business peaks in Torquay each Easter during the **Rip Curl Pro** surfing contest (Ⓦwww.ripcurl.com.au) for boardriders, the world's longest-running professional surfing contest, which has been sponsored by Rip Curl since 1973.

If you don't know a point break from a reef break, the best place to start is the **Surfworld Museum** (daily 9am–5pm; $9; ℡5261 4606) at the rear of the Surfcoast Plaza on the Surfcoast Highway – the main road into Torquay from

Distances and driving times from Melbourne					
Melbourne to	Torquay	Anglesea	Aireys Inlet	Lorne	Apollo Bay
kilometres	96km	112km	123km	140km	188km
approximate time	1hr 15min	1hr 25min	1hr 35min	1hr 50min	2hr 30min

Geelong. Advertising itself as the world's largest surfing museum, it has a wave-making tank and a big-wave exhibition, with photographs and film footage of the largest waves ever captured at Bells Beach (see below), along with interactive displays where you can check your balance on a surfboard, and countless surf memorabilia, including collections of vintage surfboards and Hawaiian shirts.

Torquay itself is a relaxed town with some good places to eat and a number of great beaches: Front and Yellow Bluff are suitable for families and are backed by a grassy reserve with barbecues, while Fisherman's Beach is worth a look for its **sundial**, made up of tiny mosaic tiles and shells representing Aboriginal Dreamtime stories. Two of Victoria's best surf beaches are **Jan Juc** and **Bells Beach**: the former lies just south of Torquay Golf Club and is the starting point for the 26-kilometre (8hr) **Surf Coast Walk**, which follows the coastline along little-used roads, joining Anglesea to Aireys Inlet (a map is available from Torquay Visitors Centre; see below). The latter – Australia's only official surfing reserve and site of the Rip Curl Pro contest – featured in the Patrick Swayze and Keanu Reeves movie *Point Break*, although the beach represented as Bells was actually in Canada.

Practicalities

The **Torquay Visitors Centre** (daily 9am–5pm; ☎1300 614 219) within the Surfworld Museum hands out tidal reports and maps of local breaks, as well as information on where to rent boards and wet suits. If you want to cut your surfing teeth, there are plenty of **surf schools** along the Great Ocean Road, including Southern Exposure (☎5261 9170, ⓦwww.southernexposure .au); West Coast Surf School (☎5261 2241, ⓦwww.westcoastsurfschool.com; and Go Ride A Wave (☎1300 132 441, ⓦwww.gorideawave.com.au), which all offer two-hour classes for around $55, or more in-depth multi-day packages.

Thanks to the transient surf community who show up for the good waves, there are plenty of **places to stay** in or around Torquay. As you'd expect, prices are cheaper during winter when only the most dedicated surfers are braving the chilly waters. Easily found by its boldly coloured murals, *Bells Beach Lodge*, 51–53 Surfcoast Highway (☎5261 7070, ⓦwww.bellsbeachbackpackers.com .au; dorms ❶–❷, doubles ❸), has helpful staff and rents out surf equipment. *Torquay Hotel*, 36 Bell St (☎5261 2001, ⓦwww.torquayhotel.com.au; ❺) has motel-style rooms close to the waves and the town. *Torquay Foreshore Caravan Park* (☎5261 2496, ⓦwww.gorcc.com.au) at 35 Bell St has on-site cabins, caravans and camping sites.

Enjoy alfresco breakfasts and lunches at *Moby* (daily 7am–4pm; ☎5261 2339), 41 The Esplanade, or *Growlers* (Mon–Fri 11am–late, Sat & Sun 9am–late; ☎5264 8455), 23 The Esplanade, which also has a bar. For a sit-down **meal**, mosey into *The Surfrider* (6pm–late, closed Tues; ☎5261 6477), 26 Bell St, for good seafood and tasty contemporary cuisine. Alternatively, *Torquay Hotel* (see above) has hearty bistro fare, including lip-smacking rib eye, and is a good place for a few quiet drinks, except on Saturday when it hosts live bands.

Lavers Hill	Twelve Apostles	Port Campbell	Warrnambool	Warrnambool via Princes Highway
235km	272km	285km	358km	307km
3hr	3hr 25min	3hr 45min	5hr 30min	3hr 30min

Anglesea to Aireys Inlet

West along the coast from Torquay is the turn-off for scenic **Point Addis** and the protected **Ironbark Basin Reserve**, which has several marked walking tracks (all 5km) taking in coastal lookouts. Before you get to Point Addis headland another car park marks the beginning of the **Koorie Cultural Walk**, a one-kilometre loop dotted with interpretive signs explaining the use of local flora and other facets of traditional life of the Wathaurong clan who inhabited the Geelong area for thousands of years.

Sixteen kilometres west of Torquay, **ANGLESEA** is an appealing seaside resort, popular with holidaying families and anglers who are attracted to the gentle shores of Anglesea River which flows through here to the sea. Its golf course is famous for its large mob of resident kangaroos. The excellent *Anglesea Beachfront Caravan Park* (℡5263 1583, 🕸www.angleseabeachfront.com.au), 35 Cameron Rd, has good facilities for children and a range of cottages, cabins and powered sites. For food, *Pete's Place*, 113 Great Ocean Rd (Wed–Sun 9am–late; ℡5263 2500) is a good spot for lunch or dinner with a pleasant timber deck and views of the river. Leaving Anglesea and skirting the coast, you'll see the pretty **Split Point Lighthouse** (tours available Sat & Sun 11am, noon, 1pm, 2pm; $12), built in 1891, overlooking the small town of **Aireys Inlet**, which has fine swimming and fishing, as well as a general store and a couple of cafés. Blazing Saddles (℡5289 7322, 🕸www.blazingsaddlestrailrides.com) is based here and runs horse-riding trails along the beach and through the Great Otway National Park.

Lorne

Forty-five kilometres southwest of Torquay, surf culture rubs shoulders with café society at **LORNE**, the premier holiday town on Victoria's west coast. Its main road is lined with clothes and surf shops, hotels and eating places, while between the road and the beach is a foreshore with a children's playground, trampolines, skatepark, pool and barbecues. The main beach is patrolled by lifeguards during summer. Lorne is also the home of the world's largest swimming race – the famous **Lorne Pier to Pub** ocean swim. This annual 1.2-kilometre event supposedly began in 1979 when a group of lifesavers dived off the pier and swam towards a nearby hotel – the last swimmer to reach the pub had to shout drinks for the rest. Taking place in early January, the race attracts several thousand competitors – for more information, visit 🕸www.lornesurfclub.com.au.

Inland of Lorne, many of the area's finest walking tracks crisscross the Lorne section of the Great Otway National Park, which takes in the lush eastern fringes of the Otway Ranges, and the numerous waterfalls and beaches around Aireys Inlet. One of the most accessible places is the **Blanket Leaf Picnic Area** – follow the signs for Erskine Falls from the town centre. From the picnic area there's a four-kilometre walk or drive to **Erskine Falls**, a stunning

---

Falls Festival

The **Falls Festival** is a three-day music and entertainment event held over New Year in the stunning Otway Ranges outside Lorne. Attracting international headlining rock and dance acts, the festival also features comedy sessions, a fayre, films and nature walks. Tickets go on sale in October through Ticketmaster (℡13 61 00) and cost around $289 for a three-day camping ticket; check out their excellent website (🕸www.fallsfestival.com) for further information.

thirty-metre waterfall cascading over one of the largest drops in the area. For a longer hike, make for the **Sheoak Falls Track** (signposted off the Great Ocean Rd, about 5km out of Lorne), a three-hour scenic loop (7km) that follows a creek downstream to the ocean-side Swallow Cave, back up to Castle Rock with awe-inspiring clifftop views, then on to the Sheoak Falls Picnic Area. There's free **bush camping** at Big Hill, to the north of Lorne, and at the River, to the south, as well as a few other sites throughout the park. For more information on camping and trails visit the tourist office in Lorne (see below) or check out the Parks Victoria website ⓦ www.parkweb.vic.gov.au.

Information

Lorne's well-stocked **visitors centre** is at 15 Mountjoy Parade (daily 9am–5pm; ☎ 1300 891 152, ⓦ www.visitsurfcoast.com), and has useful handouts on the Great Ocean Road's towns as well as park walking maps.

Accommodation

Erskine Beach Resort Mountjoy Parade ☎ 5228 977, ⓦ www.mantraerskinebeachresort .com.au. Lorne's only beachfront accommodation has 276 modern rooms including apartments compete with all the mod cons, plus there's a gym, pool, day spa and tennis courts. ❻–❾

Grand Pacific Hotel 268 Mountjoy Parade ☎ 5289 1609, ⓦ www.grandpacific.com.au. This spectacular hotel near the pier is all opulence from the outside, but inside the rooms are simple motel-style affairs, though they do have stunning views. The hotel also has smarter one- to three-bedroom apartments ($180–350) next door, which are a better bet. ❹–❼

Great Ocean Road Backpackers YHA 10 Erskine Ave ☎ 5289 1809, ⓦ www.yha.com.au.

The best budget rooms in town, with pleasant timber verandas to read on and spotless shared kitchens. Dorms ❶, rooms ❸

Lemonade Creek Cottages 690 Erskine Falls Rd ☎ 5289 2600, ⓦ www.lemonadecreek cottages.com. These self-contained weatherboard units are located out of town in lush bush, on the road to the falls. Facilities include a heated pool and tennis court. ❺–❼

Sandridge Motel 128 Mountjoy Parade ☎ 5289 2180, ⓦ www.sandridgemotel.com.au. Occupying a prime spot overlooking the main drag, the Sandridge has a range of rooms; try for one of the rooms with a balcony looking out over the sea. ❸–❺

Eating

There's no shortage of places to grab a bite to **eat**. *Ba Ba Lu Bar and Restaurant* at 6a Mountjoy Parade (daily 9am–1am; ☎ 5289 1808) is a popular Spanish tapas café and bar that dishes up great breakfasts and mains, and has a pleasant courtyard. Another old favourite is *Arab* at 94 Mountjoy Parade (daily 7am–9.30pm; ☎ 5289 1435), with great coffee and a likeable menu that includes thin-crust pizzas, calamari, and burgers. For good bar meals, head for the *Lorne Hotel*, 176 Mountjoy Parade (bistro open daily noon–9am; ☎ 5289 1409).

Apollo Bay

From Lorne the road twists and turns for over forty kilometers (keep an eye out for koalas around Kennett River; take the turn-off up Grey River Rd and look up) to **APOLLO BAY**, an unpretentious and laid-back resort, with a lively alternative scene during the summer. A fishing port and former whaling station, its setting is one of the prettiest along the Great Ocean Road, with a crescent-shaped bay set beneath the rounded, sometimes foggy Otway Ranges. Gentle updraughts make these hills popular with hang-gliders, who can often be seen floating lazily above the town. The pier and breakwater are usually the province of anglers, and at the base of the pier the Fisherman's Co-op sells fresh seafood. You can also **learn to surf** and **kayak** here with Apollo Bay Surf and Kayak (☎5237 1189, ⓦwww.apollobaysurfkayak.com.au). In March, the town hosts the three-day **Apollo Bay Music Festival** (ⓦwww .apollobaymusicfestival.com), featuring jazz, rock, blues, country and world music. The **visitors centre** at 100 Great Ocean Rd (daily 9am–5pm; ☎5237 6529) is a good resource for the area, and can provide details on the **Great Ocean Walk** (ⓦwww.greatoceanwalk.com.au), a 100-kilometre trail that heads from Apollo Bay to Glenample, a few kilometres before the Twelve Apostles, taking in national parks and beautiful coastal scenery along the way.

Apollo Bay makes a good place to break up your trip with a number of **motels** dotted along the main strip; one of the nicest is the friendly *Sandpiper Motel* (☎5237 6732, ⓦwww.sandpiper.net.au; ❹–❻), 3 Murray Sts, with a range of bright, well-appointed rooms, some with ocean views. Cafés and **restaurants** line the Great Ocean Road where you'll find lots of fresh seafood on the menu: for breakfast try *Bayleaf Café* at no. 131 (summer 6am–9pm; winter 8am–2.30pm; ☎5237 6470), while *Buffs Bistro* (noon–late; ☎5237 6403) at no. 51 is a warm and friendly place that offers a bit of everything, from seafood chowder to steaks and gnocchi – make sure you leave room for one of the huge desserts from the counter.

The Shipwreck Coast

Beyond Apollo Bay the Great Ocean Road heads inland, passing through the temperate rainforests and fern gullies of the **Great Otway National Park**. In the late 1860s, loggers spread into the Otway Ranges and built a number of small townships that remain to this day, but nowadays tourism is the area's lifeblood. A pleasant way to see the park firsthand is to follow the 800-metre boardwalk at **Maits Rest**, 15km beyond Apollo Bay, which takes you on a picturesque circuit through the ancient rainforest.

On the way to the tiny hilltop town of Lavers Hill, you pass the turn-off to the **Cape Otway Lighthouse** (9am–5pm; $14.50; daily tours from 9am; ☎5237 9240). Erected in 1848 after the ship *Cataraqui* went down off the coast of King Island to the south, it is the oldest remaining lighthouse on the Australian mainland. Only nine of the 400 passengers survived – just one of many tragedies that gave the title **Shipwreck Coast** to the 130-kilometre stretch of coastline from nearby Moonlight Head to Port Fairy, where 700 ships are known to have gone down; 200 of which have been found. For information on 25 of these wrecks (whose sites are signposted off the road) pick up a free copy of the *Historic Shipwreck Trail Guide* from visitors centres in the region. From Lavers Hill you can make the fifteen-minute detour to the **Otway Fly Treetop Walk** (daily 9am–5pm; $19.50; ☎5235 9200), a 25-metre-high walkway that allows visitors to walk through the canopy of myrtle, beech and mountain ash trees of the Otway Ranges. The 600-metre walkway also features a 47-metre-high tower, accessed by a spiral staircase, and a café.

The eastern portion of the Shipwreck Coast is dominated by the narrow **Port Campbell National Park**. Windswept, heath-covered hills overlook Bass Strait and its sometimes awesome swells. There are several places to stop along this route, the most popular being the site known as the **Twelve Apostles** just over 80km from Apollo Bay. Here, the waves of the Southern Ocean have worn the cliffs into a spectacular series of offshore limestone stacks – astonishingly this sculpting has occurred only over the last 600 years, a relatively short time in the

▲ The Twelve Apostles

20-million-year-old coastline. Originally there were a dozen stacks, but they are now down to eight, the latest having collapsed in 2005. Access to the viewing platform is via the unstaffed information centre adjacent to the car park. The best time to view them is at sunset, although inevitably this time draws the largest crowds. Stick around for a bit longer after dusk, however, and you'll be rewarded with the sight of around a thousand fairy penguins returning to their burrows.

A few kilometres further west is **Loch Ard Gorge**. In 1878 the clipper *Loch Ard*, transporting immigrants from England, struck a reef near here and went down, taking all but two of the 53 passengers with her. Most of the passengers and crew are buried in the cemetery overlooking the gorge. There are three self-guided walks beginning from the car park (ranging from 40 to 90 minutes) explaining the story of the *Loch Ard* as well as the geology of the gorge in more detail. For more information on the coast's maritime tragedies, visit the **visitors centre** (9am–5pm; ☎5598 6053) at **PORT CAMPBELL**, 12km to the west. The centre also houses the tiny **Loch Ard Shipwreck museum**, a display of artefacts retrieved from some of the ill-fated wrecks along the Shipwreck Coast. Port Campbell itself is named after Captain Alexander Campbell, the manager of Port Fairy's whaling station, and is a seriously incognito town of a couple of hundred regulars, with a pleasant beach and a jetty offering good fishing opportunities, plus a number of good cafés and motels within earshot of the water.

Just a few kilometres beyond Port Campbell is **London Bridge**, a rock formation whose two sections were connected by a central span of rock – the "bridge" – until 1990, when it suddenly collapsed, leaving two rather startled people stranded on the outer section (they were eventually rescued by helicopter). Just beyond here, the **Grotto** – another amazing natural rock formation – has a path leading down to a rock pool beneath a limestone arch.

Warrnambool

West of London Bridge, the Great Ocean Road passes through dairy country before ending just short of **WARRNAMBOOL**. Once home to sealers and whalers, it is now Victoria's pre-eminent destination for **whale watching**: southern right whales can be sighted off Logans Beach, just east of town, between May and October; follow the signs for "Whale Nursery". Warrnambool's excellent **Flagstaff Hill Maritime Village** (daily 9am–5pm; $15.95; ℡5559 4600, Ⓦwww.flagstaffhill.com) on Merri Street is a re-created nineteenth-century fishing port, with an impressive collection of shipwreck finds including the Loch Ard Peacock, an earthenware peacock washed ashore two days after the clipper *Loch Ard* went down in 1878. The highlight, however, is the nightly *Shipwrecked* ($25.50) sound-and-vision show re-telling the story of the sinking of the *Loch Ard*. Warrnambool's **visitors centre** (9am–5pm; ℡5559 4620) is also housed within the museum at 23 Merri St. On Liebig Street the excellent regional **Warrnambool Art Gallery** (Mon–Fri 10am–5pm, Sat & Sun noon–5pm; free; ℡5559 4949), houses a fine collection of colonial works, including the paintings of Eugene Von Guerard (see below), and over six hundred contemporary works. Leibig Street in the town has a number of good places **to eat** including ⚓ *Fishtales Café* (daily 7am–8pm) ℡5561 2957) at no. 63, a relaxed place with a huge menu that offers a bit of everything, from all-day breakfast, fish meals and focaccia, to Asian, Indian, Italian and over thirty choices of burger. It's also licensed and does takeaway. A few doors down at no. 77 is *Mack's Snacks* (Mon–Sat 9am–8.30pm; ℡5562 2432), Warrnambool's first café-diner, which offers a similar menu. **Accommodation** options are numerous; try *Warrnambool Beach Backpackers* (℡5562 4874, Ⓦwww.beachbackpackers.com.au; dorms ❶ or ❷ with breakfast, doubles ❸), 17 Stanley St, with a bar, pool table and kitchen; or *Downtown Motel* (℡5562 1277, Ⓦwww.downtownmotel.net.au; ❸–❹) at 620 Raglan Parade, in the centre of town, which has a heated pool, guest kitchen and a games room.

Fifteen kilometres west of Warrnambool, along the Princes Highway, is the **Tower Hill Game Reserve** (sunrise–sunset; free), which lies within a dormant volcano. After years of logging, the area was replanted in the 1950s using an 1855 landscape painting by Eugene von Guerard as a guide. More than 300,000 trees were introduced and the reserve now has an abundance of water birds, koalas, kangaroos and wallabies, as well as a Natural History Centre and a visitors centre (Mon–Fri 9am–5pm, Sat & Sun 10am–4pm) with geological and historical displays, local Aboriginal art, and a copy of Guerard's painting. There are several self-guided half-hour and hour-long walks, as well as barbecues and picnic areas.

Mornington Peninsula

Just south of Melbourne, the **Mornington Peninsula** is a favourite seaside holiday destination. The peninsula has lots to offer: elegant beachfront towns like **Sorrento** and **Portsea**, prolific bush and native wildlife in the **Mornington Peninsula National Park**, excellent surfing and swimming spots (many of them patrolled by lifeguards), lookouts, walking trails and wineries. Further southeast, and connected to the mainland by a bridge, is scenic **Phillip Island**, whose main tourist attraction is the **Penguin Parade**, the amazing spectacle of hordes of penguins waddling ashore each evening at sunset. Little-known **French Island** in Western Port Bay is a blissfully under-exploited gem – formerly the setting for a prison farm, it's now virtually undeveloped wilderness. Further southeast along the mainland, **Wilsons Promontory** is a nature-lovers' paradise. Known locally as "The Prom", it is one of Australia's best-loved national parks, renowned for mountainous bushland, wetlands and walks, as well as excellent surfing and swimming beaches.

Mornington Peninsula

Curving around Port Phillip Bay from Frankston to Point Nepean, the **Mornington Peninsula** has traditionally been popular with Victoria's less affluent holidaymakers, whose caravans and tents dot the peninsula's tea-tree-studded foreshore. The towns of Sorrento and Portsea, however, at the tip of the peninsula, remain the preserve of Melbourne's wealthy, many of whom decamp here for extended periods during the summer months. Water-based activities like surfing and swimming with dolphins are the main attractions, but when you tire of sea and sandcastles, there are some excellent wineries, crafts markets, walking trails, sweeping views and historical sites inland. For more information, visit the official Mornington Peninsula website (Ⓦwww .visitmorningtonpeninsula.org).

Regular bus services to all major towns on the Mornington Peninsula operate from Frankston, which is on the Frankston train line from Flinders Street Station (1hr), but if you want to take in wineries, beaches and Arthurs Seat you'll need your own car. Change at Frankston for trains to Stony Point (35min) for connections to Phillip and French islands. From Frankston Station metlink buses run to various points along the peninsula; #788 to Portsea stops at Mornington, Dromana and Sorrento as well as other points in between, while #782 and #783 head to Flinders and Hastings respectively. For more information call Ⓣ13 16 38 or go to Ⓦwww.metlinkmelbourne .com.au. Alternatively, you can connect with the Portsea Passenger Service bus #787 from Dromana to Sorrento Ferry Terminal for ferries to Queenscliff on the west side of Port Phillip Bay; for timetable information call ☎1800 115 666.

If you're travelling **by car**, the most direct route is via the Mornington Peninsula Freeway, which runs down the peninsula as far as Rosebud, but an alternative is taking the Nepean Highway from Melbourne and then the Mornington turn-off.

There are visitor information centres (daily 9am–5pm) at Frankston, Pier Promenade (☎1300 322 842); Mornington, 320 Main St (☎5975 1644); and Dromana, 359b Point Nepean Rd (☎1800 804 009).

Frankston to Cape Schanck

The peninsula starts at **Frankston**, 40km south of Melbourne, beyond which the peninsula's western coast is a succession of clean, safe and beautiful beaches, although all become crowded and traffic-snarled in summer. Fifteen kilometres further on, the old fishing port of **Mornington** has few attractions, although the lookout at the Matthew Flinders obelisk at Schnapper Point has great views over the sometimes choppy bay, and a handy café and restaurant; there's also a popular craft market on Main Street every Wednesday (9am–3pm). Four kilometres along the Nepean Highway, near Mount Martha, **Briars Park** (9am–5pm; free; ☎5974 3686) comprises an 1840s homestead named after the former occupants' family home on the island of St Helena (10am–4pm; $5.10 entry with tour guide only; guides work on a voluntary basis so may not always be available: phone to check) with a collection of furniture and memorabilia given to the owner, William Balcombe, by Napoleon Bonaparte who reportedly stayed with the family during his exile at St Helena, and an enclosed wildlife reserve with woodlands and extensive wetlands. The **visitors centre** near the homestead will put on a short film giving you an overview of the Balcombe's pioneering days and the history of the homestead, as well as a rundown on the present-day facilities of the park. There is also a wetlands display with turtles and lizards. To the west of the visitors centre are the starting points for two walks through the woodlands, while the adjacent **wetlands**, visited by more than fifty species of waterbirds, can be observed at close distance from two bird-hides accessed via a boardwalk from the visitors centre; pick up a map of these walks from the centre.

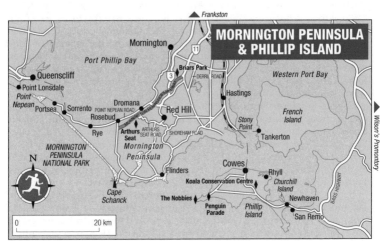

Beyond here, the coast road leads to **Dromana**, where seaside development begins in earnest. Inland from Dromana, the granite outcrop of **Arthurs Seat** rises to a height of 305m, providing breathtaking views of Port Phillip Bay. You can drive up to the summit along a winding road dotted with some great lookouts. Before you get to the top you'll pass the entrance to **The Enchanted Maze Garden** (daily 10am–6pm; adults $15, 3–15 yr-olds $9; ☎5981 8449, ⓦwww.enchantedmaze.com.au), which combines three traditional hedge mazes with theme gardens plus a maize maze (mid-Feb to April), a sculpture park and a children's animal farm. Alternatively, you can have a drink or a bite at the top at *Arthurs Hotel* (Mon–Fri 10am–9pm, Sat & Sun 9am–9pm; ☎5981 4444), with live jazz on Fridays.

Interspersed among the peninsula's bushland, orchards, craft outlets, berry farms and enormous French provincial-style houses are over 200 **wineries**, which produce superb Pinot Noir and Shiraz, as well as good whites. The most notable wine-growing area is **Red Hill**, southeast of Arthurs Seat, and in recent years many gourmet restaurants have opened. Overlooking the hills and calm waters of Western Port Bay, *Red Hill Estate* (daily 11am–5pm; ☎5931 0177, ⓦwww .redhillestate.com.au), 53 Shoreham Rd, Red Hill South, has tastings, sales and light lunches, with dinner on Friday and Saturday evenings at the award-winning **Max's** restaurant. Nearby, at 33 Shoreham Rd, the *Montalto Vineyard and Olive Grove* (daily 11am–5pm; ☎5989 8412, ⓦwww.montalto.com.au) offers both wine and an area of **wetlands** that's home to over ninety species of birds and other wildlife. Another cracking winery is *Moorooduc Estate* (Mon & Thurs–Sun 11am–4pm; ☎5971 8506, ⓦwww.moorooducestate.com.au), at 501 Derril Rd, Moorooduc, at the northern end of the peninsula. Out back, the cellar door dispenses good Pinot and Chardonnay, while *Jill's*, the upmarket winery restaurant (Sat lunch & dinner, Sun lunch), serves a fabulous range of quality local produce – from roast free-range chicken to fresh fruits, vegetables and cheeses. For more details, see the *Peninsula Wine Country Annual*, available online at ⓦwww.visitor.com.au or from tourist visitors centres and attractions in the region; or the Mornington Peninsula *Wine Touring Map*, available at information centres. Also in Red Hill, **Ashcombe Maze and Lavender Gardens** (daily 10am–5pm; $15; ☎5989 8387, ⓦwww.ashcombemaze.com.au) at 15 Shoreham Rd is Australia's oldest and most famous **hedge maze**, with 25 acres of gardens, woodlands and waterways, plus a circular rose maze and a café.

As well as wineries, the peninsula's **community markets** selling local produce and crafts attract many city-dwellers; most are monthly affairs, and there's usually one every weekend. One of the biggest and best is Red Hill Community Market, Australia's oldest community market, held on the first Saturday of every month (Sept–May 8am–1pm), at Red Hill Recreation Reserve, Arthurs Seat Road, 10km east of Dromana.

West of Red Hill, near Rye, are the **Peninsula Hot Springs** (daily 9am–9pm; ☎5950 8777, ⓦwww.peninsulahotsprings.com), 140 Springs Lane, off Browns Road, Victoria's only natural thermal springs. Here you can bathe in mineral-rich pools heated to a relaxing 50°C from natural sources far underground, and pad around in fluffy dressing gowns while waiting for relaxing spa and massage treatments. Entrance to the public pools costs $24 Tuesday to Thursday and $30 all other times, with treatments starting at $76.50 for a 45-minute massage up to $450 for one-day packages.

Further south, on the ocean side of the peninsula, **Cape Schanck** (daily 10am–5pm; park entrance $4.40) is the site of a 21-metre-high, red-topped lighthouse, which has protected sailors since 1859. From here, a timber staircase and boardwalk lead from the dramatic basalt cliffs down to the sea along a narrow neck of land, providing magnificent coastal views. The three **light-house-keeper's cottages** offer the most scenic **accommodation** on the peninsula (☎5988 6184, ⓦwww.austpacinns.com.au; ❻), each with a cosy lounge and kitchen. There's a small maritime museum ($10) at the lighthouse, which is open daily for tours at half-hour intervals (10am–5pm; $14).

Sorrento

Near the tip of the peninsula (90km from Melbourne) **SORRENTO** is the area's oldest and most affluent town. This is where Melbourne's big money relaxes – in the wide, tree-lined residential streets, the spectacular cliff-top properties hidden behind high fences, and in the town centre's abundant antique shops, galleries, cafés and restaurants.

Two kilometres before the town on the Point Nepean Highway is the **Collins Settlement Historic Site**, in Sullivan Bay. This is where, in 1803, Captain David Collins attempted the first permanent European settlement of the Melbourne area, only to abandon the site less than a year later because of its chronic lack of water. One of the convicts in the expedition was the infamous William Buckley who, having escaped, was adopted by the local Aborigines and lived with them for 32 years (see box, p.223). You can walk along the cliffs and around the pioneer cemetery; there's a signposted turn-off from the main road.

From Sorrento, **ferries** (☎5258 3244, ⓦwww.searoad.com.au) run across the mouth of the bay to Queenscliff on the Bellarine Peninsula (see p.221), departing every hour from 7am to 6pm (40min), returning from Queenscliff at the same hours. Tickets for passengers only are $10 one-way and $20 return; bikes are an extra $2. For two passengers with a car, tickets are $63 ($7 for every additional adult), one-way, depending on the season. Tickets can be purchased from the passenger lounges at Sorrento and Queenscliff. Cars should be at the terminal thirty to forty-five minutes prior to departure.

The standard of **accommodation** in Sorrento is good: *Hotel Sorrento* (☎5984 8000, ⓦwww.hotelsorrento.com.au; ❼–❽), 5 Hotham Rd, occupies a great spot on a hill near the jetty and has a choice of stylish rooms, some with bay views, while *Carmel Of Sorrento* (☎5984 1356, ⓦwww.sorrentobeach motel.com.au; ❺–❻), 142 Ocean Beach Rd, is a charming B&B right in the middle of town. Alternatively, if you want a bit of action you should head for *Bayplay Adventure Lodge*, 46 Canterbury Jetty Rd (☎5984 0888, ⓦwww .bayplay.com.au; ❸), in Blairgowrie, which offers budget accommodation near the beach and a wide range of activities including sea-kayaking trips, surf lessons and horse riding, as well a being a PADI dive resort, running courses from its shop in Portsea. For **food** just take a wander along Ocean Beach Road where you'll find cafés, takeaways and restaurants. *Spargos* (daily 9am–late;

Dolphin tours

Swimming with **dolphins** and **seals** has become one of the area's prime attractions, so much so that tour operators are obliged to follow a code of practice to ensure they don't adversely affect the animals. Two long-established operators are the environmentally conscious Polperro Dolphin Swims (☎5988 8437, mobile ☎0428 174 160, ⓦwww.polperro.com.au), who take the smallest maximum number of people, and Moonraker (☎5984 4211, mobile ☎0419 205 060, ⓦwww.moonrakercharters.com .au). Both depart from Sorrento Pier twice daily during the season (Sept/Oct–May), weather permitting, for a four-hour trip ($105–115 per swimmer, including wetsuit and snorkelling equipment; $50 for sightseers).

☎5984 3177) at no. 113 is a good place for breakfast and lunch as is *Shells* (daily 7.30am–4.30pm; ☎5984 5133), at no. 95, while on the foreshore *The Baths* (Mon–Fri 11.30am–late, Sat & Sun 9am–late; ☎5984 1500), 3278 Point Nepean Rd, has great seafood and lovely views of the bay, as does *Hotel Sorrento* (see above; open for breakfast, lunch & dinner), whose fine dining menu offers above-average pub food.

Portsea and the Mornington Peninsula National Park

A few kilometres further on, **PORTSEA** is quieter and more private than Sorrento, with the houses of its wealthy inhabitants contentedly secluded in the coastal scrub. In summer, Front Beach and Shelley Beach are for sunbathers, while on the other shore surfers and boardriders make for the swell of Portsea Ocean Beach, which also attracts a good number of hang-gliders. Portsea is a mecca for **divers**, with excellent dives off Port Phillip Heads; trips operate from the pier throughout the summer and there are a couple of good dive shops, including Bayplay Adventure Lodge (see opposite). Each year around January 20, Portsea hosts the **Portsea Swim Classic**, an open-water race that attracts both young and old to the 1.2-kilometre course; for more information, visit ⓦwww.portseasurf.com.au.

The tip of the peninsula, Point Nepean, is now classified as **Point Nepean National Park**, part of a patchwork of parks sprinkled over the southern end of the peninsula, collectively known as **Mornington Peninsula National Park**. Here the historic **Fort Nepean** has tunnels, bomb-proof rooms, gun emplacements, fortifications, glorious views of the Port Phillip Heads and spectacular cliff-top walking tracks leading off into secluded bushland. Built at the same time as Fort Queenscliff opposite (see p.221), it is where the first Allied shots were fired during both World Wars – in 1914, a warning shot was fired across the bow of a German freighter and, in 1939, there was a similar response to an unidentified ship (later discovered to be the *Tasmanian Woniora*.

The visitors centre and a car park (daily 9am–5pm; free; ☎03/5984 4276) are 1km west of Portsea. Entrance into the national park costs $7.90. To get to **Point Nepean**, 7km from the visitors centre, you can either rent a bike ($16.50 for 3hr) or take the Transporter "train" – actually a few carriages pulled by a tractor ($13.50 one-way, $16.50 return; fare includes the park admission fee), which departs from the visitors centre at 10.30am, 11.30am, 12.30pm, 2pm and 3pm; during summer the service runs half-hourly. Alternatively, you can drive the 2.5km to Gunners car park and walk the rest of the way.

The Transporter runs to Point Nepean, with four drop-offs for walks: the first, the **Walter Pisterman Heritage Walk** (1km), leads through to the Port Phillip Bay shoreline; the second (1km) heads to the top of Cheviot Hill, with views across to the Bellarine Peninsula, then continues to **Cheviot Beach** where on December 17, 1967, **Harold Holt**, Australia's then prime minister, went for a swim in the rough surf of Bass Strait and disappeared, presumed drowned: his body was never found. The third walk, the **Fort Pearce and Eagle's Nest Heritage Trail** (2km), crosses through defence fortifications. A fourth walk takes you around **Fort Nepean**, right at the tip of the peninsula.

Phillip Island

Just under two hours' drive from Melbourne, and connected to the mainland by a 640-metre bridge, **PHILLIP ISLAND** is one of Victoria's most popular destinations, largely on account of the **Penguin Parade**. However, the island also has large colonies of seals and koalas, fine coastal scenery, children's activities, good swimming beaches, and enough nooks and crannies to create surfable waves all year round.

The first European to set foot on its shores was the English explorer George Bass in 1798. Since his visit, the island has undergone a number of name changes: originally called Westernport by Bass, it became Snapper Island, then Grant Island after Lieutenant James Grant visited in 1801, before finally being christened Phillip Island in honour of the First Fleet's Captain Arthur Phillip. A favoured hunting ground for whalers and sealers, the island later became a sheep and cattle run, and a farming region for chicory, a coffee additive that was grown and roasted in kilns for the first time in 1870 – you can still see the peculiar square-shaped chicory kilns dotted around the island. Each year, Phillip Island switches gear for the 500cc **Australian Motorcycle Grand Prix**, held in October over three days (Ⓦbikes.grandprix.com.au), when accommodation on the island becomes scarce.

Massive investment has boosted Phillip Island's infrastructure in recent years, but even now getting around poses problems. From Southern Cross Station, there is a V/Line **bus** direct to **Cowes** (Mon–Fri 3.50pm; 3hr 20min; $10), the main settlement on the island, but no public transport once you get there. If you're short of time, a **bus tour** from Melbourne is a good way to see the penguins, and most tours also take in other island attractions as well. One of the best operators is the long-established Autopia Tours (Ⓣ9419 8878, Ⓦwww.autopiatours.com.au), who pick you up from central Melbourne or St Kilda. Their daily one-day tour ($109 including entrance fees and dinner) takes in the Wildlife Park, Koala Conservation Centre and Penguin Parade, as well as Seal Rocks and the Nobbies. Travelling by **car**, the island is ninety minutes away from Melbourne via the Monash Freeway or Princes Highway, both of which join the South Gippsland Highway beyond Dandenong: follow the road to Lang Lang and then the Bass Highway to Anderson where the road heads directly west to San Remo and the bridge across to the island. **NEWHAVEN**, the first town you come to after crossing the bridge, has a large **tourist information centre** (daily 9am–5pm; Ⓣ1300 366 422, Ⓦwww.visitphillipisland.com), where you can book

▲ Bushwalkers, Darby River, Wilson's Prom

accommodation, pick up a free map and buy tickets for the Penguin Parade ($20), Churchill Island ($10), the Koala Conservation Centre ($10), or a combined parks pass for all three ($34), as well as ferry cruises.

The Penguin Parade

Despite the abundance of fur seals, koalas, wallabies, emus, and lyrebirds that inhabit this sweep of land in southeast Victoria, none draws such a crowd as the Little Penguins (also known as Fairy Penguins), the smallest of the penguin species, found only in southern Australian waters. The enormously popular **Penguin Parade** (nightly at sunset, $20, credit card bookings ℡5956 8300, Ⓦwww.penguins.org.au) takes place at **Summerland Beach**, near the western end of the island. Each evening at sunset, people rush to see the thousand or so cute little penguins emerging from the surf and waddling to their nesting areas on the foreshore. It's an impressive spectacle, although the penguins are almost outnumbered by the hordes of tourists who look down from concrete stands onto the floodlit beach. The parade takes about fifty minutes, after which (or before) you can move onto the extensive boardwalks over the burrows and continue watching the penguins' antics. The crowds are smaller in winter, when you should bring rugs, as winds blowing in from Bass Strait can make the experience unbearably chilly, plus something to sit on (there's only concrete tiers). If you hang around long enough, you get a much closer view of the penguins – some of their burrows are close to the road, meaning the birds have to take the longer route along the sides of the boardwalks. To escape the majority of the crowds, you can choose the "Penguin Sky Box" option ($50) – an exclusive, elevated viewing-tower with a ranger on hand to answer questions.

All the money goes back into the excellent **Penguin Parade Visitors Centre** (daily from 10am; admission included in the parade ticket) which has a simulated underwater scene of the hazards of a penguin's life, interactive displays, videos and even nesting boxes to which penguins have access from the outside, plus a café and souvenir shop.

Around the island

A few kilometres beyond the Penguin Parade, at the western end of the island, are **The Nobbies**, two huge rock-stacks linked to the island at low tide by a wave-cut platform of basalt, affording views across to Cape Schanck on the Mornington Peninsula. Two kilometres off the coast, **Seal Rocks** are two rocky islets known for their thriving colony of Australian fur seals, estimated to number around 5000. You can see the seals year round through the telescopes on the cliff edge ($2), though numbers peak during the breeding season between late October and December. From the car park at the new **Nobbies Centre** (daily 10am to 1hr before sunset) a boardwalk leads along the rounded clifftops to a lookout over a blowhole.

Other highlights of the island include the **Koala Conservation Centre** on the Phillip Island Tourist Road between Newhaven and Cowes (daily 10am–5pm; $10), where elevated walkways allow visitors to observe koala at close range. Opposite here, **A Maze'n Things** (daily 10am–5pm; adults $29, 4–16 yr-olds $19.50; ℡5952 2283, Ⓦwww.amazenthings.com.au) has a mini-golf course and fun park with an enormous three-dimensional maze. **COWES** is the main town on the island with a wide sheltered beach that's good for bucket-and-spaders. The Esplanade has some good alfresco eateries, try *Harry's on the Esplanade* (Tues–Sun noon–2.30pm, 5.30pm–late; ℡5952 6226) for good seafood and views, or *Isola di Capri* (daily lunch and dinner; ℡5952 2435) on the corner of Thompson Street and The Esplanade, a family-run Italian with adjacent gelateria. Chapel Street is dotted with **motels**; *Coachman Motel* (☎5952 1098, ⓦwww.coachmanmotel.com.au; ❹) at no. 51 offers spacious units and studios and has a heated pool and spa. While round the corner *The Castle Villa by the Sea* (☎5952 1228, ⓦwww.thecastle.com.au; ❺–❻), 7–9 Steele St, is a delightful boutique hotel. Alternatively if you're looking for seclusion and stunning views head to ⚑ *Cliff Top* (☎5952 1033, ⓦwww.clifftop.com .au; ❼–❽) at Smiths Beach, on the south of the island, arguably the best accommodation on the island with seven exquisitely decorated rooms. Incidentally Cowes is where the words of *Waltzing Matilda*, Australia's best known and much-loved national song, were penned.

Churchill Island

One kilometre north of Newhaven and accessible via a narrow bridge is tiny **CHURCHILL ISLAND**. First used by the Bunurong Aborigines for hunting shark and oysters, the island was visited in 1801 by Lieutenant James Grant, who cleared and planted Victoria's first crops. It was then purchased by Samuel Amess, a building contractor and former mayor of Melbourne, in 1872, who built a home on the island, which still stands today: you can wander through the heritage-listed weatherboard homestead in English-style gardens and its **working farm** (daily 10am–5pm; adults $10, 4–15 yr-olds $5; ☎03/5956 7214) with Highland cattle, sheep, horses and free-roaming hens and ducks. The farm puts on a range of daily activities including milking Daisy the cow, sheep shearing and blacksmith demonstrations, while a leisurely walk leads around the small island (2hr) from the Churchill Island Visitors Centre (free), with views of the unspoilt coastline; the centre also has a café.

French Island

Across from Phillip Island is the towering shape of **FRENCH ISLAND**, named for the French scientific expedition, led by Nicholas Baudin, which visited in 1902. Previously, the first known European to sight the island was George Bass, who entered Western Port Bay in 1798 but mistook it for a promontory of the mainland. In 1802, it was named Western Island after Lieutenant John Murray spied it from the **Lady Nelson**. Subsequently inhabited by sealers, it became Victoria's own Alcatraz when it housed a prison farm from 1916 to 1975, but these days French Island is known for its raw natural beauty and rich wildlife. Salt marshes and mangroves ring the coastline, while the interior is mostly heathland with magnificent wildflower displays in spring. Over two-thirds of the island is national park, whose inhabitants include sea eagles, mutton birds, pelicans and the rare potoroos: not so rare are the mosquitoes – make sure you bring some repellent. The island also has Australia's largest population of **koalas**. Indeed, so abundant are the marsupials that they are exported to zoos in Australia and around the world.

Largely flat, the island is a cyclist's and walker's paradise (you need a permit to bring a car onto the island), and there are plenty of half- and full-day **trails** coiling inland and around the coastline, including a gentle three-kilometre hike up to the Pinnacles, which affords good views over wetlands to the west, Western Port Bay and of Phillip Island. All walks start from **Tankerton Foreshore Reserve** on the west of the island, and guides to routes are available from the information board located next to Tankerton jetty. The **French Island National Park office** on Bayview Road (☎5980 1294) also has information on local walks and activities, or visit Parks Victoria at ⓦwww.parkweb.vic.gov.au. You can bring your own bike (mountain bikes are advisable due to the wet, sandy conditions) or rent one from the French Island general store (☏5980 1209; $16 per day) or *Tortoise Head Guest-house* (see below), both located near the Tankerton Jetty.

The **McLeod Prison** and associated farm (daily 9am–5pm; $5 per adult, minimum entry $20) once housed over a hundred inmates serving the last periods of their sentences. From all reports the prison was quite comfortable – located amid extensive natural bushlands, inmates were consoled by a nine-hole golf course, basketball and tennis courts, and it was the first Australian prison to introduce television in the 1950s. It now offers rooms in the old cells (see below), guided tours of the prison facilities and bicycles for rent.

Arrival and getting Around

Access to French Island is via **ferry** ($20 return, bikes $8), although cars are not allowed on board. From Phillip Island, Inter Island Ferries (☏9585 5730, ⊛www .interislandferries.com.au) depart Stony Point daily at 8am and 4.15pm, plus 10.15am and noon Tuesday, Thursday, Saturday and Sunday, returning at 9.30am and 4.30pm; and from Cowes jetty daily at 8.45am, returning at 5.25pm. Unless you plan on getting around the island by bike it might be easier to take an afternoon **tour**, which lasts about four hours and includes a history of the island and its flora and fauna, plus a visit to the McLeod Eco-Farm. French Island Bus Tours ($38 including Devonshire tea; ☏5980 1241, ⊛www.frenchislandtours .com.au), run on Tuesday, Thursday and Sunday, while French Island Eco-Tours ($40; ☏1300 307 054, ⊛www.frenchislandecotours.com.au) run tours on Thursday and Sunday. For both, take the Inter Island Ferry from Stony Point at noon to Tankerton jetty; the tours meet the ferry and drop off at the jetty at the end of the tour.

Accommodation

For **accommodation**, the *McLeod Eco-Farm and Historical Prison* (☏5980 1224, ⊛www.mcleodecofarm.com), on McLeod Road, has a range of bunkrooms (❸) and guesthouse rooms (❹) in the former prison cells and officer's quarters. The rate includes three meals using organic produce grown on the farm, and transfer to and from the jetty 20km away. Another value-for-money option is the *Tortoise Head Guesthouse* (☏5980 1234, ⊛www.tortoise head.net; ❸–❹) near the jetty on Tankerton Road. The only camping on the island is at *Fairhaven Campsite*, which offers very basic camping – pit toilet and no showers. Camping is free but you will need to get a permit beforehand; phone ☏5980 1294 for more information. The site is a five-kilometre walk from the jetty and you will need to bring a gas stove as fires are not permitted; it also pays to also include fresh water which is scarce on the island. The general store is roughly 2km away.

Wilsons Promontory National Park

Forming the southernmost point of the Australian mainland, **WILSONS PROMONTORY NATIONAL PARK** (known locally as "The Prom") is one of Australia's best-loved national parks, renowned for bushland, granite mountain ranges, wetlands, mountain walks, and excellent surfing and swimming beaches. For most of the nineteenth century, this remote and relatively inaccessible location was only used by sealers, whalers and cattle-grazers, but by the 1880s, the park was a regular haunt of naturalists, who secured its position as a national park. Named in honour of prominent London businessman, Thomas Wilson, it became a commando training camp during World War II and is today an important refuge for a diverse range of native wildlife, with around half of all

Victoria's bird species and a third of its mammals, including the threatened long-nosed potoroo and eastern pygmy possum. Other fauna, such as wombats, emus, kangaroos and wallabies, are commonly sighted around visitor areas and near walking tracks. In recognition of its characteristic land forms, plants and animals, the park was designated a Biosphere Reserve by UNESCO in 1982.

Tidal River, located thirty kilometres inside the park boundary by a small river on Norman Bay, is the park's only service area, with a general store, takeaway food, fuel and free barbecues, and the chief focus for tourism and recreation. The drive to it is especially beautiful, for along the way it's possible to see large mobs of kangaroos, usually grazing or resting in the shade, and often emus and wombats. From Tidal River, you can get a closer view of the wildlife by exploring on foot, with myriad short **walking tracks** zigzagging through the park's many ecosystems and habitats. **Squeaky Beach Track** (1.5hr) heads through a tea-tree canopy to a pure quartz sand beach named for the sound its sand makes underfoot, while the walk to the top of **Mount Oberon** (558m; 2hr), which looms over Norman Bay and Tidal River, has great views over the coast, offshore islands and Bass Strait. One of the best wildlife-viewing opportunities is the walk at **Millers Landing** on the southern shore of Corner Inlet (2hr) near the park entrance, where you can see swamp wallabies and birdlife, including egrets and cormorants. Other popular walks include the **Lilly Pilly Gully Nature Walk** (2hr) through heathland, eucalypt forest and rainforest, or longer treks to Tongue Point to the west. You can also explore the northern part of the Prom, an officially designated wilderness, or take an overnight hike to one of the eleven outstation campsites (accessible only on foot) such as Sealers Cove, Refuge Cove, Waterloo Bay and Five Mile Beach.

Practicalities

Approximately 220km southeast of Melbourne, Wilsons Promontory National Park is a three-hour drive from Melbourne. You can reach it by following the South Gippsland Highway to Meeniyan, then turning right onto Route 189, which takes you all the way to the park entrance. Once you get into the park, it's 30km to Tidal River. There is no public transport directly to Wilsons Promontory.

An **entrance fee** is payable before entering The Prom at the gate that marks the entrance to the park. A variety of passes are available: day pass for a car ($10.20); two-day pass for a car ($16.20); five-day pass for a car ($30.50); day pass for a motorbike ($2.70). An obvious starting point is the Tidal River **Visitors Centre** (daily 8.30am–4.30pm; ☎5680 9555), which has audiovisual presentations, displays, maps and *Discovering the Prom* ($14.95), a handy reference if you're about to tackle one of the overnight walks. Visit the Parks Victoria website at ⓦ www.parkweb.vic.gov.au for more information on the park including **maps**.

If you want to **stay** overnight, you have to arrange accommodation through the visitors centre, although it's virtually impossible to find a bed on spec during peak periods such as Christmas, weekends and public holidays, as places often book up months in advance. Accommodation is in basic motor huts ($60 for four beds). Capable of holding up to five hundred people, the camping site (non-powered sites $22.50 for 1 car and 3 adults) at Tidal River operates on a first-come, first-served basis and gets packed in summer. For **overnight walks** you will need to book way in advance as some campsites have limited numbers. You will also need to obtain a permit to camp ($7.10); contact Parks Victoria (☎13 19 63) or the visitors centre to make a booking.

The Dandenong Ranges

The peaceful and inviting hills of the **Dandenong Ranges**, 30km east of Melbourne, have been a popular retreat for city dwellers for over a century. Modest in height (their most elevated point, Mount Dandenong, is only 633m), they are famous for their undulating woodland scenery, pretty gardens, interesting fauna and excellent walking possibilities. There are also a few worthwhile tourist attractions: the historic **Puffing Billy** steam train; the lovely gardens and sculptures of the **William Ricketts Sanctuary**, and the towering mountain ash trees, varied wildlife and observation points of the **Dandenong Ranges National Park**.

Parts of the Dandenongs are easily accessible as a day-trip from the city by **public transport**. Trains run from Flinders Street Station to Upper Ferntree Gully and Belgrave, from where buses go to many other destinations in the ranges, including the villages of Olinda, Sassasfras, Emerald and Gembrook – see the relevant sections for more details. If you're travelling **by car**, head east on the Monash Freeway and get off at the Ferntree Gully Road exit, then follow the route along the Burwood Highway to Upper Ferntree Gully, from where you're ideally placed to explore the area – the drive from Upper Ferntree Gully via the Mount Dandenong Tourist Road to the quaint villages of Sassasfras and Olinda and SkyHigh Mount Dandenong is particularly scenic.

The **Dandenong Ranges Visitors Centre** is at 1211 Burwood Highway in Ferntree Gully (daily 9am–5pm; ☎9758 7522, ⓦwww.dandenongrangestourism .com), and has walking guides and maps and can help with a range of accommodation. If you're travelling by train, the office is next door to Upper Ferntree Gully station.

Dandenong villages and gardens

The winding **Mount Dandenong Tourist Road**, lined with mountain ash, stretches from Upper Ferntree Gully in the south to Montrose in the north. Along it are a number of picturesque little villages, many with small cafés, galleries or craft shops that make for a pleasant pit-stop, while there are amazing views of Melbourne and beyond atop the ranges from the SkyHigh lookout. Travelling by public transport, take **bus** #694 (Mon–Sat) from Belgrave Station (via Kallista) or #698 (Mon–Fri) from Upper Ferntree Gully Station.

Eight kilometres from Upper Ferntree Gully, **SASSAFRAS** has a couple of antique and craft shops as well as a few good options for afternoon tea: *Miss Marples Tearooms*, 382 Mount Dandenong Tourist Rd (daily 11am–4.30pm; ☎9755 1610), is decorated in homage to Agatha Christie's greatest female sleuth and doles out scones with lashings of cream and jam; *Tea Leaves* at no. 380 (daily 10am–5.30pm; ☎9755 2222) has over three hundred teas available for purchase as well as various tea-making paraphernalia; while the hospitable *Sassafras General Store* at no. 391 serves up coffee, cakes, Devonshire teas and handmade chocolates. Worth a look is too Bluestone Candles at no. 381 (daily 11am–5pm; ☎9755 2281), which has the largest range of candles and candle-ware in Australia. Sassafras is also the start of the 16-kilometre Dandenong Ranges Tourist Track to Emerald; starting from behind the community hall the walk takes in a number of pleasant picnic grounds along the way.

A couple of kilometres east off the Mount Dandenong Tourist Road, along Sherbrooke Road are the **Alfred Nicholas Memorial Gardens** (daily 10am–5pm; $6.50) in Sherbrooke. Once Australia's finest private gardens they have been restored to some of their former glory by Parks Victoria, and with

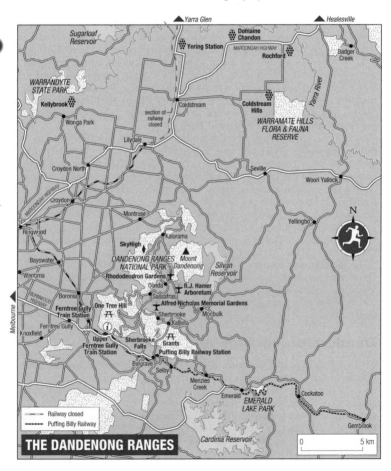

THE DANDENONG RANGES

waterfalls and an ornamental lake they make a particularly nice spot to relax. Bus #694 stops near the entrance.

Four kilometres north of Sassafras is **OLINDA** (ⓦwww.olindavillage.com .au), the highest and most attractive village on the road. With a number of boutique B&Bs in the area, this former logging settlement is a popular stop-over for those visiting the park, and gets packed at weekends with day-trippers from the city who come here for Devonshire teas and to browse the art and craft shops. Olinda is also home to the vibrant 40-hectare **National Rhodo-dendron Gardens** (daily 10pm–5pm; $6.70; ☎13 19 63), with more than 15,000 rhododendrons, 12,000 azaleas, daffodils and spectacular cherry and Japanese maple trees that are perfect for lazing under in spring when they flower; and the **R.J. Hamer Arboretum** (open access 24hr; free), a vast expanse of woodland that has a number of good walking tracks and over 150 species of native and exotic trees. The arboretum is also home to the paintings *Golden Afternoon in Olinda* and *View from Farmer's, Olinda* by late nineteenth-century landscape artist Arthur Streeton, who lived in the village. Some of the town's many lunch options include *Pie in the Sky*, 43 Olinda–Monbulk Rd (Mon–Fri 10am–4.30pm, Sat & Sun 9.30am–5pm; ☎9751 2128), or *Olinda Fish Café*, 23 Main Rd (Tues–Sun 10.30am–8pm; ☎9751 1634), which serves up huge portions of fish and chips. Alternatively try the smorgasbord accom-panied by yodelling and thigh-slapping at the Bavarian *Cuckoo Restaurant*, 508 Mount Dandenong Tourist Rd (Mon–Thurs noon–3pm, Fri & Sat noon–3pm & 7pm–late, Sun 11.30am–3pm & 6.30–10pm; bookings advised). For good old-fashioned sweets like gobstoppers, humbugs and Dutch liquorice, make a beeline for the Olinda Sweet Co, at 37 Monash Ave (daily 11am–5.30pm; ☎9751 1788). If you plan on **staying over** in Olinda bear in mind that accommodation caters very much for couples on weekend retreats and that prices jump considerably at weekends. Central places include; *Como Cottages* (☎9751 2264, ⓦwww.comocottages.com.au; midweek ❻; weekends min 2-night stay ❾), 1465 Mount Dandenong Tourist Rd, which offers 1, 2 and 3-bedroom cottages, some with balconies and four-poster beds, in leafy surroundings; and the *Loft in the Mill* (☎9751 1700, ⓦwww.loftinthemill .com.au; ❹–❽), 1–3 Harold St, whose eight charming rooms housed within a replica flour mill come with features such as spa baths, four poster beds or open fire places.

Puffing Billy

Perhaps the most enjoyable and comfortable way to get a taste of the Dande-nongs is by the **Puffing Billy** (3–6 daily; ☎9757 0700, ⓦwww.puffingbilly .com.au), a narrow-gauge steam railway which has run more or less continually since entering service in the early 1900s. The railway starts in **BELGRAVE**, 40km east of Melbourne, then winds the 24km through thick forests and lush fern-filled gullies to Gembrook (adult $33.50 one way/$51 return; child $16.50/$26 return), with other stops at Menzies Creek, Emerald, Lakeside and Cockatoo. Special lunch and dinner packages are also available. Belgrave itself is a large town with supermarkets, pubs and local shops and amenities.

If you want to break up the two-hour round trip, **Emerald Lake Park** (daily: mid-March to April 9am–6pm; May–Oct 9am–4.30pm; Nov to mid-Dec 9am–6pm, mid-Dec to mid-March 8am–8pm; free, parking $2 per hour or $6 all day; ⓦwww.emeraldlakepark.com.au), adjacent to Emerald station, has over 15km of bush walks, paddle boats for rent ($15 for 30min), a water slide and free swimming pool, and picnic and barbecue facilities, as well as a model railway (Tues–Sun 11.30am–4pm; $5.50; 3–15yr $3.50). The park is a pleasant weekday escape, but it gets very busy at weekends.

Dandenong Ranges National Park

Stretching north of the railway line between Upper Ferntree Gully and Mount Evelyn in the north, the mountain ash forests of the **Dandenong Ranges National Park** (Ⓦ www.parkweb.vic.gov.au) are well worth a visit. Covering an area of 3500 hectares the park is divided into several areas, of which **Sherbrooke Forest** (a 15min signposted walk from Belgrave station) and **Ferntree Gully** (a 10min walk from Upper Ferntree Gully station) are the most accessible if you don't have your own transport. The park provides a number of opportunities for bushwalking and is equipped with picnic areas, many with free barbecues. The most accessible is Ferntree Gully picnic ground which also has a children's playground, and is the start of the popular **1000 Steps and Kokoda Track**, a walk that commemorates those who fought in Papua New Guinea during World War II; bronze plaques dot the 3.5-kilometre route to One Tree Hill picnic ground.

Sherbrooke Falls is a popular destination within the Sherbrooke Forest section – an easy 2.5-kilometre return walk signposted from the Sherbrooke Picnic Ground, off Sherbrooke Lodge Road (reached from the Mount Dandenong Tourist Rd). Alternatively, you can try your luck at spotting the beautiful lyrebird – named after the lyre-shaped tail of the male – on the magnificent seven-kilometre **Eastern Sherbrooke Lyrebird Loop** (2hr), which sets off from Grants Picnic Ground; this is one of the few places in Victoria where you might get to see one of these elusive birds in the wild. The walk also takes in other colourful birdlife including rosellas, kookaburras and honeyeaters. For a shorter stroll, the **Hardy Gully Nature Loop Walk**, also leaving from Grants Picnic Ground, takes you into the thick bush on a walk of less than an hour. Walking maps for all of the park's numerous trails are available from the Dandenong tourist office in Ferntree Gully (see p.191).

Up in the Doongalla section of the park is the newly developed **SkyHigh Mount Dandenong observatory** (Mon–Thurs 10am–10pm, Fri 10am–10.30pm, Sat 8am–11pm, Sun 8am–10pm; cars $4; Ⓣ 9751 0443, Ⓦ www.skyhighmtdandenong.com.au) one of the park's most popular destinations on account of its spectacular views. On a clear day you can see Port Phillip Bay, the Mornington Peninsula and across to You Yangs Park (see p.217). The area itself also has a café and bistro, a maze ($6), and gardens. To get there by car, take the Mount Dandenong Tourist Road then turn left at Ridge Road, or take bus #694/698 from Ferntree Gully or Belgrave stations.

William Ricketts Sanctuary

Just off the Mount Dandenong Tourist Road towards the north end of the park is the **William Ricketts Sanctuary** (daily 10am–4.30pm; $6.70; Ⓣ 13 19 63, Ⓦ www.parkweb.vic.gov.au). Ricketts, an eccentric sculptor, worked here for many years until his death in 1993 aged 94. Set within the moss-covered rocks and damp fern beds of the sanctuary are various kiln-fired clay figures of people and animals that controversially blend Christianity with indigenous characters, inspired by Ricketts' experience of living among Aboriginal people in central Australia.

The Yarra Valley

A n hour's drive northeast of the city, the Yarra Valley is Victoria's wine district. A patchwork of historic vineyards and rich farmland, this former backwater now boasts more than eighty of the state's best **wineries**. It's a major wine tourism destination, and most vineyards provide tastings and cellar-door sales, and many offer winery tours. More and more are opening their own restaurants, where you can marry mouthwatering local fare with fine homegrown wines.

If you can drag yourself away from the cellars, there are also plenty of non-alcoholic attractions, from scenic **Kinglake National Park**, north of the valley, to **Healesville Sanctuary**, an outstanding wildlife park to the south. In and

Black Saturday bushfires

February 7, 2009 will be etched forever on most Victorians' minds as the start of Australia's worst **bushfires** in history. The day dubbed **Black Saturday** killed over 170 people and thousands of wild animals, decimated over a million acres of bushland, wiped out townships and destroyed 1800 homes. The state's worst affected areas were northeast of Melbourne in the Kinglake and Yea–Murrindindi regions, encompassing Marysville, Toolangi, Kinglake, Kinglake West, Strathewen, Steels Creek and Narbethong. In the Gippsland region, southeast of Melbourne, a fire was started deliberately in Churchill and quickly spread to Callignee and Traralgon South.

A heatwave had already rendered the land tinder-dry, and residents in Victoria were told to prepare for extreme conditions with temperatures exceeding 47 degrees and winds of up to 120kmph. Many of the towns devastated were set in hilly, forested country, including the picturesque village of **Marysville**. Established in 1863, with a population of just over 500, Marysville had experienced many bushfires during its 146-year history, but none like that in February which killed one in five residents and reduced the town to ashes. To the west, flames moving over 100kmph swept through the small hamlet of **Kinglake** so quickly people didn't even know they were in danger. Fires pushed by westerly winds were expected to miss the Kinglake area but changed suddenly to southwesterly winds with catastrophic results.

Temperatures within the firestorms were so hot the energy released would have supplied Victoria with electricity for two years. Survivors described how birds began falling from the sky seconds before fireballs sounding like jet engines ripped through their homes. The CFA (Country Fire Association) battled to contain spot fires up to 15km away from the main fire front, which were created by embers whipped up by winds. Many fires continued to blaze out of control for weeks afterwards. National Parks in the area, including Kinglake and Yarra Ranges, were closed to visitors as police and forensic officers sifted through the aftermath. The riskiest months are December, January and February. For safety tips go to Ⓦwww.fireready.vic.gov.au.

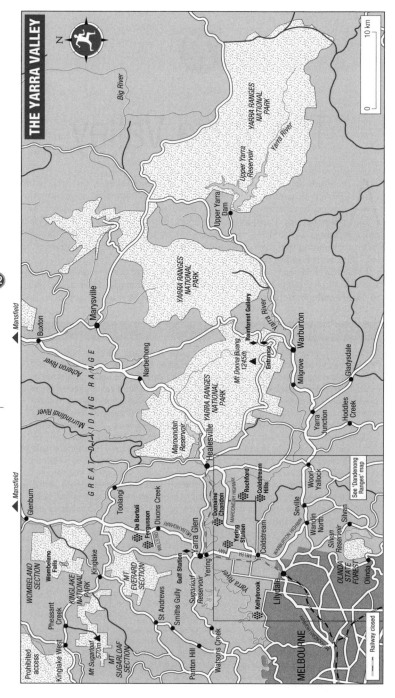

THE YARRA VALLEY

N

0   10 km

Big River

Murrindindi River

Acheron River

Yarra River

Yarra River

Yarra River

G R E A T   D I V I D I N G   R A N G E

Glenburn

Mansfield

Mansfield

Buxton

Marysville

Narbethong

YARRA RANGES
NATIONAL
PARK

Upper Yarra
Reservoir

Upper Yarra
Dam

YARRA RANGES
NATIONAL PARK

Toolangi

Maroondah
Reservoir

Healesville

Mt Donna Buang
1245m

Entrance

Rainforest Gallery

Warburton

Milgrove

Gladysdale

Hoddles
Creek

Yarra
Junction

YARRA RANGES
NATIONAL PARK

Pheasant
Creek

Mt Sugarloaf
570m

MT
SUGARLOAF
SECTION

Prohibited
access

Kinglake West

WOMBELANO
SECTION

Wombelano
Falls

Kinglake

KINGLAKE
NATIONAL
PARK

MT
EVERARD
SECTION

Smiths Gully

St Andrews

Panton Hill

Watsons Creek

Dixons Creek

De Bortoli
Fergusson

Yarra Glen

Gulf Station

Sugarloaf
Reservoir

Yering

MELBA HIGHWAY

Rochford

Domaine
Chandon

MAROONDAH HIGHWAY

Coldstream
Hills

Yering
Station

Coldstream

MEL RA
HWY

Woori
Yallock

Seville

WARBURTON HIGHWAY

Wandin
North

Silvan

Silvan
Reservoir

OLINDA
STATE
FOREST

Olinda

Lilydale

Kellybrook

Yarra River

See 'Dandenong
Ranges' map

MELBOURNE

Railway closed

around you'll find a healthy selection of walking and cycling tracks in the magnificent **Yarra Ranges National Park**. Climax of the region's vibrant calendar of seasonal events is the annual Grape Grazing Festival (Ⓦ www.grapegrazing.com .au), held in February to celebrate the start of harvesting, when around twenty wineries combine in a summer celebration of wine, food and music.

Arrival and information

The southwestern gateway to the Yarra Valley is the Melbourne outer suburb of Lilydale, about 35km from the city centre. If you're coming by **car**, take the Eastern Freeway from Fitzroy to Springvale Road and turn right; the Maroondah Highway to Lilydale is about 2km south down Springvale Road. Lilydale is also a one-hour **train** journey from Flinders Street Station on the Lilydale line. **Bus** #685 travels to the valley's two main townships: Yarra Glen and Healesville (though to visit the Healesville Sanctuary, it's best to take the daily bus departing from Lilydale). There's also a daily bus #684 from Melbourne to Eildon in the north via Healesville and Marysville; while the V/Line bus service to Mansfield passes through Lilydale and Yarra Glen daily (for further information, call V/Line on ☎ 13 61 96).

Touring the vineyards by public transport would be impossible, but several companies offer **winery tours** of the region, starting from around $145 for a basic one-day tour from Melbourne, including lunch, and taking in four or five wineries: try Link Tours (☎ 9699 8422, Ⓦ www.linktours.com.au), Victoria Winery Tours (☎ 5428 8500, Ⓦ www.winetours.com.au) or Yarra Valley Winery Tours (☎ 5962 3870, Ⓦ www.yarravalleywinerytours.com.au). Alternatively, for an exciting birds-eye view of the pretty Yarra Glen countryside, you can take to the skies in a **hot-air balloon** before gently descending into a vineyard to enjoy a sparkling wine breakfast: contact Go Wild Ballooning (☎ 9739 0772, Ⓦ www.gowildballooning.com.au), Balloon Sunrise (☎ 9730 2422, Ⓦ www.hotairballooning.com.au), or Global Ballooning (☎ 1800 627 661, Ⓦ www.globalballooning.com.au) for details – packages cost around $260 during the week and $295 at weekends.

For **tourist information** head to the Yarra Valley Visitors Centre at Healesville on Harker Street (bus #685), just off the Maroondah Highway, (daily 9am–5pm; ☎ 5962 2600, Ⓦ www.visityarravalley.com.au), which is well stocked with winery and walking maps, information on places to eat, bus timetables, as well as being able to book accommodation and tours. The area is a popular weekend break all year round for Melbourne urbanites so it's wise to book your accommodation in advance if you're planning to visit over the weekend.

Lilydale to Yarra Glen

The suburbs of Melbourne have expanded to swallow the town that was once LILYDALE, which is less than an hour's drive east of Melbourne's city centre. The only attraction of note is the small **Museum of Lilydale** (☎ 9294 6313) at 33 Castella St, which has everything you might wish to know about famous Australian soprano Dame Nellie Melba, but was closed for refurbishment at the time of writing. Melba, when she wasn't touring, spent much of her time in the small township of **Coldstream**, just north of Lilydale. Her former home, Coombe Cottage, is set behind a vast hedge at the junction of Melba and Maroondah highways, and is now privately owned.

Heading north along the Melba Highway, you'll come to the turn-off for the ⚘ **Yarra Valley Dairy** (daily 10.30am–5pm; ☎ 9739 1222, Ⓦ www.yvd .com.au), a converted milking shed on McMeikans Road in the tiny settlement of **YERING**. There's a huge array of cheese on sale here, every-thing from washed rind to Persian feta and goat's cheeses, which you can try before you buy. If you decide you want to stay in Yering, *The Gatehouse* (℡9739 0822, ⓦwww.villaraedward.com.au; ❻–❼) at 26 Melba Highway, has two modern self-contained suites with kitchen, spa bath and courtyard garden, plus in-house DVDs and a breakfast basket.

A few kilometres further up the highway, the small agricultural township of **YARRA GLEN** lies in the centre of the Yarra Valley. On Bell Street, the main drag, you'll find a couple of takeaways, a bakery and the National Trust-classified *Yarra Glen Grand* (℡9730 1230, ⓦwww.yarraglengrand.com.au; ❺), a beauti-fully restored nineteenth-century hotel with boutique rooms and a bistro that does stylish pub grub. Alternatively, *Acorn Cottage* (℡9730 1858, ⓦwww.acorncottage.com.au; weekdays ❺; weekends ❺–❼), 956 Melba Highway, has pleasant B&B accommodation set in landscaped gardens. On the first Sunday of the month from September to June, the **Yarra Glen Craft Market** (9am–2pm) is held at the Yarra Glen Racecourse, 200m east of Bell Street.

Just north of Yarra Glen on the Melba Highway, the National Trust's **Gulf Station** (Wed–Sun & public holidays 10am–4pm; $9; ℡9730 1286, ⓦwww.gulfstation.com.au) is a large pastoral property which was once home to the Bell family, Scottish immigrants who settled here in 1854. The pioneer working farm is the best-preserved timber complex in Victoria, with a number of hand-built buildings from the 1850s. Stocked with many of the settlers' original breeds such as Ayrshire cattle, Clydesdale horses and Berkshire pigs, it also has a glorious kitchen garden, and a magnificent avenue of quince trees which explodes with colour in September and October. At the time of writing the station was closed for refurbishment and the animals had been relocated to other properties. The buildings were open for group bookings by appointment only. Phone the number above to check the current situation.

Yarra Valley wineries

One of Australia's oldest grape-growing areas, the Yarra Valley is known as a cold-climate wine region, producing sleek Chardonnays, good Pinots and some solid bottles of Shiraz. Winemakers used to sell directly to the public at bargain prices using the cellar door outlet, often little more than a cash register sitting beside maturing barrels of wine. Nowadays wineries have become more sophis-ticated, with handmade cheeses and olives on sale to accompany the best wines, and swish restaurants on site. Others have live concerts among the vines or feature small art galleries with experimental works on display. Almost all wineries offer **tastings**, where you can sample the latest wines and buy in bulk. Unfortunately prices have risen with the more sophisticated surroundings, so prices may be only as good as your local bottle shop. But for many visitors a cellar door visit to the Yarra Valley remains a popular day-trip.

If you're planning on visiting a few wineries, be aware that local police are particularly active with the breathalyzer and will book drivers who exceed the blood alcohol limit of 0.05 (which usually equates to five 20ml tastes). You may be better off taking a tour (see p.197) and leaving the car at home.

Toolangi and the Kinglake National Park

North of Yarra Glen along the Melba Highway, the tiny timber town of **TOOLANGI** (meaning tall trees and water) surrounded by forest, is where the Australian poet C.J. Dennis wrote "The Songs of a Sentimental Bloke" in 1915,

Wineries to visit

The Yarra Valley's first vines were planted in 1838 by two Scottish brothers at Yering Station. Today there are eighty wineries dotted around the Yarra Valley, with the highest concentration found in the triangle formed by Yarra Glen, Healesville and Dixon's Creek. Some recommended wineries are listed below.

Coldstream Hills 31 Maddens Lane, Coldstream ☎5964 9410, ⓦwww.coldstream hills.com.au. Daily 10am–5pm. Cellar door tastings at a small award-winning winery known for its Chardonnay and Pinots.

De Bortoli 58 Pinacle Lane, off Melba Highway ☎5965 2271, ⓦwww.debortoli .au. Daily 10am–5pm, tours daily at 11am & 3pm. With several wineries across Australia, the De Bortoli name is huge in Australian wine. The one-day Wine Adventure tour ($125) includes a look at the vineyards and processing and includes a three-course lunch followed by tastings. The restaurant (daily noon–3pm plus dinner on Sat 7pm) specializes in authentic Italian cuisine.

Domaine Chandon Green Point, Maroondah Highway ☎9738 9200, ⓦwww .domainechandon.com.au. Daily 10.30am–4.30pm. Owned by legendary bubbly makers, Möet and Chandon, this is one of Australia's premiere *méthode champenoise* sparkling wine makers. Sample a glass in the Green Point Room ($9.50 with bread and cheese), or enjoy a light lunch while looking out onto the gorgeous sprawling vineyard. Daily self-guided tours with informative display panels (in several languages) let visitors experience the wine-making process at their leisure (30min; 11am, 1pm, 3pm).

Fergusson Wills Rd, off Melba Highway ☎5965 2237, ⓦwww.fergussonwinery.com .au, Daily 11am–5pm. First planted in 1968, this vineyard grows most of the major grape varieties. Wine tastings cost $3 or $12 with a cheese platter. The attractive restaurant, with its use of native timber, blends in with the surrounding bush (open daily for lunch and for dinner Fri & Sat).

Kellybrook Fulford Rd in Wonga Park ☎9722 1304, ⓦwww.kellybrookwinery.com .au. Mon–Sat 10am–5pm, Sun 11am–5pm. The sprawl of Lilydale has crept up to almost surround Kellybrook, the oldest licensed winery in the region, but it remains a good family-run, traditional place with old-fashioned cellar-door friendliness. Also produces a good range of ciders. Restaurant open lunch Thurs–Sun, dinner Fri & Sat.

Rochford corner of Maroondah Highway & Hill Rd ☎5962 2119, ⓦwww.rochfordwines .com.au. Daily 10am–5pm. A cool, architect-designed winery with regular concerts held in the surrounding gardens, and a large, airy restaurant (daily noon–3pm; two-course $55) that relies almost entirely on superb local produce. There is also an informal café (daily 10am–5pm).

Yering Station 38 Melba Hwy ☎9730 0100, ⓦwww.yering.com. Mon–Fri 10am–5pm, Sat & Sun 10am–6pm. Established in 1854, this was Yarra Valley's first vineyard. A large complex dominated by a sweeping wall hewn from local stone, with magnificent views along the Yarra Valley, it has wine-making facilities, a glass-walled restaurant, a wine bar and art gallery. On the third Sunday of every month (9am–2pm), the station's heritage-listed Old Barn hosts a Farmers' Market, which attracts food enthusiasts from Melbourne and elsewhere who stock up on a gobsmacking range of local produce. Next door is the original building, **Chateâu Yering**, now the magnificently luxurious *Chateau Yering Hotel* (ⓦwww.chateauyering.com.au; ⓞ) where a night in a sumptuously decorated room won't leave you much change from $600. If you can't afford to stay, you could consider splashing out at the hotel's excellent *Eleonore's Restaurant* and *Sweetwater Café*.

a bawdy tale of larrikin Bill and his "ideal bit o'skirt", Doreen. In the same year, Dennis and his wife, Olive Herron, carved out of the Toolangi forest the pleasant **Singing Gardens of C.J. Dennis** (Mon & Thurs–Sun 10am–5pm;

$2.50, free if you eat in the tearooms; ☎5962 9282), at 1694 Main Rd. The gardens, named after Dennis's last published work, are filled with giant Australian mountain ash, European trees and flowers and are particularly spectacular in spring when the gardens blossom with azaleas, and rhododendron. Tours around the gardens include stories of "Den", and snatches of his poetry while Devonshire teas and lunches are available from the **tearooms**.

Nearby, the Toolangi Forest Discovery Centre on the town's Main Road (usually Mon–Fri 8.30am–4.30pm; free; ☎5962 9318) introduces visitors to the forest ecosystem and has a 1.5-kilometre Sculpture Trail. Nine sculptures were presented to the centre in 1996 after a UNESCO-sponsored event invited Asian-Pacific artists to represent their culture's relationship to the environment; today eight of these sculptures remain, along with two new additions, all in various states of natural decay. The centre can also provide details on a local rainforest boardwalk.

West of Toolangi lies the huge **Kinglake National Park** (Ⓦ www.parkweb .vic.gov.au), an immense tract of eucalyptus forest and native bush with walking trails, picnic and barbecue spots, and lookouts. Sadly, at the time of writing much of the 22,000 hectares of park, including the township of Kinglake, was devastated by the **Black Saturday** Victorian bushfires (see box, p.195), and was closed to visitors. It is hoped that in the near future sections of the park will be open to the public, such as Jehosophat Gully in the Mount Everard section, and two small waterfalls – Masons Falls and Wombelano Falls in the Mount Sugarloaf and Wombelano sections respectively, but check what the current situation is with the visitors centre on p.197 before setting out.

Healesville

The small town of **HEALESVILLE**, nestling beneath the forested slopes of the Great Dividing Range has a main street lined with cafés and tea places; a number of good restaurants and pubs; and several craft stores, junk and antique shops to poke around. On Sundays and public holidays, the **Yarra Valley**

▲ Wine tasting in the Yarra Valley

Tourist Railway operates half-hour rides on a scenic nine-kilometre circuit from Healesville Station out towards Yarra Glen (hourly 10am–4pm; adults $9, children $7; ☎5962 2490). The town's main attraction, **Healesville Sanctuary** (daily 9am–5pm; $23.60 adults, $11.80 4–15yr olds; free guided tours if booked in advance; ☎5957 2800, ⓦwww.zoo.org.au), 3km east of town on Badger Creek Road, is one of Australia's outstanding conservation parks, and shouldn't be missed. Established in 1921 as a research institute for native fauna, the sanctuary takes advantage of its bushland setting to display the largest collection of Australian wildlife in the world. It also has a long and proud tradition of caring for injured and orphaned animals – over 1500 are received each year; some are returned to the wild, while those that are threatened or endangered join the park's education and breeding programmes. Visitors can experience close encounters with a number of native Australian fauna including platypuses, koalas, dingos, red kangaroos, Tasmanian devils and wombats, or go on meet-the-keeper sessions to learn more about the animals. There are also popular aerial presentations featuring birds of prey such as eagles, owls and falcons.

If you want to stay in Healesville, check out *Tuck Inn* guesthouse (☎5962 3600, ⓦwww.tuckinn.com.au; ❺–❻) at 2 Church St, ideally situated in the heart of town, with five stylish en-suite rooms and a cooked breakfast. For food try the excellent *Giant Steps/Innocent Bystander* (daily 10am–10pm; ☎5962 6111) at 336 Maroondah Highway, a striking wood and glass building that houses a bakery, pizzeria, cheese room and cellar door. Alternatively, the grand **Healesville Hotel** (food available daily noon–9pm; ☎5962 4002), at no. 256, does above-average classic pub food, with a more formal menu available in the dining room.

Yarra Ranges National Park

East of Healesville lie the spectacular mountain ash forests and fern gullies of the **Yarra Ranges National Park** (ⓦwww.parkweb.vic.gov.au), home to forty native mammals including the endangered Leadbeater's possum. Access to the park is limited, as it's an important catchment for Melbourne's water supply, but many areas remain open and accessible. At the southern end of the park, walking tracks fan out from the car park of Mount Donna Buang (1245m); one leads for 3km (1hr 30min; moderate to hard) to the Rainforest Gallery (free), a spectacular 40-metre long walkway and observation platform at canopy height surrounded by forests of mountain ash trees, some over 60m tall, and 400-year-old myrtle beech trees. At the summit of the mountain itself is a lookout tower with great views of the surrounding area; in winter the snowy slopes are popular with skiers and tobogganists with six designated slopes open (weather permitting; $25–35 for cars; ⓦwww.lakemountainresort.com.au); toboggan rental available. This southern section of the park is easily reached by car, taking the Mount Donna Buang Road from the pretty town of Warburton, whose cool climate and hill-station atmosphere attracts droves of urban dwellers seeking respite from the city. The town is also the final stop on the **Warburton Trail**, a 40-kilometre cycling track that follows the former Warburton Railway from Lilydale. For more information go to ⓦwww.railtrails.org.au.

Sections of the Yarra Ranges National Park were badly affected during the **Black Saturday** bushfires and the park was closed to visitors at the time of writing. Check with the Yarra Valley visitors centre on p.197 for the current situation.

Macedon Ranges

S eventy kilometres northwest of Melbourne, the Macedon Ranges feature panoramic views, pleasant townships like **Macedon** and **Woodend**, and, most famously, the spine-tinglingly eerie **Hanging Rock**, an austere lump of lava mythologized in book and film. Further west, **Daylesford** is known for its vibrant and easygoing lifestyle, with a high population of gays, lesbians, greens, hippies and established migrant communities, while more wealthy types come to neighbouring **Hepburn Springs** to take in the waters at the Hepburn Spa Resort. Nestled within an extinct volcanic basin, the region around Daylesford and Hepburn Springs has hundreds of natural mineral springs, each with their own distinctive flavour, flowing through the surrounding hills – the reason why these two towns are collectively known as the "Spa Centre of Australia". Every weekend, tourists flood the area to indulge in the languid comforts of the spas and retreats, but you'll also find fine food, galleries, antique and knick-knack shops, and kilometres of well-marked trails vectoring forests, national parks and waterfalls.

From Melbourne, the Macedon Ranges can be reached by daily **train services** to either Macedon (1hr; $10.80/$15.40 off-peak/peak return) or Woodend (1hr 10min; $12.40/$17.40) from Southern Cross Station. Arriving at Woodend, you can take a connecting **bus** to Daylesford (45min; $6.20 return). For further details, contact V/Line on ☎13 61 96, ⓦwww.vline.com.au. Alternatively, you can **drive** by taking the Calder Freeway (part of the CityLink toll system) to Macedon or Woodend, from where Daylesford is only 45km away.

Woodend and Hanging Rock

Around an hour's drive from Melbourne, the bucolic township of **WOODEND** retains a quiet, country town feel despite the number of visitors. With characterful cafés, bookshops and pubs, as well as a microbrewery, it makes a good base for exploring the surrounding ranges and sights. Six kilometres northeast from here, the eerie, boulder-strewn **Hanging Rock** (105m) provided the setting for Joan Lindsay's novel **Picnic at Hanging Rock**, filmed by director Peter Weir in 1975, about the mysterious disappearance of three schoolgirls and a teacher. Created by a volcanic eruption six million years ago, and featuring formations named the Black Hole of Calcutta, the Chapel and the Eagle, it is, thanks to the film, possibly the most internationally famous sight in Victoria. What is less known is that it was also the hideout of "Mad Dan Morgan", a notorious nineteenth-century bushranger. Entry to the reserve (daily 9am–5pm) costs $4 per person or $10 per car, and there's a discovery centre, café and picnic area with coin-operated barbecues at the base of the rock.

Hanging Rock is also the venue for a number of events including two **horse-racing meetings** (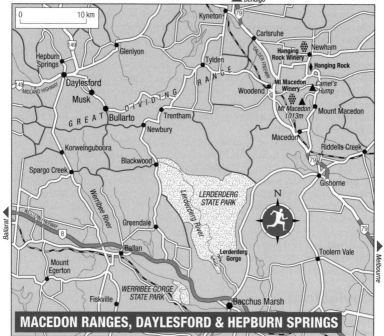www.hangingrockracingclub.com.au): one on New Year's Day, the other on Australia Day (January 26). On the last Sunday in February, the **Harvest Picnic** (adults $18, under-15s free; www.harvestpicnic.com.au), is a hugely popular food-and-wine **festival** attracting over a hundred small producers, performance artists, celebrity chefs and thousands of people eager to try the huge range of cheeses, boutique beers and preserves. In October/November several wineries band together for the Macedon Ranges **Budburst** (www.budburst.com), a celebration of local produce and wines, which begins with a street party in neighbouring Kyneton. See the festival website for information on tickets, transport and participating wineries.

There are more than two dozen **wineries** around the Macedon Ranges, and lovers of cold-climate wines (especially the Pinot Noir and the sparkling) will find the quality excellent. The visitors centre in Woodend (see below) does a handy **wine touring map**. Two particularly outstanding wineries are the *Hanging Rock Winery* at 88 Jim Rd, Newham (daily 10am–5pm for tastings; ☎5427 0542, www.hangingrock.com.au), famed for its Sauvignon Blanc and sparkling wine, and *Mount Macedon Winery* at 433 Bawden Rd, Mount Macedon (Sat & Sun 11am–5pm for tastings; ☎5427 2735, www.mountmacedonwinery.com.au).

Practicalities

For more information and maps, the well-stocked **Woodend Visitors Centre** (daily 9am–5pm; ☎5427 2033, www.visitmacedonranges.com) is on the High Street, on the left as you drive out of town towards Hanging Rock.

MACEDON RANGES, DAYLESFORD & HEPBURN SPRINGS

You'll need your own **transport** to get around the area as local bus services are very patchy. To get to Hanging Rock from Woodend you could get a cab (approximately $16) from Woodend Taxis (☎5427 2641).

As a small town, **places to stay** are limited and it's advisable to book ahead if possible. The *Seven Chimneys*, 45 High St (☎5427 1952, ⓦwww.the7chimneys .com.au; ❹–❺) is an attractive B&B on Woodend's main street, with three doubles (one with en suite) and one twin room. Alternatively, ⚐ *Holgate Brewhouse* (☎5427 2510, ⓦwww.holgatebrewhouse.com; ❹–❺, rates include breakfast), 79 High St, has ten comfortable en-suite rooms within a historic coaching inn, as well as a bar, on-site brewery and restaurant. *Macedon Spa Motel* (☎5426 4044, ⓦwww.macedonspa.com.au; ❻–❼), 652 Black Forest Drive, on the way into town, has 36 rooms each with spa bath, while on-site facilities include a restaurant, heated pool and day spa.

Eating in Woodend represents good old-fashioned country value. For a quick breakfast or lunch, try a quiche or a delicious dessert at *Maloa House Gourmet Delights*, 95 High St (Mon–Sat 9am–5.30pm, Sun 10am–5.30pm; ☎5427 1608). Book lovers may want to indulge in a white hot chocolate and cake at the bookshop-cum-café *Literary Latte* at 81 High St (Mon–Fri 9am–4.30pm, Sat 8am–4pm; ☎5427 3399). For something more substantial, try the Mod Oz menu with one of the pub's award-winning beers at the *Holgate Brewhouse* restaurant (see above), which also does tasty bar meals (closed Mon for lunch).

Mount Macedon

Just east of Woodend lies **Mount Macedon**, an extinct thousand-metre-high volcano that has 30km of good walking tracks and a number of picnic grounds. In autumn, the park is particularly beautiful as the deciduous trees form spectacular russet avenues. Because of the abundance of pasture and water, snakes – some quite venomous – are found in the area.

On the summit of Mount Macedon, a huge **memorial cross** was erected by William Cameron in 1935 to commemorate his son and others killed in World War I. The structure that stands today is a replica of the original cross, which suffered damage in the Ash Wednesday bushfires that swept through the area in 1983, killing seven people, scorching land and destroying a number of houses. On a clear day there are great views across to Port Phillip Bay in the southeast.

Near the car park is a **café** (Mon–Wed 11.30am–3pm, Thurs & Fri 11.30am–4pm, Sat & Sun 10.30am–5pm) with pleasant views from where you can set forth on the **Macedon Ranges Walking Trail**. The route can be broken up into walks of a couple of kilometres, or you could tackle the entire 29-kilometre trek all the way to Macedon; pick up a map from the visitors centre in Woodend. On the easy drive to the summit via Mount Macedon village, you pass sprawling homesteads and a number of plant nurseries, before passing the parking area of **Camels Hump** (20min return), a lava outcrop that has a great view north to Hanging Rock. Alternatively you can walk the 4.5km to the memorial cross from the car park via Cameron Picnic Ground.

Daylesford

Forty-five kilometres west of Woodend, **DAYLESFORD** sports well-preserved Victorian and Edwardian streets and is a beacon for those who have left the rat-race behind: alternative lifestylers of every description call Daylesford home.

The **Daylesford Museum** (Sat & Sun 1.30–4.30pm; $3; ☎ 5348 1453), next door to the tourist office on the main Vincent Street, traces the town's origins in the 1850s goldrush. The museum's ramshackle collection of gold-mining ephemera is housed in a former School of Mines, while the adjoining yard has numerous rusting items of farm equipment and a tiny post office – once claimed to be the smallest in Victoria.

Down the hill from the museum, surrounded by trees, is the picturesque **Lake Daylesford**, with ducks and geese, barbecues, two cafés and the luxriouxs award-winning **Lake House** hotel and restaurant (see p.206) along its quiet shores. The *Bookbarn @ Daylesford* (daily 10am–5pm; ☎ 5348 3048), 1 Leggatt St, is a secondhand bookstore and café that serves cakes, cheese, antipasto plates and wine out on a little deck. The sixteen-kilometre (6hr) **Tipperary Walking Track** runs from the lake to Hepburn Mineral Springs Reserve (see p.206), passing through undulating open-forest country and several old gold-diggings; the trail can be broken up into smaller walks. Also beginning from here is the 70-kilometre **Federation Track** to Ballarat (see p.208) across wooded hillsides, deserted mines, and burbling creeks and gullies. The walk, which usually takes around three days, and is part of the 260-kilometre Great Diving Trail, has several camping areas if you want to pitch a tent; otherwise, basic accommodation in cottages, motels or dormitories can be arranged. You can pick up a map for these walks from the Daylesford Visitors Centre (see below).

Wombat Hill rises above the town to the east. At the top, the **botanical gardens**, established in 1861, contain magnificent elms, conifers and oaks, and a lookout tower with views of the local countryside. The views are best seen on foot, although there's a pleasant circular driveway around the gardens. Just below the gardens, the **Convent Gallery** (Mon–Fri 10am–5pm; $5; ☎ 5348 3211, ⓦ www.theconvent.com.au) is on the corner of Daly and Hill streets. A former convent, religious retreat and gold commissioner's residence, it now has three levels of galleries displaying contemporary and traditional arts and crafts, jewellery and textiles, plus a café and a stylish bar and gift shop at the front of the complex.

The old Daylesford **train station** is down the road from Wombat Hill, where the Midland Highway enters town. On Sundays the Central Highlands **Tourist Railway** runs from here through the Wombat State Forest to the nearby towns of Musk ($8 return) and Bullarto ($10 return), a return journey of just under an hour (10am–2.45pm). Also on Sundays, the station car park is the site of a lively antiques, crafts and produce **market** (8am–2pm).

Practicalities

On Vincent Street, the main drag, you'll find several good cafés, and a **visitors centre** (daily 9am–5pm; ☎ 5321 6123, ⓦ www.visitdaylesford.com.au) with information on accommodation, including a useful publication listing gay- and lesbian-run establishments. It also stocks pamphlets on local health practitioners, walking trails and mineral springs, and has a handy selection of maps. From here, **buses** travel four times daily (Mon–Fri) to neighbouring Hepburn Springs.

While accommodation in Daylesford is plentiful, the tourist boom has meant that prices are inflated, especially at weekends. The *Royal Hotel*, on the corner of Vincent & Albert streets (☎ 5348 2205, ⓦ www.daylesfordroyalhotel.com; ❹–❼), is a lovingly restored Victorian-era pub with heated rooms, some with spa facilities and balcony access. For comfortable B&B/motel-style accommodation in town, *Central Springs Inn* (☎ 5348 3134, ⓦ www.centralspringsinn.com.au; ❸–❺ weekdays, ❺–❻ weekends), corner of Howe and Camp streets, offers a range of rooms – some with spa bath and open log fires – and good breakfasts in two historic buildings. Close to the lake, *Motel Daylesford* (☎5348 2763, ⓦwww .lakesmotel.com; ❹), 1–3 King St, has four units each with balcony. For complete indulgence head to the ★ *Lake House* (☎5348 3329, ⓦwww .lakehouse.com.au; ❾ including breakfast and dinner), overlooking the lake, with day spa and tennis courts.

The main street of Daylesford, between Central Springs and Albert roads, offers several good **eating** options with *Frangos & Frangos* (Fri 11am–late, Sat 10am–late, Sun 10am–4pm; ☎5348 2363) at 82 Vincent St, serving contemporary food in relaxed surroundings, and its sister café, *Koukla* (daily 8am–late) offering an inventive range of pizzas, pastas and other mains. For lunch try the delightful deli-cafés *Gourmet Larder* at no. 57a (daily 9am–5pm; ☎5348 4700) or *Cliffy's Emporium* (daily 9am–5pm, Sat closes 10pm; ☎5348 3279), 30 Raglan St, on the road near the old station. Alternatively, *Electric Sitar* at 4/27 Albert St (Wed–Sun 4–9pm; ☎5348 1676) does groovy lip-smacking takeaway curries. For more regular fare opt for the *Royal Hotel* (see p.205) which does bistro meals until 9pm. Don't leave without trying the delicious hot chocolate and other calorie-laden delights at ★ *Sweet Decadence* café at 87 Vincent St (daily 9.30am–5pm; ☎5348 3202), which also makes exquisite handmade chocolates on the premises. Down by the lake the *Boathouse Café* (daily 9am–4pm; ☎5348 1387) occupies a superb spot overlooking the lake with a sunny deck. The best table in town, however, is at the *Lake House* (see above; booking advisable), with a dynamic menu that samples Victoria's best regional food and has a sublime wine list.

Hepburn Springs

Leaving Daylesford, Vincent Street heads on to **HEPBURN SPRINGS**, a few kilometres north. At the height of the 1848 revolution in Europe, many Italian and Swiss settled around here, drawn by the lure of gold, the climate and the health-giving qualities of the natural mineral springs. For more than a century, Australia's only mineral spa resort has been a major destination for affluent tourists, although in recent years it has attracted more alternative types.

As you enter the town, you'll pass the first sign of Hepburn Springs' Italian heritage: the National Trust-listed **Old Macaroni Factory** on the left. Built in 1859, it was the first pasta factory in Australia; visitors can call ahead to arrange a tour of the frescoed interior (Sat & Sun 10.30am; $10; ☎5348 4345, ⓦwww .macaronifactory.com.au). Further down the hill, on the corner of Tenth Street, **The Palais** is a lovingly restored 1920s theatre hosting everything from torch-song performances to gypsy swing bands, and has a good-value restaurant and bar (Thurs–Sun 6pm–late).

At the bottom of Tenth Street, you'll pass through the Soldiers Memorial Park to the **Hepburn Mineral Springs Reserve**. There are four springs bubbling out in the immediate area, and a visit to any of them, taking with you a few empty containers, is a must. Hand pumps dispense the water, with each spring having an acquired, effervescent taste. Most have a more robust flavour than the bland, filtered variety you can buy in shops, and all are better tasting than the local tap water which, ironically, tastes awful (the local council can't afford to upgrade the town's water-treatment facilities).

The renovated **Hepburn Bathhouse and Spa** (☎5348 4399, ⓦwww .hepburnbathhouse.com), built in 1894, lies at the centre of Hepburn Mineral Reserve. Facilities include a relaxation and spa pool (daily 9am–8pm; entry

Mon–Thurs $15, Fri–Sun $30), aromatherapy steam rooms, flotation pool and heavy mineral salt pool (Mon–Fri 10am–8pm, Sat & Sun 9am–8pm; entry Mon–Thurs $50, Fri–Sun $70); there is also a day spa with a range of treatments and packages available using its extensive private facilities.

Accommodation options in Hepburn Springs range from the luxurious *Peppers Springs Retreat* (☎5321 6200, ⓦwww.peppers.com.au/springs; ❾) to *Continental House* (☎5348 2005, ⓦwww.continentalhouse.com.au; ❹–❺), at 9 Lone Pine Ave, which offers a real slice of the alternative lifestyle and a variety of rooms in a rambling house that includes yoga classes, open fires and a strictly vegan menu or self-catering kitchen. *Wildwood* YHA (☎5348 4438, ⓦwww .yha.com.au; dorms ❶–❷, rooms ❸) 42 Main Rd, represents the best value, with dorm rooms, singles and doubles, some with views into the lush paddocks or bush out the back. For **food**, the bright and busy ⁂ *Red Star Café* (Mon–Thurs & Sun 8am–5pm, Fri & Sat 8am–late; ☎5348 2297) on the main road is your best bet for delicious brekkies and lunches, and is licensed, while *Lucini's Historical Pasta Restaurant* (Fri–Sun noon–3pm, 6pm–late) at the Old Macaroni Factory serves up delicious freshly made pasta dishes and other Italian fare.

Ballarat

J   ust over 100km west of Melbourne, the town of **Ballarat** (a combination of the Aboriginal words "Balla" and "Arat", meaning "to rest on one's elbow") holds a pivotal place in Australia's history. In the 1830s, white pastoralists fanning out from Port Phillip Bay were quick to appreciate the grazing potential of the lightly wooded hills and plains to the northwest. But in August 1851 the town's fortunes changed for ever. Gold was discovered nearby, which brought immense wealth to the town but also led to the country's only civil uprising – the bloody **Eureka Rebellion** (see p.211) – as put-upon prospectors revolted against the authorities. By the decade's end, Ballarat had grown into a prominent Australian city: gorgeous Victorian architecture lined its wide tree-lined avenues, and the city took on the airs and graces of a prosperous and conservative provincial centre.

With gold long gone – the last seam was exhausted in 1918 – tourism and information technology have now taken over as Ballarat's major sources of income (IBM has its Southeast Asian headquarters here), while a large student population from the excellent University of Ballarat has challenged the town's more insular inclinations.

Arrival and information

The Ballarat **Visitor Information Centre** (daily 9am–5pm; ☎446 633) is located at the Eureka Centre (see p.212) on the corner of Eureka and Rodier streets and is well stocked with maps, brochures, transport timetables and accommodation information; it also has a route map of the Eureka Trails (see p.211). There's an additional information centre in the foyer of the **Ballarat Fine Art Gallery** at 40 Lydiard Street North (9am–5pm).

Trains run frequently from Southern Cross Station to Ballarat Station (1hr 25min; $20 off-peak return) every day, centrally located in Lydiard Street. If you're **driving**, the quickest route is to take the West Gate Freeway out of Melbourne, then turn onto the Western Ring Road before taking the Western Highway to Ballarat; the trip takes just over an hour. A longer, but more gentle, drive is the approach from the south, via Geelong, on the Midland Highway.

Accommodation

The well-preserved and often refurbished **hotels** of Ballarat are a great chance to experience Australian pub rooms with the bonus of a bit of luxury. Cheaper package deals for weekends are a good bet, though many hotels may require reservations of at least two nights.

The Ansonia 32 Lydiard St ☎5332 4678, ⓦwww.questansoniaballarat.com.au. This sprawling boutique hotel includes a fine-dining restaurant and attractive communal areas including a library and a guest lounge. The building's historic character has been fused with contemporary design and modern luxuries. ❺–❻

Craigs Royal Hotel 10 Lydiard St ☎5331 1377, ⓦwww.craigsroyal.com.au. Forty-one indulgent suites and rooms in a Victorian-era heritage hotel. The rooms are plush with en suites and much-needed heating for the chilly nights. Doubles ❻

George Hotel 27 Lydiard St ☎5333 4866, ⓦwww.georgehotelballarat.com.au. This quaintly terraced hotel was once a rallying point for police planning to lay siege to the Eureka Stockade. Rooms upstairs were undergoing major renovations at the time of writing (due to reopen April 2009), and rates had yet to be established.

The Menzies 5–7 Hummfray St ☎5331 3277 or 1800 100 210, ⓦwww.ballarat.com/menzies. Aimed at business travellers, the Menzies has wireless internet and office facilities. Decor is plain but the one- or two-bedroom apartments include well-equipped kitchens and lounge areas, while some also have spa baths; two-storey townhouses are also available. ❺–❻

Sovereign Hill Lodge Magpie St ☎5337 1159, ⓦwww.yha.com.au. Small hostel adjacent to the Sovereign Hill complex offering a range of YHA dorms as well as en-suite motel-style rooms. Kitchen/common areas are roomy and rates include reduced entry to Sovereign Hill. Dorms ❶–❷, rooms ❸–❺

The Town

Reminders of Ballarat's glory days as a wealthy gold-mining centre can still be seen in elegant sandstone and Victorian buildings on and around **Lydiard Street**. Further south is Ballarat's most popular attraction, **Sovereign Hill**, a re-creation of the mining shafts, hotels and shops of the goldrush era. Beyond Ballarat, the tacky but endearing **Kryal Castle** warrants a visit, as does the Arch of Honour, a solemn memorial to those killed in arms.

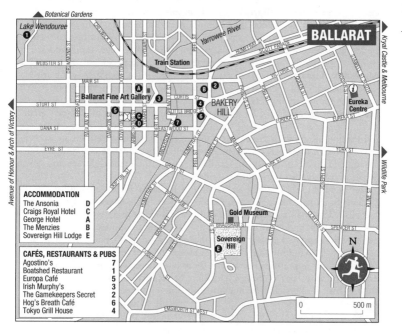

ACCOMMODATION

The Ansonia	D
Craigs Royal Hotel	C
George Hotel	A
The Menzies	B
Sovereign Hill Lodge	E

CAFÉS, RESTAURANTS & PUBS

Agostino's	7
Boatshed Restaurant	1
Europa Café	5
Irish Murphy's	3
The Gamekeepers Secret	2
Hog's Breath Café	6
Tokyo Grill House	4

▲ Panning for gold at Sovereign Hill

Lydiard Street and around

The heart of Ballarat contains one of Australia's best-preserved nineteenth-century streetscapes, **Lydiard Street**. Running from the centre up past the train station, the street has several two-storey terraced shopfronts, with verandas and decorative iron lacework, mostly from the period 1862–89. Among the stately buildings, the former **Mining Exchange** (1888) has been renovated to its original splendour, and the architecture of Australia's oldest theatre, **Her Majesty's Theatre** (1875) at no. 17 also proclaims Ballarat's goldrush-era heyday. In addition there is a collection of fine hotels on Lydiard Street that once watered thirsty diggers, amongst them **Craig's Royal Hotel** at no. 10 and the **George Hotel** at no. 27, which are still an integral part of Ballarat's architectural heritage. Sadly, during the 1970s, the council forced most of the old pubs to pull down their verandas on the grounds that they were unsafe, so very few survive in their original form. An excellent free map detailing three short self-guided **heritage walking trails** of the CBD, Lydiard Street and Sturt Street is available from the visitor centres.

The highlight of the street is the superb **Ballarat Fine Art Gallery** at 40 Lydiard St North (daily 9am–5pm; $5; ☎5320 5858, ⊛www.balgal.com.au). Established in 1884, this is Australia's largest and oldest regional gallery, home of one of Australia's greatest cultural icons – the original Eureka flag. For over a century, the flag was kept out of sight in a gallery cupboard, but it is now framed and displayed in a dimly lit, shrine-like room, the blue and white-starred fabric frayed but still impressive. Elsewhere, there is a fine collection of colonial from 1887 to present day, including Heidelberg School paintings (see p.85) by artists such as Tom Roberts and Arthur Streeton, and contemporary art and works by members of the talented Lindsay family, who lived in nearby Creswick. One room of the gallery is given over to a reconstruction of the Lindsay household's sitting room. The gallery's temporary exhibitions are usually first-rate.

A short distance west of Lydiard Street, the man-made **Lake Wendouree** was once the site of the 1956 Olympics rowing events, but in recent years has been reduced to a vast dry dirt bowl on a number of occasions with redundant ("no swimming") signs and jetties – a stark reminder of Australia's drought and water shortage. On the western side you'll see the austere Ex-Prisoners of War Memorial, a grim tribute to Australians captured during the Boer, Korean and two world wars that includes a black granite wall engraved with the 35,000 prisoners' names. Nearby are the **Ballarat Botanical Gardens**, established in the 1800s and featuring the striking Robert Clark Conservatory (daily 9am–5pm), with giant California redwoods, and a dazzling variety of flowers, shrubbery and gardens that are re-landscaped every year. Each year in March, the Begonia Festival (Ⓦ www.ballaratbegoniafestival.com) is held here, celebrating gardening and all things flower-related, in particular the humble begonia. For those who are less green-fingered there are music and art shows, children's workshops and a street parade along Sturt Street. Opposite the gardens, a terrific adventure playground, complete with a fortress-like cubbyhouse, makes for kiddie nirvana. On weekends and public holidays, visitors can take a ride past the gardens on the western side of the lake on a tram along Wendouree Parade (noon–5pm; $3). To get to the lake and gardens by **bus**, take #16 from Ballarat Station.

The Eureka Trails and Centre

Starting at the Fine Art Gallery, which was the site of the former government camp, the 3.5-kilometre (1hr) **Troopers Trail** follows the path the troops took during their march to the Eureka Stockade (see box, below) and makes up one of the two **Eureka Trails**, the other being the shorter **Diggers' Trail**. The former winds its way through the city along the Yarrowee River and through Ballarat's older residential suburbs, while the latter begins at Bakery

The Eureka Rebellion

The **Eureka Rebellion** is one of the most celebrated events of Australian history, provoked by conditions in the goldfields where diggers had to pay exorbitantly for their right to prospect for gold without having any permanent right to the land they worked or the right to vote. Checks for licences were ruthless and brutal and corruption was rife – police officers were entitled to half of the fine imposed on unlicenced diggers. The administration in Ballarat was particularly repressive, and in November 1854, sparked by the death of a young digger named James Scobie outside the Eureka Hotel, local diggers formed the Ballarat Reform League and burnt their gold licences. Under the leadership of Peter Lalor, a group of a hundred miners barricaded themselves in a flimsy stockade on the Eureka Lead (now the site of the Eureka Centre), above which fluttered a blue flag featuring the Southern Cross.

Just before dawn on the morning of December 3, almost three hundred troops summoned from Melbourne slipped out of the government camp and made their way through the sleeping city. Upon reaching the stockade, they loaded muskets, fixed bayonets and charged. In less than fifteen minutes, more than thirty miners lay dead and 114 had been taken prisoner. Four troopers also died in the assault. Public opinion, however, sided firmly with the miners. Thirteen were charged with high treason but acquitted three months later, and within the year Peter Lalor had been elected to the Victorian Parliament and the miners had earned the right to vote; the licence fee was eventually abolished. When Mark Twain visited Ballarat he succinctly eulogized the uprising with "It was a revolution – small in size, but great politically; it was a strike for liberty, a struggle for a principle, a stand against injustice and oppression. It is another instance of a victory won by a lost battle."

▲ Koala at Ballarat Wildlife Park

Hill, where many diggers pledged a legion to the Ballarat Reform League and burnt their licences, and continues past the site of the Eureka Hotel and on to the former Eureka Lead (goldfield); both trails are signposted and finish at the **Eureka Centre** (daily 9am–5pm, last entry 4pm; $8; ☎5333 1854, ⓦ www.eurekaballarat.com) on the corner of Eureka and Rodier streets. Opened in 1998, the centre was built close to where the stockade is thought to have stood, and features a number of dull figures of soldiers and diggers, and multimedia galleries highlighting the main events behind the rebellion; it also houses the Visitor Information Centre (see p.208). On the roof the huge **Eureka Sail** guarantees that the building can be seen for miles; inside, a fragment of the original flag has pride of place in the centre's central Contemplation Space. If you don't want to walk to the centre, take **bus** #8 (Mon–Sat) or #9 (Sun) from Ballarat Station or Curtis Street just east of Lydiard Street.

Sovereign Hill and around

Ballarat's undoubted highlight, **Sovereign Hill** (daily: winter 10am–5pm; summer 10am–5.30pm; $37.50, includes Red Hill Mine Tour and Gold Museum; ☎5337 1100, ⓦ www.sovereignhill.com.au), is on Bradshaw Street just south of the city centre. To get there it's a fifteen-minute walk from Sturt Street, or take bus #9 from Ballarat Station or Curtis Street. Alternatively V/Line trains from Southern Cross Station runs a courtesy "Goldrush Special" bus which picks up passengers from Ballarat Station in the morning and drops them back in the afternoon, and entitles tickets holders to ten percent of the admission price; call ☎13 61 96 for more information.

Open for around forty years, this 25-hectare reconstruction of the gold-mining township of Ballarat in the 1850s is complete with working mineshaft, over two hundred actors dressed in period costume, horse-drawn carriages and a Chinese Temple. Activities such as wheelwright and blacksmith demonstrations, riding in horse-drawn carriages, gold pannings and pourings, mine tours, candlemaking, and music shows at the Victoria Theatre run throughout the day, while the evening ninety-minute sound-and-light show "Blood on the Southern Cross" (twice nightly; $45; booking essential on ☎5337 1199) lavishly re-creates the Eureka Rebellion. On entry to Sovereign Hill, visitors are given a map and an itinerary of activities – it's worth spending a few minutes plotting your day before continuing. Bear in mind as well that some activities cost extra. The site has plenty of cafés, restaurants, picnic areas and accommodation (see p.209).

Directly opposite here, the interesting **Gold Museum** (daily 9.30am–5.20pm; free with Sovereign Hill entry, $9 on its own; ☎5337 1107) tells the story of Ballarat's rise to fame during the 1850s goldrush and the decades that followed and is crammed with coins, nuggets, alluvial deposits and temporary exhibitions.

A few kilometres east of the museum, on the corner of Fussell and York streets, the award-winning **Ballarat Wildlife Park** (daily 9am–5.30pm; $22; ☎5333 5933; bus #8 or #9) has a large collection of Australian wildlife including koalas, wombats, Tasmanian devils, goannas, saltwater and freshwater crocodiles, snakes and wallabies, some of which roam freely. Tours are free, and run daily at 11am, plus there are animal shows on Saturdays and Sundays from 1.30pm to 3.30pm.

Eating

Food options in Ballarat are better than many towns of this size in Australia due to the strong international community that stretches back to the days of the goldfield. You shouldn't need to stray too far from Lydiard or Sturt streets for a tasty meal.

Agostino's 1 Eastwood St ☎5338 8818. Popular restaurant serving good old-fashioned Italian pasta, pizza and risotto. Mon–Fri 11am–10pm, Sat & Sun 5pm–late. Moderate.

Boatshed Restaurant 27A Wendouree Parade ☎5333 5533. Relax with a sophisticated meal by scenic Lake Wendouree or enjoy a bottle of wine as swans and ducks float past (water permitting). Daily 7am–10pm. Moderate.

Europa Café 411 Sturt St ☎5331 2486. Warm and welcoming café-bar that's popular throughout the day serving coffee, all-day breakfasts, pides, tapas and lunches. Pleasant place at night, too, for dinner and drinks. Mon–Wed 7.30am–6pm, Thurs & Fri 7am–late, Sat & Sun 8.30am–late. Cheap to moderate.

The Gamekeepers Secret corner of Mair & Humffray sts ☎5332 6000. Safari in this fabulous African-themed restaurant for a menu thick with generous steaks and creative pasta. Weekday lunches for $15 and delicious cake and coffee deals make for good value. Daily 11am–11pm. Inexpensive to moderate.

Hog's Breath Café 8 Victoria St ☎5333 3655. A vegetarian's nightmare. Large portions of ribs, steaks, burgers and fish dishes: if it had a pulse it's here. Daily 11.30pm–late. Inexpensive to moderate.

Tokyo Grill House 109 Bridge Mall ☎5333 3945. Head to this teppanyaki diner for a tasty dinner and the frenetic spectacle of having your food cooked while you watch. Tues–Sun 6pm–late. Expensive.

Drinking

Bars and **pubs** cluster around Lydiard and Sturt streets, but there are a few good options to be found by wandering further out. The likeable **Irish Murphy's** at 36 Sturt St (daily noon–late; ☎5331 4091) is a good Emerald Isle pub filled with regulars. A modish middle-aged set frequent the **Gamekeepers**

BALLARAT | Eating • Drinking

Secret, on the corner of Mair and Humffray streets (see p.213), with an inviting bar area, decent wine list and several beers on tap. The cosy, but cool front bar of the **George Hotel**, at 27 Lydiard St (see p.209), is a good spot for a drink to warm up for an evening out.

Around Ballarat

An unmistakeable sight on the Western Highway 8km east of Ballarat, **Kryal Castle**, on the slopes of Mount Warrenheip (Mon–Fri 10am–4pm, Sat & Sun 9am–5pm, $20; ℡5334 7388, ⓦwww.kryalcastle.com.au), is an ersatz castle-cum-medieval theme park whose mishmash of exhibits includes a gloriously tacky dungeon, children's playground and maze. For a kooky night out, try their "Castle Cabaret" nights ($50) that boast a three-course meal, magic and comedy, or for that truly gothic experience you can stay the night in one of its suites with spa bath (❺–❼).

Five kilometres west of Ballarat on the Western Highway, the Arch of Victory heralds the entry to the 22-kilometre **Avenue of Honour**, a beautiful if sobering stretch of road. Flanking either side are nearly 4000 ash, elm, poplar, maple and plane trees, one for every local soldier who fought in World War I.

The Bellarine
Peninsula

The journey southwest of Melbourne along the Princes Freeway to Geelong may lack the drama of the Great Ocean Road but it does have a number of excellent attractions that make for a good day out, as do the pleasant beach towns of the Bellarine Peninsula. The first real reason to make a stop is **Werribee Park**, a glorious mansion and gardens, adjacent to which lies **Werribee Open Range Zoo**, where you can roam safari-style among an interesting variety of animals. Continuing westward brings you to the small but rewarding **You Yangs Regional Park** and eventually, around 75km from Melbourne, **Geelong**, Victoria's second-largest city and gateway to the Bellarine Peninsula. Don't come looking for extraordinary natural landscapes or brilliant sunsets, however, because Geelong's attractions are predominantly man-made. Long the centre of Australia's wool industry, the city's main draws are its historic National Wool Museum and revitalized waterfront, but you'll also find a modicum of other sights: an excellent art gallery, lovely botanic gardens and fine examples of colonial architecture. In addition, Deakin University and the Gordon Institute have attracted a younger population, and there's a small arts community and healthy band scene (Jet hail from here), which lend a patina of hipness to the city. Beyond Geelong, the **Bellarine Peninsula**, a stubby knuckle of land pointing across Port Phillip Bay to Melbourne, has blossomed in the last decade, and offers the graceful beachfront town of **Queenscliff**, quaint fishing villages, some of Victoria's finest views, great food and wine, and activities such as swimming with dolphins and surfing.

West to Geelong

Just beyond Melbourne the western outskirts along the Princes Freeway lapse into drab suburbia until you approach Werribee, just over thirty minutes by car from the city. Here, the stately **Werribee Park** adjoins the grassy plains of **Werribee Open Range Zoo**, while further west, the **You Yangs Regional Park** makes for a picturesque detour coupled with nearby **Serendip bird sanctuary**. Werribee is also a destination on the Bay West Trail, a 55-kilometre scenic route between Williamstown (see p.97) and Werribee that takes in a number of attractions along the way; follow the brown signs for Route 11; maps are available from the **Werribee Visitors Centre** (daily 9am–5pm; ☎9742 0906), 177 Watton St, in the town centre, along with information about the surrounding region of Wyndham, including bus timetables and accommodation.

Werribee Park and around

Mention Werribee to city folk and the first thing they will say is "poo farm", thanks to the large water treatment farm located on the outskirts – but don't let that put you off paying this pleasant town a visit. A few kilometres south of the town along the K Road is Werribee Park Tourism Precinct where you'll find **Werribee Park** (May–Oct Mon–Fri 10am–4pm, Sat & Sun 10am–5pm; Nov–April daily 10am–5pm; $13.50 ☎8734 5100, ⓦwww.werribeepark.com .au), an award-winning estate and Italianate mansion set in ten hectares of formal gardens. Finished in 1877 by Scottish squatters Thomas and Andrew Chirnside, who struck it rich on the back of sheep, the sixty-room house is the largest private residence in Victoria. Guides in period costume show you inside the ornate homestead with impeccably restored bedrooms and reception rooms and around the tranquil Victorian-era lawns and adjoining **Victoria State Rose Garden** (daily 10am–5pm; free). Featuring over 5000 rose bushes, the garden is a splendid place to while away a sunny afternoon, especially between November and April when the flowers are in bloom. If you fancy a self-guided tour, headsets ($4) providing a commentary on the park are

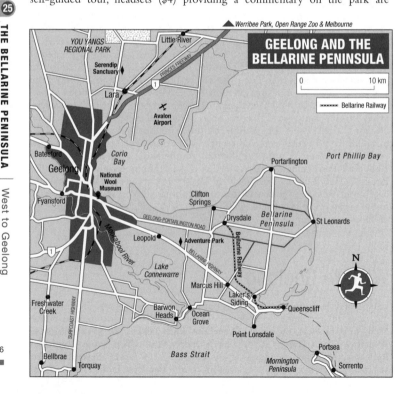

▲ Werribee Park, Open Range Zoo & Melbourne

GEELONG AND THE
BELLARINE PENINSULA

0   10 km

━━━━━ Bellarine Railway

available at the entrance. From March to May the grounds host the **Helen Lempriere National Sculpture Awards**, where visitors can wander through the gardens displaying the finalists' exhibits. If you're interested in staying in the formal gardens the **Sofitel Mansion & Spa hotel** (☎9731 4000, ⓦwww .mansiongroup.com.au; ❼–❾), a former seminary, has luxurious boutique-style accommodation and a spa; you can also dine at *Joseph's*, the hotel's upmarket restaurant with a modern Australian/French-inspired menu and well-matched wine list. The hotel even has its own winery, the small **Shadowfax** (☎9731 4420, ⓦwww.shadowfax.com.au), which offers cellar-door sales (daily 11am–5pm), plus glimpses of the wine-making process and tastings (Sat 4pm; $10) along with gourmet food from the deli. Drawing the crowds at weekends are delicious wood-fired pizzas (Fri–Sun only), and live jazz sessions every Sunday afternoon.

Also set within the tourist precinct are the extensive grounds of **Werribee Open Range Zoo** (daily 9am–5pm; $23.60; ☎9731 9600, ⓦwww.zoo.org .au). Developed around the picturesque Werribee River, the zoo is home to Australian and African herbivores including lions, cheetahs, hippos, rhinos, giraffes, zebras, monkeys, meerkats and other creatures. The magnificent savannah-like conditions are designed to resemble as closely as possible the natural habitats of the animals, which roam freely and can be seen on a 45-minute safari **bus tour** (10.30am–3.30pm; included in entrance fee), conducted by trained guides. Visitors can also take the Volcanic Plains Walk which gives an insight into the endangered grasslands of the Western Basalt Plains and allows views into the Australian exhibit, with kangaroos, emus and wallabies. If you really want to get close to the animals, the zoo offers the "Slumber Safari" ($270 per person) with meals served in an African-inspired lodge kitted out with 1920s-style furnishings, and a night in a luxury canvas tent with king- and queen-sized beds. **Werribee Park Shuttle**, a private bus service, provides transport to Werribee Park (mansion, zoo and Shadowfax) from Melbourne, departing from the Victorian Arts Centre, St Kilda Road, at 8.30am & 10am ($25 return; advance booking required on ☎9748 5094; ⓦwww.werribeeparkshuttle.com.au). To get to the park by **public transport**, catch a Werribee line train from Flinders Street Station to Werribee from where buses make the short trip to the precinct.

You Yangs Regional Park

Some 25km west of Werribee, the **You Yangs Regional Park** (daily 8am–4.30pm) is a small but rugged volcanic range with abundant birdlife and several walks around the central 348-metre Flinders Peak, climbed by Matthew Flinders in 1802; scramble to the top (approx 45min return) for fine views across the bay and down towards Geelong. The park was once used by the local Barrabool tribe as hunting grounds, and scattered here and there you'll find rock hollows enlarged by Aborigines to ensure water was available during the driest spells. The You Yangs are around 40 minute from Melbourne and only accessible if you have your own transport: take the marked turn-off on the Princes Freeway at Little River. The park has plenty of shaded picnic areas with barbecues.

Serendip Sanctuary

A short drive from You Yangs park is the small **Serendip Sanctuary**, at 100 Windermere Rd in Lara (daily 10am–4.30pm; free; ☎13 19 63; no public transport). A refuge for endangered Victorian birds, the sanctuary is renowned for its captive breeding programme of brolgas, magpie geese and Australian bustards. The wetlands can be viewed on four self-guided walks (pick up a map from the information centre) ranging from 800m to 1400m, along walkways, with bird hides and observations areas along the way. Kangaroos and other marsupials, including the rare Pademelon wallaby, can also be viewed here in special enclosures.

Geelong

Industrial **GEELONG** is not a particularly attractive city – the fact that the **National Wool Museum**, 26 Moorabool St (Mon–Fri 9.30am–5pm, Sat & Sun 1–5pm; $7.30, combined Ford Museum entry $11.50; ☎5227 0701), is the main attraction will give you some idea of the place. Housed in an imposing late-nineteenth-century bluestone building, the museum proves that Australia really did ride on the sheep's back. Inside, displays demonstrate the importance of the wool industry to the city, with life-like reconstructions of typical shearers' quarters, turn-of-the-twentieth-century looms (still in use), and evocative sound and image shows. Geelong's other major industry was the production of the Ford motor car, and if you so desire you can visit the **Ford Discovery Centre** (daily except Tues 10am–5pm; $7, plus Wool Museum $11.50; ☎5227 8700, ⓦwww.forddiscovery.com.au), on the corner of Gheringhap and Brougham streets, to look behind the scenes of the car manufacture and design industry, with a huge car museum, and a good deal of marketing thrown in.

Many of the town's best Victorian buildings are on **Little Malop Street**, three blocks south of the National Wool Museum in the city centre, including the elegant **Geelong Art Gallery** (Mon–Fri 10am–5pm, Sat & Sun 1–5pm; free; ☎5229 3645, ⓦwww.geelonggallery.org.au), which has an extensive selection of over 4000 works including important pieces from nineteenth-century Australian artists such as Tom Roberts and Frederick McCubbin, plus contemporary Australian paintings and sculpture.

Geelong's waterfront

Neglected for many years, **Geelong's waterfront** from Rippleside Park to Eastern Beach has recently undergone a $170 million makeover, with the shipping traffic and industrial skyline to the north now offset by stunning ocean views across green expanses. The promenades, rotunda, fountains and Art Deco-style swimming pool (on Eastern Beach, where swimming is also permitted inside an enclosure) have been renovated, as has a lovely nineteenth-century **carousel**, featuring about thirty sculpted wooden horses, and one of only a few working carousels left in the world.

Nestled among the lawns and trees are Geelong's historic **Botanic Gardens** (daily 7.30am–5pm; free; free guided walks Wed 10.30am & Sun 2pm). Begun in the late 1850s, they are the fourth oldest in Australia after those in Sydney, Melbourne and Hobart. The gardens feature a "twenty-first century" section showcasing local indigenous species, succulents and cactuses, an 1851 dragon tree and other plants that thrive in dry conditions. This latest garden provides a stark contrast to the lush green lawns of the heritage nineteenth-century gardens, which boast rare and endangered plants, fountains, a geranium conservatory, sculptures and the **Tea House** (daily 11am–4pm), where you can enjoy refreshments with excellent views of the lawns.

▲ Painted bollards, Geelong

The new-look waterfront features more than a hundred brightly **painted bollards**, the work of local artist Jan Mitchell, depicting some of Geelong's historic characters, from footy players to old-fashioned bathers. A designated "bollard walk" along the waterfront from Limeburners Point, east of the swimming pool, to Rippleside Park, takes in the prominent **Cunningham Pier**, which was built in the 1880s to load wool and gold onto tall ships, and is now home to a rather touristy restaurant. Close to the pier, you can't miss the enormous "shark fins" carved from stone. A number of **bicycle trails** head off from here along the western shore and further afield – pick up a map from the visitors centre.

The bay is host to sailing festivals and regattas, including January's **Skandia Geelong Week** (Ⓦ www.geelongweek.com.au). Held since 1844 and recognized as the largest sailing regatta in Australia, it attracts more than 500 yachts of all shapes and sizes, and over 100,000 visitors. The four-day festival starts with racing in Melbourne, before the massive fleet – joined by visiting tall ships – heads for Corio Bay in the traditional Williamstown to Geelong race. As well as sailing, there are aerobatic displays, street theatre, live music and a fireworks show.

Practicalities

Avalon **airport** (Ⓦ www.avalonairport.com.au), Melbourne's domestic passenger terminal and home to low-cost carrier Jetstar (Ⓣ 13 15 38, Ⓦ www .jetstar.com.au), is 15km from Geelong and accessed via Avalon Airport Shuttle ($17; Ⓣ 5278 8788, Ⓦ www.avalonairportshuttle.com.au), which can drop you in various destinations around the Bellarine Peninsula. The easiest way to get to Geelong from Melbourne is by **train** (hourly from Southern Cross Station; 1hr; $6.20 one-way); the train station is situated northwest of the centre. By **car**, it's an uneventful hour's drive southwest of Melbourne on the Princes Freeway.

As well as the **Visitor Information Centre** (daily 9am–5pm; Ⓣ 5222 2900, Ⓦ www.visitgeelong.org) in the museum – see opposite – which provides lots of brochures and city and regional maps, there's a helpful staffed **tourist information stall** in the Market Square Shopping Centre along Moorabool Street (Mon–Sat 9am–5pm), and a booth on the waterfront (daily 10am–4pm), in front of the carousel. For details of what's going on in the city and southwest Victoria, pick up a copy of the free **What's On** magazine from visitors centres. For the latest club and gig listings check out **Forte** (free), available fortnightly from pubs, record stores and cinemas.

Accommodation

There's plenty of **accommodation** around Geelong, though rooms in summer can book up quickly. Also at this time some hotels and B&Bs may require a minimum booking of two nights at the weekend.

Corio Villa 56 Eastern Beach ☎ 5221 3838, ⓦ www.coriovilla.com.au. If you looking for luxury with no expense spared then a night at Corio Villa will not disappoint. Exquisitely restored mansion set in beautiful stately grounds with views of the bay. A popular venue for celebrity weddings and fashion magazine photoshoots. ❾

Four Points Sheraton 10–14 Eastern Rd ☎ 5223 1377, ⓦ www.fourpoints.com/geelong. Some of the best rooms in Geelong can be found at the *Sheraton*'s luxury waterfront tower, and offer grand spa baths and large-screen TVs. Service is impeccable and there's also a decent restaurant and gym. ❻–❽

Irish Murphy's 30 Aberdeen St ☎ 5221 4335, ⓦ www.irishmurphys.com; bus #35/#36. One of only two places offering backpacker-style accommodation in Geelong, this cheerful pub offers basic six-bed dorm accommodation and also roomy twins.

Entertainment most nights from pub quizzes to live bands (Thurs–Sun), when the noise levels can rise. ❶

Mercure Geelong Corner of Gheringhap & Myer sts ☎ 5223 6200, ⓦ www.mercuregeelong.com.au. At the top of the hill, this hotel affords excellent bay views with recently refurbished modern rooms, though some areas still have a 1970s feel. Good online deals available. ❼–❽

The National Hotel 191 Moorabool St ☎ 5229 1211, ⓦ www.nationalhotel.com.au. Conveniently located backpackers offering small, but clean dorms ($28) above a large, old pub. The first floor has a kitchen and lounge (rooms are on the second and third floors), while downstairs the restaurant offers cheap noodle dishes with $7 specials Tues–Thurs. The pub is also a popular venue for live bands (see opposite). Free linen provided. ❷

Eating

Geelong has a great range of popular **dining** options, with restaurants to suit most budgets. Pakington Street to the west of the city centre (**bus #35/#36**) is fast becoming Geelong's trendiest eating and shopping strip, with a number of good Italian eateries along the Geelong West end – try *Giuseppe's Café* at no. 149 (Tues–Sat from 5pm; ☎ 5223 2187), which dishes out good Italian dinners – while the slightly more affluent Newtown end with its gift shops and boutiques is a great place to enjoy a spot of café culture: the bright and bold *Relish One-3* (Mon–Fri 7.30am–4pm, Sat & Sun 8am–4pm; ☎ 5229 4466), at no. 13/321 is a good pit stop. For the tastiest burgers this side of Geelong head across the road to ⚑ *Burger Inc* (daily noon–8.30pm; ☎ 5222 7776), at no. 320, which serves delicious gourmet burgers for around $10. There's also a branch in the city centre at 51 Moorabool St. Also in the city the *Lambys Restaurant and Bar* (Mon–Wed & Sun 9am–5pm, Thurs, Fri & Sat 9am–late; ☎ 5223 2536), next door to the Wool Museum, does a roaring trade with risotto, pasta, steak and the like on the menu. The waterfront is the place to head for just-off-the-boat seafood: for dinner with a French twist try *La Parisien*, 15 Eastern Beach Rd (Mon–Sat noon–2.30pm & 6pm–10.30pm, Sun noon–10pm; ☎ 5229 3110), or below it, the *Wharf Shed Café* (Mon–Fri

11am–11pm, Sat & Sun 9am–11am; ☎5221 6645) serves huge burgers and gourmet pizzas, as well as more fishy delights, and has a pleasant terrace overlooking the bay.

Drinking

There are plenty of **pubs** in which to slake your thirst, but the *National Hotel* (see opposite), also hosts local, and the occasional international, rock, funk and hip-hop acts, while *The Barking Dog*, 126 Pakington St (☎5229 2889, ❽www .thebarkingdog.com.au) often has live folk, rock or blues, plus a DJ every Friday, and serves affordable meals. The same people own *Barwon Club Hotel* (the "BC"), 509 Moorabool St (☎5221 4584, ❽www.barwonclub.com.au), another popular pub band venue. If you fancy a pint, including several Irish beers, and a male-dominated crowd, try *Irish Murphy's* (see opposite) which hosts a quiz night every Wednesday. Alternatively, there's *The Bended Elbow*, 69 Yarra St (☎5229 4477, ❽www.geelong.bendedelbow.com.au) a British ale house with live bands (Fri & Sat), good food specials and a great rooftop beer garden and nightclub.

Bellarine Peninsula

While it's not as exciting as the popular Mornington Peninsula (see p.181), which it faces across Port Phillip Bay, new development has invigorated the **Bellarine Peninsula** in the past couple of years, making it a popular escape from the city, as well as a sought-after residential area. Picturesque and palm-tree fringed, with a number of good wineries and safe, family beaches, the peninsula has just enough sights to make a weekend trip worthwhile. The most obvious attraction is the quiet seaside resort of **Queenscliff**, with its historic buildings, fishermen's cottages and Victorian hotels, while nearby is an evocative light-house and a collection of interesting small coastal hamlets.

From Geelong, take a McHarry's Buslines **bus** (☎5223 2111, ❽www .mcharrys.com.au) from the train station for Ocean Grove and Barwon Heads, Point Lonsdale via Queenscliff, St Leonards via Portarlington. Pick up a timetable from the Victoria Visitors Centre (see p.223). Regular **ferries** link Queenscliff and Sorrento on the Mornington Peninsula – see p.184 for details.

Queenscliff

The Bellarine Highway runs 31km southeast from Geelong to **QUEENSCLIFF**, which sits at the tip of the Bellarine Peninsula. From its humble beginnings as a sea pilot's station and fishing village, Queenscliff (named after Queen Victoria) became a fashionable resort in the 1880s before falling out of favour early in the twentieth century. Since the 1990s, it has enjoyed a remarkable revival in popularity; quaint sailors' cottages and fine examples of Victorian-era buildings abound (such as the grand *Queenscliff* and *Royal* hotels), while running down the centre, Hesse Street is home to a plethora of lifestyle stores and modish cafés, with even more poodles than Sorrento or Portsea.

Facing the fort at Point Nepean (see p.185), **Fort Queenscliff** demonstrates the town's strategic position near the narrow entrance to Port Phillip Bay. Planned during the Crimean War, but not completed until 1885, it was built in response to the perceived threat of a Russian invasion, and was used again during World War I and II. Guided **tours** of the fort (Sat & Sun 1pm & 3pm; 1hr; $10; ☎5258 1488) allow you to see tunnels built during the goldrush period, muzzle-loading cannons and the unusual "Black Lighthouse", the only one in Australia built of black stone which works in tandem with the Point Lonsdale lighthouse (see opposite) to guide ships safely through the Port Phillip heads. Further north on Wharf Street, the **Queenscliff Maritime Museum** (Mon–Fri 10.30am–4.30pm, Sat & Sun 1.30–4.30pm; $5; ☎5258 3440) focuses on the many shipwrecks caused by "The Rip", a fierce current at the entrance to Port Phillip Bay between Point Lonsdale and Point Nepean. The treacherous, churning stretch of water, with its strong currents and whirlpools, has accounted for numerous shipwrecks over the years along the Victorian coastline. Follow signs from Point Lonsdale Road to the **Rip View Lookout** at Point Lonsdale (see opposite) where you can watch container ships or cruise liners make their entrance to Port Phillip Bay.

Rail enthusiasts will want to take the restored steam-powered **Bellarine Railway**, originally opened in 1879 as part of Australia's defences against a Russian invasion and operating a regular passenger service until 1931. Today it runs from the old Queenscliff Railway Station to Drysdale (1hr 15min), a pleasant town 20km northwest (Sun 11.15am & 2.45pm, plus Tues & Thurs during school holidays; $12 one-way, $20 return; ☎5258 2069, ⓦwww.bpr .org.au), or to Laker's Siding, 5km from the station (35min; $12 return). Coming back the train departs Drysdale 12.15pm and 3.45pm, and Laker's Siding 2pm. Alternatively you could take a bike onboard and cycle the 17km back to Queenscliff (part of the Bellarine Rail Trail; see box, below) – doing it the other way round is an uphill slog. From October to May the railway hosts the Blues Train (6.30–11.30pm $76 return and meal; ⓦwww .thebluestrain.com.au), a round trip with performances by Melbourne's leading blues and jazz musicians. The **Queenscliff Sunday Market** is held on the last Sunday (9am–2pm) of each month from August to April on Symonds Street, selling everything from household bric-a-brac to local jams and handicrafts. The last weekend in November sees crowds flocking to

Activities in Queenscliff

Queenscliff offers a whole range of activities both in and out of the water. **Boat rides** can be organized through Swan Bay Boat Hire, 1195 Queenscliff Rd, with hourly and daily rates (from $18/$145; ☎5258 1780) that vary slightly, depending on the boat.

Alternatively you can **swim with dolphins and seals** off the bay; Sea All Dolphin Swims (ⓦwww.dolphinswims.com.au) is a reliable tour operator with boats departing from the Queenscliff boat harbour near the car ferry (mid Oct–April daily 8.30am & 1pm weather permitting; $120 swimmers, $65 sightseers; bookings essential on ☎5258 3889). There's also great **scubadiving** available: Queenscliff Dive Centre ($195 for a one-day Scuba Experience; ☎5258 1188, ⓦwww.divequeenscliff.com .au), 37 Learmouth St, offers trips to wrecks.

For something land-based, rent a bike from Big4 Beacon Resort ($10–25; see opposite) and follow the **Bellarine Rail Trail** (map available from the information centre), a fabulous track running 33km from Queenscliff to Geelong through farming and coastal countryside, sharing some of the journey with the Bellarine Railway (see above).

If you're after a rather less energetic activity, try the **Queenscliff Day Spa**, 2 Hobson St (call ☎5258 4233 for an appointment; ⓦwww.queenscliffdayspa.com .au), where you can indulge in a range of facials, spas and body treatments, as well as a three-hour "Coast Experience" combining aromatherapy, body brushing, exfoliation, massage and hydrotherapy.

Buckley takes his chance

In 1803, during an exploration expedition to Port Phillip Bay led by Captain David Collins, an English convict, **William Buckley**, escaped. He was adopted by the local Wautharong Aboriginal tribe, who lived around the Barwon River, and stayed with them for over thirty years. When the "wild white man" turned up at John Batman's camp at Indented Head, he was dressed in animal skins and could scarcely remember how to speak English; his survival has been immortalized in the phrase "**Buckley's chance**".

In his day, there was huge reluctance on the part of the government to pardon Buckley, despite the fact that he later played an important role in building relations between Aborigines and white settlers. A committee was established in 2003 to promote the bicentenary of his escape, and educational resources on his story have been made available to schools in the Geelong region.

Queenscliff Music Festival (ⓦwww.qmf.net.au) for three days of live Australian music, from folk, blues and world.

Practicalities

Buses from Geelong stop outside the Post Office on Hesse Street, just a block before the excellent Victorian **Visitor Information Centre** at no. 55 (daily 9am–5pm; ⓣ5258 4843), which offers plenty of advice on local sights and activities. The few good **accommodation** options in Queenscliff book up quickly. The elegant, stately *Queenscliff Hotel*, 16 Gellibrand St (ⓣ5258 1066, ⓦwww.queenscliffhotel.com.au; ❽), has good bed-and-breakfast, and dinner packages, while the conveniently located, *Vue Grand*, 46 Hesse St (ⓣ5258 1544, ⓦwww.vuegrand.com.au; ❼–❾), is a gorgeous nineteenth-century house with well-appointed rooms, and a fine-dining restaurant. For a bit more personal attention the *Lathamstowe* guesthouse, 44 Gellibrand St (ⓣ5258 4110; ❾) offers bed and breakfast in a heritage-listed mansion. *BIG4 Beacon Resort* (ⓣ5258 1133, ⓦwww.beaconresort.com.au; ❹–❻), 78 Bellerine Highway, offers a range of tent sites (❷–❸), cabins and holiday homes, and has a heated pool. There are a number of **places to eat** along Hesse Street which boasts cafés and fish-and-chip eateries, while *Harry's*, at *Esplanade Hotel* (open daily for lunch & dinner; ⓣ5258 3750), 2 Gellibrand St, has excellent seafood and great sea views from its balcony.

Bellarine Peninsula coast

From Queenscliff it's about 5km west to peaceful **Point Lonsdale** (also just known as "Lonnie") and its 120-metre-high lighthouse (tours Sun 9.30am–1pm; $6; bookings on ⓣ5258 3440; under-fives not permitted) at the edge of the foreshore reserve overlooking "The Rip". Built in 1902, it's visible for 30km out to sea and has sweeping views across to Point Nepean on the Mornington Peninsula. Beneath the lighthouse, on the edge of the bluff, "Buckley's Cave" is where the famous **William Buckley** reputedly made his home (see box, above).

With your own transport, you can head 10km or so west down the highway from Queenscliff to the **Adventure Park** (Oct–April: daily 10am–5pm; closed Tues & Wed Nov, Feb & March; adults $32, children under 1.2m $27, under-3s free; ⓣ5250 2756, ⓦwww.adventurepark.com.au), 1251 Bellerine Highway, Wallington, which boasts Victoria's only water park, and is a big hit with kids and adults alike. Spread over fifty acres of picturesque parkland, it has over twenty rides and provides everything from giant water slides and a raging river to mini-golf, go-karts and paddleboats.

Fifteen kilometres west of Queenscliff, **Ocean Grove** and **Barwon Heads** face one another across the Barwon River – the former is the largest town on the peninsula and has one of Victoria's safest surf beaches – a gorgeous twelve kilometre long stretch of sand – and a pleasant summer climate cooled by breezes blowing in from Bass Strait, while the latter (made popular as the fictional seaside backwater of "Pearl Bay" in **SeaChange**, a hit TV series made in the late 1990s) is a pretty town with a long sandy river foreshore which offers safe swimming, jetties, a collection of good eateries and bars, golf courses, heritage walks, delightful rock pools and a popular surf beach – Thirteenth Beach. Barwon Heads is also home to the **Jirrahlinga Koala and Wildlife Sanctuary** on Taits Road (daily 9am–5pm; $14; ℡5254 2484, ⓦwww.jirrahlinga.com.au), where koalas, dingoes, wombats, snakes and other native fauna are found.

North of Queenscliff, **St Leonards** was founded in 1840 as a fishing base for Geelong. Formerly a haven for retirees, the town has glammed up, attracting a hipper and younger set of holidaymakers and city folk seeking a more relaxed lifestyle. Further north, at the hillside setting of **Portarlington**, there's the beautifully preserved, steam-powered **Portarlington Mill** at 5 Turner Court (Sept–May: Wed, Sat & Sun noon–4pm; closed June to mid-Sept; $2.50; ℡5259 2804). Four storeys of solid stone, this National Trust property was built in 1857 and is well worth visiting if you're interested in seeing how bluestone (basalt) was once put to industrial use. Apart from a safe family beach and splendid views across the bay to the You Yangs Regional Park (see p.217), Portarlington is also within close proximity to some of Victoria's best **wineries**, including Kilgour Estate, 85 McAdams Lane (℡5251 2223, ⓦwww.kilgourestate.com .au), Scotchmans Hill, 190 Scotchmans Rd, Drysdale (℡5251 3176, ⓦwww .scotchmanshill.com.au), and the glorious Spray Farm, 2275 Portarlington Rd (℡5251 3176, ⓦwww.sprayfarm.com.au), with its heritage architecture and steep grounds leading down to Corio Bay. Visit ⓦwww.winegeelong.com.au for details of wineries further off the beaten track. If you're looking for somewhere **to eat**, hold out for *Port Pier Café* (summer daily 9am–11pm; winter Wed–Sun lunch & dinner only; ℡5259 1080) on Portarlington's beach front, which serves great Spanish food and freshly caught Portarlington mussels; the quiet narrow strip of beach is popular with picnicking families.

Contexts

Contexts

History

T he region surrounding the Melbourne that we know today has been inhabited for thousands of years, though the city itself has existed for only a fraction of that time. What follows is a concise account of the city's history, from the trials and tribulations of the first settlers, to the state of the city in the twenty-first century.

Melbourne's original owners

Melbourne and Victoria's original inhabitants were the **Koories**, who have lived in the region for over 50,000 years. Semi-nomadic hunters and gatherers, they had a close relationship with the land, living a mostly comfortable life that was threatened only in times of scarcity. To protect themselves against the cold, Koories built fires and turf huts, and donned great possum-skin cloaks. For leisure, they played a game where two competing teams attempted to catch a round ball made of possum skins that was kicked high into the air (a forerunner to Aussie Rules football).

Victoria's Aboriginal people also had a highly ordered social life, sophisti- cated traditional cultures, and around ten separate languages spoken by over thirty different dialect or sub-language groups. In the Port Phillip region, five different groups shared adjoining territories, a common language, and an integrated culture and belief system, forming a nation or confederacy known as the "Kulin". Periodically, groups from the Kulin would gather in areas around present-day Melbourne. But although the Aboriginal way of life had evolved over thousands of years, they were ill-prepared for Gubba (white) invasion.

Tentative beginnings

European involvement with Australia began in the early seventeenth century, when Portuguese, Spanish and Dutch expeditions mapped parts of the coast- line, although the land's forbidding climate and seeming barrenness discouraged Western powers from taking much of an interest in the country the Dutch called "New Holland". After the voyage of a British party under **Captain James Cook** in 1770, which claimed the eastern seaboard for King George III, in 1788 Europe's first settlement on Australian soil was established with the arrival of the **First Fleet** in Botany Bay, near present-day Sydney.

The first Briton to attempt to populate the Melbourne area, **Captain David Collins**, sailed from London on the HMS *Calcutta* along with a party of marines and free settlers and a few hundred convicts, arriving in Port Phillip Bay in 1803 at the site of what is now Sorrento. Less than a year later, after declaring the location unsuitable due to its lack of fresh water, Collins abandoned the settlement and took his party to an island across the Bass Strait, named Van Diemen's Land (now Tasmania). Across the Bass Strait, a number of Van Diemen's Land armers, including John Batman and Thomas and John Henty, looking for favourable pastures, had sought permission from authorities in London and Sydney to graze livestock on the mainland. Impetus was also spurred by the glowing reports of suitable land received from whalers active in the Bass Strait. However, the pastoralists' requests were consistently refused as the authorities in both London and Sydney believed it would prove too expensive. Tired of being bossed around, **Edward Henty** (Thomas's son) set out with his family and began squatting at Portland Bay on the southwest coast in 1834, thereby establishing the district's first permanent settlement.

Into the frontier

John Batman, a barrel-chested former bushranger, continued to harbour plans for a pastoral settlement in Victoria. In May 1835, together with a consortium of graziers, public servants and merchants, he set out to buy land from the local Aborigines. Leading a party on the sloop *Rebecca*, he reached Indented Head on the Bellarine Peninsula in Port Phillip Bay and proceeded to walk around Corio Bay, noting that the fertile countryside was "beyond my most sanguine expectations". After reaching the mouth of a river (later to be called the Yarra), he continued along one of its tributary streams until meeting a local Dugitalla tribe with whom, on June 6, 1835, a **treaty** of his own making was signed. Batman claimed to have procured 240,000 hectares (600,000 acres), which he paid for with £200 worth of goods (knives, tools and trinkets), promising similar payments each year. Today historians suggest that the Aborigines believed Batman was simply handing over gifts in return for visitation rights, but Batman thought he was actually buying the land.

Batman returned to Van Diemen's Land on June 9, leaving a small party at Indented Head to look after the land he had "bought". Days later, ensconced in the *Launceston Hotel*, Batman proclaimed he was "the greatest landowner in the world". His braggadocio was tempered, however, by the refusal of officials in Hobart and Sydney to recognize the settlement without permission from the British colonial authority. Until further instructions were received, those settling at Port Phillip were to be treated as trespassers.

Despite this setback, **plans for settlement** continued apace and by the end of June, Batman and his backers had formed a syndicate, called the Port Phillip Association, to send livestock to the mainland. However, it was another group led by the visionary **John Pascoe Fawkner** that played the major role in the establishment of Melbourne. The son of a convict and a member of Captain David Collins' party that landed in Sorrento, Fawkner had made his way in Van Diemen's Land as a baker, bookseller, newspaper owner (he would subsequently publish Melbourne's first newspaper, the *Melbourne Advertiser*) and publican of the *Launceston Hotel*. In April 1835, he bought the schooner *Enterprize* to ferry a new party of settlers to Port Phillip. The trip was planned for August 4 that year, but, having organized and financed a small group to accompany him, Fawkner was forced to disembark due to his own financial problems. The *Enterprize*, under the command of Captain John Lancey, continued without him, reaching the Yarra on August 29 and berthing at a natural rock barrier in the riverbed, near present-day William Street, where fresh water was guaranteed. Fawkner and his family arrived on October 11, with Batman – whose popularity as the city's traditional founder continues today – following on November 9.

Growing pains

In September 1836, orders arrived allowing settlement (although Batman's purchase was declared "invalid"), sparking a monumental **land grab** as increasing numbers of settlers from Van Diemen's Land, New South Wales and immigrants from Britain flocked to the new location. Sir Richard Bourke, governor general of New South Wales, visited in 1837, choosing the site for the city. He was accompanied by surveyor-general **Robert Hoddle**, who famously mapped out the blueprint for Melbourne's spacious grid in a couple of hours, recording that, "in 1837, Governor Bourke entered my tent and gave me his list of names for the streets". Up until then, Melbourne had gone by a number of names – Dutti-Galla, Doutta Galla, Batmania, Bearbrass, Bearport, Barehup, Bareheep and Bareberp were all considered at one time or another – before it was decided in 1837 to name the town after William Lamb, second Viscount Melbourne and prime minister of Great Britain.

In 1839, **Charles La Trobe** arrived to administer the district, which one writer had called "unquestionably the most drunken region on the face of the earth". A precocious scholar and butterfly collector, La Trobe spent fifteen years in office, steering Victoria to self-government and establishing major public works such as the State Library of Victoria and other cultural institutions, intended to create a stable democracy and turn an uncouth frontier town into an urbane colonial city.

Under his guidance Melbourne rapidly began taking shape. The development was concentrated on the north bank of the river, as the south was an unstable floodplain – only since the 1970s have any buildings of consequence been built on this side. The city's population grew quickly, and such was the tumult on the streets that many people were gored or crushed to death by sundry drays, bullocks and horses. By 1840, the number of citizens had reached 10,000. **Aboriginal people** also began drifting into the settlement, as their land was taken and they became increasingly attracted to tobacco and alcohol. Largely seen as a degenerate people by the European populace, Aborigines did mostly menial work, trading goods such as feathers and skins, or acting as pastoral labourers. Although less violent than other settlements in Australia (predominantly due to John Batman's treaty and the Port Phillip Protectorate, which outlined laws to protect Aborigines), the massacres by white settlers, as well as poisoned waterholes and European diseases such as dysentery and measles, saw the Aboriginal population of Melbourne decline from around 15,000 in 1834 to 2000 in 1850. Alcohol abuse also reduced numbers, and by the mid-1850s there were few Aborigines left in the city.

In 1842, Melbourne was declared a town and, five years later, a city. The **Port Phillip District** separated from New South Wales (of which it was still part) in 1849 and, two years later, officially broke from the state when it was declared an independent colony, just nine days before gold was discovered.

The goldrush

The **discovery of gold** near Ballarat in 1851 irrevocably changed Melbourne's character. With its strongly rural atmosphere, the city had previously struggled to attract immigrants, but the goldrush saw shiploads of fortune-seekers flooding in from around the world. Melbourne was transformed into a convulsing, sprawling and increasingly violent metropolis crammed with gaudy shops, brothels, flashy gold-diggers, opportunists and no-hopers. Most migrants didn't stay long in the city but scurried off in search of gold; their desertion stripped Melbourne of much-needed labour, even forcing Governor La Trobe to feed and groom his own horses.

However, within a year, Melbourne's merchants were busy turning a profit from those returning from the goldfields. The city's population exploded, and Melbourne became the fastest-growing and richest port in the British Empire. Growth came at a price, though; with no infrastructure, city streets began accumulating filth at an astonishing rate, and it was not uncommon for citizens to walk ankle deep in mud or faeces in the downtown area. Sir Charles Hotham, who became Victoria's governor in 1854, wrote of the place before his death in office two years later: "It is a vile hole, and I shall never like it."

Among other things, the year 1854 also saw the first edition of *The Age* newspaper and the beginning of the Victorian rail network, with passenger and goods services between Flinders Street and Port Melbourne. It also heralded the miners' uprising in Ballarat. Known as the Eureka Rebellion, the stand of the miners represented a giant step in the march to liberty and democratic freedoms in the newly formed state.

Boom and bust

The 1860s to 1880s were years of great optimism and prosperity in "**Marvellous Melbourne**". The city, driven by gold and untramelled industry, took over from Sydney as Australia's financial centre. Rail lines and cable trams were introduced on Melbourne's streets, telephones were installed, and a night-time football match was played under electric lighting at the Melbourne Cricket Ground (MCG). Grandiose public developments such as the Royal Exhibition Building (built especially to stage the Melbourne International Exhibition of 1880–81) and the Melbourne Town Hall were constructed on goldrush profits, suburbs from St Kilda to Collingwood began to develop, and large tracts of the city centre were set aside as public parks and gardens. Always deferential towards the "Mother Country", Melbourne's well-to-do modelled themselves on middle-class English society, adopting the fashions, the furniture, and the carefully enunciated speech, while filling their gardens with imported shrubs and trees.

By the 1890s, however, Melbourne's star waned, as the city was rocked by a series of strikes, sparking a devastating depression and the beginning of the "**grey nineties**". Melbourne's earlier laissez-faire prosperity, fuelled by dubious financial speculation, had drawn manpower from the land, decreasing primary production. As land became unsaleable and wool and wheat prices slumped, companies were bankrupted and fortunes lost overnight.

The twentieth century

By the turn of the century Melbourne had recovered and financial stability returned. Following the unification of Australia's six colonies in 1901, the city became the country's political capital (the first session of the new Parliament was held in the Royal Exhibition Building) and remained so until the specially constructed capital city of Canberra was completed in 1927. Stability continued through World War I and beyond, until the city's prosperity was shattered by the Great Depression of the 1930s. With unemployment rife, many people were put to work building a series of public works, including St Kilda Road, the Shrine of Remembrance and the Great Ocean Road.

By the early 1930s, Melbourne had bounced back again and began a period of intense **industrial development**. Warehousing and manufacturing moved outwards from the city and into the suburbs, and families attached to these industries went to the outskirts for work and cheap housing. Following World War II, Melbourne continued its programme of development, beginning a huge **immigration push** that attracted waves of refugees and migrants from around the world – their arrival helped transform the city from a culturally suburban, stereotypically British backwater into a sophisticated international melting pot. As the inner suburbs became crowded and accommodation scarce, Melbourne built thousands of houses in the outer suburbs for low-income earners. The drift outwards continued until the 1960s, when new city-centre developments and the revitalization of inner-city suburbs such as Carlton and Fitzroy by Melbourne's growing band of bohemians, intellectuals and further waves of immigrants, helped reverse the trend.

The undoubted highlight of this era was the city's hosting of the **1956 Olympic Games**. After initial apprehension about Melbourne's ability to stage such an event (at the time, with a population of just 1.6 million, the city was considered rather provincial), the "friendly games", as they became known, were a resounding success: not only did they lead to the Melbourne Cricket Ground (MCG) being transformed into Australia's largest and most famous stadium, but the event also put the city firmly on the world map.

Progress continued until the **1990s**, when Australia fell into recession. Melbourne, in particular, hit an all-time low as unemployment rose to record levels, factories closed, the property market collapsed and some of the city's largest financial institutions went under. The Labor government was unable to handle the state's finances, leading to a lack of trust among voters, who in 1992 elected a conservative Liberal/National party coalition under Jeff Kennett.

Kennett in power

Bold and occasionally boorish, Victoria's premier **Jeff Kennett** wielded almost complete control of parliament, and set about invigorating Melbourne by investing heavily in infrastructure. Dubbed the "Mitterrand of the South", he was keen to demonstrate that Melbourne was a "world-class" city, and new developments such as the Melbourne Museum and Federation Square sprung up all over town. To fund these works, the government oversaw savage budget cuts to health and education. Kennett also came under fire for Melbourne's gambling culture, as well as for harassing the media (he once shovelled sand over a group of reporters), and for making changes to the office of the auditor-general, which had previously investigated government officials' dubious tender processes and credit-card abuse. But despite Kennett's Thatcherite approach to the economy and propensity for antagonizing various sections of the community, his popularity as premier remained high, and he was widely recognized as Australia's most effective politician at both a state and federal level at the time. His activist government continued to celebrate the state's cultural, racial and religious diversity, and his lead against the fledgling One Nation Party – a new and xenophobic force in Australian politics – won him many admirers on both sides of the political fence.

Melbourne's Aboriginals

The **Aboriginal population** in Melbourne had, since the 1850s, steadily grown, with up to 15,000 Aborigines living in the city today. State-wide community organizations, schools and health and legal centres boosted Aboriginal esteem and provided widespread employment. In addition, Victorian and federal legislation have given control of some heritage and cultural sites to Aborigines. In 1998, the Melbourne City Council recognized the past suffering of Victorian Aborigines by issuing a formal apology during National Sorry Day, an event that's been held annually ever since then. In 2008, Prime Minister Kevin Rudd gave a speech apologising for the mistreatment of the Stolen Generations, which he referred to as "blemished chapter in our nation's history".

The new millennium

In September 1999, arrogantly riding high in the polls and sporting a massive parliamentary majority, Kennett lost the "unloseable election" to rank outsider **Steve Bracks** of the Labor Party. Kennett's unexpected demise was largely due to his government's neglect of rural Victoria (he once memorably described Melbourne as the vital heart of the state and rural towns as the "toenails"). Bracks inherited a buoyant economy, efficient services, low unemployment and, unbeknown to Kennett, a massive budget surplus of $1.8 billion, which he proceeded to rapidly spend in rural and regional Victoria. At the same time he concentrated his party's efforts on improving the key areas of health and education. Bracks also continued the work of the former premier in encouraging **new developments** across the city, particularly along the river in the form of the Docklands project – set to transform the waterfront.

Re-elected in 2002, Bracks's government had to struggle with an ailing economy, union unrest and a fall in immigration, but succeeded in upgrading transport routes and pushing through environmental initiatives. Melbourne's staging of the 2006 Commonwealth Games also helped to boost his popularity and, despite adopting, at times, a Kennett-style lack of concern for certain sections of the community, Bracks won his third election in 2006. However, in 2007 he resigned unexpectedly, citing family commitments as the reason, and **John Brumby**, Bracks' former State Treasurer, was sworn in as the new Premier. Since then the Brumby government has come under fire several times, especially in its decision to approve a pipeline that would take billions of litres of water from the ailing Murray-Darling Basin to supply the city. Melbourne's future remains rosy, however, and Victoria is the country's fastest growing state: it is estimated that the population (currently nearly four million) will increase by one million within the next two decades. To cope with this increase the government's **Melbourne 2030** plan will see more sites given over to "activity centres"; mixed-use retail, commercial and residential hubs such as the Docklands development, which will provide the 600,000 homes needed.

Books

Most of the following books are still in print, although some may be hard to find unless you visit a library, or secondhand or specialist bookshop. The Australian publisher is provided plus the UK and US publishers where available.

General introductions

Melbourne – Biography of a City (Hill of Content). The best and most detailed account of Melbourne's founding and subsequent growth, with a good sprinkling of photographs and illustrations.

History and culture

R. Barrett *The Inner Suburbs – The Evolution of an Industrial Area* (Melbourne University Press). The stuttering development of Collingwood and Richmond during the nineteenth century makes for a fascinating and grimy read, especially the warts-and-all picture of wealthy industrialists pouring noxious wastes into the Yarra.

C.P. Billot (ed) *Melbourne's Missing Chronicle – John Pascoe Fawkner* (Quartet). This private journal of John Pascoe Fawkner, the industrious former publican and early Melbourne settler, traces the city's formative years in 1835–36. Somewhat scrappy but disarmingly candid, it's an invaluable work for anyone interested in Melbourne's history and the life of one of the city's founders.

Michael Cannon *Old Melbourne Town* (Loch Haven). Interesting analysis of Melbourne life up until the discovery of gold. Cannon's sequel, *Melbourne After the Gold Rush* (Loch Haven), is equally good, concentrating on Melbourne's transformation from a small shantytown into a hectic and overcrowded metropolis.

Patricia Clancy and Jeanne Allen (ed) *The French Consul's Wife: Memoirs of Céleste de Chabrillan in Gold-Rush Australia* (Melbourne University Press, Aus & UK). This racy memoir of the immigrant Céleste de Chabrillan (former Parisian courtesan, circus performer and dancer) and her encounter with mid-nineteenth-century Melbourne has insightful and deliciously impertinent descriptions of society during the goldrush era.

Maree Coote *The Melbourne Book – A History of Now* (Hardie Grant). Writer and designer Maree Coote puts her professional knowledge to good use with this richly illustrated and well-researched tome, combining interviews, photographs and anecdotes to give a unique view of the city. It gives background information on landmarks, personalities and everything that makes the city special.

Graeme Davidson *The Rise and Fall of Marvellous Melbourne* (o/p). Scholarly and sometimes difficult to read, but worth persisting with to gain an idea of the "Marvellous Melbourne" era, during which the city became the wealthiest and most advanced in Australia.

Tim Flannery *The Birth of Melbourne* (Text Publishing). Handy look at early Melbourne through diary entries, newspaper clippings and letters from the likes of John Batman, Mathew Flinders, Rudyard

Kipling and Alexandre Dumas. The material collated by naturalist and author Tim Flannery is often fun and entertaining, and conveys a city built on dispossession, ecological mismanagement and the greed of sleazy entrepreneurs.

Andrew Hoyne, Jason Loucas and Andrew Anastasios *St Kilda In Your Face* (Hoyne Design). This gorgeous volume of photographs and text romps around Melbourne's famous seaside suburb lovingly exploring its places and many characters.

Janet McCalman *Sex and Suffering: Women's Health and a Woman's Hospital* (Melbourne University Press, Aus & UK; Johns Hopkins University Press, US). A powerful and moving social history of the lives and suffering of Melbourne women since the 1850s, focusing on the nursing and medical staff at the Women's Hospital in Carlton.

Gary Presland *Aboriginal Melbourne: The Lost Land of the Kulin People* (o/p). Fascinating and readable short study of a vanished country and a remarkable way of life, with accounts of the Kulin lifestyle and the effects of white settlement on the Aboriginal population and culture.

Jill and Jeff Sparrow *Radical Melbourne 1 & 2* (Vulgar Press). These two volumes, covering the nineteenth and twentieth centuries respectively, examine political activism in Melbourne. Solid, sometimes secret, histories of the city, supported by rarely seen images from the archives of the State Library of Victoria.

Art and architecture

Maie Casey *Early Melbourne Architecture, 1840 to 1888* (Oxford University Press). Smallish but useful photographic representation (with brief notes) of the city's more architecturally interesting nineteenth-century buildings. Sadly, over one-third of the buildings included in the book have since been altered or demolished.

Leon van Shaik (ed) *Architectural Monographs No 50: Tom Kovac* (o/p). Nicely illustrated study of the Melbourne work of the enigmatic and provocative Tom Kovac, analysing nineteen completed and unfinished projects, including the Melbourne Museum and Federation Square. The results are witty and consistently entertaining.

Granville Wilson and Peter Sands *Building a City* (Oxford University Press). Meticulously researched and comprehensive general history of Melbourne's architecture.

Food and wine

Stephanie Alexander *The Cook's Companion* (Viking). Superb culinary collection of ingredients from one of Melbourne's finest chefs. Designed to be a gift from one generation of cooks to the next, this attractive (if very heavy) package is the "bible" in many Australian kitchens.

Max Allen *Sniff, Swirl, Slurp* (Mitchell Beazley). An abundance of helpful advice on how to get the most enjoyment out of drinking wine. Allen's skill lies in the fun way he describes the quaffing process, whether it be a bold red or crisp white.

Allan Campion and Michelle Curtis *The Foodies' Guide to Melbourne* (Hardie Grant). Released annually, this is one of the better food guides, spotlighting everything from delis and markets to Indian takeaways, picnic sites and late-night supper spots.

Teague Ezard *Ezard* (Hardie Grant). This book traces how the style of Teague Ezard, known for his bold and imaginative Asian-inspired dishes, melded into the Melbourne food landscape. Apart from revelling in Ezard's enthusiasm for developing amazing flavours, you'll also be taken through the art of stir-frying, steaming and pasta making.

Greg and Lucy Malouf *Arabesque* (Hardie Grant). The Melbourne restaurateur couple's first foray into the publishing world is an award-winning and widely acclaimed book larded with the flavours of North Africa and the Middle East. Look out for their second offering, *Moorish: Flavours from Mecca to Marrakech*, which covers similar territory.

Fiction

Peter Carey *The True History of the Kelly Gang* (Alfred A Knopf). Ironically titled novel by Booker-prize winner Peter Carey about the Australian outlaw Ned Kelly masterfully combines several journals supposedly written by the man himself for his unborn daughter, in the process establishing a new and vivid mythology of Australia's most enduring legend.

J.R. Carroll *The Clan* (Pan Macmillan Australia). Admirable for its brutal, bare-knuckle approach, *The Clan* tells the story of the notoriously lawless Beattie clan, whose youngest son is killed by the police in a back alley. It's all here – epic family struggles, hold-ups, retribution and a Melbourne quite unlike any you imagined before.

Katie Falkiner (ed.) *All Change Please* (Cardigan Press). The third instalment in a series of antholo-gies from new Melbourne writers (many students from RMIT). In a canny piece of marketing, stories vary in word length to suit various tram journeys around the city. Look out for the latest fourth instalment, *Allnighter*, bedtime stories with weird and dark themes.

Adam Ford *Man Bites Dog* (Allen & Unwin). A laugh-out-loud funny novel for young adults that follows

a local postman into Melbourne's subcultures of performance poetry and accidentally deceased pets.

Helen Garner *Monkey Grip* (McPhee Gribble, Aus). Prize-winning first novel set in Melbourne during the 1970s, about the passionate, volatile relationship between an inner-city artist type and a junkie. A meandering but worthwhile story, with much of it set in the skanky-bohemian areas of Fitzroy and Carlton, including key scenes at the Fitzroy Pool (see p.156). Made into a so-so film in 1982 that featured, interestingly, Garner's daughter Alice.

Frank Hardy *Power Without the Glory* (Mandarin). One of Austral-ia's greatest and most controversial novels, *Power Without the Glory* is the semi-fictional account of the life of John Wren, a legendary criminal figure who lived in Collingwood in the 1930s. Hardy, who collected much of his material while working as a Melbourne journalist, had enormous difficulty in getting the work published, and was later sued (unsuccessfully) by Wren's wife for defamation.

Joan Lindsay *Picnic At Hanging Rock* (Vintage). This tale about the mysterious disappearance of three schoolgirls and their teacher whilst on a trip to Hanging Rock has secured the rock formation as one of Victoria's most famous sights: its popularity no thanks to Lindsay's suggestion that it was a true story. The final chapter which explains the disappearances was later published as *The Secret of Hanging Rock*.

Norman Lindsay *The Magic Pudding* (Angus and Robertson). A whimsical tale of some strange men and their grumpy, flavour-changing and endless pudding; a children's classic with very adult humour.

Shane Maloney *Stiff* (Text Publishing, Aus; Arcade, UK & US). Mixing a benighted central character (private detective and single parent Murray Whelan) with drugs, Turks and killer cars, *Stiff* is a fast and often funny thriller set in various Melbourne suburbs. First in a series that includes *The Brush-Off, Nice Try, The Big Ask* and the latest instalment, *Something Fishy*.

Elliot Perlman *Three Dollars* (Picador, Aus; Faber & Faber, UK; MacMurray & Beck, US). Stirring read that goes straight for the jugular in its depiction of economic rationalism and downsizing in modern Melbourne. Collected *The*

Age Book of the Year award for 1998. His more recent endeavour *Seven Types of Ambiguity* and the award-winning short story collection *The Reasons I Won't be Coming* are also both worth seeking out.

Christos Tsiolkas *Loaded* (Vintage, Aus & UK). Convincingly maps out ideas on homosexuality, ethnicity, sex, drugs and music from the perspective of Ari, the unemployed son of Greek migrants. Think Jean Genet and William Burroughs with toothache and you're already halfway there. Made into the film *Head On* (see p.238).

Arthur Upfield *The Great Melbourne Cup Mystery* (ETT Imprint). A thriller about the Melbourne Cup might not sound like an intriguing prospect, yet Upfield has done a fine job in capturing Depression-era Melbourne, its seediness, corruption and underworld goings-on.

Arnold Zable *Café Scheherazade* (Text Publishing, Aus). Set around a famous Acland Street cake shop (see p.124) this delicious, warm book explores Melbourne's Russian Jewish community. Zable's interest in the migrant experience can also be seen in his more recent *Scraps of Heaven*.

Film

Ava Gardner's wrongly attributed words famously haunted Melbourne for years. "A great place to make a film about the end of the world," she reputedly quipped in 1959, during the shooting of Stanley Kramer's apocalyptic *On the Beach* (in fact, the remark was penned by a local journalist). At the time there was little film production in Melbourne, a far cry from the **beginning of the twentieth century**, when the city was pioneering the latest film technology. In 1900, over two thousand people packed the Melbourne Town Hall to watch *Soldiers of the Cross*, an evangelistic film made by the Salvation Army about early Christian martyrs. Six years later, John and Nevin Tait produced *The Story of the Kelly Gang*, one of the first feature-length fictional films in the world. But as the Hollywood silent era churned out miles of celluloid and "more stars than heaven" (as MGM claimed), Melbourne, like the rest of Australia, succumbed to the waves of overseas imports arriving on its shores.

The city's film culture was revived in the 1950s with the founding of the **Melbourne International Film Festival** (see p.148), which helped develop an interest in alternative cinema and fostered a modest "underground" of film-makers, who took their lead from the French New Wave. During the postwar years, Melbourne also became the engine room of Australian film studies. The National Film Theatre and the Australian Film Institute were founded in Melbourne, while publications such as *Lumiere* and *Cinema Papers* (both now defunct), Australia's former premier film magazine, went into circulation. In addition, the first film studies department was instituted at La Trobe University, and the first film school introduced at Swinburne Institute of Technology (now at the Victoria College of the Arts on St Kilda Road). Melbourne and Australia's film renaissance was given a further boost in the 1970s, when state and federal government bodies started actively supporting the domestic film industry, a process that continues in fits and starts today.

By the early 1990s, however, Victoria's film business was in the doldrums. A welcome sign of improvement came in 1993, when Film Victoria established the **Melbourne Film Office** to entice film and television projects to the state. Production in Melbourne has since boomed, partly because the city sells its streets at a far lower price than Sydney, but also because of its "every-city" appeal. With the completion of the Central City film studios at Docklands in 2004, scores more films are earmarked for production in the city.

The list of films that follow doesn't pretend to be exhaustive, but it should give you an idea of some of the films available with distinctive Melbourne qualities, or those that have their source in the city. Most can also be rented from DVD outlets around the city and suburbs.

Angel Baby (1995). Made with the help of the Australian Film Commission, *Angel Baby* sets out to unsettle, with a story of romance between two mentally disabled lovers. Starring a young Jacqueline McKenzie and John Lynch as the oddball couple, it's somewhat reminiscent of *Benny and Joon*, the Johnny Depp and Mary Stuart Masterton film.

The Big Steal (1990). Director Nadia Tass's charming romantic comedy of a high-school boy's infatuation with a girl and Jaguar cars, and getting even with a shonky used-car dealer.

The Castle (1997). Salt-of-the-earth saga about the battling Kerrigan family taking on big business to save their home from an airport runway extension. The nods and winks at Aussie culture might not always make sense, but the more you know about Melbourne, the funnier it gets.

Chopper (2000). This semi-biopic of Mark "Chopper" Read, psychotic ex-crook and best-selling author, is a gem. Stylish, brutal and horribly funny, the film proved enormously popular in Australia, largely because of the masterly portrayal by one-time comedian Eric Bana, later of *Black Hawk Down*, *Hulk* and *Troy* fame. Filmed in a number of inner-city locations, the characters and action were so realistic that worried residents, not knowing what was going on, regularly called in the police.

The Club (1980). David Williamson's satirical play studies the intrigue and machismo within the ranks of Collingwood, the most famous AFL club in Australia. Perfectly adapted for film by director Bruce Beresford.

Crackerjack (2002). Mick Molloy again, this time playing Jack Simpson, who joins an inner-city bowling club facing closure to take advantage of the free parking. It's a cracking story, with Molloy naturally saving the day, not to mention popularizing the term "swear jar", and marijuana biscuits. Ever since, bowls clubs have become irresistible to the grunge crowd, who have now found a way to drink, smoke, wear thongs and get a bit of "sport" back into their lives.

Crackers (1998). Low-budget film tracing the humorous goings-on within the tightly knit Dredge family, a bunch of whackos who come together for Christmas festivities.

Death in Brunswick (1991). Directed by John Ruane and starring Sam Neill, this black comedy revolves around Neill's no-hoper cook who works at a nightclub in the multicultural melting pot of

Brunswick. New Zealand-born, Melbourne-based comedian John Clarke is a scene-stealer at every turn.

Dogs in Space (1987). Unintentionally hilarious film about the punk-rock era of the late 1970s. Directed by Richard Lowenstein and starring the late Michael Hutchence, the film vainly attempts to capture glorious "youth" in all its waywardness. Over the years it's built up something of a cult, with ageing Melburnians in their Doc Martens still swearing by it.

Head On (1998). A raw and explicit story of a young "wog" (superbly played by hunky Alex Dimitriades) crashing through 24 hours of his life fuelled by vast quantities of sex, drugs and booze. Wonderfully photographed scenes of the seedier side of the city and deft insights into 1990s youth culture in multicultural Melbourne. Based on the cult Christos Tsiolkas novel *Loaded* (see p.236).

Hotel Sorrento (1994). Filmed on location at Sorrento, south of Melbourne, *Hotel Sorrento* comes over all deep and meaningful in its examination of the dysfunctional Moynihan family, particularly the rotten relationship between three sisters living very different lives. There's plenty to admire here – the performances, poisoned interactions and political musings on Australia's place in the world – but the final result is patchy and uneven, a film never quite sure of its own ambitions.

Kenny (2006). The eponymous hero is a Melbourne plumber who installs Portaloos, whose family and ex-wife give him a hard time. A heart-warming "mockumentary" of the quintessential Aussie bloke. Network Ten's 2008 TV spin-off, *Kenny's World*, followed Kenny on a tour of toilets around the world.

Love and Other Catastrophes (1996). Lightweight romantic comedy that follows the adventures of a group of students at a Melbourne university. Apart from the odd laugh and a reasonably good soundtrack, it's most notable for introducing a bunch of fresh-faced actors like Frances O'Connor, Radha Mitchell and Matt Day to the screen.

Love's Brother (2004). Starring the always watchable Giovanni Ribisi and Aussie ex-pat Adam Garcia, this is an old-fashioned romantic fable about two brothers from Italy, mixed identity and the first espresso machine in Australia. Set in Hepburn Springs, Victoria's glorious spa country, *Love's Brother* starts out with an inventive premise and some good insights into life in an Italian community in Australia in the 1950s, but unfortunately dissolves into caricature and tedium.

Mad Max (1979). Where would Australian cinema be without George Miller's apocalyptic masterpiece? The story of a cop (Mel Gibson) who seeks revenge after witnessing the brutal deaths of his partner and family by gang leader Toecutter, it has provided the template for road warrior movies ever since and struck a chord with audiences worldwide.

Malcolm (1986). Nadia Tass (see *The Big Steal* opposite) directed this delightful comedy about a social misfit inventor finding fulfilment as a criminal's offsider (assistant). Humorous, with great scenes of Melbourne and its rapidly disappearing W-class trams.

Mallboy (2000). Directed by local filmmaker Vincent Giarrusso and set in Melbourne's western suburbs, *Mallboy* is a gritty coming-of-age story in which a young tearaway aimlessly hangs out at the mall, thieving, smoking and generally playing up. Leaden at times, but

excellent performances from the central characters.

Metal Skin (1994). Writer/director Geoffrey Wright's follow-up to the critically-acclaimed *Romper Stomper* (see p.240) is an oppressive affair about a couple of "rev-heads" cruising the suburban streets of Melbourne. Violent, gloomy and filled with a collection of mostly unlikeable characters, it nonetheless features two remarkable performances from Aden Young and Ben Mendhelson and, if you can stick it out, a particularly gripping finale.

Ned Kelly (1970). Watchable "star" vehicle for Mick Jagger, who is ambitiously (and not altogether unsuccessfully) cast here by director Tony Richardson to play the totemic Australian outlaw Ned Kelly. Much emphasis is placed on the class conflict at the heart of Ned's story, and there are several good Irish ballads by Mick, Waylon Jennings and Kris Kristofferson among others. The story of Ned's short life was updated in 2003 again as *Ned Kelly* and filmed in Ballarat and the tiny Victorian country town of Clunes. This time, Heath Ledger plays the whiskery bushranger and Naomi Watts his love interest (Orlando Bloom also pops up as one of Ned's accomplices). Sentimental and dull, the film was pilloried for its mythologizing, and unsurprisingly sank without trace.

On the Beach (1959). Director Stanley Kramer's classic Cold War flick has Melbourne as the last place on earth that hasn't choked on the radioactive fallout of World War III. Gregory Peck, Ava Gardner, Anthony Perkins and Fred Astaire all give outstanding performances. Remade into a drab TV mini-series in 2001, starring Amande Assante, with the story set in 2006 after China's invasion of Taiwan triggers another world war.

One Perfect Day (2003). Promoted as the "techno answer to *Moulin Rouge*", *One Perfect Day* is an ambitious foray into Melbourne's dance culture. Tommy Matisse, played by Dan Spielman, is a gifted violinist who finds himself exploring clubland after a family tragedy. As with any fashionable scene, the club sequences already seem dated and despite great Aussie acting this film failed to impress at the box office.

Picnic at Hanging Rock (1975). Those who have seen this can never forget the haunting image of the virginal Miranda, immaculately dressed in white, spookily vanishing between the ageless boulders of Hanging Rock. Directed by Peter Weir, this is the pick of Australia's New Wave cinema – a classic turn-of-the-twentieth-century tale of vanishing schoolgirls, repressed sexuality and menacing landscapes.

Proof (1990). Jocelyn Moorehouse's quietly paced though chilling analysis of loveless sex, betrayal and broken marriages, with a blind photographer (Hugo Weaving) caught in the middle.

Romper Stomper (1992). Bleak and intense tale of neo-Nazis in Footscray and their running battles with the Vietnamese community. The film divided audiences on its release, with many railing against its random acts of pitiless violence.

Glossary of Melbourne terms

AFL Australian Football League, or "Aussie Rules", or simply "footy".

Ankle biter Small child.

Anzac Australia and New Zealand Army Corps; every town has a memorial to Anzac casualties from both world wars; Anzac Day is April 25.

Arvo Afternoon.

Barrack To cheer for (as in your favourite footy team).

Bathers Swimming costume (see "swimmers", "togs").

Beer o'clock Time to leave work.

Biffo A fight.

Bingle Mishap or car crash.

Blowies Blowflies.

Bludger Someone who doesn't pull their weight, or a scrounger – as in "dole bludger".

Blue A fight; also a red-haired person.

Bonzer Great, as in "we had a bonzer time".

Bottle shop Off-licence or liquor store.

Buckley's No chance; as in "hasn't got a Buckley's".

Budgie smugglers Speedos (swimming briefs).

BYO Bring Your Own; café or restaurant which allows you to bring your own alcohol.

Cactus Broken, useless, as in "the car's cactus".

Carked it Dead, died.

Chewy Chewing gum.

Chuck a wobbly Have a temper tantrum.

Chrissie Christmas, which also involves "prezzies" or presents.

Chunder Vomit.

Connies Melbourne's late, lamented tram conductors.

Crap on Talk too much, often nonsense ("geez, you crap on sometimes").

Dag Friendly term for decidedly uncool person.

Dob in To tell on, to nominate someone for an unpleasant task.

Doing a Melba Reference to Dame Nellie Melba, famous Australian operatic soprano who retired, then made a series of comebacks.

Drongo An idiot, fool.

Dunny Toilet; usually an outside pit toilet.

Esky Portable, insulated box to keep food or beer cold.

Footy AFL.

The G Affectionate term for the Melbourne Cricket Ground (MCG).

G'day Hello, hi.

Grey Ghost A parking inspector.

Grog Alcohol.

Grommet Young surfer.

Gubba Europeans.

Gunzels Tram enthusiasts.

Gutless wonder Coward.

Hangy Hangover.

Harry Holt To "bolt", or leave unexpectedly (comes from ex-Australian prime minister Harry Holt, who disappeared, presumed drowned, while swimming off the Victorian coast).

Hip and shoulder Footy term for legal tackle.

Hook turn Driving manoeuvre (see p.28).

Hoon A yob, delinquent.

Icey-pole Ice lolly/popsicle.

Koorie Collective name for Aboriginal people from southeastern Australia.

Lollies Sweets and hard candy.

Loo Toilet.

Lay by Practice of putting a deposit on goods until they can be fully paid for.

Milk bar Corner shop, and often a small café.

More pull than a Collins Street dentist Often heard during the Spring Racing Carnival, and used to describe a tearaway racehorse.

Mulga The country.

Mystery bag Meat pie.

No worries That's OK; it doesn't matter; don't mention it.

Nuddie The nude.

Onya Good for you!

Op shop Short for "opportunity shop"; a charity shop or thrift store.

Pashing Kissing or snogging.

Pokies Poker machines, slot or fruit machines.

Pot 285ml or 10oz glass of beer.

Prang An accident, usually minor.

Rack off Go away, get out of here.

Rattler A train or tram.

Rego Vehicle registration document.

Root Vulgar term for sexual congress, often substituted with "pork".

Rooted To be very tired or to be beyond repair; as in "your car's rooted, mate".

Sangers Sandwiches.

Scull To down a drink (usually beer) quickly.

She'll be apples It will be okay.

Shirtfront Another footy term for a tackle.

Shonky Something or someone deceptive or unreliable.

Sickie Taking a day off work when you're not actually sick.

Silverhairs Retirees.

Slab 24-can carton of beer.

Smoko Tea break.

Snag Sausage usually cooked on a barbecue.

Snot block Vanilla slice.

Southerly buster Melbourne's much-welcomed cooling breeze.

Sticky-beak A closer look.

Swimmers Swimming costume.

Tanty Temper tantrum for children.

Thongs Flip-flops or sandals.

Tinnie Can of beer.

Togs Swimming costume.

Toorak tractor A 4WD used only for city driving.

Top drop An enjoyable drink, usually referring to alcohol.

Top shelf Really good person, as in "He's top shelf".

VB Victoria Bitter, the state's thirst-quenching lager.

Vegemite Blackish-brown yeast spread used on sandwiches. Aussie version of Marmite.

Wag To play truant.

Waxhead Surfer.

Weatherboard Wooden house.

White mice Football umpires, also known as "white maggots".

Wog Derogatory description for those of Mediterranean descent.

Write off A total loss.

Wuss To be weak, lacking commitment.

Zonked Tired, exhausted.

Travel store

Available from all good bookstores

ROUGH GUIDES

Small print and
Index

A Rough Guide to Rough Guides

Published in 1982, the first Rough Guide – to Greece – was a student scheme that became a publishing phenomenon. Mark Ellingham, a recent graduate in English from Bristol University, had been travelling in Greece the previous summer and couldn't find the right guidebook. With a small group of friends he wrote his own guide, combining a highly contemporary, journalistic style with a thoroughly practical approach to travellers' needs.

The immediate success of the book spawned a series that rapidly covered dozens of destinations. And, in addition to impecunious backpackers, Rough Guides soon acquired a much broader and older readership that relished the guides' wit and inquisitiveness as much as their enthusiastic, critical approach and value-for-money ethos.

These days, Rough Guides include recommendations from shoestring to luxury and cover more than 200 destinations around the globe, including almost every country in the Americas and Europe, more than half of Africa and most of Asia and Australasia. Our ever-growing team of authors and photographers is spread all over the world, particularly in Europe, the USA and Australia.

In the early 1990s, Rough Guides branched out of travel, with the publication of Rough Guides to World Music, Classical Music and the Internet. All three have become benchmark titles in their fields, spearheading the publication of a wide range of books under the Rough Guide name.

SMALL PRINT

Including the travel series, Rough Guides now number more than 350 titles, covering: phrasebooks, waterproof maps, music guides from Opera to Heavy Metal, reference works as diverse as Conspiracy Theories and Shakespeare, and popular culture books from iPods to Poker. Rough Guides also produce a series of more than 120 World Music CDs in partnership with World Music Network.

Visit www.roughguides.com to see our latest publications.

Rough Guide travel images are available for commercial licensing at www.roughguidespictures.com

Rough Guide credits

Text editor: Ros Belford
Layout: Umesh Aggarwal
Cartography: Ed Wright
Picture editor: Sarah Cummins
Production: Rebecca Short
Proofreader: Helen Castell
Cover design: Chloë Roberts
Photographer: Karen Trist
Editorial: Ruth Blackmore, Andy Turner, Keith
Drew, Edward Aves, Alice Park, Lucy White,
Jo Kirby, James Smart, Natasha Foges, Róisín
Cameron, Emma Traynor, Emma Gibbs, Kathryn
Lane, Christina Valhouli, Monica Woods, Mani
Ramaswamy, Harry Wilson, Lucy Cowie, Helen
Ochyra, Amanda Howard, Lara Kavanagh, Alison
Roberts, Joe Staines, Peter Buckley, Matthew
Milton, Tracy Hopkins, Ruth Tidball; **Delhi**
Madhavi Singh, Karen D'Souza, Lubna Shaheen
Design & Pictures: **London** Scott Stickland,
Dan May, Diana Jarvis, Mark Thomas, Nicole
Newman, Emily Taylor; **Delhi** Ajay Verma, Jessica
Subramanian, Ankur Guha, Pradeep Thapliyal,
Sachin Tanwar, Anita Singh, Nikhil Agarwal,
Sachin Gupta
Production: Vicky Baldwin

Cartography: **London** Maxine Repath, Katie
Lloyd-Jones; **Delhi** Rajesh Chhibber, Ashutosh
Bharti, Rajesh Mishra, Animesh Pathak, Jasbir
Sandhu, Karobi Gogoi, Alakananda Bhattacharya,
Swati Handoo, Deshpal Dabas
Online: **London** George Atwell, Faye Hellon,
Jeanette Angell, Fergus Day, Justine Bright, Clare
Bryson, Aine Fearon, Adrian Low, Ezgi Celebi,
Amber Bloomfield; **Delhi** Amit Verma, Rahul Kumar,
Narender Kumar, Ravi Yadav, Debojit Borah,
Rakesh Kumar, Ganesh Sharma, Shisir Basumatari
Marketing & Publicity: **London** Liz Statham,
Niki Hanmer, Louise Maher, Jess Carter, Vanessa
Godden, Vivienne Watton, Anna Paynton, Rachel
Sprackett, Libby Jellie, Laura Vipond, Vanessa
McDonald; **New York** Katy Ball, Judi Powers,
Nancy Lambert; **Delhi** Ragini Govind
Manager India: Punita Singh
Reference Director: Andrew Lockett
Operations Manager: Helen Phillips
PA to Publishing Director: Nicola Henderson
Publishing Director: Martin Dunford
Commercial Manager: Gino Magnotta
Managing Director: John Duhigg

Publishing information

This fourth edition published September 2009 by
Rough Guides Ltd,
80 Strand, London WC2R 0RL
14 Local Shopping Centre, Panchsheel Park,
New Delhi 110017, India
Distributed by the Penguin Group
Penguin Books Ltd,
80 Strand, London WC2R 0RL
Penguin Group (USA)
375 Hudson Street, NY 10014, USA
Penguin Group (Australia)
250 Camberwell Road, Camberwell,
Victoria 3124, Australia
Penguin Group (Canada)
195 Harry Walker Parkway N, Newmarket, ON,
L3Y 7B3 Canada
Penguin Group (NZ)
67 Apollo Drive, Mairangi Bay, Auckland 1310,
New Zealand
Cover concept by Peter Dyer.

Typeset in Bembo and Helvetica to an original
design by Henry Iles.
Printed and bound in Singapore by SNP Security
Printing Pte Ltd
© Rough Guides 2009
No part of this book may be reproduced in any
form without permission from the publisher except
for the quotation of brief passages in reviews.
256pp includes index
A catalogue record for this book is available from
the British Library
ISBN: 978-1-84836-099-0
The publishers and authors have done their best
to ensure the accuracy and currency of all the
information in **The Rough Guide to Melbourne**,
however, they can accept no responsibility for
any loss, injury, or inconvenience sustained by
any traveller as a result of information or advice
contained in the guide.

1   3   5   7   9   8   6   4   2

Help us update

We've gone to a lot of effort to ensure that the
fourth edition of **The Rough Guide to Melbourne**
is accurate and up-to-date. However, things
change – places get "discovered", opening hours
are notoriously fickle, restaurants and rooms raise
prices or lower standards. If you feel we've got it
wrong or left something out, we'd like to know,
and if you can remember the address, the price,
the hours, the phone number, so much the better.

Please send your comments with the subject
line "**Rough Guide Melbourne Update**" to
@mail@roughguides.com. We'll credit all
contributions and send a copy of the next edition
(or any other Rough Guide if you prefer) for the
very best emails.
Have your questions answered and tell others
about your trip at
@community.roughguides.com

Acknowledgements

Karoline Thomas would like to thank all those who helped her with updating this latest edition of the *Rough Guide to Melbourne* including Wayne Brown for early use of home and computer and Martin, her driver/navigator/photographer all rolled into one, who never once complained even when she insisted on doing one more walk or reading every piece of information that happened to be pinned or nailed to a board. Thanks also to Ros Belford for her diligent editing, support and understanding, Sarah Cummins for the pictures and Umesh Aggarwal for typesetting. Finally, she would like to thank Jack, who accompanied her to every bar, café, hotel, museum and national park and never once kicked up a fuss.

Readers' letters

Thanks to all the readers who have taken the time to write in with comments and suggestions (and apologies if we've inadvertently omitted or misspelt anyone's name):

Sarah-Jane Brooks, Douglas Dickson, Stuart Goodall, Clive Paul, Heidi van Spaandonk, Jill Wookey.

SMALL PRINT

Photo credits

Index

Map entries are in colour.

INDEX

Map symbols

maps are listed in the full index using coloured text

	Freeway			Waterfall
	Main road			Spring
	Minor road			International airport
	Unpaved road			Domestic airport
	Pedestrianized street			Lighthouse
	Path			Vineyard
	Railway			Visitor centre
	Ferry route			Post office
	River			Building
	Chapter boundary			Church/cathedral
	Point of interest			Cemetery
	Mountain peak			Park
	Gorge			

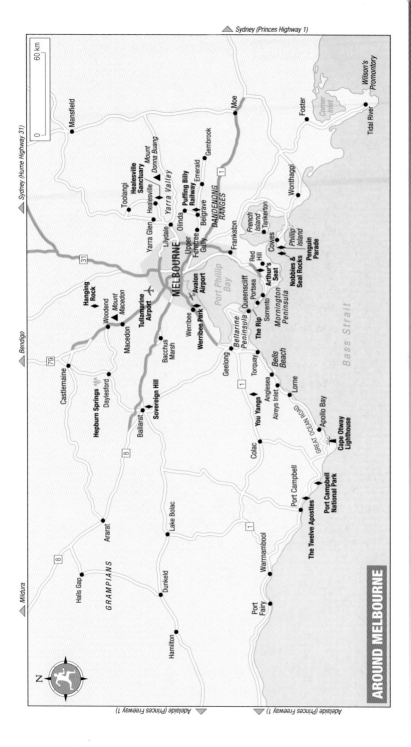

AROUND MELBOURNE

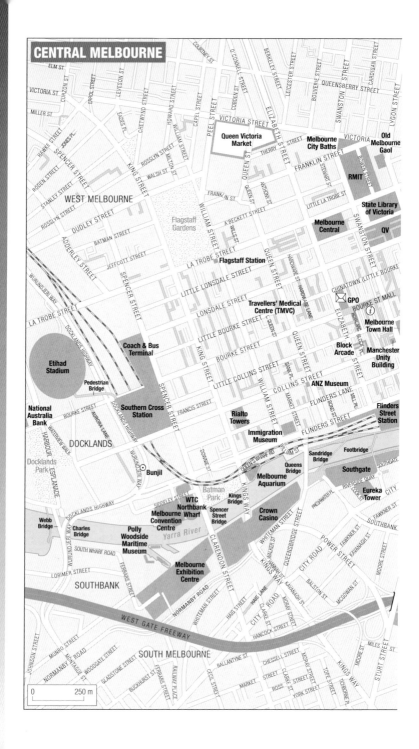

CENTRAL MELBOURNE

ELM ST

VICTORIA ST

MILLER ST

COURTNEY ST

O'CONNELL STREET

BERKELEY STREET

LEICESTER STREET

BOUVERIE STREET

QUEENSBERRY STREET

SWANSTON STREET

CARDIGAN STREET

LYGON STREET

CURZON ST

ERROL STREET

LEVESON ST

CHETWYND STREET

HOWARD STREET

CAPEL STREET

CORDEN ST

PEEL STREET

VICTORIA STREET

ELIZABETH STREET

STREET

VICTORIA

**Queen Victoria
Market**

THERRY ST

**Melbourne
City Baths**

**Old
Melbourne
Gaol**

HAWKE STREET

JONES PL

SPENCER STREET

EADES PL

ROSSLYN STREET

WILLIAM STREET

KING STREET

MILTON ST

WALSH ST

QUEEN ST

ANTHONY ST

FRANKLIN STREET

STEWART ST

RMIT

RODEN STREET

STANLEY STREET

WEST MELBOURNE

FRANKLIN ST

LITTLE LA TROBE ST

SWANSTON STREET

**State Library
of Victoria**

ROSSLYN STREET

DUDLEY STREET

A BECKETT STREET

QUEENS ST

**Melbourne
Central**

QV

BATMAN STREET

MELBES ST

ADDERLEY STREET

JEFFCOTT STREET

**Flagstaff
Gardens**

WILLIAM STREET

LA TROBE STREET

QUEEN STREET

Flagstaff Station

WURUNDJERI WAY

DOCKLANDS HIGHWAY

SPENCER STREET

LITTLE LONSDALE STREET

HARDWARE ST

HARDWARE LANE

CHINATOWN (LITTLE BOURKE

✉ **GPO**

LA TROBE STREET

LONSDALE STREET

QUEENS ST

**Travellers' Medical
Centre (TMVC)**

ELIZABETH

BOURKE ST
MALL

ⓘ

**Melbourne
Town Hall**

**Coach & Bus
Terminal**

LITTLE BOURKE STREET

KING STREET

BOURKE STREET

QUEEN STREET

BANK PL

**Block
Arcade**

SWANSTON

**Manchester
Unity
Building**

**Etihad
Stadium**

**Pedestrian
Bridge**

SPENCER STREET

LITTLE COLLINS STREET

WILLIAM STREET

QUEEN STREET

MARKET STREET

COLLINS STREET

BANK PL

ANZ Museum

**Flinders
Street
Station**

**National
Australia
Bank**

BOURKE STREET

WATERVIEW WALK

AURORA LANE

DOCKLANDS HIGHWAY

**Southern Cross
Station**

FRANCIS STREET

**Rialto
Towers**

**Immigration
Museum**

WILLIAM STREET

FLINDERS LANE

FLINDERS STREET

KING ST

ELIZABETH ST

DEGRAVES ST

**Docklands
Park**

HARBOUR ESPLANADE

DOCKLANDS

WURUNDJERI WAY

DOWNIE ST

Bunjil

QUEEN WHARF RD

**Sandridge
Bridge**

Footbridge

SOUTHGATE

**Queens
Bridge**

**Melbourne
Aquarium**

Southgate

RIVERSIDE QUAY

CITY

PRICEWATERS

**Eureka
Tower**

**Webb
Bridge**

WURUNDJERI WAY

**Charles
Bridge**

DOCKLANDS HIGHWAY

SIDDELEY STREET

**WTC
Northbank
Melbourne
Convention
Centre**

**Batman
Park**

**Kings
Bridge**

KINGS WAY

**Spencer
Street
Bridge**

**Crown
Casino**

WHITEMAN STREET

QUEENSBRIDGE STREET

POWER STREET

FAWKNER ST

KAVANAGH ST

SOUTHBANK

FAWKNER ST

MOORE STREET

**Polly
Woodside
Maritime
Museum**

Yarra River

CLARENDON STREET

KINGS WAY

CITY ROAD

SOUTH WHARF ROAD

**Melbourne
Exhibition
Centre**

KANAVAGH ST

BALSTON ST

CITY ROAD

MCGOWAN ST

LORIMER STREET

FERRARS STREET

NORMANBY ROAD

WHITEMAN STREET

HAIG STREET

HAIG LANE

CITY ROAD

MORAY ST

KAVANAGH ST

SOUTHBANK

JOHNSON STREET

MUNRO STREET

NORMANBY ROAD

MONTAGUE ST

WOODGATE STREET

GLADSTONE STREET

FERRARS STREET

RAILWAY PLACE

WEST GATE FREEWAY

HANCOCK STREET

CECIL STREET

SOUTH MELBOURNE

BALLANTYNE ST

CHESSELL STREET

STREET

MORAY STREET

CLARKE ST

STREET

ROSS ST

YORK STREET

MARKET

KINGS WAY

TOPE STREET

MILES ST

MOORE STREET

STURT STREET

TICHBORNE PL

| 0 | 250 m |

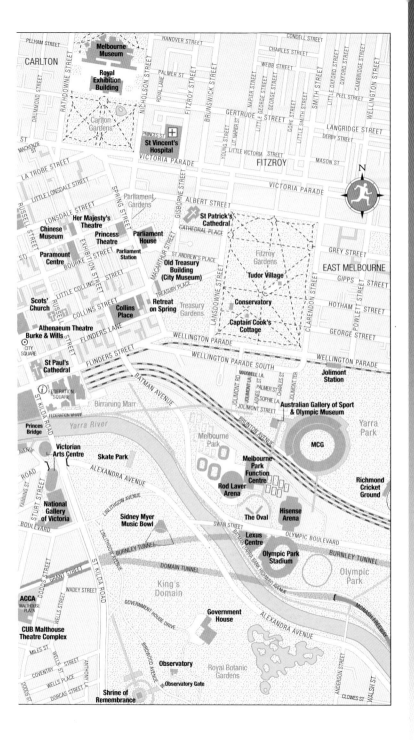

connex

CRAIGIEBURN

Roxburgh Park
UPFIELD P
Broadmeadows
Gowrie P
Jacana
Fawkner P
Glenroy
Merlynston P
Oak Park
Batman
Pascoe Vale
Coburg P
Strathmore
Moreland P
Glenbervie
Anstey
Sunbury P
Essendon
Brunswick P
Diggers Rest P
#FLEMINGTON RACECOURSE
#Showgrounds
Moonee Ponds
Jewell P
Watergardens P
Ascot Vale
Royal Park
SYDENHAM
Keilor Plains P
Flemington Bridge
St Albans P
Newmarket
Ginifer P
Macaulay
Albion P
Kensington
V/LINE
North Melbourne
Melton P
*Flagstaff
Melbourne Central
Rockbank
Deer Park
Ardeer
Sunshine
Tottenham
West Footscray
Middle Footscray
Footscray
South Kensington
Parliament
Seddon
Southern Cross
City Loop
Yarraville
Spotswood
Flinders Street
Newport P
Seaholme P
North Williamstown P
Laverton
Altona P
Williamstown Beach
Aircraft
Westona
WILLIAMSTOWN P
Hoppers Crossing
WERRIBEE

PORT PHILLIP

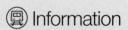

Information

Ticketing zones

City Saver | Zone 1 | Zone 2 | Connecting tram | Connecting bus | Connecting V/Line train | Connecting V/Line coach | Premium Station | Host Station | Parking

Premium Station:
Customer service centre is staffed from first train to last, seven days a week.
Host Station:
Customer service staff at station during morning peak.

*Flagstaff Station is closed on weekends and public holidays.

#Line to Showgrounds and Flemington Racecourse is only open for special events.

For train, tram and bus information
call **131 638 / (TTY) 9619 2727** or
visit **metlinkmelbourne.com.au**

Melbourne Train Network

metlink

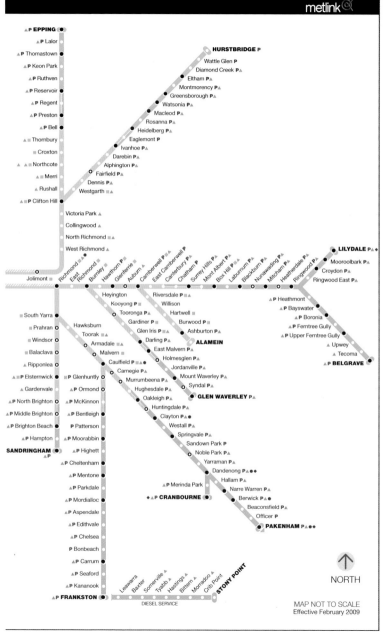

EPPING

Lalor

Thomastown

Keon Park

Ruthven

Reservoir

Regent

Preston

Bell

Thornbury

Croxton

Northcote

Merri

Rushall

Clifton Hill

HURSTBRIDGE

Wattle Glen

Diamond Creek

Eltham

Montmorency

Greensborough

Watsonia

Macleod

Rosanna

Heidelberg

Eaglemont

Ivanhoe

Darebin

Alphington

Fairfield

Dennis

Westgarth

Victoria Park

Collingwood

North Richmond

West Richmond

Jolimont

Richmond

East Richmond

Burnley

Hawthorn

Glenferrie

Auburn

Camberwell

East Camberwell

Canterbury

Chatham

Surrey Hills

Mont Albert

Box Hill

Laburnum

Blackburn

Nunawading

Mitcham

Heatherdale

Ringwood

LILYDALE

Mooroolbark

Croydon

Ringwood East

Heyington

Kooyong

Tooronga

Gardiner

Glen Iris

Riversdale

Willison

Hartwell

Burwood

Ashburton

ALAMEIN

Heathmont

Bayswater

Boronia

Ferntree Gully

Upper Ferntree Gully

Upwey

Tecoma

BELGRAVE

South Yarra

Prahran

Windsor

Balaclava

Ripponlea

Elsternwick

Gardenvale

North Brighton

Middle Brighton

Brighton Beach

Hampton

SANDRINGHAM

Hawksburn

Toorak

Armadale

Malvern

Caulfield

Glenhuntly

Ormond

McKinnon

Bentleigh

Patterson

Moorabbin

Highett

Cheltenham

Mentone

Parkdale

Mordialloc

Aspendale

Edithvale

Chelsea

Bonbeach

Carrum

Seaford

Kananook

FRANKSTON

East Malvern

Holmesglen

Jordanville

Mount Waverley

Syndal

GLEN WAVERLEY

Carnegie

Murrumbeena

Hughesdale

Oakleigh

Huntingdale

Clayton

Westall

Springvale

Sandown Park

Noble Park

Yarraman

Dandenong

Hallam

Narre Warren

Berwick

Beaconsfield

Officer

PAKENHAM

Merinda Park

CRANBOURNE

Leawarra

Baxter

Somerville

Tyabb

Hastings

Bittern

Morradoo

Crib Point

STONY POINT

DIESEL SERVICE

NORTH

MAP NOT TO SCALE
Effective February 2009

© State of Victoria, 2009

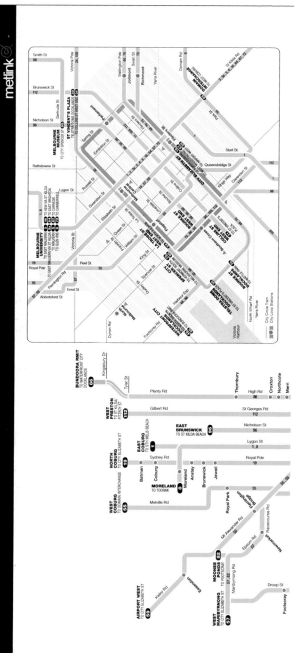

YARRA TRAMS

Melbourne Tram Network

metlink

NORTH

MAP NOT TO SCALE
Effective January 2009

© State of Victoria, 2009

300109

Information

For train, tram and bus information call
131 638 / (TTY) 9619 2727 (6am–10pm daily)
or visit **metlinkmelbourne.com.au**

For Yarra Trams customer feedback and lost
property call **1800 800 166** (6am–10pm daily)
or visit **yarratrams.com.au**

Ticketing zones

City Saver
Zone 1
Zone 2

72
▲
Connecting bus
Nearest train station
Tram terminus

Routes: 1, 3 (Mon–Fri), 3a (Sat–Sun), 5, 6, 8, 16, 19, 24 (AM/PM peaks),
30, 31, 48, 55, 57, 59, 64, 67, 70, 72, 75, 78 (until 7pm), 79 (after 7pm),
82, 86, 95 (Mon–Fri), 96, 109, 112

VERMONT SOUTH
TO CITY SPENCER ST

BOX HILL
TO PORT MELBOURNE
Box Hill

WATTLE PARK
TO BOURKE ST DOCKLANDS

NORTH BALWYN
TO CITY LA TROBE ST WEST END
TO WATERFRONT CITY DOCKLANDS

CAMBERWELL
TO MELBOURNE UNIVERSITY

KEW
TO MELBOURNE UNIVERSITY
VIA ST KILDA

GLEN IRIS
TO MELBOURNE UNIVERSITY

TOORAK
TO MORELAND

MALVERN
TO MELBOURNE UNIVERSITY

EAST MALVERN
TO MELBOURNE UNIVERSITY
TO MELBOURNE UNIVERSITY VIA ST KILDA

CARNEGIE
TO MELBOURNE UNIVERSITY

EAST BRIGHTON
TO MELBOURNE UNIVERSITY

Burwood Hwy
Union Rd
Balwyn Rd
Warrigal Rd
Whitehorse Rd
Riversdale
Camberwell
Burwood
Harptree
Glenferrie
Cotham Rd
Riversdale Rd
Burke Rd
Gardiner
Glen Iris
Glen Rd
Malvern
Wattletree Rd
Waverley Rd
Caulfield
Hawthorn Rd
Glenhuntly
Elsternwick
Glenhuntly Rd

Doncaster Rd
Hawthorn
High St
Koroyong
Glenferrie Rd
Toorak
Toorak Rd
Armadale
High St
Dandenong Rd
Balaclava
Balaclava Rd
64

NORTH RICHMOND
TO LUNA PARK/
ST KILDA BEACH
TO PRAHRAN

Westgarth
Clifton Hill
Victoria St
North Richmond
Bridge Rd
Swan St
Burnley
Church St
East Richmond
South Yarra
Commercial Rd
Prahran
Windsor
Chapel St
Malvern Rd
PRAHRAN
TO NORTH RICHMOND

St Kilda Rd

DOMAIN INTERCHANGE
TO WEST COBURG

Canterbury Rd
Park St
Clarendon St
Ferrars Rd
Victoria Ave

LUNA PARK/ST KILDA BEACH
TO NORTH RICHMOND

ST KILDA BEACH
TO EAST BRUNSWICK

ST KILDA/
FITZROY ST
TO WEST PRESTON

STH MELBOURNE
BEACH
TO EAST COBURG

PORT MELBOURNE
TO BOX HILL

PORT
PHILLIP

FOOTSCRAY
TO MOONEE PONDS

Abbotsford St

CITY CENTRE
see main inset

Tullamarine Airport

Museum of Modern Art at Heide & Montsalvat

BILLA ROAD
LINCOLN ROAD
MOUNT ALEXANDER ROAD
PASCOE VALE ROAD
TULLAMARINE FREEWAY

BUCKLEY ST

COBURG

THORNBURY

MORELAND ROAD

NICHOLSON STREET

NORMANBY AVENUE

BRUNSWICK

ST GEORGES RD

HIGH STREET

NORTHCOTE

WAVERLEY STREET

MOONEE PONDS

Moonee Valley Racecourse

MARIBYRNONG ROAD

ASCOT VALE ROAD

BRUNSWICK ROAD

SYDNEY ROAD

LYGON STREET

NICHOLSON STREET

WESTGARTH STREET
HEIDELBERG ROAD

PARKVILLE

Royal Park

Melbourne General Cemetery

QUEENS PARADE

MILLER STREET

Flemington Racecourse

RACECOURSE ROAD

Melbourne Zoo

ALEXANDRA PARADE

EASTERN FREEWAY

Yarra Bend Park

BALLARAT ROAD

FLEMINGTON ROAD

ROYAL PARADE

JOHNSTON STREET

HODDLE STREET

STUDLEY PARK ROAD

DYNON ROAD

CARLTON

FITZROY

COLLINGWOOD

VICTORIA STREET

DOCKLANDS HIGHWAY

VICTORIA STREET

WHITEHALL STREET

Fitzroy Gardens

Etihad Stadium

Southern Cross Station

Flinders Street Station

MCG
Yarra Park

BRIDGE ROAD

RICHMOND

DOCKLANDS

FLINDERS STREET

SPENCER STREET

Yarra River

King's Domain

SWAN STREET

West Gate Bridge

WEST GATE FREEWAY

Royal Botanic Gardens

SOUTH EAST FREEWAY

PORT MELBOURNE

GRAHAM ST

BAY STREET

SOUTH MELBOURNE

KINGS WAY

STURT STREET

SOUTH YARRA

TOORAK ROAD

TOORAK

ORRONG ROAD

ALBERT PARK

ALBERT ROAD

Albert Park Lake

QUEENS ROAD

PUNT ROAD

COMMERCIAL ROAD

WILLIAMS ROAD

Station Pier

BEACONSFIELD PARADE

Melbourne Sports & Aquatic Centre

Albert Park

PRAHRAN

HIGH STREET

WINDSOR

NELSON PLACE

Commonwealth Reserve

FITZROY STREET

DANDENONG ROAD

CHAPEL STREET

HOTHAM ROAD

NEPEAN HIGHWAY

WILLIAMSTOWN

St Kilda Pier

ST KILDA

BARKLY STREET

Point Gellibrand

Shelly Beach

St Kilda Botanical Gardens

GLEN EIRA ROAD

Port Phillip Bay

Elwood Beach

ORMOND ESPLANADE

ST KILDA STREET

NORTH ROAD

NEW STREET

N

0   2 km